HOPE & SCORN

HOPE

&

SCORN

EGGHEADS, EXPERTS,
AND ELITES IN
AMERICAN POLITICS

Michael J. Brown

THE UNIVERSITY OF CHICAGO PRESS
Chicago & London

The University of Chicago Press, Chicago 60637

The University of Chicago Press, Ltd., London

© 2020 by The University of Chicago

Published 2020

Printed in the United States of America

29 28 27 26 25 24 23 22 21 20   1 2 3 4 5

ISBN-13: 978-0-226-71814-9 (cloth)

ISBN-13: 978-0-226-72770-7 (e-book)

DOI: https://doi.org/10.7208/chicago/9780226727707.001.0001

Library of Congress Cataloging-in-Publication Data

Names: Brown, Michael J. (Michael James), author.
Title: Hope & scorn : eggheads, experts, and elites in American politics / Michael J. Brown.
Other titles: Hope and scorn
Description: Chicago : The University of Chicago Press, 2020. | Includes bibliographical references and index.
Identifiers: LCCN 2020004026 | ISBN 9780226718149 (cloth) | ISBN 9780226727707 (ebook)
Subjects: LCSH: Intellectuals—Political aspects—United States. | United States—Politics and government—20th century. | United States—Politics and government—21st century.
Classification: LCC E169.12 .B743 2020 | DDC 320.973/0905—dc23
LC record available at https://lccn.loc.gov/2020004026

♾ This paper meets the requirements of ANSI/NISO Z39.48-1992 (Permanence of Paper).

CONTENTS

INTRODUCTION

Years ago I was teaching high school civics. Gathering material on the role of television advertising in presidential campaigns, I watched a clip from the first contest in which such ads were prominent: Illinois governor Adlai Stevenson against General Dwight Eisenhower, 1952. A Stevenson ad, "I Love the Gov," opens with an unidentified woman singing: "I'd rather have a man with a hole in his shoe than a hole in everything he says." These curious lyrics led me to a famous photo of Stevenson taken at a Labor Day campaign stop in Michigan. As Stevenson crossed his legs, a photographer at the foot of the stage snapped a candid shot of what the *New York Times* called "an old-fashioned schoolboy hole right through to the sock."[1]

Shortly after stumbling over Stevenson's shoe, I traveled to a speech and debate tournament where I heard the "original oratory" finalists. One student gave her speech about Richard Hofstadter's half-century-old *Anti-Intellectualism in American Life*, finding it to be a powerful summons to intellectualism in an American culture that emphasizes matter over mind. Her remarks so impressed me that I bought Hofstadter's volume for the Amtrak ride home. Within a few pages I encountered a figure suddenly familiar: Adlai Stevenson. Hofstadter, it seemed, was preoccupied with the man.

Hofstadter saw the 1952 election as a battle between intellect and anti-intellectualism. Stevensonians like him regarded their candidate as one of the finest minds in American politics. Eisenhower, by contrast, was a figure of little intellectual substance but great likability. "Eisenhower's decisive victory was taken both by the intellectuals themselves and by their critics," Hofstadter concluded, "as a measure of their repudiation by America."[2]

With Hofstadter in mind, I returned to Stevenson's shoe. It could evoke Depression days when newspapers plugged holes in soles, reminding voters that Stevenson's Democrats stood for the New Deal. A message that Stevenson's campaign mobilized, however, was the distinction between the hole in his shoe and the holes in Eisenhower's thinking—the "hole in everything he says" or, as Stevenson put it, "better a hole in the shoe than a hole in the head."[3] This rhetoric suggested that Stevenson was so focused on ideas and issues that he did not worry about the state of his sole—an intellectual attention not shared by his opponent.

Stevenson's standing as an intellectual—he was the original "egg-head"—was also a liability.[4] Eisenhower supporters contrasted the general's practical know-how with what they characterized as Stevenson's merely vicarious experience through reading books.[5] This line of attack deployed a long-established distinction drawn between intellectuals' abstract considerations and the practical, shoes-on-the-ground concerns that Eisenhower's campaign thought most important to voters.

How long-established? I was at the time also working with ninth graders on ancient philosophy, starting with pre-Socratics like Thales of Miletus. In the *Theaetetus*, Plato relates the story of how Thales, a philosopher and astronomer, was so intent upon looking at the stars that he fell into a well. As a Shakespearean jest goes: "O Thales, how shuldest thou have knowlege in hevenly thinges above, and knowest nat what is here benethe under thy feet?"[6] A hole in one's shoe could indeed suggest a preoccupation with higher things, but what use was such thinking, especially for politics, if it led to tumbling head over tunic into a well?

Fifty-six years after Stevenson versus Eisenhower (round one—they faced each other again in 1956), the 2008 presidential election offered another contest between a cerebral Democrat from Illinois and a Republican whose reputation rested upon military service. The campaign between Barack Obama and John McCain was about many things: Obama's race, the presidency of George W. Bush, the September 2008 economic collapse, the wars in Iraq and Afghanistan, the rise of social media. In the welter of election commentary, however, one strand caught my attention: the parallel some drew between Stevenson and Obama. "Barack Obama: Egghead?" was the question in the *Huffington Post*. A Princeton political scientist reported that "friends and colleagues comment on the possibility that Obama could become the egghead candidate"—a concern for those fearing his electoral fate would replicate Stevenson's. The day after Obama's sizable victory, however, Michael Schaffer of the *New Republic* declared: "We're All Eggheads Now."[7]

A half century after Stevenson lost handily—a half century during which the country had purportedly been growing more hostile to intellect with each passing sound bite—the egghead candidate defeated the military hero. The conventional wisdom that over "the past four decades, America's endemic anti-intellectual tendencies have been grievously exacerbated," as Susan Jacoby put it months before Obama's election, must not have been the entire story.[8]

If debate over intellectuals in public life were confined to *Huffington Post* columnists and Princeton political scientists, it would be a circular affair—discussion of intellectuals among intellectuals. But in Stevenson's era, Obama's, and our own, the uncertain place of the intellectual in American political culture has produced comment from ordinary citizens as well as putative intellectuals. Writing to the *Washington Post & Times Herald* in December 1957, Louise Williams of Silver Spring, Maryland, objected to how "'egghead' has been used in describing many people of great ability—one was Adlai Stevenson. Please call these illustrious people intellectuals, highbrow, or something else denoting their ability—not 'egghead.'" Williams found that term "ignoble," "undignified," and downright "ugly." Fifty-one years later, responding to the *Huffington Post* article, the commenter "sanang" wrote: "I'd take a [sic] 'egghead' anytime over an empty one." Another commenter, "phughez," criticized "the egghead epiphany that a candidate like Obama needs to dumb himself down in order to 'connect' with the average voter." It was, rather, the Bush administration that "made an art form of condescension—and pandering—and lying." Better an egghead's lecture, phughez suggested, than a huckster's bill of goods. "Redrover666," however, said that "Americans preferred to listen to Bush trying to string together sentences than Gore and . . . Kerry talk down to them." Another replied: "If you are feeling 'talked down to,' instead of . . . voting for the one that panders to make you feel better about your lack of knowledge, you could . . . learn something about the real issues effecting [sic] you and the rest of us."[9]

Americans were not of one mind about the quality that Hofstadter called "mind," and presidential politics made this multiplicity particularly visible. Did candidates' intellects qualify them to lead, or did intellect drive a troublesome wedge between candidates and the people they would represent? Just as American political culture has appeared to be on a particular trajectory with respect to these questions, it has changed course. The most recent shift was especially abrupt: after twice electing constitutional law professor Obama, the country pivoted to what journalist Conor Lynch called "Donald Trump's glorious victory for anti-intellectualism."[10]

Such vicissitudes point to the inadequacy of claims about the fortunes of intellectuals in public life simply rising or falling. Complex dynamics are at work beneath the surface of these electoral about-faces, dynamics that flow from the uncertain role of intellectuals in a democracy.

* * *

In the half century following World War Two, Americans engaged in a series of fierce debates about the place of intellectuals in public life— debates conditioned by the unique moments in which they occurred but unified by a set of persistent questions concerning the fraught relationship between intellectuals and democratic politics. In a culture infamous for anti-intellectualism, these debates were not as one-sided as one might think. Instead, intellectuals have been both targets of scorn and vessels of hope.

Looking at debates about the role of intellectuals shifts the focus from their fortunes—rise, fall, or disappearance—to Americans' efforts to determine what an intellectual is and ought to be.[11] Rather than asserting a particular definition of the intellectual, I view that definition as contested ground. Those seeking to claim the title for themselves, those seeking to impose it on others, and those struggling to create social and political change asked: What are intellectuals, what are their obligations to society, and how, if at all, are they compatible with democracy? Americans offered an array of responses to these questions. Many offered answers in deed as well as in word—they sought to enact the role of the intellectual even as they continued to think about what that role might mean. This book holds up a series of telling moments when the foci, participants, and terms of debate about the role of intellectuals in public life changed, charting a path from the "egghead" to the "public intellectual." These moments reveal shifting anxieties about and aspirations for democracy in America over the last half century. For some, intellectuals were models of civic engagement. For others, the rise of the intellectual signaled the fall of the citizen.

In this story, intellectuals are the topic of debates, not only participants in them. British historian Stefan Collini wrote of "the *question* of intellectuals," that is, "the ways in which the existence, nature, and role of intellectuals have been thought about and argued over, including claims about their absence or comparative insignificance."[12] Here Collini's question of intellectuals appears on the American side of the Atlantic.

Americans have attended to the question of intellectuals because it leads to questions deeper still. As Collini observed, "The spell cast by the actual word 'intellectuals' is extraordinary, an indication that the term must be serving as a kind of place-holder for a whole collection of cultural attitudes."[13] Debates about intellectuals bear upon attitudes toward democracy in America—the character of popular political participation or the lack thereof—and, beyond it, the nature of authority in the public sphere.

"Democracy" and "the intellectual" are protean things: moving targets that move in relation to one another. Whether intellectuals are deferred to or despised, whether they hold power or rail against it—these are fault lines pointing to larger fissures in the structure of democracy. Intellectuals have functioned as canaries in the democratic coal mine. Anxiety about the disappearance or absence of intellectuals in public debate is anxiety about the extent to which such absence points to the attenuation of democratic civic culture.[14] Conversely, anxiety about the prominence of intellectuals as spokespeople or experts in public affairs is anxiety about the extent to which such prominence points to a drying up of broader democratic engagement and accountability. Debates about the role of intellectuals are also debates about the nature of the democratic public sphere. Will it be a sphere in which claims are adjudicated on the basis of detached reason, a sphere in which the invocation of moral wisdom carries the day, or one where plural forms of reasoning and moralizing are themselves the causes of contention?[15]

Argument and, indeed, anxiety over intellectuals' role have persisted because their authority is evident but ambiguous. If intellectuals are meant to hold authorities—government, corporate, others—accountable, by what authority of their own do they do so, and how is that authority different (uneasily, in a democracy, greater) than that of ordinary citizens?[16] Intellectuals' authority has overlapped with forms of authority based on race, class, and gender that have made American democracy, at best, an uneven playing field and, at worst, no democracy at all. And yet intellectuals have also challenged these same concentrations of power. Not only the nature of intellectuals' authority but also its sources are unclear: how are individuals authorized to act as intellectuals? Ambiguous in nature and unclear in origin, intellectuals' authority has been hotly contested—by both the "power elite" and "ordinary Americans." For all their differences, American CEOs and their lowest-paid employees have, strikingly, held this in common: contempt for eggheads. Both perceive intellectuals' authority as a threat to their own. Can both be right? Its uncertain implications for the distribution of power in our democracy explain why the role of the intellectual has not only been subject to contest, but *worth* contesting for many Americans—and not just aspirants or claimants to the title "intellectual."

* * *

Though increasingly intense after World War Two, debates about the role of intellectuals were not new. The actual and perceived closer proximity of intellectuals to power fueled arguments in the second half of the twentieth century, but their antecedents were as old as Plato's *Republic*. If the powerful were wise or the wise powerful, Plato claimed, there would be justice in the polity. The separable nature of wisdom and power allowed misrule, so uniting the two in the person of the philosopher king presented a solution. It also presented a tantalizing prospect for intellectuals, depicting their political power as normative and positioning cognitive excellence as the best credential for rule. Plato's vision is, however, an authoritarian prospect for those with democratic commitments. His *Republic*, after all, ends in dictatorship.[17]

This tension between intellectuals' special claims to authority and democratic principles, which diffuse authority throughout the body politic, has been a focal point in American debates. Some have shared Plato's lament, pointing to the United States as a place where the gap between wisdom and power is widest. In the 1920s, American thinkers characterized their society as a "business civilization" uniquely hostile to the ministrations of intellect. Progressive Era intellectuals like Walter Lippmann called on "intelligent men of [their] generation" to seize the "vast opportunity of introducing order and purpose" to national life amid the upheavals of industrial capitalism and the melee of mass democracy.[18]

Political leaders were not deaf to this call. Even Warren G. Harding—a president not renowned for valuing intellect—vowed to consult "the 'best minds' of the nation, regardless of party affiliation." He called his Marion, Ohio, home the "Great Listening Post," inviting "men and women . . . eminent in the discussion of our foreign relations" to join him there.[19] It was FDR's "Brains Trust," however, that offered intellectuals a seat at the table of power, and New Deal policies institutionalized an expanded role for intellectuals in government.

Federal agencies grew to carry out the New Deal, a growth far exceeded during World War Two. By war's end, the domestic apparatus of government was larger, and the national security state had come into being. Among the new institutional homes for specialist minds was the president's Council of Economic Advisers, created in the Employment Act of 1946 to make good the Keynesian commitment to full employment. As cold war succeeded world war, foreign policy and national defense roles proliferated. Lippmann wrote in 1921 of the need for "organized intelligence" whereby "the disinterested expert first finds and formulates the facts for the man of action."[20] The National Security Act of 1947 established a new intelligence organization: the CIA. It was part of a growing defense establishment recruiting intelligence analysts, geographical-area experts, and game theorists. Intellectuals as experts were on the rise.[21]

The 1944 Servicemen's Readjustment Act, commonly known as the GI Bill, further altered intellectuals' prospects. It opened the door to college for legions of demobilizing troops, and enrollments swelled along with the number of academic jobs. By the time the Cold War was in full swing, intellectuals could find themselves working directly for government or in post-secondary institutions where their students' tuition or research center's funding came partly from government outlays. Philosophers were not king, but they were increasingly populating the court.

These changing institutional positions and the increased public visibility related to them pointed to a real and perceived attainment of power by intellectuals, raising the stakes of debate over their role. The Cold War heightened those stakes further. On the one hand, a contrast between outspoken American intellectuals and Soviet thinkers moldering in gulags bolstered America's image as a free society. These outspoken intellectuals challenged the Cold War, however, when they spoke out against state policy. A fierce debate about the loyalty of American thinkers persisted from the onset of the Cold War through Vietnam. The McCarthy hearings, blacklists, and loyalty oaths required of college professors were all incursions into American intellectual life, enforcing boundaries on dissent and raising the bar for loyalty.[22] The Cold War raised the question of whether intellectuals ought to take sides. To whom or to what were they responsible?[23]

As some intellectuals gained power, others charged that they were no longer responsible to truth. Critics like Noam Chomsky saw intellectuals legitimizing the imperial state—speaking lies *for* power rather than truth *to* it. As Chomsky framed it, American intellectual life was a clash between those seeking truth and those serving power, with the former becoming voices in the wilderness.

Depiction of intellectuals as bearers of inconvenient truths clashed with another rendering taking shape during the Cold War, one showing intellectuals as distinctly prone to falsehoods. The concept of totalitarianism, developed in the writings of Hannah Arendt and others, linked the showdown with communism to the fight against Nazism—totalitarianisms both. From this discourse there emerged a view of intellectuals as servants of the totalitarian enterprise—previously alienated, powerless thinkers drawn to state power like moths to a flame. The totalitarian intellectual was the stooge of the dictator or the dupe of intoxicating ideologies like fascism or Marxism. In French thinker Raymond Aron's *The Opium of the Intellectuals* (1955), being captivated by ideology defined the intellectual. Rejecting Marxism, Aron was therefore not an "intellectual" himself—no matter how many books he wrote.[24]

The deployment of "intellectual" as a term of abuse for those on the left outlived the early Cold War. The critique of communism bequeathed to the neoconservative critique of Left liberalism a set of arguments for attacking the interventionist state, its advocates, and its agents. Sociologists were pointing to the emergence of what Alvin Gouldner described as "a New Class composed of intellectuals and technical intelligentsia" challenging "the groups already in control of the society's economy, whether these are businessmen or party leaders."[25] This New Class became a target for new conservatives. Characterizations of intellectuals as power-hungry bureaucrats and decadent elites dovetailed with the attacks on "big government" that were a hallmark of the resurgent Republican Party in the 1970s and '80s. Pushing against intellectuals with one hand, conservatives built their own formidable apparatus of intellectual institutions—think tanks, foundations, and academic alliances—with the other.[26]

At the same time, critics were pointing to gendered and racialized constructions of the intellectual. As feminist and African American thinkers challenged the boundaries of a category that had largely been the province of elite white men, they created a set of new possibilities for "the intellectual" in American life. These included the possibility that women, people of color, and others historically excluded from the domain of "the intellectual" would now occupy it—and their previously marginalized forebears in intellectual achievement be recognized. They also included reshaping that domain itself, a reshaping driven not only by reconsideration of who got counted as an intellectual but also what modes of thought, sources and kinds of authority, and practices served intellectuals' purposes.

The relationship between intellectuals and communities was a focal point in these debates. Cornel West invoked Italian philosopher Antonio Gramsci's concept of the "organic intellectual" to describe African American intellectuals like bell hooks and himself. Conversation among and about these scholars canvassed the possibility that intellectuals were not only those who spoke *to* or *for* a community but also those who spoke *from* or *with* one.

This emphasis on intellectuals' roles in specific communities occurred in the wake of lamentations over the academic character of American intellectual life. As intellectual activity became more focused on college campuses, the campuses embraced postmodern theory that, critics charged, was too esoteric for broader civic debate. Beginning in the late 1980s and picking up steam thereafter, the term "public intellectual" sought to describe and applaud those who addressed an audience beyond the academy in language suited to broad comprehension.

The decades after World War Two saw not only an intensification of debates about the place of intellectuals in American political culture, but also a proliferation of the conceptions of the intellectual deployed in them. This multiplication helps to explain why debate about intellectuals has been ongoing, unresolved, and intensifying. The question of intellectuals remained unsettled when the very term at its heart was the site of continued conflict. Never had the role of the intellectual been more plural than in this period.

With each passing decade, debates about American intellectuals produced a multiplicity of sometimes contradictory constructions of their roles in public life. There were attempts at empirical description: policy intellectuals, think-tank intellectuals, literary intellectuals, and academic intellectuals. There were labels meant to valorize: action intellectuals, dissident intellectuals, or simply experts. There were labels meant to condemn: mandarins, moralists, or elites. There were those, like egghead, meant to ridicule. There were labels imported from Europe: organic intellectuals, specific intellectuals, and New Class intellectuals. There were those arising from American debate: connected critics, prophetic pragmatists, and public intellectuals. This proliferation of labels, this multiplication of potential roles for intellectuals in the public sphere, signaled both the extent to which the role of the intellectual was indeterminate and the extent of Americans' efforts, nevertheless, to determine it.

* * *

Two narrative frames have surrounded American intellectual life: a story of general decline and of a uniquely American anti-intellectualism. These stories compound one another—prolonged and pervasive anti-intellectualism drives intellectuals' decline over time. Moving debates about the role of intellectuals in public life to the center of vision, however, shows how the decline and anti-intellectual accounts obscure the picture. Indeed, these accounts are themselves positions in debates about intellectuals, performing polemical and normative work alongside purportedly diagnostic or descriptive efforts.

A number of well-known titles about American intellectual life over the last half century highlighted the anti-intellectualism and declension themes: Richard Hofstadter's *Anti-Intellectualism in American Life* (1963), Russell Jacoby's *The Last Intellectuals* (1987), Richard Posner's *Public Intellectuals: A Study of Decline* (2001). While these books contributed, often richly so, to the study of American intellectual life, they tended to take one particular conception of the intellectual as fixed, rather than addressing the contested definition of the intellectual over time.[27] As Edward Said observed in 1993: "In the outpouring of studies about intellectuals there has been far too much defining of the intellectual."[28] This emphasis on specifying what the intellectual is, or what intellectuals as a group are, has imposed fixity on histories that are in fact less determinate. By moving from definitions of the intellectual to debates about them—including debates that take the form of proliferating definitions—the elusive, unstable character of the role of the intellectual remains visible, rather than being submerged under any particular conception of it.

Narratives of decline exemplify this tendency to overlook changing conceptions of the intellectual. These tales take one particular definition and trace the downfall of those who fit it. The result may be question-begging. Shifting the focus to debates instead of downfalls reveals not a story of decline so much as ongoing, high-stakes argument over what an intellectual is and ought to be. The anti-intellectual account offers a more static picture of American intellectual life. Whereas decline narratives must logically begin with some high point—the Founders, the American Renaissance, the heyday of the New York Intellectuals—and trace a downward trajectory, the anti-intellectual account posits a perennial animus between American culture and American intellectuals. This animus has been attributed to the democratic character of American life, which makes problematic the presence of those who, by dint of intellectual qualifications, might claim (or have conferred upon them) a kind of *aristocratic* distinction.

Alexis de Tocqueville pointed to this tension between intellect and democracy in Andrew Jackson's America. Underlying Tocqueville's observations, gleaned from travels around the country, was a conviction that democracy is inherently at odds with the life of the mind, which meant for him the cultivation associated with the leisured, learned classes of Europe to which he belonged. Democracy tended to be practical, present oriented, and engendering of conformity, while intellectual life, at its best, was theoretical or reflective, took the long view, and encouraged originality. Democratic culture militated against intellectual authority. "It is not simply that in democracies the confidence in the superior knowledge of certain individuals has been weakened," Tocqueville wrote. "The general idea that any man whosoever can attain an intellectual superiority beyond the reach of the rest is soon cast in doubt."[29]

Tocqueville's view of democratic America is the seedbed for a flowering of complaints about the role (or lack thereof) of intellectuals in American public life. The notions that Americans elect beer buddies rather than big brains, that public discourse is superficial, and that voices of learning are drowned out by cacophonous consumerism all have a Tocquevillean pedigree. Rather than settling the question of intellectuals, however, these are contested positions in ongoing debates about the proper role of intellectuals in American democracy. Are politically influential intellectuals a threat to or ally of popular rule? Are intellectuals of or apart from the people? Are intellectuals catalysts for democratizing social change or checks upon it? The meaning of "political" here is broad. It includes elections and policymaking but also embraces a larger conception of the political that recognizes the deeply entwined character of culture and politics. After World War Two, debates about the role of intellectuals in American political culture became a defining feature of that culture.

* * *

The following pages trace a history that runs from the "egghead" to the "public intellectual." Comprehensively covering this ground is a Hercu-

lean labor not attempted here. Instead, each chapter focuses on a significant moment when debates about the role of intellectuals became particularly voluble, their stakes heightened or changed, and concerns animating
them shifted. Using this series of revealing moments makes granular analyses of particular debates possible, while allowing the pervasiveness and
evolution of such debates to appear over time. Each of these moments takes
one or two figures as a starting point but embraces the contributions of
many voices—including those of people not identifying as intellectuals—
to debate. These are moments that elicited those voices while highlighting
persistent themes, like populism and elitism, authority (moral and expert),
and political commitment versus rational detachment.

To examine intellectuals' roles concretely as well as conceptually,
these moments are grounded in human stories. They are at the intersec-
tion of thought and action, where individuals write about what intellectuals should do and try, haltingly, to do it. Actions, in turn, illuminate
how those undertaking them conceived of their role. This approach brings
familiar figures like Hofstadter into view from less familiar angles: thinking, acting on that thought, and rethinking—all in response to other intellectuals, ordinary people, and contemporary events. A recurrent question,
moreover, has been whether intellectuals can work to implement their
social vision or criticism while remaining intellectuals, rather than having become in some exclusive way something else—for example, activists.

This particular model of the intellectual—focused on individuals wrestling with how to bring their thought to bear on public life—is not the only
one. Indeed, its limitations are clear in the chapters ahead. An alternative model displaces individuals, focusing instead on collective intellectual
work and experience: intellectualism rather than intellectuals. Contemporary social movements like Occupy Wall Street, Me Too, and Black Lives
Matter center on ideas without centering "the intellectual." They suggest
that debates about the role of the intellectual in American political culture
may ultimately lead not to definition of that role but to moving beyond it.

Indeed, at any historical moment, debates about the role of the intellectual do not exhaust all possible constructions of that role. The same is
true of the debates surveyed here: focused primarily on writing, speaking,
and acting with respect to politics, they encompass a limited range of intellectual practices. With historians and philosophers looming large in the
storytelling, that range becomes more limited still.[30] A host of intellectual
activities—the production and criticism of literature, music, and art, for

instance—have been vital to conceptions of intellectuals' role but appear only through the central preoccupation, here, with politics.

Constructions of "the intellectual" have also been limited by the racialized, gendered, and elite assumptions that have shaped debates about them. Well before and ever since the term "intellectual" came into American use, there were women, working people, and people of color who exemplified any normative definition of that term. They were nonetheless regularly excluded from the most elite—and by virtue of that status most visible—strand of debates about intellectuals' place in politics. Though some as Jewish Americans dealt with prejudice, the midcentury white men in the opening chapters here faced no barriers of racism or sexism, and though a handful of them came from working-class backgrounds, they were ultimately marked as intellectuals by their affiliation with elite institutions: prestigious universities, premier publishing houses, respected periodicals, selective fellowships, and significant government positions. Indeed, when the so-called "new black intellectuals" of the late 1980s and early 1990s, like Cornel West, bell hooks, and Henry Louis Gates Jr., were denoted as such, it was by these same prestigious publications and in connection to these same elite universities. Standing in a long African American intellectual tradition, this cohort was "new" in the sense of being newly recognized by the culturally powerful institutions through which intellectuals received their imprimatur—in its Latin origins, a permission to print.[31]

Print has indeed been the medium most associated with intellectual work. West, however, is among those who have pointed to musical and oral improvisation as, among other non-print modes of expression, bearers of vernacular intellectual practice that is woven into lived experience—the "doings and sufferings" of people, as he put it.[32] That West often characterized the latter as "everyday" or "ordinary people" implies a distinction between them and "intellectuals" that does not rest on intellect or on dealing with and expressing ideas but, rather, on social location. "Ordinary" means not professional thinkers, which, in turn, has often meant academics.

The chapters ahead examine debates that were historically delimited, bounded by an array of assumptions that make them outdated in important ways, and rightly so. With respect to democracy and politics, however, these debates raise questions that endure. The problem of what as well as who an intellectual is has persisted, and that persistence points to the deeply contested character of authority in the democratic public sphere.[33]

In debating the role of intellectuals, Americans faced the uncertain meaning of their democracy and sought to shape that meaning.[34]

These debates operated on multiple levels and in several forms. Most publicly, they surfaced as dueling views in print or on air. They also registered in epistolary exchanges, where arguments about the public, political role of intellectuals occurred in relative privacy. Archival sources yield rich material in this vein. Hofstadter and Arthur M. Schlesinger Jr. received correspondence from other intellectuals but also from those making no claim to that title. The latter argued with them, contested their authority, and offered encouragement. In short, they participated in debates about the role of the intellectual, demonstrating that such debates were a terrain upon which intellectuals and other people met, since all had a stake in their outcomes. More private still, these debates took the form of individuals' struggles within their own thinking about the role they should play in public life. These struggles register in archival sources and in changing public statements over time.

Taking a broad view of what counts as participation in debates, I consider not only writing and speaking but other forms of intervention as well. If intellectuals run for political office, advise presidents, or try to create political parties—these are all forms of articulating a role for themselves in public life (or, as critics charged, betraying a conception of intellectual life that precludes such activity). Indeed, the dialectical relationship between debates and practices, thinking and doing—particularly pronounced among self-reflexive intellectuals—means that discussing roles and living them have been thoroughly enmeshed. Six moments form the nuclei of the chapters that follow—instances when intellectuals undertook some new form of action or endeavor, sparking debate about whether they were abandoning the role of the intellectual, expanding it, epitomizing it, or transforming it.

The curtain opens on Richard Hofstadter's engagement with Stevenson's 1952 and 1956 campaigns, years that saw the advent of "the egghead" amid Joseph McCarthy's anti-intellectual brand of anti-communism. Hofstadter identified a timeless hostility between the democratic and the intellectual, with the latter frequently vulnerable to periods of "'democracy' with a vengeance." For him, the role of the intellectual in American political culture was something akin to that of a Roman centurion standing guard along the Rhine, ever mindful of the barbarians at the gate, perennially "manning the barricades of civilization."[35]

Overcoming Hofstadter's suspicion of popular politics, H. Stuart Hughes sought to mobilize public opinion with his 1962 campaign for the US Senate in Massachusetts. Hughes's campaign embodied competing conceptions of the intellectual, for although he considered himself "a cosmopolitan, polyglot man of letters"—or, as his memoir put it, a "gentleman rebel"—he increasingly promoted his authority as "a specialist, particularly on contemporary European problems."[36] In the context of the Cold War, even a humanistic intellectual felt compelled to claim the mantle of expertise in order to warrant a public hearing.

While Hughes searched for intellectuals' public authority, Arthur Schlesinger Jr. and Noam Chomsky turned debate over Vietnam into an argument about intellectuals' responsibilities. For Chomsky, Schlesinger was the prototypical mandarin: an intellectual who wielded power in the service of national interests at best amoral and at worst criminal. For Schlesinger, Chomsky was the prototypical moralist: an ideologue who abandoned analysis for absolutism. Vietnam was the occasion for their dispute, but different models of the intellectual—and their peril and promise for democratic political culture—were near the heart of it.

Chomsky took to the streets to protest American policy. Looking to move beyond such protests, historian and social critic Christopher Lasch struggled to reconcile what he regarded as the canons of intellectualism with the messiness of political work, testing the idea that the two could be joined. Feminist intellectuals like Berenice Fisher, Toni Cade Bambara, and Ellen Willis challenged constructions of the intellectual advanced by Lasch and others, providing their own accounts of what that role could mean in the context of democratic and movement politics.

While some intellectuals pursued social change, others acted upon the belief that intellectuals themselves were the greatest threat to the social fabric. Irving Kristol was a potent exponent of the charge, resting on work by Joseph Schumpeter, that intellectuals were engaged in a struggle with business. While business amassed financial capital, a "New Class" of intellectuals used cultural capital and seizure of the public sector to advance their position. Kristol and other conservatives in the 1970s and '80s made it their task to oppose this New Class—becoming, ironically, intellectuals against intellectuals.

In the 1990s, observers declared that an increasingly visible cohort of African American scholars—hooks, West, and others—were the answer to lamentations over the absence of intellectuals in public life that intensified in the wake of Jacoby's *The Last Intellectuals*. Members of this cohort forged their roles as intellectuals in light of feminist and African American precedents and in the wake of postmodern critiques destabilizing the truth in which intellectuals were supposed to traffic. They faced the particular obstacles placed before African American and women intellectuals and were at the center of debate about a new role: the public intellectual. Forging a practice of public intellectualism that sought to align with democracy rather than being, as Hofstadter's intellectualism was, in tension with it, this cohort found that, even when intellectuals embraced the public, the role of public intellectuals was far from clear.

The moments surveyed in these chapters are entrances to the question of intellectuals in American political culture after World War Two rather than an inventory of it. Alternative entry points, from the travails of Henry Kissinger to those of Angela Davis, would serve too. The particular moments are less important, however, than the set of questions raised by them. They are instances when individuals moved from more conventional forms of intellectual activity, such as writing and teaching, to less conventional ones—running for office, working for government, supporting political campaigns, engaging social movements, building institutions, gaining visibility, and, in some cases, achieving celebrity. These actions elicited comment about the role of intellectuals from the actors themselves, other thinkers, and everyday people. The individuals in the pages that follow were not only participants, in both deed and word, in debate about the role of intellectuals in American political culture—they were occasions for it.

1

MANNING THE BARRICADES
OF CIVILIZATION

Decades after his death, Richard Hofstadter was widely invoked by critics trying to make sense of the political scene. When the Tea Party emerged in 2010, *Newsweek* placed Hofstadter on its "What You Need to Read Now" list. Writer Jon Meacham dubbed such moments "'Hofstadters,' when commentators turn to Richard Hofstadter's 1964 essay 'The Paranoid Style in American Politics' for an intellectual frame in which to view conspiracy-minded fury." *Slate*'s David Greenberg noted that from "'tea parties' to the 'birther' frenzies . . . allusions to Hofstadter have never seemed more widespread." Hofstadter was "the pundits' favorite historian." In 2015–16, pundits again reached for Hofstadter, to illuminate Donald Trump's rise. "Trump has succeeded in unleashing an old gene in American politics," wrote Evan Osnos in the *New Yorker*: "the crude tribalism that Richard Hofstadter named 'the paranoid style.'" "Trump's style perfectly embodies the theories of [this] renowned historian," declared *Salon*.[1]

While Hofstadter wrote on a variety of subjects—social Darwinism, academic freedom, political parties, and the antebellum tariff debate, to name but a few—his work on the political culture of popular protest has most endured. Sam Tanenhaus, writing for the *New Republic*, claimed that Hofstadter "was the first serious thinker to recognize (in 1954!) that a new 'dynamic of dissent' in American politics had come into being via Sen. Joseph McCarthy and that the forces he unleashed were 'powerful enough to set the tone of our political life' for years to come."[2]

The Hofstadter summoned by these commentators is a historian as psychologist, peering deep into the American mind to glimpse the psychic underpinnings of our politics. Hofstadter's concepts and the memorable terms, like "paranoid style," he used to convey them sound like diagnoses. Meacham's "Hofstadters" calls to mind the naming of diseases after the physician who discovered them. If intellectuals' role is to clarify political issues by organizing them under a conceptual rubric, their work indeed resembles physicians' organization of disparate symptoms under the heading of a larger syndrome, connecting troubles the patient experiences but does not fully understand.

Hofstadter belonged to a group of social analysts—including Robert Merton, Seymour Martin Lipset, David Riesman, and Daniel Bell—who proposed "status politics" as a way of understanding political behavior. "Political life is not simply an arena in which the conflicting interests of various social groups in concrete material gains are fought out," Hofstadter wrote. "It is also an arena into which status aspirations and frustrations are, as the psychologists would say, projected." Political debates, "or the pretended issues of politics, become interwoven with and dependent upon the personal problems of individuals."[3] Status politics stood in contrast to interest politics, the clash of opposing economic forces that both Hofstadter's predecessors in American historiography—progressive historians like Charles Beard—and Marxist thinkers had placed at the heart of political behavior. Status politics provided the key, Hofstadter argued, to understanding Goldwaterism, McCarthyism, Progressivism, and Populism.

Interested in the formation of political orientations and identities, Hofstadter wondered whether "'cultural politics' and 'symbolic politics'" were ultimately better terms than "status."[4] Today it is common to speak of "cultural politics" and the importance of "symbolic issues." Flag burning, abortion, and gay marriage have been infused with powerful symbolic (as well as concrete) meaning, dividing the culture and, as a result, driving wedges through the electorate. Moving from status toward cultural or symbolic politics, Hofstadter was developing a profile of what later observers would dub "the culture wars." Examining culture wars in his own time, he traced them throughout the American past too.[5]

Hofstadter went beyond studying culture war; he also waged one. To diagnose those who practiced status politics was to dismiss them. Emphasizing the resentful, anxious origins of populism in his own day and before it, Hofstadter suggested that such politics might be more readily treated than debated. Psychologizing the American populist Right, Hofstadter undermined its standing as a legitimate political force. "Much of Hofstadter's work," historian Jack Pole noted, "is both a critical and diagnostic account of the times."[6] Embedded in his analyses of "paranoid style," "anti-intellectualism," and "pseudo-conservatism" was a normative view of liberal politics and a counterattack against those who threatened it.

MANNING THE BARRICADES OF CIVILIZATION

Hofstadter waged culture war on behalf of an intellectualized public sphere, a domain he found both fragile and under threat—from within as well as without. It was a sphere he knew best from his semesters at Columbia University and his summers at Wellfleet on Cape Cod. A counterpoint to the right-wing world summoned in his writings, it was a realm where intellectuals were respected rather than scorned, politics was rational rather than emotional, and the life of the mind was left free to pursue its own dictates rather than being dictated to by the climate of public opinion or the prevailing views of university trustees. Hofstadter wrote of the person who exhibits the paranoid style: "He is always manning the barricades of civilization."[7] In his work as a widely read historian and intellectual, Hofstadter was manning the barricades of civilization too. He looked out over the walls of the university at an America populated by volatile masses, and he made it his role as an intellectual to guard the intellectualized public sphere against these potential barbarians at the gate.

The 1950s were a critical decade in debates about the role of intellectuals in American political culture. Hofstadter is a bellwether for this period, as reflected in his literary output between 1948's *The American Political Tradition and the Men Who Made It* and 1963, when *Anti-Intellectualism in American Life* was released and Hofstadter gave the Herbert Spencer Lectures at Oxford, which later became the essay "The Paranoid Style in American Politics." In between, *The Development and Scope of Higher Education in the United States*, "Democracy and Anti-Intellectualism in America," *The Development of Academic Freedom in the United States*, *The Age of Reform: From Bryan to F.D.R.*, and "The Pseudo-Conservative Revolt" are a formidable body of writing on the place (or, rather, the plight) of intellect and intellectuals in a democracy.[8]

In addition to his *ideas* from this period, Hofstadter's *actions* bear upon the role of intellectuals in the public, political arena. He both constructed a framework for the interplay of intellectuals and American democracy and acted within it, providing a model of what an intellectual in the world that Hofstadter theorized might do. "In many ways Richard Hofstadter was the historian he admired," wrote Philo A. Hutcheson.[9] In many ways, too, Hofstadter was the intellectual he summoned in his writings. In his view of history and society, intellect needed its champions. He worked in this period to be that champion.

Hofstadter produced a theory of society and an interpretation of the American past that both illuminated the place of intellectuals and served their cause. Critics wondered which of these imperatives drove his work: the desire to understand society and history or the need to interpret them in a way that would aid intellectuals in his own time.[10] This criticism addressed Hofstadter the scholar but not necessarily the intellectual. Norms for that more ambiguous enterprise were what Hofstadter tried to locate in his work. One quality he and other liberals of the 1950s included among the desiderata—if not requirements—for intellectuals was a lively sense of irony. An ironic feature of the cultural climate of their decade was that intellectuals came under attack and felt themselves most embattled at a time when, as columnist George Sokolsky wrote by way of skewering them in 1955, "they never had it so good."[11]

* * *

Introducing their "Our Country and Our Culture" symposium in the spring of 1952, William Phillips and Philip Rahv, editors of *Partisan Review*, noted "that American intellectuals now regard America and its institutions in a new way. Until little more than a decade ago, America was commonly thought to be hostile to art and culture," but "the tide has begun to turn, and many writers and intellectuals now feel closer to their country and its culture." In that intervening decade, Americans had witnessed European culture give rise to World War Two and be left in ruins by it. American culture, philistines and all, looked healthy by comparison. The United States was now "the protector of Western civilization."[12] After 1945 America seemed the last, best hope of humankind—a vision that had endured since the Puritan City on a Hill but one that American intellectuals had not always shared.

Not only were intellectuals drawing closer to America in this period, but America was drawing closer to them. The Servicemen's Readjustment Act of 1944, better known as the GI Bill, expanded the college student population by allocating billions of dollars to veterans' education, and the academic job market grew accordingly. By 1948 intellectuals like Lionel Trilling, who had previously moved in the ambiguous zone between college teaching and periodical writing, could find themselves tenured full professors. For Trilling, that meant a permanent place at Columbia University.

In 1946 Hofstadter also arrived at Columbia, leaving the University of Maryland. His move to New York coincided with his marriage to Beatrice Kevitt.[13] After the death of his first wife, Felice Swados, Hofstadter had sent their son Dan to live with family in Buffalo. Now, with his new wife and his son, Hofstadter took up residence in Morningside Heights, the neighborhood he would call home for the rest of his life. Postwar America appeared to be a site of stability and growth for the country as a whole, for intellectuals as a class, and for Richard Hofstadter personally.

Such good times, however, were themselves cause for unease among intellectuals. The "affirmative attitude toward America which has emerged since the Second World War" raised the question of whether affirmation was appropriate for the intellectual. If intellectuals abandoned criticism, would they still be intellectuals? Moreover, if intellectuals felt less alienated in American society, would they be dropping the distance necessary for a detached, critical perspective on it?[14]

Partisan Review's editors signaled an intellectual shift that offered one means of navigating these questions—a shift with significant consequences for the relationship between intellectuals and democracy. While intellectuals felt more comfortable with the United States, they were "not prepared to give up all criticism" of a nation that had "not suddenly become ideally beneficent." They wanted to affirm America without abnegating intellectuals' critical role. In mass culture, the editors identified a target that might allow them to shoot both ways. They found, looming larger all the time, "a new obstacle: the artist and intellectual who wants to be a part of American life is faced with a mass culture which makes him feel that he is still outside looking in."[15]

Turning their fire on mass culture, intellectuals diverted it from the structure of American capitalism, which had been under critical assault in the 1930s and, before that, during the Progressive Era. This shift was an implicit affirmation of the basic institutions of American democracy, which the *Partisan Review* editors described as "not merely a capitalist myth but a reality which must be defended against Russian totalitarianism."[16] In a linear, progressive view of history—in which the critical project of intellectuals is to move history along its path of progress—this new focus on mass culture implied that America had advanced far enough on the economic and political fronts, especially after the New Deal and in the face of Stalin's Russia, to leave culture as the last bastion of backwardness. Taking a different view, Christopher Lasch argued that "intellectuals shifted their attention to the criticism of popular culture" not "because capitalism had eliminated . . . economic injustices . . . but because the possibilities of a political attack on capitalism appeared by the middle forties to be so greatly diminished." As crusading anti-communism intensified, criticism of mass culture marked a damming up of intellectuals' critical energies behind a set of political barriers.[17] Cultural criticism could, however, be more than evidence of progress in political economy, on the one hand, or political repression, on the other: it could be a bridge by which intellectuals spanned their dueling desires to remain critical, detached, and even alienated while affirming and integrating with an America that, in the dawning Cold War, looked like the best of all actual, if not necessarily possible, worlds.

When their critical vision turned from the economic power of the few to the cultural threat of the many, intellectuals found themselves staring uneasily at democracy. The *Partisan Review* editors came to the troubling realization that since "political democracy seems to coexist with the domination of the 'masses,'" it involved "serious cultural consequences." The democracy/mass-culture trade-off was a devil's bargain, for mass culture tended "to exclude everything which does not conform to popular norms; it creates and satisfies artificial appetites in the entire populace. . . . Its overshadowing presence cannot be disregarded in any evaluation of the future of American art and thought." The editors confronted the "paradox" that in the United States, "cultural freedom is promised and mass culture is produced."[18]

Intellectuals were left affirming American democracy while deploring democratic American culture—a situation that bound them to an inescapable elitism. In the 1930s, intellectuals had often aligned with the "common man" against the abuses of capitalism. With the shift to mass-culture debates, however, intellectuals severed themselves from the common people—now the "mass" whose culture was the problem.[19] That culture threatened to stamp out intellectualism, replacing it with consumerism. In a market society, the preferences of the many were pitted against the tastes of the intellectual few. Reacting against mass culture, intellectuals were asserting that their tastes should matter, if not predominate.[20]

The question of mass democracy was more than a matter of taste, however. Intellectuals saw in the American masses not only philistines in full bloom, but also seeds of totalitarianism. There "was a sense of alarm about how a democratic society could become a fascist one," Hofstadter's Columbia colleague William Leuchtenburg recalled. There was "fear that people who start out with a liberal or centrist cast of mind can become overwhelmed." No single work did more to raise this specter than Hannah Arendt's *The Origins of Totalitarianism* (1951).[21] The masses, she argued, were composed of "atomized, isolated individuals." Atomization deprived

people of their intellectual bearings: "they lost the whole sector of communal relationships in whose framework common sense makes sense." They
became susceptible to conspiratorial thought, which offered some modicum of coherence in an otherwise seemingly inexplicable train of events.
Totalitarianism and its propaganda offered a ready-made way of understanding the world to a mass society in which intellect had ceased to provide one. "Before the alternative of facing the anarchic growth and total
arbitrariness of decay or bowing down before the most rigid, fantastically
fictitious consistency of an ideology," Arendt argued, "the masses probably
will always choose the latter."[22]

Intellectuals, rather than arresting this descent into totalitarian fiction,
too often abetted it. Totalitarianism "attracted the intellectual elite and
the mob alike"—a mode of expressing both groups' hatred for middle-class
liberalism. Intellectuals' alienation, their anxiety as a class whose status
was ambiguous at best, made them potential extremists who might stop
at nothing "in forcing the recognition of [their] existence on the normal
strata of society."[23]

If Arendt despaired of intellectuals staving off totalitarianism, she did
see hope in individualism. "Total power," she wrote, "can be achieved and
safeguarded only in a world of conditioned reflexes, of marionettes without the slightest trace of spontaneity." American intellectuals themselves
were worried about an "Age of Conformity," as Irving Howe later put it.
That a woman intellectual gave this concern its most powerful articulation was ironic, since both the option of and aspiration to nonconformity,
necessary conditions for anxiety about conforming, were most accessible
to men—women were *supposed* to conform.[24] For Arendt, the preservation
of intellectual independence, of individuality, was an essential political
act. Critical intellectuals, individuals thinking for themselves, could block
the totalitarian threat by maintaining minds that were immune to it. But
individuality could not necessarily be preserved through impeccable alienation, for Arendt connected such alienation to resentments that led intellectuals to join with the masses in a blind rage against bourgeois society.

In 1952, then, American intellectuals found themselves in a postwar
climate pregnant with—to use their lexicon—"complexity," "irony," "paradox," and even "tragedy." Their country and its democratic institutions
seemed like the best hope for freedom, but their culture still seemed alien
and threatening. They sought to affirm American liberal principles against
Soviet totalitarianism, but they needed to retain their critical indepen-

dence and detachment in the process. They celebrated democratic freedom, but worried about the alignment of democracy and mass culture. Democracy was necessary for freedom, but democratized culture contained the potential for a mass society that could easily become totalitarian. Even as intellectuals embraced the ideals of American democracy, they looked with suspicion upon the millions who populated it. The elitist implications of this view were lost on neither the intellectuals nor their critics in the popular press. Amid a swirl of Cold War tensions, Senator Joseph McCarthy's accusations, Korean War casualties, and elections pitting "the New Dealers" against "the car dealers," as Adlai Stevenson put it, many intellectuals came to view the preservation of critical intellect itself as their primary political task.

* * *

In 1952 Richard Hofstadter was not in tune with the editors of *Partisan Review*. While they observed that "intellectuals now feel closer to their country," Hofstadter was most alert to the persistent distance, if not the clash, between intellectuals and the American people. Perhaps they were reading different things. The editors sprinkled their pages with quotes from literary luminaries, culminating in Edmund Wilson's remark that he felt "a revival of democratic . . . creativeness" in the air.[25] Hofstadter's essays were adorned more often with quotes from Texas congressmen and *New York Daily News* columnists. He had one eye on proceedings within "the house of intellect" but could not divert the other from the angry crowd gathering at its doorstep.[26]

Before the international Cold War turned hot on the Korean peninsula in 1950, the domestic Cold War had already inflicted casualties on the ideals of freedom and tolerance that intellectuals were affirming in the wake of World War Two. On March 21, 1947, President Harry Truman issued an executive order requiring loyalty oaths from federal employees and instituting background checks on those applying for government employment. In 1948 the Alger Hiss case arose from and fueled fears of communist subversion—particularly by intellectuals—in the State Department. Adlai Stevenson, whom Hofstadter would support vigorously in the presidential election a few years later, testified before the House Un-American Activities Committee (HUAC) on Hiss's behalf.

In 1949 the University of California's Board of Regents required employees to sign a loyalty oath indicating that they were neither members of nor believers in organizations, like the Communist Party, seeking to topple the government of the United States. The oath controversy raised questions about academic freedom in the United States, and in 1950 thirty-one professors who refused to sign lost their jobs.[27] In addition to sparking the loyalty-oath program, anti-communism in California also propelled Congressman Richard M. Nixon of HUAC to the United States Senate in the 1950 elections.

If Hofstadter shifted his gaze from the West Coast to the Midwest, he could see a heretofore obscure senator from Wisconsin named Joe McCarthy speaking to a crowd in Wheeling, West Virginia, on February 9, 1950, in a speech that would become infamous for McCarthy's allegation that he held in his hand a list of communists who had infiltrated the State Department. University professors and State Department officials alike were in the crosshairs of domestic anti-communism.

A marked shift in Hofstadter's thinking took place amid these events. It was evident in the different emphases of his 1948 book, *The American Political Tradition and the Men Who Made It*, and his next several books, notably 1955's *The Age of Reform*.[28] In the former he is highly critical of the tradition of free-market acquisitiveness endorsed by even putative political adversaries throughout American history, while in the latter he is critical of the Populists and Progressives, who challenged such laissez-faire capitalism. The change in Hofstadter's thinking between 1948 and 1955 was not, however, a movement toward embracing American capitalism. It was, rather, a shift in terms of what he perceived as the most significant threat to the free play of intellect in American political culture: no longer the dominance of market modes of thought, but the dangers of popular protest. While Hofstadter's sense of the threats to intellect changed, his concern for the status of intellect remained the same.

This concern had been at the center of his thinking since the 1930s, when he was deeply critical of capitalism and searching out alternatives to it. That search led Hofstadter in 1938 to join the Columbia graduate unit of the Communist Party, which he quickly left, citing the party's anti-intellectualism. "People like us," he told his brother-in-law Harvey Swados, "grow up to believe in a certain set of values—freedom of individual intellectual inquiry, scientific attitudes of mind, respect for facts, a certain cultural latitude—which [Communist leaders like] the Stalins, Browders, Cannons and Schactmans dislike and will, if given a chance, stamp out." Hofstadter might have written this sentence in 1952, substituting the names of the anti-communist McCarthy, Eisenhower, Roy Cohn, and Nixon for the Communists he criticized in 1939. The 1950s seem a decade when Hofstadter's commitment to the ideal of intellectual freedom came to the fore. But a look at Hofstadter in the 1930s finds him already railing against inhospitable conditions for intellect at a time when he was at his most radical politically. It finds him concerned about the vulnerability of critical thought. Hofstadter's commitment to intellectualism thus preceded his migration to liberalism. As biographer David S. Brown observes, Hofstadter's "first skirmishes with anti-intellectualism . . . were fought against the left."[29]

Hofstadter's attention to the intellectual climate of politics, to the mentality of political movements, shaped his critique of the American political tradition—a durable, widespread emphasis on business prosperity that he dubbed "a democracy in cupidity." Unlike those who applauded the practical (i.e., purportedly non-ideological) character of this consensus, Hofstadter, Lasch wrote, saw it "as a form of intellectual bankruptcy."[30] As in Hofstadter's brush with the Communist Party, the issue was not only the specific policies that flowed from the business bent, but also the intellectual climate it produced. The beliefs and assumptions associated with Hofstadter's "entrepreneurial view," as Arthur Schlesinger Jr. called it, had excluded other views, had made it difficult, in fact, to even find another viewpoint.[31] Prosperous industrial societies like the United States "have a kind of mute organic consistency," Hofstadter wrote. "They do not foster ideas that are hostile to their fundamental working arrangements. Such ideas may appear, but they are slowly and persistently insulated, as an oyster deposits nacre around an irritant." Bold ideas "are confined to small groups of dissenters and alienated intellectuals, and except in revolutionary times they do not circulate among practical politicians."[32]

The Liberal Imagination, published in 1950 by Hofstadter's Columbia colleague Lionel Trilling, echoed his concern about America's inhospitality for ideas—but pointed to progressive ideals rather than business-mindedness as a source of the problem. The liberal imagination was, for Trilling, one "mature" enough to contemplate "variousness and possibility, which implies the awareness of complexity and difficulty." Achieving it required outgrowing "the simple humanitarian optimism which, for two decades, has been so pervasive." Trilling had in mind the spirit of the New Deal and the postwar reconstruction effort, in which he saw not just the belief that collective action could improve the human condition but the assurance that it would do so. Such blithe belief in progress was not only "politically and philosophically inadequate," Trilling wrote, but "a kind of check on the creative faculties."[33]

In Hofstadter's *American Political Tradition*, the most creative figure is Wendell Phillips: "The Patrician as Agitator." For Hofstadter's Phillips, "there was no higher office . . . than exercising *the moral imagination* necessary to mold the sentiments of the masses into the form suitable for the next forward movement of history." In Hofstadter's hands, Phillips emerges as one whose growing sense of "variousness and possibility" approximates Trilling's conception of the liberal imagination: "he was a keener observer and had a more flexible mind than most of his colleagues," rising "high above the intellectual limitations" of other reformers.[34]

Hofstadter's sketch of Phillips reveals much about his stance on intellectuals' political role. For Hofstadter, Phillips "introduces a contrast between the agitator and the practical politician," with the agitator coming off better than the political figures in the rest of the book. "The work of the agitator . . . consists chiefly in talk; his function is not to make laws or determine policy, but to influence the public mind in the interest of some large social transformation," Hofstadter wrote. This work "is vastly different from the responsible politician's and rightly so."[35]

While much of this sketch accords with persistent themes in Hofstadter's writing—the rare virtue of the flexible mind, the marginal position of the critical thinker, and the value of such thinkers to society—other elements are surprising in light of his later work. One such surprise is its view of the general public. Hofstadter reserves his criticism for elites, and his implicit sympathies lie with the people. In his later work, this formula is often reversed. In his sketch of Phillips, the people may not be wise, but they are educable. "The duty of the scholar," as Phillips's 1881 Phi Beta Kappa address at Harvard proclaimed it, "'is to help those less favored in life,' and to educate the mass of the people." Phillips lamented that a "'chronic distrust of the people pervades the book-educated class of the North.'"[36]

The people in this rendering are not menacing, but rather inertial. They are not yet masses; they are simply a mass—and a difficult one to move, even with the most vigorous agitations. In Hofstadter's view, Phillips urged to his last breath "that scholarship fulfill its duties" and "at last . . . take the side of the wage worker and the woman in their coming campaigns for justice." The cause of the people and that of the agitator-intellectual were the same: justice. The agitator-intellectual spurred the people and their politicians toward that lofty goal. Hofstadter concluded that Phillips had performed this function well, for "he had been a thorn in the side of complacency." The relationship here envisioned between the intellectual and the people resembles that between the Socratic gadfly and its Athens as horse: "the state is like a great and noble steed who is tardy in his motions owing to his very size, and requires to be stirred into life." Socrates is "that gadfly which . . . all day long and in all places [is] always fastening upon you, arousing and persuading and reproaching you."[37] In 1952 and after, the relation between the people and the intellectual in Hofstadter's work becomes less like that between horse and gadfly and more like that between wolf and prey. If Phillips had been a thorn in the side of the complacent horse, Hofstadter would become a blade drawn to hold the circling wolf at bay.

* * *

A convergence of factors intellectual and political contributed to Hofstadter's changing take on the relationship between intellectuals and democracy over the course of the 1950s. While the editors of *Partisan Review* eyed the possibility of a homecoming for intellectuals in American life in 1952, Hofstadter was becoming increasingly absorbed by that year's presidential election and, especially, the Stevenson campaign. With the Korean War, university loyalty oaths, and McCarthyism all in full swing, the country seemed poised to deliver the presidency to a Republican for the first time since 1928.

Stevenson, the "scholarly and reflective governor of Illinois" whom historian Barton J. Bernstein called "a midwestern patrician," was a reluctant candidate. As host governor to the Democratic Convention in Chicago, Stevenson delivered an "eloquent welcoming address" that impressed the crowd and won him the nomination after the third ballot. In a gesture toward the South aimed at preventing the kind of bolt Dixiecrats had made in 1948, Senator John Sparkman of Alabama—a segregationist—completed the ticket. Fifty African American delegates left the convention in protest.[38]

In the general election, Stevenson faced General Dwight D. Eisenhower, whose campaign centered on the "K1C2" strategy: Korea, communism, and corruption. Republicans aimed to expose the poor performance of the Truman administration in stopping communism abroad and rooting it out at home. Democrats ran on the legacy of the New and Fair Deals and a promise to extend them.[39]

If Hofstadter and other Columbia faculty wished to wait out the 1952 political season within the ivory tower, they were unable to do so because Eisenhower occupied the chamber at its top, serving as their university president. Senator Robert Taft of Ohio, a staunch conservative, had been the relatively centrist Eisenhower's main rival for the Republican nomination. To win Taft's allegiance and conservative support for November, Eisenhower invited Taft to his residence at Columbia. Claiming that the general made policy and other concessions in exchange for Taft's help in the fall campaign, Democrats dubbed the meeting "the surrender of Morningside Heights."[40]

The election had come to Columbia, and it marked an important moment for Hofstadter in two respects: it triggered a burst of direct political action on his part, and it left a lasting impression on his ideas about intellectuals and American democracy. Those who knew him characterized Hofstadter as temperamentally unsuited to activism. Frank Freidel, a colleague and friend to Hofstadter and sociologist C. Wright Mills when all three were at the University of Maryland in the 1940s, recalled that "later when they were at Columbia, Mills at times used to scoff at Hofstadter and always attack him as an establishment person, which he certainly was not. He was simply I think a little more thoughtful, a little less ready to get excited about things." Elisabeth Earley, who also knew him in Maryland, remembered that Hofstadter "was not an activist in any way, shape or form." He "took the spectator-interpreter-critic-analytical position more." In 1940 Hofstadter had described himself as "permanently alienated from the spirit of revolutionary movements."[41]

Active engagement in the Stevenson campaign was certainly neither radicalism nor revolution, but it was direct involvement in contemporary events—not through the writing of history with an eye to the present, but through the melee of electoral politics. In the fall of 1952, Hofstadter took to organizing committee meetings, raising funds, and firing off letters to the editor. According to Freidel, Hofstadter "was in the forefront of those professors, in fact I think the leader of the Columbia professors who were so firmly for Adlai Stevenson." Hofstadter was elected to the executive committee of the Columbia Faculty Volunteers for Stevenson, which, the *New York Times* reported on October 2, "will work in close cooperation with the regular Volunteers for Stevenson to distribute campaign literature and write letters to the press and colleagues in other universities." That same week, the *Columbia Spectator* denounced Eisenhower in Hofstadter-ian terms, calling him "a plodding, orthodox, unimaginative thinker."[42]

On October 5, Hofstadter was among "twenty-three full professors at Columbia University" who issued "an analysis of the funds of Sena-tor Richard M. Nixon and Gov. Adlai E. Stevenson, which purported to show that there were clear differences in the moral implication of the two funds." The group's actions were prompted by the revelation that Eisen-hower's running mate Nixon had accepted roughly $16,000 in personal spending money from California businessmen. Nixon ducked the scan-dal in his televised Checkers speech, which not only defended his actions but defiantly told of a booster's gift he would never give back: the cocker spaniel named Checkers that his children had grown to love. Ahead of the speech, Stevenson revealed that he himself had a personal political fund to pay holiday bonuses to state employees. The Columbia professors declared that Nixon's money "set a vicious example," while the Stevenson fund was appropriate because it paid bonuses anonymously. Speaking for the group, Hofstadter's colleague Allan Nevins "said he felt a public service would be performed by an analysis that put down the issues in 'coherent form,'" in contrast to the emotionalism of the Checkers speech. "It is an elementary rule of public morals," the group's statement read, "that no gov-ernment officer should accept gifts, contributions, or extra compensation from sources which may be affected by his official action. In guarding this rule, intelligent citizens have not always been vigilant."[43]

Their language reveals something of the professors' view of the rela-tionship between academic intellectuals and the public, political sphere. The Checkers speech had obscured a serious allegation about influence-buying in a cloud of sentiment that they aimed to dissipate, passing "mea-sured judgment" and providing "coherent form."[44] That they were not only professors but "full professors" established their credentials for judging the funds, but there was no apparent link between Hofstadter's and Nevins's academic expertise and the analysis they conducted.[45] The professors were acting not as specialists, however, but in their broader capacity as intellectuals—those who bring analytical, rigorous qualities of mind to bear on public questions. They invoked no expertise in forensic account-ing and saw no need to do so. Their endeavor was simply a model of the "vigilance" that "intelligent citizens" should maintain.

The pro-Eisenhower *New York Daily News* reported that several of the professors who signed the analysis were "prominently mentioned in the files of the House committee [HUAC] for belonging to Communist fronts, refusing to take loyalty oaths, writing for Communist publications, or signing left-wing petitions." The *Daily News* echoed a statement, put forward by the Republican National Committee, claiming that "the 'Red front boys' are lining up behind Stevenson."[46] Hofstadter was not cited in HUAC files, but he was painted with this broad red brush nonetheless. The professors had sallied forth on the strength of their intellectual credibility only to have it undermined by allegations of communist sympathy and un-American activity.

On October 16, the Volunteers for Stevenson on the Columbia University Faculties and Staff—listing Hofstadter on its executive committee—published an advertisement in the *New York Times*. Endorsed by 324 signers, it emphasized Stevenson's intellectualism as much, if not more, than his policy positions. "He has appealed not to unreasoning sentiment," it read, "but to the sober judgment of the electorate." A person of "intelligence" and "dignity," Stevenson "does not indulge in demagogy." While his opponent had "surrendered" to the "unsavory" side of his party, Stevenson had maintained the higher ground. The surrender no doubt referred to Eisenhower's Morningside meeting with Taft, but the general had also backpedaled in the face of McCarthy, famously deleting a defense of George C. Marshall—a McCarthy target—from a speech in Green Bay, Wisconsin. At stake in the election was not only a set of policies but also a style of politics. On one side was a candidate of intelligence and eloquence who appealed to public reason. On the other was a candidate who either lacked these traits or submerged them in an appeal not to reason, but to the worst tendencies of the demagogue-led mob. Eisenhower would "open the door" of the public sphere, of the executive branch itself, to these popular forces.[47] Stevenson, protecting freedom, would keep that door shut.

Newspapers around the nation reported on the advertisement. As Leuchtenburg, who signed the document, recalled, "Normally what a bunch of professors have to say doesn't get any attention at all, but this drew a lot of attention because Eisenhower was the president of Columbia."[48] The advertisement sparked a reaction from Republicans and debate about the role of professors in politics. Morningside Heights was not only contested terrain; it was apparently terrain that held strategic value for both sides.

On October 23, Faculty Volunteers for Eisenhower, feeling unable to remain silent, published an advertisement in the *New York Times* and the *New York Herald Tribune* carrying the names of 714 "members of Columbia University's faculty and staff" for Ike. Hofstadter and three other Columbia Stevensonians sprang into action. They combed the list of names, finding that only 259 of the 714 were designated as members of the teaching staff in the university directory. Hofstadter, along with philosophy professor Justus Buchler and instructors Peter Gay and Paul Seabury, took these findings to the *Times*, which reported that "twenty-three buildings and ground employees, five bookstore clerks and 103 clerical employees, such as secretaries and stenographers" were among the Eisenhower supporters. Gay "challenged the inclusion" of such people "in a group that said it was made up of 'faculties and staffs.'" He went on to designate certain categories of university employees as "legitimate" signers; counting only them, the Stevenson Columbia faction outnumbered the Eisenhower one by sixty-five. "Some people in our group walked into it," Leuchtenburg remembered, "by saying . . . these aren't professors, these are ordinary folk, which was a very inadvisable thing to say, even though true. Because here you're supposed to be liberal professors, people who are for the people, and now you sneer at them when they express their political views."[49]

The dueling advertisements and the debate about who was a "legitimate" Columbian drew mockery from the media and criticism from within Columbia itself. "The professors have shimmied down from their ivory towers and are having themselves a high old time making stump speeches, signing manifestoes, buying advertising, and working zealously at various spare time jobs in whatever Republican or Democratic headquarters happens to be nearest campus," the *Washington Post* editorialized. "Of course they are doing all this, not in their capacities of scholars and gentlemen, but merely as 'voters and citizens,' which seems to suggest that the Swiss savant, Dr. Max Picard, may have had something when he complained some years ago that almost everybody is a bit schizophrenic nowadays." Making its final dismissal, the *Post* exclaimed: "Thank Heaven, it will all be over in a few more weeks, and the professors can go back to pleasanter worries over whether they have made enough acknowledgements in their prefaces or attached enough footnotes to their texts."[50]

Columbia professor of East Asian religions W. T. de Bary assessed the consequences of the campaign—and its flurry of activity, publicity, and accusation—for the university. "There is great need for college alumni and persons in academic life to take a serious and responsible part in politics," de Bary wrote to the *New York Times*, "but when any group of alumni, faculty or students, instead of working through one or another of the existing channels of political activity, chooses to make use of the Columbia campus or the name of Columbia to advance its own cause it can only be to exploit the prestige of an educational institution dedicated to an impartial search for truth." Faculty who engaged in overt political activity *as* faculty made it "far more difficult to defend [the university's] legitimate function of promoting open discussion or the legitimate political activity of its individual members."[51]

At another moment, Hofstadter might have assented to de Bary's views.[52] Now, however, Hofstadter was at the center of electoral activism at Columbia: the analysis of the Nixon fund, the executive committee of the Faculty Volunteers, and the rapid-response scrutiny of the Eisenhower advertisement. An outlier in terms of both his personal temperament and his beliefs about universities, this activity underscores the significance he placed upon the contest. It also served as a cautionary tale for his later engagement with politics, an engagement that, while ultimately more consequential than his efforts on behalf of Stevenson, would take place largely through the book, the essay, and the lectern.

Historian H. Stuart Hughes recalled discussing the 1952 campaign with Hofstadter, who "kept citing to me, as an almost traumatic memory, how much time it had taken, how much writing time he had lost, and swore never to do that again." Hughes was a vigorous political activist throughout his life, even running for US Senate in 1962. He and Hofstadter shared a friendship that flourished during their summers at Wellfleet on Cape Cod. It is not difficult to imagine them reflecting upon their differing engagements with politics during a warm evening on the shore. Hughes believed that Hofstadter's reluctance to engage in direct political action was about "wanting to limit not his moral commitment but his time commitment or his commitment of energies." Hofstadter felt, Hughes recalled, that "there were certain types of things he could do that only he and a handful of others could do, and he'd better do them and not waste his time on other things." Hofstadter would not turn away from politics; he would be more indirect but effective in how he practiced it.[53]

Frank Freidel, whose memory of Hofstadter in 1952 corroborates Hughes's, believed that Hofstadter was anything but apolitical in the major thrust of his work. He felt very strongly, and could best express himself through essays, through books, and through personal appearances throughout the United States before academic audiences, in which again and again he would be asked to come and address large groups—not under political auspices directly, but on the themes which were obviously political. This man clearly was caught up in the Stevenson movement in this way, rather than going out and writing Stevenson's speeches. This way he's in sharp contrast to the organizer, and even in certain ways in contrast to Arthur Schlesinger, Jr. who has written political speeches for candidates.[54]

Unlike Schlesinger, Hofstadter would never be on the payroll of a politician, and 1952 was as close as he would come to such involvement. The lessons he drew from that election went beyond refocusing his mode of engaging with politics, however. The year 1952 was above all for Hofstadter a moment of profound realization about the political landscape of America itself.

A decade later, Hofstadter continued to write about the 1952 election as though it were painful and present. He viewed the contest within the frame of McCarthy's "sorties against intellectuals and universities [that] were emulated throughout the country by a host of less exalted inquisitors." In this "atmosphere of fervent malice and humorless imbecility . . . the campaign of 1952 dramatized the contrast between intellect and philistinism in the opposing candidates." The most threatening aspect of the election for Hofstadter was the idea that, like him, the American people viewed the contest as one between intellect and anti-intellectualism. They did so because they were eager to deliver, in the form of Eisenhower and Nixon, a rebuke to the intellectual class they despised. "Eisenhower's decisive victory was taken both by the intellectuals themselves and by their critics as a measure of their repudiation by America," Hofstadter wrote. Concern over intellectuals' fate "seemed . . . amply justified when the new administration got under way. The replacement, in Stevenson's phrase, of the New Dealers by the car dealers seemed to make final the repudiation of intellectuals and their values."[55]

Hofstadter's *Anti-Intellectualism in American Life* contains a rogue's gallery of clippings about Stevenson. One sees Hofstadter opening the pages of the conservative *Freeman* and reading Louis Bromfield's grouping of liberals, New Dealers, and intellectuals under the newly minted label "egghead": "A person of spurious intellectual pretensions, often a professor or the protégé of a professor. . . . A self-conscious prig, so given to examining all sides of a question that he becomes thoroughly addled while remaining always in the same spot." For Bromfield, writing at the close of 1952, "the recent election demonstrated a number of things, not the least of them being the extreme remoteness of the 'egghead' from the thought and feeling of the whole of the people." Hofstadter clipped this piece, publishing a portion of it as "Exhibit A" in his effort to put anti-intellectualism on trial.[56]

Hofstadter saw the word "egghead" as one sign of the country's contempt for intellectuals. People "seemed to be in need of some term to express the disdain for intellectuals which had by then become a self-conscious motif in American politics," he wrote. "*Egghead* was originally used without invidious associations, but quickly assumed them." Stevenson's own cranium, with its balding pate, lent the term a little descriptive flourish. The egg image suggested not only the shape of the shell, however, but its contents. The egghead was full of runny yellow yolk. In an era of Soviet expansion abroad and communist subversion at home, the cowardice implied by yellow and runny was an indictment indeed. "Nixon, a master of tasteless invective, called Stevenson 'Adlai the appeaser' and a 'Ph.D. graduate of Dean Acheson's cowardly College of Communist Containment.'"[57] Eggheads were many things, but they were decidedly not persons to be trusted with vital affairs. For Hofstadter, 1952 was not a promising year for the joining of hands between intellectuals and American democracy.

* * *

The Stevenson campaign underscored the hostility to intellect among the American public. Hofstadter's work on education in the United States, beginning in 1952 with *The Development and Scope of Higher Education in the United States* and continuing for a decade thereafter, highlighted threats to intellect from within its own precincts. *Development and Scope* was published under the auspices of the Commission on Financing Higher Education, funded by the Rockefeller and Carnegie Foundations and presided over by a dozen college administrators, industrialists, and lawyers: an elite crowd.[58] The commission's purpose, as executive director John D. Millett explained, was to address the uncertain finances of higher education amid its rapid growth after World War Two. College and university funding was hampered by "widespread ignorance of what higher education is, how it developed, and what it tries to do." The work of the commission was, in part, to correct this ignorance. In order to fund the university, taxpayers "must believe in its goals and methods."⁵⁹ Writing for the commission, Hofstadter was to be an evangelist for higher learning.

He exceeded his mandate. Hofstadter offered a narrative of decline running from the colonial period and the first half of the nineteenth century, called "The Age of the College," to "The Age of the University" commencing in the latter part of the nineteenth century. In his portrait of the old colleges, an ideal—and aristocratic—intellectual community emerges. "Education was for gentlemen," he wrote; "it was designed to create among them a common core of central knowledge that would make of them a community of the educated." Yet the community of the educated was not based simply upon the social origin of those it admitted; it had also to do with the content of their education and the quality of the college experience. Indeed, when "sons of farmers and even of artisans" attended college, "the education to which they were exposed was designed for the strengthening and adornment of the mind and not for immediate practical use or vocational advancement." These colleges nurtured what one might call a Hofstadterian realm where the "life of the mind" was both fostered and practiced in a community that valued it.⁶⁰

But that realm was vulnerable, and suited to exploit that vulnerability was democracy. Lamenting the death of the old college, Hofstadter argued that "American society was too democratic to accept completely the idea of a gentleman's education, too practical and perhaps too philistine to continue to accept complacently its classical content." The subsequent university model was the mode of higher education characteristic of American democracy. While the old colleges recognized "that a man's education and his intellectual life were fundamental parts of his character and his spiritual being," the newer institutions were "neither intellectual nor spiritual but practical, accumulative, indeed acquisitive." Universities had become "dynamic and community-centered, but the 'community' too often meant nothing more than business and technology. The feeling that the life of the mind should have an independent weight of its own in affairs was stifled rather than encouraged." In its turn toward applied knowledge, the university moved away from the formation of an intellectual community that would foster, sustain, and—of particular importance in a diverse democracy—acculturate students to the life of the mind. "In the old college," Hofstadter wrote, "the sons of plain farmers . . . rubbed elbows with the sons of the upper middle class; applying themselves to a common curriculum in the intimate atmosphere of a small school, they grew somewhat more alike because they had something in common, both social and intellectual." That shared collegiate atmosphere, an equalizing force, had been lost. "The new university curriculum sent [students] off in a dozen different directions; and its social milieu—its fraternities and clubs and 'activities'—gradually reproduced the social heterogeneity and the snobbery of the world outside."[61]

The old college thus represented an intellectual community with democratizing potential that was, ironically, undone by the pressures of the democratic market society beyond its gates. While the old college trained students to act as citizens in the public sphere—the kind of public sphere that Hofstadter and his colleagues envisioned when they subjected the Nixon fund to the "measured judgment" characteristic of "vigilant" and "intelligent citizens"—the new university prepared graduates to function as cogs in the machinery of the market economy.

Just as the intellectual community of the old college had been vulnerable to the changing currents of American society, so the graduate school—innermost bastion of intellect—had fallen to leveling forces in Hofstadter's own time. Rather than "a small group of superior, creative intellects," graduate schools had caught "the disease of bigness" and been swamped by such a quantity of students that "professionalized general ignorance and trained intellectual incapacity" were the result.[62]

As the "democratic" character of the academy increased, Hofstadter argued, its intellectual character diminished. "If it is democratic to admit to our colleges great numbers of students who lack intellectual interests and to attune the educational system to their sub-intellectual needs and capacities, there has been an excess of democracy in the conduct of American higher education," Hofstadter concluded, in one of several sentences that vibrated between a plea for embattled intellect and a scowl.[63] Intellectually inclined students were not just swamped by anti-intellectual peers; they were increasingly persecuted by them. "Many a campus is dominated by a kind of inverse snobbery in which the intellectually serious student stands as a loathsome reminder of the putative goals of higher education, and is rewarded for his role by being made a social outcast." Hofstadter believed that when "such great numbers go to college," cerebral students "are overwhelmed by philistines." This situation was "'democracy' with a vengeance."[64] The attacks on intellectuals in the Senate chambers presided over by McCarthy were repeated on campuses across the nation, abetted by football players, business majors, and frat boys.

Whether he looked to national politics or to his own findings on higher education, Hofstadter saw mounting evidence for inescapable tension between intellect and democracy. Persecuted, ridiculed, overrun, and embattled, intellect could find no refuge in American life. At its best, the academy had "offered a haven . . . to creative artists as well as to teachers and scholars." It was now, however, "cramped by limitations about which no one can afford to be complacent." For "a system of mass higher education" lost "something qualitatively" as it grew quantitatively. It was unlikely "to serve science and technology in a practical society without some cost to intellectual and spiritual values" or "to serve the American community . . . without succumbing to some of the failings of that community."[65]

Prominent among those failings was blindness to the value of intellect as an end in itself. Intellect always had to harness itself to other values—like the productivity and power fostered by technical expertise—to achieve recognition. "American writing and speaking on education" exhibited "a strange and pervasive reluctance—even when the writers and speakers are teachers and scholars—to admit that enjoyment of the life of the mind is a legitimate and important consummation in itself," Hofstadter observed, "as least as valid among the ends of life as the enjoyment of, say, sports, sex, or liquor. Education is justified apologetically as a useful instrument in attaining *other* ends."[66] Unable to stand on its own in the eyes of the culture, intellect was left vulnerable and dependent; its value was derivative, not fundamental.

Three years later, when he coauthored *The Development of Academic Freedom in the United States*, Hofstadter sounded the alarm more loudly. Searching history to highlight the fragility of conditions that nurtured intellectualism, he found the delicate ecosystems of intellectual communities repeatedly swamped by outside predators. He reached back to the medieval university, where "as national states arose, sovereigns, princes, and parliaments took upon themselves the right to meddle in the internal affairs of universities, appointing and discharging professors at will and mocking at the former pride and autonomy of the masters." He looked to eighteenth-century America, where "the colonial elite need not have been ashamed of its educational achievement," including "higher standards" and "greater liberality." Amid Jacksonian democracy and Protestant revival, however, "the little candles of the Enlightenment guttered or failed. Between 1790 and 1830 the intellectual and moral temper of the country was drastically transformed."[67] Hofstadter's message: it has happened before and—with persecution by McCarthy, Stevenson's defeat, and mass education even in graduate schools—it is happening again.

Hofstadter emerged from 1952 with a sense of both the value of an intellectualized public sphere and its fragility. Preserving a place for the free and independent operation of intellect, that sphere offered an antidote to dogmatism. It was a forum for adjudicating among interests and engaging in moral and political debate—the alternative to which, Hofstadter feared, was violence.[68] Yet an intellectualized public sphere was delicate. Hofstadter repeatedly emphasized the necessity of an intellectual *community* to nurture and safeguard intellect, and he worried that intellect in his own time lacked a secure institutional home.

For Hofstadter, Columbia provided one such place. His summers on Cape Cod, beside neighbors like Edmund Wilson and H. Stuart Hughes, provided another. But Stevenson's crushing defeat, the depredations visited upon intellectuals by McCarthy, and the threats to the academy posed by mass education and the utilitarian view of learning all underlined for Hofstadter the rarity of his own experiences at Morningside Heights and Wellfleet. Popular democracy, he came to believe, made intellect vulnerable in America. Its values were at odds with intellectual values, and its growth had often presaged intellect's decline. Hofstadter had seen the enemy, and it was popular democracy. In the years after 1952, he would fight back.[69]

* * *

In the late 1970s, historian Richard Gillam argued that Hofstadter and C. Wright Mills shared an adherence to "the critical ideal." This ideal rested on the idea that "scholars . . . must critically confront great issues of their age" and the "conviction that the critical intelligence, contending with reality, was . . . powerful and autonomous in itself." While casting intellect as "a potent force in human affairs," the ideal also narrowed the roles it could play in those affairs: "while Mills and Hofstadter were political men, they remained, first and foremost, *intellectuals* as opposed to experts, advisors, activists, captives of a party line."[70]

For Hofstadter, however, the critical ideal influenced not only the kind of public role he was willing to adopt but also the *purposes* of his public presence. In the 1930s, Hofstadter upheld the critical ideal against the constraints of the Communist Party line. In the 1940s, he "deplored" the intellectually stifling character of the American political tradition. Commitment to the critical ideal was a continuous feature of his outlook. What changed in 1952 was, therefore, not his level of commitment to that ideal but his activity in the service of it. He entered the public, political arena to practice criticism on behalf of the critical ideal. He acted as an intellectual in the service of intellectualism. Hofstadter was deeply engaged "in trying really to interpret the anti-intellectualism which was in the forefront of American politics," Frank Freidel recalled. "He's going to be remembered, I would suspect, as much as anything, first as a great historical essayist, and second for the way he fought back on behalf of the intellectuals," Freidel said. "I think Hofstadter more effectively than anyone else was able to engage in this gentle, thoughtful backfire."[71]

Hofstadter's writing and speaking served intellect on two fronts: he championed the life of the mind, and he constructed theory and history that undermined what he saw as its most dangerous foe—the populist mentality. In "Democracy and Anti-Intellectualism in America," *The Age of Reform*, "The Pseudo-Conservative Revolt," *Anti-Intellectualism in American Life*, and "The Paranoid Style," Hofstadter fired broadsides against the popular mind and its hostility to intellect. He deployed history, psychology (indeed, psychiatry), and sociology to arraign popular democracy. His work went beyond diagnosing democratic maladies; it blasted them in the name of intellect.

At the same time, his work bolstered the *status* of intellect. Not only did he write forcefully and consistently about the life of the mind, but his writings also positioned intellectuals more closely to social elites. If one of the factors that made intellect vulnerable in America was intellectuals' lack of a social and institutional home, then Hofstadter's work conjured a world where intellectuals and northeastern elites were at home with each other. In the Depression and then in the twilight of the New Deal in the 1940s, intellectuals had often lined up against big business and the elites grouped around it. Hofstadter himself had been critical of industrial capitalism. But after 1952 Hofstadter, looking southward, westward, and—in his estimation—culturally downward, saw that social elites and intellectuals had more in common with each other than with other Americans. From his vantage points at Columbia, Wellfleet, and the Carnegie- and

Rockefeller-funded Commission on Financing Higher Education, Hofstadter realized that intellectuals had in American elites a potential new social and institutional safe harbor.[72]

In his work on higher education, Hofstadter pointed out how popular democracy undermined intellectualism while aristocracy often bolstered it. From one who valued intellect as Hofstadter did, this assessment amounted to an indictment of the former and an endorsement of the latter. As early as 1948, Hofstadter celebrated Wendell Phillips not only as an agitator but, more specifically, "the *patrician* as agitator." In *The Development of Academic Freedom*, Hofstadter claimed that "the sponsorship of an enlightened aristocracy has often been identified with . . . gains in American higher education." Indeed, "the centers of aristocratic culture were far more generous in fostering higher education than were the regions in which popular democracy enjoyed a more unqualified reign." When the democratic spirit surged, as it did during the Jacksonian period, intellect came under pressure. "None of this should be taken to imply that those who stood in the democratic tradition were invariably hostile to freedom in higher education, while aristocrats were invariably tolerant," he wrote. "What does seem true is that the most enlightened aristocracies had a considerably better record than the most militantly democratic communities."[73]

Six months after Stevenson's 1952 defeat, Hofstadter took to the podium at the University of Michigan. Much of his lecture there appeared verbatim in *Anti-Intellectualism in American Life* ten years later—evidence that the book was grounded in Hofstadter's experience of the 1950s. Published as "Democracy and Anti-Intellectualism in America" in the *Michigan Alumnus Quarterly Review*, Hofstadter's words were aimed at an educated audience. As Brown reports, "The intention of the essay was as much therapeutic as explanatory—he hoped to boost the morale of American intellectuals."[74]

Surveying the terrain, Hofstadter found that "everywhere in America, intellectuals are on the defensive." Politics were discouraging, for "in the late presidential campaign a political leader who embodied the kind of traits that the intellectual would most like to see in our national leadership found the support of intellectuals of slight value." More discouraging, however, was the "failure of nerve" shown by the intellectual community itself. Educators were too willing to abandon the position that education should cultivate intellect, too quick to accept the "non-intellectual or anti-intellectual criteria that many forces in our society wish to impose upon education and which we might well consider it the bounden duty of educators to resist." He delivered a reproach meant to stiffen spines: "What . . . brings our nation's educators to such depressing disavowals of the fundamentally intellectual purposes of education? Much the same thing, I believe, that has them cringing before the onslaughts of politicians who are beyond the pale of moral decency—and that is the lack of a self-confident dedication to the life of the mind."[75]

Intellectuals and educators were hesitant to assert that the life of the mind had its own independent value because doing so, Hofstadter believed, required trimming their commitment to another important value: democracy. "There has been a historically persistent tension between our popular democracy and intellectualism that has been very sadly felt in the sphere of university and college life," he claimed.[76] Higher education should be a bastion for intellectualism, where the value of intellect is taken as a given, not as a derivative of its uses for war and profit. The value of intellect could not be subjected to plebiscite; it must be beyond the vicissitudes of democracy.[77] To argue this was to argue for limits to democracy, and that was the sticking point for those accustomed to siding with the many against the few. "Many of us have in the past made a mystique of the masses and have tended too much to attribute all the villainy in our world to the machinations of vested interests," Hofstadter wrote.[78]

That "mystique" must be dispelled. Educators would then see, Hofstadter claimed, that their retreat from the intellectual premises of higher education "has a great deal to do with our false piety for populistic democracy, our sense of guilt at daring to suggest that there is anything wrong with the mob, even when a large part of it has obviously been whipped up by demagogues to a state of frantic suspicion of everything it does not care to understand." In the clarity of this realization, intellectuals could finally "face the fact that the very idea of intellectualism implies an elite of some kind—not, to be sure, a ruthless elite with special privileges or power, but simply a group of people who have interests not shared by everyone in the community and whose very special interest is in freedom." The sooner intellectuals acknowledged the inherently elite character of intellectualism, the sooner they would cease their contortions to make intellect acceptable to popular prejudice. The sooner they would defend the truth that an "elite must maintain a certain spiritual autonomy in defining its own standards."[79]

Hofstadter closed by laying out a political blueprint for embattled intellectuals. They should do "what any group of sensible people will do whose values are under attack": neither "find some plausible reason for abandoning those values because they are not shared by the majority," nor "convince themselves that they really agree with the majority after all," but "show cohesion and firmness under fire, until the point has been reached when it is no longer profitable to encroach upon them."[80] Hofstadter stood amid the wavering ranks of intellect, imploring them to hold their ground while firing the strongest salvos he could at the oncoming popular onslaught.

He fired such a salvo in 1955's *Age of Reform*. In its opening chapters, the strands of thought from his Michigan lecture, his work on higher education, and the painful lessons of the Stevenson campaign came together in a reinterpretation of nineteenth-century Populism that carried unmistakable significance for the present.[81] As he put it, Populism "seems very strongly to foreshadow some aspects of the cranky pseudo-conservatism of our time."[82] Hofstadter's work from 1952 to 1955 had often been defensive—odes to the value of intellect and warnings of its extirpation. Now he went on the offensive, not extolling the virtues of intellectuals so much as cataloguing the vices of the people.

Hofstadter again warned intellectuals to break free from the "mystique of the masses"—a sentiment spawned in historical eras of reform that became a danger in periods of retrenchment.

> Liberal intellectuals, who have rather well-rationalized systems of political beliefs, tend to expect that the masses of people, whose actions at certain moments in history coincide with some of these beliefs, will share their convictions as a matter of logic and principle. Intellectuals, moreover, suffer from a sense of isolation which they usually seek to surmount by finding ways of getting into rapport with the people, and they readily succumb to a tendency to sentimentalize the folk. Hence they periodically exaggerate the measure of agreement that exists between movements of popular reform and the considered principles of political liberalism. They remake the image of popular rebellion closer to their heart's desire. They choose to ignore . . . the elements of illiberalism that frequently seem to be an indissoluble part of popular movements.[83]

In their fondness for the people, Hofstadter claimed, intellectuals neglected their office of instructing them. They seek "not to educate the public or curb its demands for the impossible but to pretend that these demands are altogether sensible and to try to find ways to placate them."[84] Intellectuals showed too much deference to a public opinion that they should instead be shaping.

American public opinion, particularly in the Midwest and South, had long exhibited tendencies Hofstadter found menacing. These included "isolationism and the extreme nationalism that usually goes with it, hatred of Europeans, racial, religious, and nativist phobias, resentment of big business, trade-unionism, intellectuals, the Eastern seaboard and its culture." Hofstadter thus saw in the Populist Party of the 1890s "merely a heightened expression . . . of a kind of popular impulse that is endemic in American political culture." That impulse bubbled up in the 1950s "as an undercurrent of provincial resentments, popular and 'democratic' rebelliousness and suspiciousness, and nativism." In yielding to these undercurrents, reform-minded populism had "turned sour, become illiberal and ill-tempered."[85]

In Hofstadter's view, Populists understood society in terms of myths and conspiracies—a reading of the world infused with symbols—rather than analysis. As a result, both their grasp of social problems and the solutions they proposed were flawed, since they flowed from "status politics," not "interest politics."[86] Intellectuals could "distinguish without excessive difficulty" between real reform and political symbolism, but "popular movements do not always operate with the same discrimination" and may thus go "beyond the demand for important and necessary reforms to the expression of a resentment so inclusive that it embraces not only the evils and abuses of a society but the whole society itself, including some of its more liberal and humane values."[87] Among those values liable to be resented and attacked was respect for the life of the mind.

The year that *The Age of Reform* appeared, Hofstadter published "The Pseudo-Conservative Revolt" in *The New American Right*, an essay collection analyzing the "radical right" in the twilight of Joseph McCarthy.[88] Though the Populists flourished more than a half century before the McCarthyite Right, Hofstadter viewed them as heads of the same hydra. If *The Age of Reform* looked at the popular mind with the eyes of a historian, Hofstadter now diagnosed it with the language of a clinician. The term "pseudo-conservative" and Hofstadter's "suggestive clinical evidence" for it came from *The Authoritarian Personality* (1950), an influential, controversial study by Theodor Adorno and his collaborators. Like his Populist, Hofstadter's "pseudo-conservative always imagines himself to be dominated and imposed upon because he feels that he is not dominant." He "knows no other way of interpreting his position" save elites' "conspiracy against him."[89] Unlike traditional conservatives, pseudo-conservatives sought radical change—to extinguish their oppressors and secure their own dominance.

Hofstadter denied the legitimacy of pseudo-conservatives' views by claiming that their origins were not rational and related to material interests but rather irrational and symbolic. After all, only psychological pathologies—deep resentment and insecurities—could explain why intellectuals were pseudo-conservatives' special targets.[90]

As prominent nonconformists, intellectuals became targets for those who, in their status anxiety, embraced conformity. This zealous conformity led them to "challenge almost anyone whose pattern of life is different and who is imagined to enjoy a superior social position—notably [the] '. . . sophisticated, the intellectuals, the so-called academic minds.'"[91] The isolation and persecution of intellectually distinctive students by their conformist peers, which Hofstadter described in his work on higher education, he now writ large.

His essay reframed the anti-intellectual's narrative. While it presented nonconforming intellectuals as subversive, un-American cultural outliers who posed a grave threat to national security, Hofstadter produced a counternarrative showing how conformity pressures and anti-intellectualism were themselves evidence of sickness in the culture, of widespread status anxiety and dislocation. Moreover, as Arendt and Adorno had shown, these pathologies were the royal road to totalitarianism. Intellectuals were a saving remnant who preserved the capacity for criticism, independent thought, and imagination. They were the antidote, not the problem.

Hofstadter's argument exalted intellect while discrediting its populist opponents. It suggested that the populist Right should be professionally diagnosed rather than publicly debated. It denied them a voice, and they were not prepared to go silently. In response, novelist Taylor Caldwell wrote to Hofstadter, striking at his social scientific, psychological authority: "It is very odd that in my anticommunist novel, *The Devil's Advocate*, published in 1952, and in my new novel, *Tender Victory*, published a short time ago—both of which are national and international best-sellers—I have a demon-psychiatrist who says exactly what you have just written." In Caldwell's view, psychological analysis was a tool that professionals used to manipulate laypeople, for "it is no secret that Hitler used psychiatrists, with your own jargon, to destroy opposition and drive sane men to insanity."[92]

Caldwell and her at times lurid letter may have validated Hofstadter's assumptions about anti-intellectuals. She wrote for the John Birch Society and belonged to the far Right Liberty Lobby. Her letter mocked intellectuals as "owl-eyed nitwits," saying: "There's really nothing basically wrong with them that a good bath . . . could not cure." But Caldwell also challenged Hofstadter's standing to make psychological judgments about politics like hers. "I believe that you have a right to your opinion," she wrote, "but you deny implicitly that people like myself have a right to our opinions, and you imply that we are mentally ill, or something." Caldwell refused to be diagnosed out of the public sphere. "A common and ridiculous error frequently made by men of your kidney is the pronounced conviction that you 'speak for' the American people," she wrote. "I assure you that you do not. The American people are full of sound health and vitality and commonsense."[93]

Caldwell also extended the status dialectic one step further. Right-wing critics claimed that intellectuals were subversives and should therefore be marginalized. Hofstadter counterclaimed that right-wing rhetoric was an irrational derivative of status anxiety. Caldwell now claimed that Hofstadter's argument was itself a product of status anxiety.

> Assuming that you are "projecting"—and the psychiatrists would probably agree that you are—you imagine yourself, to quote your own remarks again, "to be dominated and imposed upon because he feels that he is not dominant." Did I touch to the quick, there, my dear Professor? Who in the world is "dominating and imposing" upon you? Those who will not give you a decent salary? . . . Humiliation that you cannot make as much money as a half-literate entrepreneur?[94]

Caldwell's letter is a complex document. It evinces some of the very scorn for intellectuals that moved Hofstadter to act. But it also shows a certain egalitarianism, a refusal to accept the diagnosis given to the people by the professor without subjecting him to the same searching examination.

The question at the heart of Caldwell's challenge was who controlled the public sphere. The anti-communist crusade with its loyalty oaths, its blacklists, and its HUAC hearings was an attempt to police that sphere by ruling not just a set of opinions—those on the left—out of bounds, but a whole set of people, intellectuals, inherently suspect. In fighting back,

Hofstadter entered the public sphere backed by the authority of a venerable university, a body of social scientific theory, and the idiom of educated intelligence to blow the whistle on dangerous anti-intellectual rhetoric and the irrational effusions of status anxiety and conspiratorial thought. Would the intellectuals keep the people at bay, or would the people keep the intellectuals at bay?

To pose the question of intellectuals' relation to the people in these terms is to assume a distance, an opposition, between the two. Such distance is one thing that Hofstadter and his adversaries could agree on. Both he and those who lampooned "eggheads" regarded the Stevenson defeats as evidence of the chasm between intellectuals and the larger population. While the Bromfields and Caldwells celebrated this distance as evidence of popular good sense, Hofstadter looked upon it as an indication of rampant anti-intellectualism. But such distance also presented an opportunity for intellectuals. Popular voices might tag intellectuals with the label of "elites," but that designation was not unwelcome. If one source of intellectuals' vulnerability was their lack of social and institutional refuge, then aligning with traditional elites—members of the East Coast establishment—offered a potential port in the popular storm.

Pseudo-conservatives had in a sense done intellectuals the favor of lumping them in with cultural, governmental, and economic centers of power and prestige. According to Hofstadter, the pseudo-conservative "enjoys seeing outstanding generals, distinguished secretaries of state, and prominent scholars browbeaten and humiliated." The prominent scholar thus kept powerful company in the eyes of the pseudo-conservative. Indeed, such right-wingers "are much happier to have as their objects of hatred the Anglo-Saxon, Eastern, Ivy League intellectual gentlemen than they are with such bedraggled souls as, say, the Rosenbergs."[95] In the 1930s, Hofstadter had been as bedraggled as the Rosenbergs. Like them, he was living in New York and trying to make ends meet during the Depression. Like them, he moved in left-wing circles. And, like them, he was involved in the Jewish community, largely through his wife, Felice Swados.[96] But by the time the Rosenbergs were executed for espionage in 1953, they and Hofstadter had traveled very different paths. Hofstadter's had in fact led him into the company of eastern elites.

Hofstadter lived in New York, but he looked forward to spending summers at his house in Wellfleet on Cape Cod. This spot was not exactly a middle ground between Boston and New York geographically, but by the early 1960s it was a meeting ground between the two culturally. During summers there, Harvard and Columbia coalesced. As Alfred Kazin put it, "*la plage des intellectuels* in Wellfleet had become a continuation of Cambridge, New Haven, the Institute for Advanced Study, and the executive assistant's wing of the White House."[97] It was where Hofstadter, the son of an immigrant furrier from Buffalo, maintained a close friendship and intellectual rapport with H. Stuart Hughes, grandson of Supreme Court Chief Justice and 1916 Republican presidential candidate Charles Evans Hughes. If Boston was the seat of the genteel tradition, the capital of Anglo-Saxon intellectualism in the vein of Henry Adams and William James, then New York was the seat of intellectual cosmopolitanism, with its African American and Jewish writers, artists, critics, and scholars. At Wellfleet, the two cities—largely excluding African Americans, however—came together in a way that would have been unthinkable for Hofstadter just two decades before, when he and Swados hosted socialist sailors at their New York apartment. In the summers of the early 1960s, Hofstadter kept company with Edmund Wilson, Hughes, and Kazin on the Cape—Jews and gentiles, New Yorkers and Bostonians, eggheads and elites.

If Hofstadter emphasized the extent of McCarthy's conjoined anti-intellectualism and anti-elitism, it was not because he rejected the association himself. His writings that catalogue McCarthy's attacks on "Ivy League graduates, high-ranking generals, college presidents, intellectuals, the Eastern upper classes, Harvard professors, and members of Phi Beta Kappa"; that argue for a fundamental, "historically persistent tension between our popular democracy and intellectualism"; and that emphasize the hospitable conditions for intellect provided by aristocracy, all point toward hope for a kind of collective-security pact between the two groups tarred with the same anti-intellectual brush and endangered by the same popular fervor.[98]

But an alliance between intellectuals and aristocrats offered more than potential security. It was also in the interests of democratic society. Hofstadter believed that "in a populistic culture like ours, which seems to lack a responsible elite with political and moral autonomy, and in which it is possible to exploit the wildest currents of public sentiment for private purposes," it was possible "that a highly organized, vocal, active and well-financed minority could create a political climate in which the rational pursuit of our well-being and safety would become impossible."[99] The implication is that a "responsible elite" is necessary to check the anti-intellectual, irrational, and dangerous propensities of the people, susceptible as they are to manipulation by demagogues. In the 1930s, Hofstadter would not have regarded intellectuals—at least the ones he ran with—as likely members of such an elite. Decades later, the view was different.

The Columbia Faculty Volunteers for Stevenson had acted as responsible elites, entering the public sphere to correct errors of opinion and, in the case of the Eisenhower ad, matters of fact. Stevenson's defeat and the blowback aimed at the professors revealed that they could use allies. It also revealed the unwillingness of people to be ministered to by elites. The liberal intellectual "just does not understand how it is that dumb clucks do manage to put things together and make them run," wrote columnist George Sokolsky in 1955. "The answer is that they do. And they do it because they want to get more of the good things of life for themselves and their families." In writing awkwardly on behalf of out-of-touch elites, Sokolsky opined, "Professor Richard Hofstadter of Columbia University is having a tough time translating himself into a conservative." Clement C. Sullivan of Bayonne, New Jersey, echoed such sentiments in a 1955 letter to the *New York Times*: "The doctrinaire concept of academic freedom as understood by writers like Richard Hofstadter . . . savors strongly . . . of the philosophy underlying the Divine Right of Kings." There was, however, "this notable difference. Those who challenged the arrogant pretensions of kings were sent to the block to lose their heads, though but rarely their dignity. Today he who dares oppose the arrogance of academicians risks having heaped on his head such indignities as 'wrong-headed' and 'pseudo-educator' or having his arguments 'laughed out of court' or just plain ignored."[100]

With intellectuals circling the wagons of a responsible elite while popular forces arrayed for an attack on the institutions and individuals composing it, the distance between intellectuals and the people seemed large, indeed. While Hofstadter advised such distance, a voice within the intellectual community raised a note of caution. In a 1959 essay on *The Age of Reform*, Hofstadter's friend C. Vann Woodward surveyed the divide that had widened between the intellectuals and the people in the last decade. "Liberals and intellectuals bore the brunt of the McCarthyite assault on standards of decency," he noted. "They were rightly alarmed and felt themselves betrayed. They were the victims of a perversion of the democracy they cherished, a seamy and sinister side of democracy to which they now guiltily realized they had turned a blind or indulgent eye." Intellectuals like Hofstadter had "responded with a healthy impulse to make up for lost time and confront the problem with all the critical resources at their command. The consequence has been a formidable and often valuable corpus of social criticism."[101]

But Woodward pointed to elitist strands in this criticism, which sometimes expressed yearning for a British-style deference to the well-educated and the wellborn. Such "respect for 'betters' is un-American," Woodward argued. Instead, all should "hope that there will be future upheavals to shock the seats of power and privilege and furnish the periodic therapy that seems necessary to the health of our democracy."[102]

The tradition of popular revolt was a salutary part of American politics, warts and all. "For the tradition to endure . . . the intellectual must not be alienated from the sources of revolt," Woodward wrote. "The intellectual must resist the impulse to identify all the irrational and evil forces he detests with [popular protest] movements because some of them, or the aftermath or epigone of some of them, have proved so utterly repulsive." Walling intellectuals off from the people as part of a responsible elite was no response to the vicissitudes of popular politics. For without periodic surges of democratic upheaval, there was no way to make a responsible elite into a *responsive* elite—and a threateningly irresponsible elite might be the outcome. Woodward urged the intellectual to "learn all he can from the new criticism about the irrationality and illiberal side of Populism and other reform movements, but he cannot afford to repudiate" them.[103]

* * *

Despite Woodward's admonition, Hofstadter continued to stress the tension between popular politics and intellectualism. *Anti-Intellectualism in American Life* (1963) and *The Paranoid Style and Other Essays* (1965) sounded similar notes to "Democracy and Anti-Intellectualism in America," *The Age of Reform*, and "The Pseudo-Conservative Revolt."[104] *Anti-Intellectualism* also echoed many of the themes from *The Development and Scope of Higher Education in the United States* and *The Development of Academic Freedom in the United States*. *The Paranoid Style* included "Pseudo-Conservatism Revisited—1965" and "Goldwater and Pseudo-Conservative Politics," essays that found in Goldwater's campaign echoes of the radical Right from a decade before.

There were new themes in Hofstadter's later work on intellect—a greater focus on the intellectual as expert and on the question of alienation from power versus service to it—but it was still "conceived in response to the political and intellectual conditions in the 1950s," when "the term *anti-intellectualism*, only rarely heard before, became a familiar part of our national vocabulary of self-recrimination and intramural abuse."[105] During that decade, Hofstadter stood guard on behalf of intellectuals against popular democracy, and the distance between mind and masses loomed large.

In the space for intellect that he sought to carve out and preserve within American democracy, Hofstadter imagined one for whom "to think—really to think—is to pray." The "meaning" of this person's "intellectual life lies in the quest for new uncertainties." That quest was a kind of "piety of the intellectual," and "it is almost certain in the end to challenge something." In a time of creeping conformism, of retreat from devotion to intellect even on the part of educators, this pious thinker was all the more valuable. "It is the piety of the intellectual that puts iron into his nonconformism," Hofstadter wrote. "It is his piety that will make him, if anything does, a serious moral force in society."[106]

With these words, Hofstadter had in mind a friend who was a "distinguished sociologist." That friend was C. Wright Mills. While Hofstadter admired Mills as a thinker, the two offered strikingly different visions of the relationship between intellectuals and American life. Hofstadter took aim at popular democracy, at the conspiratorial irrationalism of the people even when it was directed against the abuses of capitalism—as it was in the Populist movement. By contrast, Mills took aim at corporate capitalism. "As for whether or not a democratic society necessarily leads to a leveling of culture," Mills wrote in 1952, "my answer is generally No. And I would of course impute the leveling and the frenzy effects of mass culture in this country not to 'democracy' but to capitalist commercialism which manipulates people into standardized tastes and then explains those tastes and 'personal touches' as marketable brands."[107] For Hofstadter, the people were often the problem. For Mills, the problem was how to liberate the people from the oppressive culture of advanced capitalism.

In that endeavor, links between intellectuals and ordinary people's politics were vital. "Without a movement to which they might address political ideas," Mills argued, "intellectuals in due course cease to express such ideas, and . . . they become indifferent." They "adapt" their thinking to the status quo in the absence of any hope of changing it.[108]

Surveying the political climate of the 1950s, Mills concluded that intellectuals no longer believed that "small groups of thinkers may take the lead in historic change." The dream of movement politics—of masses and intellectuals uniting in the causes of justice, truth, and freedom—was a dream that many intellectuals had congratulated themselves on having awakened from. Mills refused to repudiate it. For him, sweeping social change forged in an alliance between intellectuals and the people was neither an idle notion nor a nightmarish prelude to totalitarianism; rather, conditions were not ripe for it. In the absence of a politically activated audience, Mills wrote, "one tries by one's work to issue a call to thinking, to anyone now around, or anyone who might later come into view and who might listen."[109]

If Hofstadter finished the 1950s an intellectual in search of security, Mills finished an intellectual in search of a public. As the new decade began, he anticipated the political ferment that would be its hallmark. Hofstadter continued looking back to the trauma of the 1950s. He counseled intellectuals to be wary of democracy, to be a responsible elite capable of correcting and counterbalancing the irrational propensities of the people; capable, too, of safeguarding the life of the mind. He envisioned a distance between mind and masses, made both by the anti-intellectualism of the masses and the necessary elitism of mind. It was best to proceed with caution, conserving the institutions that held liberal society together. As Hughes remembered, Hofstadter's "whole attitude towards life, and an attitude we shared, [was] that the important things of life, whether they are intellectual activities or personal relations, are precarious and fragile, and you don't go running in like a bull in a china shop. I think he probably would have characterized Mills as a bull in a china shop."[110]

As the 1960s began, the bull stood poised at the china shop door. In his "Letter to the New Left," Mills said that he had "been studying, for several years now, the cultural apparatus, the intellectuals—as a possible, immediate, radical agency of change. For a long time, I was not much happier with this idea than were many of you; but it turns out now, in the spring of 1960, that it may be very relevant indeed." In 1952, the year that Hofstadter took to the public sphere on behalf of intellect and Adlai Stevenson, Mills contemplated intellectual action of a more radical kind. He reminded *Partisan Review* readers that "what in one decade is utopian may in the next be implementable."[111]

A CANDIDATE OF INTELLIGENCE

Two years before his "Letter to the New Left," C. Wright Mills wrote *The Causes of World War Three* (1958). Newly returned from Europe, he saw his country careening toward a catastrophic military conflict, not because of an inexorable spiral of events, but because of a failure of human thought.[1] It was a matter not of fate but of will—particularly the will to think.

Much of a book ostensibly devoted to the potential for nuclear holocaust surveyed the role of intellectuals in society. Beneath problems in diplomacy, technology, and politics, Mills saw problems with intellectuals. They were in "default"—abdicating their responsibilities as critics and thereby abetting the move toward war. "They believe that the human mind cannot grapple successfully with the total and ultimate issues involved," Mills wrote. Some, "perhaps in fear of being thought Unpatriotic, become nationalist propagandists; others, perhaps in fear of being thought Unscientific, become nationalist technicians." None, Mills concluded, "seems able to transcend the official terms in which the world encounter is now defined."[2] The Cold War constrained intellectuals' thinking far more than their thinking challenged it.

Mills measured intellectuals' failings against the singular role he believed they could play. Indeed, hitting the brakes on the road to World War Three and steering a new course fell to them: "Those who are articulate can become rallying points of oppositional opinion and independent judgment." Mills did not believe in fate—either in the metaphysical sense of destiny acting beyond humans' control or in the sociological sense of the world's complexity frustrating the efficacy of individuals. Building on his ideas from *The Power Elite* (1956), Mills argued that a consolidation of power in the corporate, military, and political arenas allowed for an unprecedented level of efficacy among elites, opening "the way to a greater role for reason in human affairs." The new potential power of reason created a Promethean moment: "We no longer need to accept historical fate, for fate is a feature of specific kinds of social structure, of irresponsible systems of power. These systems can be changed. Fate can be transcended."[3]

The difficulty was not that human beings were powerless; it was that power lay in the hands of an irresponsible elite, an elite that intellectuals had failed to challenge. In the age of the atomic bomb, these elites' decisions were more consequential than ever. "Yet leading intellectual circles in America" had instead "invented images of a scatter of reasonable men, overwhelmed by events and doing their best in a difficult situation." These images encouraged people "to accept public depravity without any private sense of outrage and to give up the central goal of Western humanism, so strongly felt in nineteenth-century American experience: the audacious control by reason of man's fate." Behind the sham excuses of fatalism and realism, Mills said, intellectuals despaired of the humanistic mission at the very moment when its realization had become possible and its stakes enormous. They were ceding control to elites insulated from accountability by the very idea that events were beyond control. Who, Mills asked, could hold elites accountable? "In both East and West today," he answered, "the immediate answer is: By the intellectual community. Who else but intellectuals are capable of discerning the role in history of explicit history-making decisions?"[4]

Mills urged intellectuals to pit new thinking against the conventional wisdoms of the Cold War, and to do so publicly—even if lacking a public. "If we are to act as *public intellectuals*," Mills charged, "we must realize ourselves as an independent and oppositional group" who "are called upon to state issues, to judge men and events, to formulate policies on all major public issues." Intellectuals should "feel responsible for the formulation and the setting forth of programs, even if in the beginning they are for only a few thousand readers."[5] It was a stirring call to action, and one imagines intellectuals sitting up straighter upon reading it. If Richard Hofstadter had worked throughout the 1950s to bolster intellectuals' sense of the dignity of the life of the mind, Mills now sought to incite them to political engagement. If only they would notice.

One who did was H. Stuart Hughes. The Harvard professor of European history had upheld his family's tradition of public service, working for the Department of State and the Office of Strategic Services (OSS) before returning to academia after World War Two. While Hughes's grandfather and father were noted Republicans, H. Stuart had supported Henry Wallace's Progressive Party in 1948. Like Mills and Hofstadter, he applauded

Adlai Stevenson in 1952. As Eisenhower's second term wound down and the Cold War—in the form of rising tensions over access to Berlin—wound up, Hughes was ready for a new direction.

"I have been sent a copy of Wright Mills' *The Causes of World War III*, and I am reading it avidly," Hughes told Martin Greenberg of *Commentary*. "I think it is an important book that deserves serious attention. Furthermore I have certain new ideas of my own on foreign affairs that I should like to get off my chest." He offered "to combine these two things into a fairly thorough review article," and Greenberg approved: "I hope it will trouble the prevailing apathy a little."[6]

Hughes found in Mills a "chillingly accurate diagnosis" of contemporary events. "It is true that most of our intellectuals are timid specialists without the imagination to give warning of the abyss toward which we are heading." Acting "as amateur Machiavellis, skilled at clothing the realities of power in the rhetoric of liberalism," intellectuals "were shirking their job."[7] They should have been providing "an alternative view of international reality to set against the one handed down by official spokesmen and by most of the press," for it was otherwise "nearly impossible to reach a clear-eyed assessment of where we stand." Intellectuals had to both be clearer eyed and share that vision with the public. Their influence was "considerably greater than most intellectuals imagine" and would "automatically increase if the professors and writers themselves begin to act *as though* their voices might carry to a wide public." They could restore controversy and debate "to the center of the public stage from which the politics of national consensus has for so long barred it."[8]

Mills welcomed Hughes's ringing endorsement. "What do you say to someone who has <u>understood</u> you?" he wrote Hughes. "Perhaps only that it is very largely in the hope of being read as you have read my pamphlet that one writes." Hughes replied that he looked forward to "dialogue on the numerous subjects of mutual interest and conviction." Such dialogue would be foreshortened by Mills's early death from a heart attack on March 20, 1962, at the age of forty-five.[9]

But in another fashion, their dialogue would persist. Seven days after Mills's death, Hughes formally announced that he was running for the US Senate in Massachusetts. In the days between Mills's death and his candidacy announcement, Hughes wrote to Mills's widow, the artist Yaroslava Surmach Mills: "I shall always remember him as one of the first in this country to speak out against the growing conformity and drift towards war—a great example to us all." In his political activity, Hughes followed Mills's ideas more than his example, for Mills had never been a candidate. But such a campaign fit the spirit of engagement that Mills urged: "The intellectual's first answer to the question, 'What, then ought we to do?' is: We ought to act as political intellectuals." In the spring of 1962, Hughes set out to do just that.[10]

Millsian ideas fed activist currents on the Harvard campus in these years. Hughes was involved with Tocsin, a student group for peace and disarmament, and with the Committee of Correspondence, a national antinuclear organization spearheaded by David Riesman. "It is the purpose of the CoC to end the separation so often made by intellectuals between their public concern and their professional life which has led them so often to turn their backs on the most exciting questions of our time," proclaimed a 1960 committee newsletter. As Hughes approached the starting line of his Senate race, he heard calls to intellectualized activism from many voices.[11]

Four months before launching his campaign, Hughes recalled Mills's mission for intellectuals. In notes for an address titled "Individual Responsibility in the Nuclear Age," he jotted: "What the Individual Can do—above all: get informed & start thinking for oneself & talking about it to one's friends & neighbors (C.W. Mills: each person to act as though he were a polit[ical] party)." Such activity would "combat [the] sense of futility and impotence [that were] most dang[erous] of all." Hughes asked: "What can we lose? We might as well be a bit reckless." His readiness to speak out followed Mills's suggestion: "We cannot know what effect upon either publics or elites such public work as we might well perform or refuse to perform might have. Nobody will ever know unless we try it." Mills advised that "even if we think the chances dim, still we must ask: If there *are* any ways out of the crises of our epoch by means of the intellect, is it not up to intellectuals to state them?"[12] For Hughes, this meant reclaiming a sense of public authority "as vs. [the] sense of [being a] leper in [the] McC[arthy] era." New and public thinking was needed, and Hughes could become a source of it. "We welcome new awareness of prob[lems] & *any* sort of discuss[ion], as vs. prev[ious] slumber," he wrote, "for once people start to think, God knows where they will end (as in my own case)."[13]

This turn toward overt political engagement marked a departure from Hofstadter's thinking about intellectuals and the public. Hofstadter envisioned the public as a threat to intellectuals and the university as a citadel for the life of the mind. Intellectuals were for their defense isolated from the public. For Mills and Hughes, intellectuals had to join with publics for effectiveness. "We should take democracy seriously and literally," Mills advised.[14] Hofstadter had at times seen democracy as antagonistic and elitism as congenial to intellect. In Mills's formulation, elites were intellectuals' antagonists. They were neither a "responsible elite" nor an "intellectual elite," but a "power elite." "Elite," like "intellectual," was a protean term. Sometimes it indicated intellectuals and was honorific. At other times, it indicated intellectuals but served as a term of abuse. Elsewhere, intellectuals were arrayed against elites.

It was in this last sense that Hughes viewed his long-shot, independent campaign.[15] The elites arrayed against him were his major-party opponents: Republican George Cabot Lodge II—son of the 1960 Republican vice-presidential nominee—and Democrat Edward M. "Ted" Kennedy—brother of the sitting president of the United States. Yet Hughes was no John Doe: as grandson of Supreme Court Chief Justice Charles Evans Hughes, son of a United States solicitor general, and a Harvard professor, he had his own bona fides. He nonetheless felt himself outside the circles of power his opponents inhabited. Hughes's status as both insider and outsider evoked the dual character of intellectuals as both alienated and elite. Such twoness would dog Hughes's campaign, and it would raise larger questions about the place of intellectuals in American politics. Was he a foreign-policy expert qualified to manage the technical intricacies of the Cold War or a humanistic critic bringing moral values to bear upon it? Was he a professor running to educate the electorate or a mouthpiece ready to articulate their latent views? Was he an intellectual speaking only for himself or a peace candidate speaking for a movement?

Hughes passed through the campaign as light through a spectroscope. Like one white beam revealing a chromatic spectrum, one intellectual's candidacy revealed a range of roles for the intellectual in politics. On one end of the spectrum, Hughes called himself a "latter-day Edwardian," a blend of "old-style patricians" and "left-oriented purveyors of international culture" that marked him "as someone out of tune with his times." The portrait of "mugwump culture," published a few months later in *Anti-Intellectualism in American Life*, seems to frame Hughes's fate. "It was characteristic of mugwump culture," Hofstadter wrote, "that its relation to experience and its association with power became increasingly remote." Mugwumps displayed "the intellectual and cultural outlook of the dispossessed patrician class." In this vein, Hughes and his campaign highlighted the qualities of his mind and character (the two were often conflated), sometimes linking them to his station as scion of a civically distinguished family and professor at a venerable institution.[16]

At another point on the spectrum, candidate Hughes presented himself in the role of the intellectual as technical expert. A campaign pamphlet featured two imperatives followed by one simple reason for carrying them out: "MAKE YOUR VOTE COUNT; VOTE FOR STUART HUGHES; AN EXPERT IN FOREIGN POLICY." Hughes's candidacy exhibited the history of the intellectual in American politics that Hofstadter traced, ontogeny recapitulating phylogeny. For mugwumps were succeeded by "the scholar in politics" who provided "certain serviceable skills that were becoming increasingly important to the positive functions of government. The era of the frustrated gentleman-reformer in politics was coming to a close," Hofstadter wrote, and that "of the scholar as expert was about to begin." In this vein, Hughes's campaign highlighted his foreign service and government work, his claims to expertise.[17]

The other hues of the 1962 campaign were shades of these two dominant colors. In the role of the intellectual as moralist, Hughes displayed elements of the mugwumps' custody of tradition and opposition to vulgarity—the Atomic Age vulgarity of the Cold War replacing the Gilded Age vulgarity of Tammany Hall. But was the moral voice Hughes raised against nuclear confrontation that of a mugwump speaking from a higher social stratum or a humanist speaking on behalf of higher values? As an intellectual, was Hughes the inheritor of a historically grounded American reform tradition or of a transcendent, ahistorical set of moral principles? If the latter, a difference between the intellectual's role as enacted by Hofstadter and that enacted by Hughes was that while the former was the conservator of those timeless values, the latter tried to bend the world toward them. If Hofstadter sought to keep the eternal flame of intellectualism burning in the dark night of McCarthy, Hughes set out to melt the Cold War with its heat.

As it had been for Hofstadter, the relation between democracy and intellectuals was a tense one for Hughes. Mills urged intellectuals to "take democracy seriously," and Hughes was careful to identify himself not simply as on the left but as a "man of letters affiliated with the *democratic* Left."[18] One rationale for his candidacy was to create a rallying point for a broader, more participatory peace movement. His opponents used well-oiled political machines. He used grassroots volunteers. His opponents relied on getting local party bosses in line. He ran without a party and spoke directly to the people. And yet for all his attempts to be of the people, Hughes never could manage it. He had eschewed running as a Democrat, but he was unable to find a way to run as a democrat. Perhaps it was because he ran, sometimes in spite of himself, as an intellectual.

* * *

Hughes may have found the wherewithal to launch a Senate campaign in 1962 because he had imagined himself in such a role since childhood. "I had stumbled into a full-scale acting out of my long-suppressed ideological fantasies," he wrote.[19] Hughes's youth had been saturated with politics, for his family's eminence flowed from government service. It had also been rooted in intellectual cultivation. The Hugheses took extended trips to Europe, with cathedrals, ruins, and battlefields on their itineraries. An eager student, Hughes went to Deerfield Academy and Amherst before entering Harvard for his doctorate—research for which was abbreviated by the outbreak of World War Two.

Hughes described his life in Washington after the war as "a reasonable facsimile of the living arrangements of a French intellectual." He oscillated between two identities: the civic-minded American political patrician and the literary European intellectual. They did not always mix well. Before the war, he had asked himself: "Did I truly want to be a scholar? Wouldn't I rather pursue some sort of public career in politics or diplomacy?" In an earlier time, these two had been fused; no choice was necessary. The literary qualities of the patrician class underwrote its civic engagement, for "men of intellect had laid claim to leadership too much on the ground that their social standing and their mental and moral qualities entitled them to it," Hofstadter observed. Public service and private cultivation had been complementary, but Hughes came to feel that they were increasingly opposed. "Winston Churchill and Léon Blum, radically as their mentalities differ," were, he wrote, "the last representatives of an era when the professions of statesman and man of letters were not incompatible."[20]

If intellectual proclivities led Hughes to feel distanced from political action, the ideological consequences of his thinking would remove him still further from the centers of power. Hughes was on the left—of his family, of many classmates, and of the prevailing mood in America during the dawning Cold War. "Early in the year 1932 I had converted to socialism," he recalled. "Possibly it was the spectacle of the unemployed selling apples on New York street corners that did it." By the late 1940s, Hughes's home-grown socialism had been influenced by extensive experience in Europe. Hughes was invited to join the OSS, and in 1943 he was sent to Algeria, followed by assignments in Italy, France, and Germany. In a research division of the State Department after the war, he befriended the German Jewish intellectuals Hans Meyerhoff, Franz Neumann, and Herbert Marcuse. Alluding to Thomas Mann's 1924 novel about a young man's political and philosophical education via conversation at an Alpine sanitarium, Hughes wrote that Marcuse's "informal instruction . . . transmut[ed] Foggy Bottom into a Magic Mountain for Hans Castorps like myself."[21]

After returning to the academy and writing a dissertation on the French economy under Napoleon, Hughes focused on intellectual history. His first published book, *An Essay for Our Times* (1950), used Spengler, Toynbee, Nietzsche, Kafka, and others to trace an intellectual ferment that, taking shape in Europe around 1890 and passing through both world wars, had come home to Americans like Hughes amid the deepening Cold War. He subsequently won praise for *Oswald Spengler: A Critical Estimate* (1952) and followed it with *The United States and Italy* (1953), *Consciousness and Society* (1958), and *Contemporary Europe: A History* (1961). Hughes developed a perspective shaped by this sustained engagement with Europe. "While I am American by nationality," he wrote, "my intellectual formation has been largely European." During the 1962 campaign, a journalist observed that "Hughes, even by European standards, is a man of the Left, and that means by American standards a very rare bird indeed."[22]

Hughes had been such a bird in postwar Washington, among upper-crust aspirants to positions in the emerging national security state. Hughes "exuded the distasteful aroma of 'class treason'" and "found it impossible to couch my thoughts, as a State Department official should, in the language of 'national interest.'" He considered "the welfare or presumed desires of the foreign population in question" and "tried to view events through the eyes of a Frenchman or a German, an Italian or a Russian."[23] An integral part of Hughes's intellectualism was this cosmopolitan standpoint: an outlook agile enough to imagine or even inhabit the thinking of those in other places around the globe. To be an intellectual was to be broader minded than the narrow view suggested by the "national interest."[24]

Not all intellectuals felt this to be the case. When, having returned to Harvard, Hughes in 1948 initially supported Progressive Party presidential nominee Henry Wallace, he found that "those who did not cleave to the orthodox view on the Cold War were made to feel outsiders." By supporting Wallace, Hughes "ran smack up against this unspoken taboo." That support cost Hughes his associate directorship of Harvard's Russian Research Center. The Carnegie Corporation funded the center, and it "found his presence . . . embarrassing."[25] Hughes resigned, but a cloud remained over him. The affair left him "accept[ing] the notion of political inactivity" as a professional necessity. In 1952 Hughes failed to secure tenure in Harvard's history department, an outcome for which he believed there were sufficient academic grounds, if not further political considerations. Five years later, on the strength of his subsequent scholarship and at the invitation of Dean McGeorge Bundy, he would return to a full professorship.[26]

After his dismissal, Hughes composed some reflections on "the intellectual as corrupter." To be "true to his role," the essay proclaimed, the intellectual "must always question existing society sharply." A chastened Hughes, however, sought limits for intellectuals' political agitations. He was struggling to define their role in the context of McCarthyism and the Cold War. "In a period when even merely abstract criticism may prove politically inexpedient, the teacher must lead a kind of double life." The intellectual as teacher "may not foreswear his function of critic—but he may urge his students not to follow the implications of his thought to their extreme conclusions." While critiquing prevailing "institutions and attitudes," students and teachers must still operate within their constraints. This approach enabled "the intellectual [to] conscientiously combine a proper regard for his responsibilities as a seeker after truth with a scrupulous performance of his duties as a citizen."[27] Hughes circumscribed intellectuals' critical function without abandoning it.

Yet some sentences seemed to pierce the very bounds he was trying to set. "The right of the intellectual to speak his mind and the right of the organized community to defend itself against potential subversion are both honored principles," Hughes concluded, reflecting upon the case of Socrates. "But for the intellectual . . . there can only be one answer." Intellectuals' "self-censorship," their "reluctance to rock the boat" during the Cold War, signaled a "serious confusion" of priorities. "It is not up to the intellectual himself to decide where his quest for truth should stop," came the daring crescendo; "that is the function of the public authorities." As a person, one could "maintain a prudent silence when it becomes obvious that the next step will bring on the hemlock," but as an intellectual, one was bound to "follow his thought wherever it may lead him."[28] Hughes upheld free thought as essential to the role of the intellectual, but he suggested that persons in that role might face other imperatives that, while not restraining their thinking, may nonetheless still their tongues.

In 1952 Hughes, like Hofstadter, supported Stevenson. But 1952 and the years after it were different for Hughes and Hofstadter. For Hofstadter, 1952 was a moment of activism not only to conserve the policies of the New Deal, but to champion the cause of intellect. In Stevenson, he saw a candidate who united these two aims, and he supported him with ardor. Hughes volunteered for Stevenson and wrote in 1952 that "the American intellectual needs to have more pride" and should "assert with more intransigence his own standards and the things that mark him off from his neighbors." Yet for Hughes, the 1950s were a decade of suppression. He felt suppression from without after supporting Wallace, and he engaged in suppression within, swallowing a good deal of his radicalism. "At Stanford"—Hughes remembered of his arrival in Palo Alto after leaving Harvard—"my heterodoxy went underground, unsuspected. What dissent there was took the safe and reassuring form of Stevensonian democracy." McCarthyism had "succeeded in creating a sense of guilt among thousands of intelligent and public-spirited people—a large part of the intellectual and moral elite of the nation." It "deprive[d] the government of their service and counsel during a decade when they were badly needed" and "crippled their own thought by stirring within them the demon of self-doubt." Hughes's allegiance to the Left was, if not wavering, at least dormant. He was ambivalent about the Stevensonian center, but there was no place else to go: "The Left had vanished—we were all liberal Democrats together."[29]

By 1956, the year of Stevenson's second campaign, Hughes doubted not only his political position but also the standing of intellectuals themselves. In *Commentary* he asked, "Is the intellectual obsolete?" Reporting that "the old exchange between the intellectual and his public is turning into a weary and repetitive monologue," Hughes linked the loss of intellectuals' audiences with their lack of political efficacy or "practical effect." But it was unclear which was the chicken and which the egg: did intellectuals lose influence because they had lost an audience, or did they lose that audience because what they wrote and said was not politically relevant—or acceptable? "Today a writers' manifesto could not possibly precipitate a government crisis or start a revolution," Hughes wrote. "Similarly the efforts of intellectuals to launch new political movements have proved uniformly unsuccessful."[30]

To understand the plight of intellectuals in the 1950s, Hughes looked back to the emergence of secular European intellectuals—noting, for example, Francis Bacon—whose work was neither strictly "technical" nor "merely personal" but "always bore a *public* character." The respect paid these intellectuals "did not derive simply from the splendor of their mental operations: it reflected their position as the custodians of the higher values of society." Publicness constituted their role in two senses: they *thought in public* (on the printed page or at the lectern), and they *thought about public* questions—enjoying "privileged status" because they addressed "general problems of universal concern."[31]

While the public component of intellectuals' role remained constant, the direction of their interventions changed. The Enlightenment "converted the characteristic European intellectual from a defender and rationalizer of existing institutions into their implacable critic." By the mid-twentieth century, "the most alert and active section of the intelligentsia" subjected society's prevailing assumptions to unremitting scrutiny.[32]

Yet the United States never exhibited an intellectual life fully devoted to this critical function. Instead, a youth "of brains and promise became a 'mental technician' rather than an intellectual," and "the physician ranks higher than the professor or writer in the scale of public prestige." Whereas intellectuals freely speculated on questions of broad public import, often criticizing the status quo, "mental technicians" were "experts for the business world, civil servants, and above all, pedagogues to teach routine courses." The New Deal's vaunted Brains Trust were emblematic: "They had assigned jobs to do: they were not free to speculate as their fancy directed." The same constraints applied to "those who in the postwar period have accepted the favors of government or of business"; those taking "far lower incomes in teaching or writing" knew "where their own particular values could best be cultivated." Yet government service was but one kind of constraint upon intellectuals, for Joseph McCarthy's "political collapse did not end the agitation for setting practical limitations on free speculation: it simply institutionalized it and made it respectable." Americans now accepted "a whole ramifying network of 'clearances,' denunciations, and nearly invisible taboos." These conditions made it necessary for "writers and scholars to rethink their relationship to their fellow citizens and to the state—that whole 'public' aspect of their endeavors that has never been absent from the Western intellectual tradition." Thinkers in the United States faced "a sharp choice," for "the only way to resolve the insoluble conflict between the ethic of the free intellectual and the ethic of the public servant is a withdrawal from one function or the other."[33]

Those choosing intellectualism had "a dubious future." Confronting "a public only sporadically (and then often dangerously) interested in what he does," the intellectual faced "almost irresistible pressures urging him in subtle fashion toward conformity to the role of mental technician." Disconnected from "*both* his historic functions—as the ideological bulwark of society and its utopian critic—he may . . . begin to doubt the relevance of his pursuits." Hughes did "not believe . . . that the intellectual . . . is obsolete," but he gave strong reasons for concluding the opposite.[34]

Not all greeted the prospect of intellectuals' obsolescence with lamentation. "Those brief periods in modern times during which the 'intellectual' . . . has achieved immediate political power have been periods in which fanatic ideology overmastered men's minds," wrote Russell Kirk, author of *The Conservative Mind* (1953), responding to Hughes's essay. "The ideologue is the scholar as sophist," Kirk continued; "what he seeks is not wisdom, but power," subordinating "learning to tyranny and demagoguery. . . . If only this sort of intellectual seemed to be obsolete, I do not think we would need to grieve."[35]

And yet Kirk's view was not entirely opposed to Hughes's, for both advised separation between intellectual life and positions of political responsibility. "Different casts of character and intellect, and different disciplines, generally are required for the mastery of books and the mastery of men," Kirk claimed. The example of professors, like Schlesinger, who had joined Stevenson's campaigns "scarcely was edifying." Kirk and Hughes separated the intellectual from the governmental for different reasons. Hughes felt that political service undermined intellectuals' function; Kirk thought intellectuals' functioning undermined politics. For Hughes, "intellectual" was an honorific term. Kirk used it pejoratively, for he considered intellectuals' social and political criticism little more than the peddling of pernicious ideology. Hughes measured the obsolescence of intellectuals by their lack of political efficacy. Kirk said that true intellectualism— "scholarship"—had nothing to do with political effects. "We ought never to forget that the end of scholarship is not political power, primarily, or even the improvement of society at large," he claimed. "The real mission of the scholar is the improvement of the individual human reason, for the individual person's own sake. If any 'intellectual' does that, he may forgo cheerfully an assistant secretaryship of state."[36] Kirk rejected the public component that Hughes placed at the heart of the intellectual's role.

It was the contraction of this public relevance that raised the specter of intellectuals' obsolescence for Hughes. He projected that intellectuals "of the future will be obliged to opt decisively against service to government or business—except for purely temporary arrangements which will be of an episodic or crisis character." For the most part, "intellectual life will become an increasingly lonely and misunderstood affair."[37] It is surprising that someone who made such a forecast in 1956 would summon the tremendous energy to run for Senate in 1962. Something in those six years had changed significantly. Understanding how the Hughes of 1956 became the Hughes of 1962 requires a look at Mills in 1958.

By the time *The Causes of World War Three* appeared that year, the tone of the decade had changed. Stevenson, McCarthy, and Korea were of receding importance. Paradoxically, McCarthyism had ended in both victory and defeat. McCarthy was censured by the Senate in 1954, yet that same year membership in the Communist Party was criminalized. McCarthy was out, but the anti-communism he stood for was encoded in law.

While McCarthy faded, the prospect of nuclear war rose. Tensions escalated with the creation in 1955 of the Warsaw Pact and West Germany's entry into NATO. Two years later, the launch of Sputnik demonstrated the advanced technical capacities of Soviet science and engineering. As Hughes reported, "A loss of confidence within the populations of the Western coalition has imperceptibly been gaining momentum. Since the launching of Sputnik it has become a near rout."[38] Soon Senator John F. Kennedy coined the charged political term "missile gap" to describe the perceived Soviet nuclear superiority. The public was alarmed; the international Cold War was becoming hotter than the domestic one.

For intellectuals, this shift opened up new possibilities. On the one hand, the Sputnik scramble afforded opportunities for "mental technicians," who were needed to catch up with the Soviets. As Senator Hubert Humphrey put it: "It was Soviet eggheads who got the sputniks off the ground, and it will be American eggheads who get our Nation off the ground."[39] On the other hand, the enormity of nuclear war raised pressing moral questions to which critical intellectuals might respond. Amid atomic peril, intellectuals might move from a sense of obsolescence to one of urgency.

Mills urged that move. It was time to shake off the malaise of the

McCarthy period, its defensive posture and self-doubt. It was "a time when the power of the intellectuals has become potentially very great indeed." In the shadow of the bomb, there could be no excuses. While others could "feel that their power to reason, their skills to investigate . . . are inadequate to the situations they confront," Mills wrote, "intellectuals cannot. So long as they are intellectuals, they must reason and investigate and, with their passion to know, they must confront the situations of all men everywhere." This sense of mission marked "the intellectual as a type of social and moral creature." If dissent was to be voiced, they must be the first to voice it. "Other men can mutter, with much justification, that they find nowhere to draw the line, to speak the emphatic 'No,'" Mills observed. "But it is the political and the intellectual job of the intellectual to draw just that line, to say the 'No' loudly and clearly."[40]

Calling for fewer missiles and greater "moral and political imagination," Mills turned Lionel Trilling's conception of the imagination on its head. In *The Liberal Imagination* (1950), Trilling had urged liberals to temper their optimism about progress through policy with a sense of the complex, ironic, and tragic as conveyed by modern literature. Mills was now urging liberal intellectuals—many of whom had become either so hardened against communism or so frozen by the complexities Trilling set forth that they were, Mills believed, abetting the onset of World War Three—to use imagination in restoring a sense of the possibilities of rational policymaking. Trilling offered imagination as an antidote to the hubris of human reason in a world scourged by totalitarianism. Mills offered it as an antidote to failures of policy in a world headed toward self-destruction. Thus, "to cultivate moral sensibility and to make it knowledgeable is the strategic task of those intellectuals who would be at peace. They *should* debate short-run and immediate policies, but, even more, they should confront the whole attitude toward war, they should teach new views of it, and on this basis they should criticize current policies and decisions."[41] To follow Trilling was to quiet intellectuals' ambitions; to follow Mills was to quicken them.

Hughes was ready. Like Mills, he saw lack of robust public debate as a major problem in the Cold War. In the postwar years, "rare individuals" who dissented "usually did so in the privacy of their own consciences. Public protest seemed futile: a pall of dull acceptance settled over the American soul." Intellectuals were complicit in this quiescence. Mills pointed to the "tragedians" and the "comfortable college professor[s]." Hughes did too. The former found in their paperback translations of Kierkegaard and

Dostoevsky "a reflection of their own sense of moral impotence." As for professors, Hughes linked "the lack of major public debate" to "the substantial reconciliation of intellectuals to the *status quo* (through comfortable jobs, research contracts and the like)." These intellectuals not only failed to debate the Cold War's premises; they also silenced others by challenging the standing of non-specialists to speak on war, peace, and policy. There arose "a feeling that the problems had become too big and complex for the mere individual citizen to grasp (with both the national Administration and the intellectuals aiding the process by insisting only 'experts' were qualified to express opinions)." These feelings compounded until "finally ensued a *privatization* of life, a tendency on the part of each man to retreat to the cultivation of his own suburban garden."[42]

Hughes and Mills thus identified a troubled relationship between intellectuals and the democratic public sphere, but it was the opposite of the troubled relationship that Hofstadter found. In his view, the public worked to silence intellectuals. For Mills and Hughes, intellectuals worked to silence the public. Hofstadter acted in the public sphere to defend the prerogatives of intellectuals and to expose the irrationality of their opponents. In this effort, he drew closer to elites and further from the public. By contrast, Hughes and Mills looked with favor on the possibility of forging alliances between intellectuals and the public in opposition to the policies of elites. In running for Senate, would Hughes be able to successfully establish a closer relationship between a professor and the people?

By 1962 Hughes had already committed to activism, inspired by a "decisive talk with David Riesman" in late 1959. "Our anxieties, we discovered, were the same: the difference was that while I had merely brooded, David had located like-minded people with whom to work in common." A Harvard sociologist, Riesman was known for *The Lonely Crowd* (1950), which assessed the isolation and anxiety pervasive in postwar American culture. He invited Hughes to participate in what became *The Liberal Papers* (1962), edited by James Roosevelt, a California congressman and FDR's eldest son. For that project, ten congressional Democrats and "forty-six intellectuals, scientists, and scholars" sought "to bridge the gap between the realm of free study and that of political action."[43]

Riesman also bridged the gap between academe and activists, connecting Hughes to Russell Johnson, Peace Education Secretary of the American Friends Service Committee's (AFSC) New England Regional Office, who visited Hughes's home. "We hope to attract many people from the university communities around New England who can be put under a real sense of urgency to give voice to their private concerns," Johnson told Hughes. "I would judge, on the basis of the opinions voiced in your home the other night, that there is a real opportunity and responsibility here."[44]

Before 1959 was out, Clarence Pickett, co-chair of the National Committee for a Sane Nuclear Policy (known as SANE), invited Hughes to join the organization. "The Committee has taken the lead in conducting a broad public education and political action program on the moral and scientific problem of nuclear war, weapons testing and fallout," Pickett wrote. Hughes accepted Pickett's invitation, later crediting the group with "launching . . . the first important nonconformist effort" that broke "the post-McCarthy slumber."[45]

"Slumber" and "sane" are revealing. Time and again, Hughes characterized the peril of nuclear war as a matter of mental states—a slumber to be solved by awakening, an insanity to be ended by asserting what is sane. As Charles A. Barker of the Baltimore Seminar on Arms Control described his group's aims to Hughes: "A general effort to devaluate the prevailing *mentality* of conflict will be the larger goal." Intellect was not only a solution to the Cold War crisis; it was the terrain on which that crisis existed. Hughes's notes for a 1959 lecture, "War and the Mind of Man: The Erosion of the Political Response," lamented the "intellect[ual] laziness of conventional wisdom on for[eign] policy." James Roosevelt claimed that the need for greater engagement between policymakers and intellectuals arose "because of the disillusionment with many of the seemingly *mindless* policies that we . . . were following." As Riesman and Michael Maccoby put it, "Old agendas and ways of regarding the world will have to be scrapped and new ones discovered." The critical front in the fight against nuclear war, it seemed, was not technological, economic, or even diplomatic; it was intellectual.[46]

The best troops, therefore, were intellectuals. Yet their strategic and even tactical objectives remained unclear. One approach was for peace-minded intellectuals to exchange ideas among themselves and their slowly growing circle. The Committee of Correspondence, for example, launched a newsletter that was largely by and for intellectuals, but it had wider aspirations. Hughes envisioned it as "a peace clearing-house, strategy board, movement, or nucleus of a 3rd party" engaged in "a rad[ical] attack on the nature of a soc[iety] that creates such apathy tow[ard] war & peace."[47] Again, the key problem cited by Hughes was a mental state: apathy. He suggested combating it by moving beyond intellectuals to engage a "move-ment."

If intellectuals focused their efforts mainly on other intellectuals, after all, what effect would they have? Jean Mosher of Mill Valley, California, posed this question in a letter to Hughes. "The correspondence between you learned gentlemen is of undisputed value to you, and to the small and already well-informed segment of the population which reads your publi-cation," she wrote, referring to the newsletter. But what about the rest of the people? Mosher advised that "the Letters to the Editor column is recog-nized as being a widely-read section of the newspaper, and represents a rel-atively unused source of expert communication with the general public." Hughes's reply indicated his new approach. "I quite agree with you about writing letters to the editor," he responded. "Indeed, I would be doing more of that myself right now if I were not so heavily involved in my indepen-dent campaign for the United States Senate. At least that should qualify as bringing the viewpoint of the Committee of Correspondence to a wider audience."[48]

The "wider audience" pointed to something wider still: together, Hughes felt, intellectuals and ordinary citizens might forge a movement. Doing so required a rapprochement with democratic politics, toward which Hughes was moving—haltingly. He wrote in 1959 of the "'price paid for democracy'—I am more than willing to pay it . . . but think it is a heavy price indeed." An early 1960 *Daedalus* essay made his ambivalence clear. Attempts "to combine elitism and democracy—things compatible perhaps in a Periclean or Jeffersonian sense of popular government led by 'the best,' but, under contemporary conditions, radical opposites"—would misfire since "contemporary democracy and contemporary mass culture are two sides of the same coin." The best American intellectuals could do was "to make our peace with mass culture in at least a few of its more bearable manifestations," since they could not transform it. "I think that only cer-tain cultural values are susceptible of large-scale dissemination and that certain other values, traditionally regarded as distinguishing features of the educated man, when subjected to such a process simply become diluted beyond recognition," Hughes wrote. Intellectuals, in short, were a group apart.[49]

Even if Hughes thought it impossible for the whole population to share intellectuals' values—detachment, cosmopolitanism—it was possible to envision a more intellectually attuned democracy. Numbed by Cold War politics, the American people had become, Hughes claimed, "lazy-minded and passive spectators." But "how different things were a couple of generations ago!" Though less "educated than their American counterparts of today," European workers at the turn of the century "were convinced that the lengthy and largely incomprehensible speeches of their leaders and teachers were of moment to them. The complex reasoning of these people from a loftier cultural sphere really mattered," for workers believed it could "make a difference in their own lives." The difference between that past public and the contemporary one rested upon the prevailing political cultures. If 1900 was a time of open political conflict, 1959 was the opposite. Its politics rested "on material prosperity" and, most importantly, "on weariness, on apathy, on passive acceptance, on a tacit agreement not to discuss potentially 'divisive' issues—on what still needs to be called 'conformity.'"[50]

Hughes was so preoccupied with lack of dissent on foreign policy that his pessimism about the prospects for an engaged public ignored the civil rights movement, in which Rosa Parks's arrest, the ensuing Montgomery Bus Boycott, and the Little Rock Nine had already happened. It is difficult to imagine the final blast of his *Daedalus* article resonating with these African American activists: Americans, he charged, "have lost our capacity for indignation, our ability to feel a cosmic anger with what we see going on around us."[51] In Montgomery and elsewhere, many ordinary people had already demonstrated their capacity for indignation—and action rooted in political and moral values alike.

Perhaps just after dispatching his *Daedalus* piece, Hughes finally noticed the rising dissent. "Suddenly," he wrote, "in the spring of 1960 I realized with a shock that a new student generation had sprung into life. In the widespread demonstrations against racial segregation a new age group had won its political spurs." Hughes saw activism on campuses, where "picketings and meetings . . . involved only a minority of college students. But this minority was soon recognized as the intellectually active and devoted which in each generation takes the moral lead."[52] Hughes posited a connection between intellectual activity and moral leadership, but hidden beneath his celebration of student demonstrators was a crucial question: Does intellectual capability or sensibility create a claim to moral leadership over others?

From many quarters, the answer was a resounding no. A *Life* editorial located Riesman, Hughes, and the Committee of Correspondence on "the unhelpful fringes" of American politics. *Life*, by contrast, represented the mainstream. It quoted Hughes finding "no alternative to the renunciation of thermonuclear deterrence" and saying: "We may end in transcending more than one of the loyalties that most Americans take for granted." The editors suggested that Hughes's intellectualism was little more than romanticism, a dangerous flaw in a time demanding sober realism. Indeed, "the Kremlin blackmail strategy has already succeeded with Messrs. Riesman and Hughes," who advocated reducing America's military posture based on "an 'act of faith' in Communist intent." They were both "Utopian and defeatist"; their "romantic" intellectualism disqualified them from—if not necessarily moral, then certainly political—leadership.[53]

John Martinson of the AFSC, a peace activist and an ally of Hughes and Riesman, had a different issue with the equation of intellectualism and moral leadership. A few days after *Life* came out, Martinson told Hughes that he had hurt the peace movement. "I really wonder if C. of C. [Committee of Correspondence] is strong enough to withstand the McCarthyite smear tactics that seem to be in the cards," he wrote. "I know it's going to be doubly hard if we have to go around apologizing for Stuart Hughes." Martinson was not questioning Hughes's intellect but his fitness as a spokesperson. "We have this nice little radical peace proposal going among the intellectual community," Martinson wrote. "Not completely thought out perhaps, but representing a fair amount of clear-headedness on the subject of war & peace. And then you liberals come along and screw up the works, not so much by your fuzzy minds, but simply by an incredibly poor choice of words that allows people like the *Life* editorial writers to completely distort your true feelings and smear your associates."[54]

Martinson questioned why Hughes couched his arguments in terms of transcendental values rather than American ones. "Couldn't you just as legitimately ask people to fulfill the finest values of the American heritage by acting as an American . . . ? Is there something contradictory about my 'American-ness' and my loyalty to humanity?" Martinson, who was so deeply involved in organizing that he eventually ran an AFSC office from his Minnesota home, expressed frustration that Hughes, rather than someone like himself, had risen to prominence as a mouthpiece for the peace effort. "Oh that God had given you a silver tongue instead of a silver spoon when you were born. Or that he had given some of the rest of us the advantages of an Ivy League education and a platform in the Harvard History dep[artment] to speak from."[55] It was not intellectual capability, but rather elite status, Martinson suggested, that gave Hughes a leadership role and attention from *Life* magazine.

From outside the nascent peace movement, *Life*'s editors attacked Hughes's intellectualism. From inside, Martinson attacked his leadership. But Hughes was undeterred. The new activism provided "a chance to leap over a ten-year span and take up again where we left off when the ideological blight descended upon America."[56] The 1950s, in other words, were over. The tone of lamentation and frustration characteristic of Hughes after the Wallace campaign, the painful reflection upon the status of the intellectual in society, the years of doubt were over. It was time to resume political action.

* * *

After John F. Kennedy was elected president, his Senate seat was open for a special election that shaped up as a battle between notable Massachusetts political families. Young Ted Kennedy faced strong competition for the Democratic nomination from Edward McCormack, the state attorney general and "favorite nephew" of John McCormack, speaker of the US House of Representatives. According to *Time*, "Eddie was . . . the favorite of Massachusetts' intellectual community" as well. On the Republican side, George Cabot Lodge—"another smiling scion of another famous Massachusetts family"—faced Congressman Laurence Curtis.[57] Not everyone was pleased with the slate of candidates. "Massachusetts deserves better for candidates than a millionaire's subsidized son, a ward he[e]ler's nephew and a fifth generation Brahmin do-gooder," wrote one frustrated couple to Hughes, whom they mistakenly viewed "as a straight thinking strong talking republican in the Coolidge Hoover Nixon tradition."[58]

Since returning to Harvard and embarking upon peace activism, Hughes had steadily increased his public profile. He debated foreign and defense policy with Henry Kissinger and Herman Kahn on campus and over the airwaves, and he was an outspoken critic of the April 1961 Bay of Pigs invasion. "I addressed a large and enthusiastic protest meeting on Cuba at the Friends' Meeting House," he wrote his mother that spring. "I had a TV news interview on both Algeria and Cuba, and then went to a Harvard protest meeting on the Cuban policy. It was amusing to hear our late colleagues, Schlesinger and Bundy"—members of the Kennedy White House—"getting flayed by speaker after speaker, to the cheers and jeers of a large and enthusiastic audience." Though as a boy he had played neighborhood football with and admired the future President Kennedy, Hughes was not about to withhold criticism of his administration's "overcautious" liberalism and "excessively nationalist" foreign policy. After a decade of keeping his activist instincts at bay, Hughes found new opportunities for speaking out "exhilarating."[59]

Discussion of a run for Senate "started at a lunch in late February of 1962 with two or three workers in what is loosely called the 'peace movement,'" Hughes recalled. "One asked me what I thought should be the main thrust of their effort in this election year. I answered, casually, that we might try the experiment of senatorial candidacies in perhaps ten key states. 'That's a funny coincidence,' came the reply. 'I was just about to ask you to run for the Senate from Massachusetts.'" Hughes wrote that he "had been trapped in my own rhetoric. Yet something in me responded to the prospect with excitement and even delight."[60] He also reported that many in Boston "feel as I do that it is a disgrace to have such second-rate candidates."[61] Did Hughes mean that the other Senate candidates had second-rate minds, second-rate morals, or second-rate qualifications?[62] His campaign would ultimately suggest all three—at least about Kennedy. Hughes's own senatorial bid "would be a lot of work and there would be no chance of my getting elected, but as a gesture I think it would be important and worth doing."[63] But if Hughes's candidacy was *only* a gesture, voters might not be convinced that he was worth supporting. This possibility split Hughes's identity as a candidate, with the Hughes of the symbolic gesture tending to be a moralist and the Hughes who was "in it to win it" emphasizing his expertise in foreign affairs.

Even before Hughes officially launched his campaign, reactions trickled in. Many celebrated the gesture. "Nothing is to be lost and perhaps a great deal to be gained by carrying the struggle for an intelligent foreign policy beyond academic confines to the electorate," wrote Jerome S. King of Williams College. "Whatever the results in November the public, both state and national, will be the richer for your campaign." Murray L. Bob of El Cerrito, California, offered his services to the campaign, noting that "since the point of your candidacy is, as I take it, not to 'win' but to spread winning ideas, my remoteness from the scene of battle is perhaps not too important." The scene of battle was indeed unclear, as Hughes knew the symbolic gesture could reach far beyond Massachusetts.[64]

The further it reached, however, the more it stretched, and the meaning of the symbol as well as the content of the gesture became both crucial and contested. For some observers, Hughes was himself the symbol—not of the peace movement, but of a certain quality of mind or type of character in public life. "I have heard you speak at the Cambridge Unitarian church . . . and found your talks very interesting, informative and just the kind of honest thinking we need in our government," wrote Susan Magri. "Your type of person would also help to attract others of your caliber to government service, and perhaps thus help the dishonest members to try to be more honest and informed on all sides of the issues." Joseph Duval wrote Hughes: "Your picture in our Pennsylvania newspapers indicates that you are a man of intelligence (some things, you know, show on the surface)." Though others would observe that Hughes failed to communicate *effectively*, Lawrence Martin wrote: "You talk *well*, and I hope the avenues of communication will give you a chance to be heard." William H. Gribble of Kansas City had been a student of Hughes's. "Your intellectual integrity was always an inspiration to me," he wrote. "It is indeed elevating to see men of your stature enter political life."[65]

These correspondents emphasized Hughes himself, rather than anything specific that he might do. Others pointed to Hughes's potential for educating the public. "Yours is a lonely voice of sanity in the midst of the fog of fear and distortion . . . churned up by our opinion makers," wrote Gray Adams. "I hope that you will have opportunity, between now and November, to voice your point of view," wrote Ruth Dadourian of Hartford; "maybe you will educate a few people." Barbara Sessions of Boston assured Hughes that his campaign would reach people "who want to have a voice but do not know what to do—people outside the academic and intellectual worlds where a certain awakening has taken place.—In fact, as I look forward to your campaign I think of it as a 'Sleepers, wake!' sort of affair." Hughes himself had written, "People who always play it safe make no contribution to awakening or enlightening their countrymen."[66]

One writer, Paul Gagnon, cautioned Hughes against dismissing as sleepers those who were already awake. He hoped the campaign "will be more than . . . a forum for your beliefs on disarmament and world peace. . . . [F]or many 'ordinary' Americans [already] understand the relationships among these issues more than the smart give them credit for." Gagnon was encouraging Hughes to bet on the intelligence of "ordinary Americans"—no matter their education. "I hope you share my faith in the existence of grown-ups in what too many academics consider unlikely places," he wrote.

My father was a truck-driver, my mother a clerk. They have not 12 years of school between them, but they laugh at the solemn explanations of the public divinities, know why the press, radio and television cannot be frank, know why MacArthur should not have gone to the Yalu, why the Cuban invasion was a fiasco. They are, in short, far more literate and sophisticated in politics than most academics I know and less entangled in dogma, whether conservative or liberal. They hunger for a grown-up discussion of every issue, for somebody to force other candidates and mass media to leave off their insolent *bourrage de crane* [brainwashing].

Though ambivalent about academics, Gagnon said Hughes's campaign "fills me with hopes," for he believed that Hughes could speak with knowledge on any issue. Indeed, "for one who represents, unavoidably, the university and intellectual community, nothing else will do."[67]

The Hughes campaign began at Boston's Hotel Bellevue on March 27, 1962. "We are in this campaign to put a particular point of view across, to get as much support as possible, and to win," Hughes told reporters. Foreign affairs was to be the central, but not the only, message. "My stand on peace and disarmament is to propose a series of independent American initiatives to halt the arms race," Hughes said. He favored "reducing tensions in the cold war danger spots throughout the world and . . . giving full support to the UN. On the domestic front, I commit myself to an extension of public welfare legislation and to more vigorous measures than are at present being taken for extending full equality to all Americans."[68]

At this moment, Hughes's *An Approach to Peace* arrived, coincidentally, on bookstore shelves. "The book was definitely not written as campaign literature (its extreme frankness may actually do me damage)," he observed. Like Mills's *Causes of World War Three*, Hughes's book called upon intellectuals to take public, political action. "Since our leaders are failing to do the job, it is up to some of us private citizens to present an alternative view of international reality," he claimed. "We need calm and quiet figures—men with a talent for telling unpleasant truths in a tone that will forestall both anger and panic, men equipped to lay bare our illusions, but gently and humanely." They "should be without vulgar ambition and with little regard for popularity, for surely the task I am suggesting is . . . unpopular." Essayist Hughes read like a want ad to which candidate Hughes responded.[69]

Approach was read in light of its author's campaign. Donald Mintz of the *Washington Star* described Hughes as "neither fuzzy nor soft-minded. Prof.

Hughes is not an emotional peace-marcher." Hughes's thoughts "on the place and responsibilities of the intellectual in modern society are almost literally mandatory reading for those who consider themselves members of this group which so often manages to be simultaneously exalted and denigrated by itself and by others." Writing in the *Nation*, Theodore Roszak described *Approach* as summoning "a tiny band of the dedicated prepared to be martyred at the hands of unenlightened public and official opinion until the people and their leaders hear and are educated." Hughes may not have intended *Approach* as a campaign book, but it became one.[70]

A campaign was an uncommon mode of expression for an intellectual, but Hughes and Mills had each urged intellectuals to stimulate new lines of thought. To do so, intellectuals had to be public, had to reach other people. And if reaching and provoking others was the end, were not those who sought it obliged to use the most effective means of attaining it? "What we, as intellectuals, ought to do with the formal means of communication—in which so many now commit their cultural default—is to use them as we think they ought to be used," Mills advised. "We should assume that these means are among *our* means of production and work."[71] By launching a campaign, Hughes was taking hold of the formal means of communication. He was pursuing a highly effective way of reaching those people that public intellectuals needed to reach; he was generating media exposure.

But while Hughes's campaign might have garnered more attention than (and *for*) his book, the question of what his campaign was drawing attention to remained. For there may be a trade-off between the promulgation of a message and the integrity of it. A book might reach fewer people than a campaign, but what if the people reading it gained a clearer sense of Hughes's message than those who knew him only through the campaign? As an intellectual committed to public action, Hughes had to weigh the message and the medium, the clarity of expression and its spread.

In the first weeks of the campaign, Hughes expressed confidence that his message was spreading and that it remained intact. "It is still too early to say just what my candidacy will accomplish, but I know that at the very least it has already stirred a number of stagnant pools and injected into the campaign of 1962 an issue of peace and disarmament which might otherwise have lain neglected." Hughes's favorable assessment was bolstered by letters from beyond the Massachusetts electorate. F. C. Hunnius of Toronto reported that "we in Canada are greatly encouraged by your courageous and imaginative decision to contest the coming election." Hughes reminded

Dr. Sunder Mansukhani of "listening to Nehru. As an Indian and Asian and a staunch admirer of the United States, I can assure you that millions in Asia and Africa will hope and pray that people like you may take charge of affairs in America and (let us hope) in Russia too."[72]

Yet Hughes began to face pressures upon the content of his message, and on him as its messenger. The exigencies of running for office only increased in proportion to the spread of news about him, and Hughes recognized the tension between his desire to advance provocative ideas and his goal of winning votes. "As a minimum position for my campaign, I am suggesting an abandonment of 'first strike capability' and an unequivocal pledge on our part never to use a nuclear weapon first," he said. "This, I think, is a position bolder than that of any leading figure now on the political scene but still sufficiently moderate to reassure many citizens who hesitate to take the plunge with me." Hughes had to both modulate his message on nuclear weapons and find a balance between that central issue and the other issues of the day. Campaign manager Jerome Grossman emphasized this tension. "Please do not underestimate the emotional dynamism of the parochial school issue," he warned. He also advised Hughes "not [to] underplay (I know you will not overplay) your ancestry. Regardless of all the talk about dynasty, your ancestry proves to a great many voters that you are basically safe and therefore it is somehow okay for them to listen to you." In the hothouse of an increasingly high-profile race, the integrity and centrality of the message Hughes sought to convey was under stress. So was Hughes. "From the more personal standpoint," he confided, campaigning "has reduced me to near-exhaustion."[73]

One aspect of Hughes's effort was to encourage new thinking among others; another was to provide such thinking himself. He was, therefore, an example of what he called for. But he was also a symbol. Hughes's Harvard affiliation, his formal style of speech, his horn-rim spectacles, his first initial and full middle name: all of it stood for the figure of the intellectual, a character freighted with hope and hostility in Cold War America. Alfred C. Klahre of Maui spoke to both sides of this contested character when he offered Hughes a "suggestion: Project the young, good-looking 'Prof.' image (you can do it); not the 'egghead' image." Klahre noted that "most people have been exposed to a young, dynamic 'Professor' in their youth whose memories they cherish." Professors, however, were not always cherished. "Harvard University has become recognized as the 'birthplace of the eggheads,'" read an editorial in the *Telegraph-Forum* from Bucyrus,

Ohio. The editors objected to what they characterized as Hughes's view that "everybody is going to play and live off the national welfare," suggesting that "Harvard better find the 'professor' a job where he had to 'earn' his money based upon his abilities to produce. In most private industry he could qualify for 'the most eligible man to be fired.'"[74]

If Hughes had to find a public identity somewhere between the detestable "egghead" and the lovable "Prof," he also had to strike a balance between commitment and detachment. Detachment and disinterestedness were often cited as constitutive qualities of the intellectual, which Hughes underscored with such phrases as "a clear-eyed assessment of where we stand."[75] An assessment was clear-eyed when not clouded by biases arising from self-interest, prejudice, or ideology. The disinterested intellectual hovered above the fray, detached. But a public, political intellectual—who might be waging a political campaign, building a social movement, or both at once—required not detachment but commitment.

Hughes did his best to muster both. "The basis of commitment," he wrote in remarks for students, is "always only partly intellect." Since the facts of a matter were potentially limitless, and there would inevitably be reasons to doubt one's beliefs, commitment to those beliefs had "an emot[ional] involvement . . . at its center." It required a leap of faith. This "need for commitment" also arose from the "emptiness . . . of life without it," from the "meaninglessness of living without a vision of a better world."[76] Hughes wanted Americans to be "clear-eyed" when they looked at foreign affairs, but he did not want them blinded to visions of a better world as a result.

On the campaign trail, however, Hughes was better at demonstrating detachment than commitment. Allen Forbes Jr. wrote to the campaign about the tension between the two:

> There is an inherent contradiction to Stuart. Here is a candidate who was recently a man of academic, intellectual stature ensconced in a secure, prestigious position at Harvard, his future comfortable, assured, and yet he has chosen to desert this pleasant world for the almost diametrically opposed vicious, rough-and-tumble world of politics. . . . One is entitled to assume that for him to make so drastic a move, to bring about such a total dislocation of his own life and his family's life as well, he must have undergone some overpowering, obsessive experience, that he has been transformed into a man-with-a-mission sort of thing.

But after hearing him speak several times he gives only the impression
of a detached, dispassionate, intellectual on an academic exercise.

Forbes wanted more evidence of commitment: "dynamism, conviction,
drive, enthusiasm." So did David Riesman, who wrote Hughes: "I hope
some in your audience will realize that, though you speak calmly and with
wit and detachment, you wouldn't be doing this at all if you didn't feel pas-
sionately." Detachment made Hughes appear as though he did not have a
horse in the race; supporters were encouraging him to behave more like he
was a horse in the race.[77]

Hughes, however, resisted horse-race politics. "My own interpretation
is that the ideas behind the campaign are far more important than my own
personality," he told his staff. "All of us—and myself in particular—should
behave in character, and not try to act in a way that goes against the grain
just because it happens to be in the current political tradition. After all,
one of the things we are trying to do is to set a new political model; we
should not even by implication suggest that we approve of current American political behavior."[78] Hughes was committed to elevating political
conduct and debate, even if it cost him votes.

In this effort, Hughes risked talking over the public, on the one hand,
and talking down to it, on the other. Luliova Barker of the Women's International League for Peace and Freedom heard Hughes at a Boston Common rally and found his speech wanting. "It seems to me that you have
lived so much 'in the ivory tower' that you do not realize how the average
person feels," she said. "How much do you meet the 'average' man? Do you
know what he thinks and why? If not, how can you expect to influence
him and bring him into the peace movement?" Barker urged that Hughes
"approach people where they are; that is only good psychology." Edith Bunker of Roxbury cautioned Hughes that "one of the reasons Mr. Stevenson
lost out (besides his heart not being in it) was that his wonderful speeches,
idealism and great sense, was too difficult in word usage for the average
voter to understand. . . . I am not suggesting that you talk down to people.
But to use simple words in place of long ones, if the simple ones will do as
well." Barker and Bunker were urging Hughes to speak neither over and
above, nor down at, but directly to people.[79]

To the extent that his campaign aimed to educate the public, however, it was difficult for Hughes to effectively inform his audience about
nuclear weapons within the context of a Senate race. Hughes's "style of

delivery was better suited to an indoor situation and a college audience, than to a political rally," reported an observer. Hughes showed "no trace of talking down to the audience, which is good, but there was some evidence of talking over the threshold of political attentiveness."[80] Hughes supporter Jim Lieberman put the issue more strongly to the candidate:

> You want to wake people up to issues, and you have chosen the best way to do so: but you will throw away what you have gained if you insist that you are an educator rather than a candidate—if you try to make the electorate listen to a lecture, rather than interacting with the people as a candidate—the best!—running a race as people expect it to be run— only with integrity. The people will not vote for a man who expects to lose, and I suspect they will not even listen to him very much.[81]

Detachment and commitment, ideas and personality, educating and engaging—Hughes had to negotiate all these binaries in a campaign that was torn between running above the race and running in it.

The campaign gained definite structure and purpose from its drive to get the 75,514 signatures necessary for a place on the ballot. After a large force of volunteers—mostly college students—fanned out across Massachusetts to ring doorbells, Hughes submitted 118,437 valid signatures. Suddenly, Hughes was big news. "The political surprise of the year erupted last week," reported *Newsweek*, noting Hughes's "Egghead Appeal": his strength "in the suburbs . . . and his popularity with intellectuals had Kennedy Democrats particularly concerned." Coverage focused not on the importance of Hughes's message, but on his potential to throw the race to Lodge.[82]

Yet Hughes's message did get out. "To educate the country, Hughes is available to out-of-state correspondents. He has not turned down a request for an interview yet," reported the *Baltimore Sun*. On *Meet the Press*, Hughes was asked by William F. Buckley and others whether he was soft on the Soviets or "at all disturbed" that his stances on foreign policy resembled theirs, why he hadn't "been a strenuous anti-Communist," and what he thought his electoral chances were. Afterward, Hughes's headquarters was flooded with mail from across the country that ran "7 or 8 to 1 in [Hughes's] favor, with many of the letter writers including contributions." These letters suggested that Hughes was indeed educating the public and stimulating new thinking. Mary Farquharson of Seattle offered "congratulations for your contribution to adult education as you campaign for the U.S. Senate." She found it "refreshing to get a little common sense plus a high degree of sophisticated knowledge." Similarly, Richard Frantz of Waukesha, Wisconsin, assured Hughes that his "courageous stand will do something to educate some people." Alan Kapelner of New York wished "there were more like you in the great tradition of intellectual dissenter, a tradition sadly evaporating these regimented days." A reverend in Florida wrote that "not since the pre-election speeches of Adlai Stevenson have I been so moved as by your honest and forthright answers."[83]

While reaching television viewers around the nation, Hughes was having difficulty reaching voters in Massachusetts, particularly working-class ones. His campaign volunteers were most often students and "lawyers, business men, doctors, teachers, engineers, house-wifes [sic], etc. They are the upper-middle class liberals. . . . Conspicuous by their total absence are Negro and labor leaders." Hughes might only preach to a choir of academics and peace activists in liberal protestant churches, upper-middle-class living rooms, and college campuses. "I hope most of your support does not come . . . from the so called egg heads as the general populace feels they are 'far out' in their thinking anyway and that factor might hinder your candidacy," wrote one supporter. Another suggested that the "campaign schedule is much too much weighted toward suburban communities . . . and you are not spending enough time in the working class areas." Hughes had opposed campaigning mostly in the suburbs but felt constrained by requests from his earliest and most active organizers—many of whom were suburbanites—that he visit their neighborhoods. He vowed to spend October visiting industrial plants.[84]

The question ran deeper than campaign scheduling, however. Hughes's conception of working-class voters—at times anthropological, at times novelistic—was an obstacle too. Hughes recalled a garment workers' dance in New Bedford where a young woman, "her opulent figure enveloped in a knitted dress, offered to introduce me around the room. To each friend in turn she whispered the magic words, 'You know, dollar-fifty and thirty-five hours'"—Hughes's proposal for wages and hours—"as though it were a very special kind of secret." He noticed a "look of incredulity . . . mingled with delight, on the face of the old and toothless woman whose hand I happened to be shaking. It was as though she had suddenly been offered a box of candy." His depiction of the elderly woman is almost Dickensian, and he sexualizes the working-class woman in a way that he does not middle-class women. One imagines Hughes jotting notes in a field journal. "As I walked down factory assembly lines, the workers had greeted me with friendly curiosity," but "among clerical employees things were invariably stickier—thereby giving unexpected confirmation to a romantic notion of the working class that I thought I had long since outgrown." Here was not simply a case of Hughes being too intellectual in manner—"too cerebral, abstract and unimpassioned," as one observer alleged—to relate to working people.[85] It was class, not intellectualism, that formed the main barrier between Hughes and these voters.[86] As a "latter-day Edwardian" and "gentleman rebel," Hughes may have viewed these voters not just as people who performed different work than he did, but as a different sort of people entirely.[87]

Although his "domestic program was rather of a militant welfare-state variety, with a strong emphasis on the rights of Negroes and of labor," Hughes was unable to garner much support among these constituencies. "At the NAACP candidates' night, a young Negro politician from Ward 12 sitting next to me was very much impressed by you and complained about the fact that you had never been to Ward 12," reported a volunteer. Would a Hughes visit there turn out differently than his evening in New Bedford? "Outside the liberal suburbs and the college towns, Beacon Hill and the Berkshires, my candidacy never quite became real," Hughes observed, suggesting it would not.[88]

In October, the campaign assembled an impressive group of "Artists and Writers for Hughes," underlining the message that intellectuals were overwhelmingly behind him. "For the first time in American history, sculptors, painters, poets, musicians and writers have joined together to support a political candidate," the campaign reported. The invitation to a cocktail reception for Hughes simply said: "An intelligent man deserves an intelligent hearing; intelligent citizens deserve to know an intelligent candidate." Hughes may not have secured the popular vote, but he did claim to have the intelligent one.[89]

Ted Kennedy was winning the support of those Hughes failed to reach. In fact, Kennedy was winning the support of most people. His position was so commanding that he refused to participate in two televised debates. His aide Gerard Doherty said Kennedy would not share the stage with Hughes, whose campaign was "frivolous." Hughes struck back, arguing that Kennedy was afraid to "meet me in a face-to-face confrontation on the vital issues of war and peace. I have spent more than twenty years in the study of twentieth century history and politics. I was a lieutenant colonel in the wartime Office of Strategic Services. I was a division chief in the U.S. State

Department after the war. I have written six books on Western history and public affairs in the twentieth century." In asserting his right to be heard, Hughes had recourse to his expertise.[90]

On October 22, the ground beneath the campaign shifted dramatically when President Kennedy announced the presence of Soviet missiles in Cuba and an American naval blockade of that island. Hughes sent a telegram to the president, "strongly urg[ing] that the United States refrain from military action in Cuba. . . . We need to show patience and a willingness to negotiate differences on the basis of international law." The following day, Hughes issued a peace plan, reminding Americans that "when we think of the panic we feel when we contemplate Soviet offensive potential in Cuba, we should also remember that for years we have maintained almost 100 offensive bases all around the Soviet Union." The crisis might underline Hughes's message in the most vivid way possible: the conduct of the Cold War was leading toward a catastrophic nuclear exchange.[91]

But in the minds of most Massachusetts voters, while the crisis evoked the danger of nuclear war, it also pointed to the peril of Hughes's plan to reduce America's military posture. "My wife and I were grateful for the sound of your quiet voice when it emerged astonishingly last week from a radio quivering with martial noises," wrote Peter Shepherd to Hughes on October 29. On the same day, Allan Ryan Jr. told Hughes he could "no longer work in your behalf," for "recent Cuban events have evoked an increasing sentiment that negotiations alone are not enough." Ultimately, there were more like Ryan than like Shepherd. "[A] Boston Globe poll taken before the blockade showed a possible Hughes vote of 7%." But when "the news media reported that Hughes had opposed the blockade, the polls showed a sharp drop to around two percent." Whereas the onset of the crisis seemed to vindicate Hughes's claim that nuclear war was the most pressing issue before the nation, its resolution—Kennedy's naval deployments seemingly led to victory over Khrushchev—appeared to vindicate the view that power, not diplomacy or unilateral initiatives toward disarmament, was the best policy.[92]

It was a turning point for the campaign. "No one, least of all Professor Hughes himself, believes that he has a chance of winning—particularly after the apparent success of the President's Cuban policy," reported the *Berkshire Eagle*. "One Boston newspaper ran a cartoon picturing Hughes entering a classroom with an umbrella labeled 'appeasement' under his arm. The caption ran something like 'Egg in his Head.'" As Karl Miller of the *New Statesman* concluded, "The success of a tough, threatening line in Cuba means that it will be very hard for Stuart Hughes, who was urging last week that the nation 'pull back' and submit the situation to the UN, to win as many votes as he once won signatures." On Election Day, Hughes received "a paltry 50,000 votes, 2 percent of the total cast."[93]

Though the Cuban Missile Crisis undoubtedly cost Hughes votes, it was only the final stress upon a candidacy that was beset from the start with tensions and contradictions arising from the uncertain place of the intellectual in American politics. First among these was the opposition between authority founded in expertise and that rooted in moral clarity. Hughes often dismissed reliance upon expertise, saying that it stifled democratic participation. It was "a smoke screen, since basic quest[ion]s are simple & moral," he wrote. "That only 'experts' are in a position to voice valid opinion about major issues is a fallacy," Hughes told voters. "With effort, individual citizens can be informed. The facts are available with vigilant newspaper and other reading, and our sense of human values is as good as any expert's. We can and should make our voices heard." When Pierre Salinger invoked the authority of experts to tell the citizens of Marblehead, Massachusetts, that they should approve a civil defense program, Hughes was critical. Salinger "made no attempt to present the program on its merits," he claimed, "but simply mentioned numerous glamorous and prestigious authorities to which he apparently assumed the citizens of Marblehead would bow: the Department of Defense, extensive analysis, scientists, engineers, military experts, electronic computers." The program was defeated by a vote of the Marblehead Town Meeting.[94]

Given his repeated rejection of expertise, it was noteworthy that Hughes and his campaign so often touted his standing as an expert. An early pamphlet described Hughes as a "foreign policy expert-statesman-veteran-writer-teacher"—expert listed first, teacher last. An expert possesses the specialized knowledge to make decisions for other people; a teacher shares knowledge so that people can make decisions for themselves. Another pamphlet was simply titled "For United States Senate Stuart Hughes, an Expert in Foreign Policy." On *Meet the Press*, when Lawrence Spivak asked Hughes why voters should support him, he replied: "I think I know more about foreign affairs. . . . I have been a specialist, particularly on contemporary European problems, now for a matter of 20 years." Even as Hughes questioned authority founded in expertise, he invoked it for himself.[95]

Of all the foundations for an intellectual's authority, of all the reasons why Hughes deserved an audience or, in this case, a vote, expertise was the most tangible. In the crucible of a campaign, it is not surprising that Hughes fell back upon this form of authority, even if he objected to it in principle. But Hughes also tried to root his authority in grounds less tangible. He sometimes claimed to be speaking on behalf of humane values or universal truths, opposing them to the amoral logic of the Cold War. He described the role of senator as French thinker Julien Benda had characterized that of intellectuals, who "gaz[ed] as moralists upon the conflict of human egotisms," and "preached, in the name of humanity or justice, the adoption of an abstract principle superior to and directly opposed to these passions." Similarly, Hughes felt "emphatically that a United States Senator should be primarily a spokesman for the interests of the whole country—or even of humanity—rather than the representative of the narrow interests of a single state." By contrast, Ted Kennedy's signature slogan was: "He Can Do MORE for Massachusetts." When Hughes made specific reference to Massachusetts, he spoke not of earmarks but of ideals. He told voters that "Massachusetts was once the source of moral leadership" and could "again be the conscience of America." Hughes put himself forth not as a prospective representative of the state but as the representative of values that transcended nations and states.[96]

The Hughes campaign also claimed authority based on the quality of the candidate's mind, apart from any particular expertise. This claim emphasized Hughes's cognitive excellence rather than clarity of conscience. "He has been designated by scholars in the field as one of the clearest-thinking minds on European history," proclaimed a leaflet. "Here is a candidate of intelligence . . . who can speak without confusion." Another simply read: "Stuart Hughes for Senator: An Open Mind for an Open Future." One supporter hoped that Hughes would "prove the impossible in your campaign: that an intelligent and objective thinker can be elected to the high office you seek." Hughes's mind—open, clear, intelligent, objective—was contrasted to Kennedy's. "Harvard, the greatest institution of its kind in the world, ought to be more insistent on turning out graduates who can think in a more logical fashion than Teddy Kennedy," wrote Louise Reilly to Hughes. Reverend O. R. Williams of Youngstown, Ohio, found it "heartening . . . to know we have a man of your stature, and penetrating mind" in politics.[97]

Williams paired Hughes's mind with his stature, the latter connoting social status more than mental acuity. Regard for the quality of Hughes's mind was, indeed, often tangled up with regard for the quality of his pedigree. Rabbi Baruch Korff claimed that Hughes "is endowed with inherent leadership and wisdom and is motivated by intellectual honesty that . . . towers far above the candidates with vested interests of party and ward heelers." This comment evoked the contest between ethnic, urban bosses and old-stock gentlemen reformers for the control of municipal governments in the Progressive Era, a period Hughes's description of himself as a "latter-day Edwardian" conjured. At a time when the Boston Irish political machine and, in particular, Joseph P. Kennedy's money were regarded as delivering reliable, if not legitimate, votes, Hughes was not above coloring his opponents green, contrasting tribal, ethnic politics with his cosmopolitan, universalistic approach. He told his mother that Edward McCormack "has a lot of Irish charm" and described the Democratic primary as an "all-Irish struggle" and "a local clan battle."[98]

Karl Miller noted that "Hughes is a handsome man of distinguished lineage who is able to regard Roosevelt as a 'real aristocrat' and the Kennedys as a mock-dynasty of *arrivistes.*" The *Boston Sunday Herald* described Hughes as combining "family eminence with academic brilliance."[99] Within an aristocratic worldview, family eminence and academic brilliance were not so much combinable as inseparable. The "best"—in the sense of social status—were also the "best"—in terms of the intellectual and moral virtues. Intelligence and morality, in short, had a definite class location, and Hughes was of that class. Although he professed independence from his family (and, ideologically, that certainly was the case), he could not achieve independence from his family name, a name that nonetheless conferred a certain legitimacy.

"H. Stuart Hughes must . . . convince [people] that he is worth listening to," advised one supporter late in the campaign.[100] Whether his demand for a hearing was grounded in expertise, moral clarity, mental acumen, or social pedigree—all qualities that swirled about the concept of the intellectual—Hughes was consistently seen as distant from the people whose votes he sought to win and whose thought he sought to stimulate. The expert was cordoned off from others by specialization. The moral conscience of a people floated above them. The uncommon cast of mind was just that: uncommon; and the gentlemen reformer was defined by the binary that divided the few from the many. Only in one dimension of his identity as an intellectual was there a level path between Hughes and other people: his role as an educator.

The educator seeks to impart insight, information, and skills to others, not to be their expert or moral conscience, but to engender expertise and moral consciousness in them. Such purposes were at the heart of the Hughes campaign, both in its explicit talk of voter education and in its expressed desire to bring forth new thinking. The problem for Hughes was not practicing education; it was practicing politics as education amid the melee of a campaign. What space there might have been was restricted by Kennedy's refusal to debate and by Lodge quitting after only the second of six scheduled debates. Taking to the airwaves required money, and raising money required soliciting donors rather than communicating with voters. When Hughes did speak over the radio, on television, or at a rally, he often did not have sufficient opportunity to expound upon his views. As a result, "confusions and misunderstandings of Hughes' programs plagued the campaign from beginning to end."[101]

Even when Hughes could fully explore a question, voters may have been more focused on learning where he stood rather than on interrogating where they themselves did. "Can an experienced statesman and teacher challenge the traditional politics with a campaign based on issues, not personalities?" asked a Hughes poster. "Yes! Politics can once again become an open forum for the exchange of ideas." Such a politics would include as well as inform voters' ideas. This election, however, proved to be about their perceptions of the candidates—and Hughes was found wanting. The tension between education and electoral politics dogged the Hughes campaign and was captured in notes from a staff meeting that asked, "Should we attempt to reach more people or a few people intensively? Must we practice peace education as well as politics?" The minutes finally indicated "Consensus: not reached."[102]

* * *

"Does your candidacy help toward the creation of a peace party such as you advocate in your current book?" reporter Allen Klein asked Hughes. "This is my hope," he replied. "I would prefer not to call it a peace party, however. It should be thought of rather as a New Left, with a militant emphasis on public welfare and equality at home." Hughes hoped that his campaign would mark the onset of a new, respectable radicalism in America. He felt that "despite his unorthodox views," he would be "widely accepted as a thoroughly 'respectable' candidate." Hughes was "upset that his student volunteers have been pictured as beatniks" and believed that "the average citizen" would find his campaign "more concrete and responsible" than demonstrations.[103]

Hughes's 1962 campaign belonged to a peace movement focused on the Cold War's nuclear standoff. The demonstrations that rocked the nation half a decade later were also part of a peace movement, but one focused on the war in Vietnam. During the earlier movement, candidate Hughes had contained the tension between the intellectual as expert and the intellectual as moral conscience within himself. By the later movement, that tension had splintered into warring camps of intellectuals, those who held to the ideal of disinterested expertise and those who labeled this putative amorality a most dangerous form of immorality.

THE MORALIST AND THE MANDARIN

While H. Stuart Hughes ran against Ted Kennedy in Massachusetts, John F. Kennedy ran the federal government from Washington. The president had assembled a brain trust said to rival FDR's. There were economists, like John Kenneth Galbraith and Walt Whitman Rostow. There were managerial "whiz kids," like McGeorge Bundy and Robert McNamara.[1] And there was Arthur M. Schlesinger Jr., a Pulitzer Prize–winning American historian.

If Schlesinger's skills differed from those of other Kennedy intellectuals, it was because his role—what Robert Kennedy described as "a sort of roving reporter and troubleshooter"—did too.[2] Tasked to work on Latin American and, later, Italian affairs, Schlesinger also drafted speeches for Kennedy on domestic policy. He had a hand in preparing for the Bay of Pigs invasion and for the Kennedy Presidential Library. He wrote memoranda and delivered remarks. If there was a unifying thread to this activity, it was Schlesinger's work crafting and communicating the administration's "messaging."

Schlesinger's literary skill served Kennedy from his presidential campaign through the posthumous construction of his legacy in A Thousand Days: John F. Kennedy in the White House, which won Schlesinger a second Pulitzer in 1966.[3] In the White House, Schlesinger provided thinking that he hoped would inform presidential action. At other times, he furnished the rationale for action taken without clear thought. Whether he shaped the vision of the Kennedy presidency, articulated a vision shaped by others, or attempted to paper over a failure of vision, Schlesinger regarded himself as one of "the President's men."[4]

After Kennedy's assassination, Schlesinger resigned and turned from serving the president to criticizing him. Even as he dissented from Vietnam policy that his Kennedy cohort—Bundy, Rostow, and McNamara—

continued to carry out, Schlesinger did so in a way that suggested he was still one of them. He portrayed the growing split over Vietnam as a respectful disagreement among colleagues, calling it in 1966 "the kind of issue which is sufficiently complex so that men who are equal in patriotism or liberalism can conscientiously come up with different conclusions."[5] Vietnam meant a policy debate within the inner circle, not a policy divide that would tear this circle apart. It was a puzzle that people sharing the same outlook and values—Kennedy people—might simply have different approaches to solving.

The emphasis on treating Vietnam as a problem—rather than, as others alleged, a crime—was characteristic of the Kennedy cast of mind. Kennedy "saw the human struggle, not as a moralist, but as an historian, even as an ironist, [though] irony was never permitted to sever the nerve of action," Schlesinger wrote. He respected Kennedy as a thinker, but admired him as one whose thought was always directed toward action: "When [Kennedy] was told something, he wanted to know what he could do about it." Thinking done with a view toward action was responsible and sober. It was the sort of thinking that people did when they held power. "I run for the Presidency of the United States because it is the center of action," Kennedy said. Action was not simply a virtue; it was a whetstone for sharpening the intellect.[6]

Schlesinger directed his attention to fixing America's Vietnam problem, not to assigning blame for it. His early writing on Vietnam had the tone of a policy analyst weighing options, assessing outcomes, and calculating costs. Those who lacked this instrumental orientation were, for Schlesinger, rigid and moralistic. They sought to impose fixed categories upon a plastic world. In this camp he placed John Foster Dulles, communists, and, by the late 1960s, the New Left.[7] This last group lacked the corrective weight of responsibility. They did not exercise power; their thinking was not disciplined by the requirement to act. Schlesinger was prepared to see New Left critics as muddled because he saw them as irresponsible.

One such critic was Noam Chomsky. While Schlesinger set out for the New Frontier, Chomsky engaged in pathbreaking work of his own—in linguistics. His early titles demonstrate his immersion in technical matters: "A Note on Phrase Structure Grammars" (1959), "Some Methodological Remarks on Generative Grammar" (1961), and "Context-Free Grammars and Pushdown Storage" (1962). These academic attentions did not diminish Chomsky's political consciousness. In 1961 he achieved tenure at MIT and, like H. Stuart Hughes, signed an open letter of opposition to the Bay of Pigs invasion.[8]

As military involvement in Vietnam eclipsed the confrontation with Cuba, Chomsky's activism shifted. "I had, from childhood, been deeply involved intellectually in radical and dissident politics, but intellectually," he recalled. "At this point, I was feeling so uneasy with the usual petition-signing and the like that I couldn't stand it any longer, and decided to plunge in."[9] That plunge took the form of protest marches, an arrest, and in 1970 even a trip to Hanoi. It also registered in Chomsky's writing.

Among his first plunges in print, 1967's "The Responsibility of Intellectuals" attacked Kennedy intellectuals as the "arrogant and deluded men of whom Schlesinger gives such a flattering portrait" in A Thousand Days. Chomsky targeted Schlesinger's admission that he had lied to the press regarding the Bay of Pigs: "It is of no particular interest that one man is quite happy to lie in behalf of a cause which he knows to be unjust; but it is significant that such events provoke so little response in the intellectual community." Chomsky wondered at "the offer of a major chair in the humanities"—in 1966 Schlesinger became the Albert Schweitzer Professor at the City University of New York—"to a historian who feels it to be his duty to persuade the world that an American-sponsored invasion of a nearby country is nothing of the sort."[10] Among mainstream intellectuals, Chomsky saw violations of what he regarded as their responsibility—to speak truth—bringing acclaim, not censure.[11] The double meaning of "the responsibility of intellectuals" to which this contradiction pointed would mark Chomsky's thought for the next half century. "The phrase is ambiguous," he wrote in 2011: "does it refer to intellectuals' moral responsibility as decent human beings in a position to use their privilege and status to advance the causes of freedom, justice, mercy, peace, and other such sentimental concerns? Or does it refer to the role they are expected to play, serving, not derogating, leadership and established institutions?" Implicitly locating himself in the first category while overtly criticizing the second, Chomsky—like Raymond Aron appraising Marxists—could write about Schlesinger and other intellectuals as though he were not one.[12]

Chomsky and Schlesinger were on a collision course, and the crash came in 1969–70 with ad hominem exchanges in Commentary, the Listener, and elsewhere, including their books. Beneath the invective, their debate illuminated competing conceptions of the intellectual's role in politics, raising questions about the relationship between intellectuals and power, the difference between "the responsibility of intellectuals" and intellectuals acting "responsibly," and the definition of the intellectual itself.

In certain respects, more united than divided Chomsky and Schlesinger. They were professors whose academic lives and reputations sprang from Cambridge, Massachusetts. They were members of Harvard's Society of Fellows and the Institute for Advanced Study in Princeton. They testified to the Senate about the lessons of Vietnam on May 10, 1972. They appeared on Nixon's "Enemies List."[13] Yet their differences overshadowed these similarities, and those differences revealed not only fundamentally opposed views of American policy but also distinct visions of what an intellectual should be.

Chomsky and Schlesinger quarreled about Vietnam but clashed over worldviews, applying competing philosophical frames to the backdrop of war. Schlesinger asked whether entering a war served American interests; Chomsky asked whether doing so was just. Schlesinger focused on geopolitics and tactical effectiveness. Chomsky concentrated on individual responsibility—moral choices made by people, particularly intellectuals whose role it was to speak truth and unmask falsehood. When Chomsky and Schlesinger looked at American involvement in Vietnam, they peered through different lenses. Ultimately, each saw the other as a character—the villain—in the drama of American politics.

For Chomsky, Schlesinger was the prototypical mandarin: an intellectual who acted in the service of national interests that were at best amoral and at worst criminal. For Schlesinger, Chomsky was the prototypical moralist: an ideologue who abandoned analysis for absolutism. In the intellectual struggle over Vietnam, Chomsky and Schlesinger did not find their bitterest enemies among hard-line hawks; each saw the greatest threat in the type represented by the other.

* * *

Schlesinger was a junior, and the Arthurs M. Schlesinger shared more than a name. Both taught history at Harvard. Though the son had "a good deal more polemical temperament," the father, "in a quiet way, had always been something of a political activist." The latter's "faith in reasoned democracy and . . . dislike of absolutisms inoculated" his son "at an early point against apocalyptic politics."[14]

As a student at Exeter, Schlesinger Jr. sharpened his pen. One essay was called "Highbrow: A Term of Respect." The term was "'applied by yokels,

100% Americans, Hoover Republicans, and other dull fellows to those whose perceptions were keener than their own.'" The talented Schlesinger entered Harvard at sixteen and was graduated in 1938. After a year of study in England, he joined Harvard's Society of Fellows and finished *The Age of Jackson*, which established him as a historian and allowed him to "avoid the Ph.D. mill."[15]

Schlesinger's time at Harvard "reinforced the anti-utopianism I inherited from my father," leading to "a darker and wiser" liberalism. A major influence on Schlesinger's tempered thought was Reinhold Niebuhr. In *The Nature and Destiny of Man* (1941–43) and *The Children of Light and the Children of Darkness* (1944), Niebuhr bolstered Schlesinger's "sense that irony was the best human and historical stance—an irony which does not," as Kennedy demonstrated, "sever the nerve of action." Schlesinger viewed irony and the doctrine of original sin, both important to Niebuhr's thinking, as a corrective to the liberalism of his youth. Influenced by John Dewey, that liberalism "had a particular weakness for the idea that the troubles of the world were due not to human frailty but to human ignorance and to unjust institutions."[16] Schlesinger favored a tough-minded reckoning with perennial problems like human frailty—but not a reckoning that resulted in paralysis. Instead, facing Niebuhrian facts seemed to gird Schlesinger for battle. Followers of Dewey and those of Niebuhr were both committed to acting in the world, but Schlesinger accused Deweyans of optimism about the efficacy of their action. By contrast, Niebuhrians, like Camus's Sisyphus, had "no illusions"—a frequent Schlesinger phrase—about their boulder finally reaching the top of the hill. Deweyans were nonplussed when it rolled back down.

While attracted to the idea of action in the face of irony, Schlesinger was also simply attracted to action, particularly political action. His historical research took him to Washington, DC, where talk "never ceases to excite—the endless gossip about power, the endless temptations of inside-dopesterism; above all, the size of the stakes." Schlesinger "envied the New Dealers with all their opportunities and responsibilities!"[17] He wanted to get in the political game for the sheer appeal of the game itself, not only because it was the right move for a Niebuhrian agent without illusions.

Schlesinger felt himself under no illusions regarding World War Two. In vigorously supporting American intervention, he demonstrated a disposition toward war that flowed from the Niebuhrian outlook, in which warfare may be a necessary response to inevitable human depravity.[18] This attitude was manifest again in Schlesinger's militant anti-communism. It appeared in the Kennedy White House, when Schlesinger harbored serious questions about the Bay of Pigs invasion but failed to articulate them forcefully enough to slow the momentum of action. Perhaps he felt the burden of proof lay not with those who advocated war, but those who opposed it—they had better ask themselves whether they were under any illusions. This attitude appeared again as Kennedy expanded American involvement in Vietnam, which Schlesinger initially viewed as a tough-minded policy. During the long years of the Vietnam conflict, Schlesinger's disposition toward war was tested and reshaped in the crucible of debate with critics like Chomsky. Schlesinger rejected the use of force on behalf of crusading moralism, but he remained open to it as a realist's response to an imperfect, often brutal world.[19] In the end, the moralistic crusader and the tough-minded Niebuhrian alike could tilt the intellectual terrain toward war.[20]

Writing editorials and speeches for the Office of War Information—a foretaste of his White House work—Schlesinger realized that he "was deplorably adept at a ghostwriter's duplicity."[21] At war's end, Schlesinger wrote for *Fortune, Life, Collier's,* and the *Saturday Evening Post,* and he began to enjoy renown as a writer of both scholarly and more popular pieces (the scholarly pieces more popular than most and the popular pieces more scholarly). Schlesinger used his prominent pen to savage conservatives and communists alike.

Schlesinger's Cold War commentary showed how intellectualized conceptions of irony and tough-mindedness could become not so much a philosophy as a posture. Tough-mindedness could begin to look like vulgar toughness. In their effort to establish a vital center in American politics, Schlesinger and other anti-communist liberals advanced their version of hardheaded realism against the soft idealism of intellectuals who, they charged, had been bedazzled by, or sentimentally clung to, Marxist utopianism. Against this softness of the socialists, Schlesinger's liberalism struck a distinctly manly pose. "American liberalism has had a positive and confident ring," he wrote in *The Vital Center* (1949). "It has stood for responsibility and achievement, not for frustration and sentimentalism; it has been the instrument of social change, not of private neurosis."[22]

"The Future of Socialism" (1947) mingled an insinuation of intellectuals' homosexuality with the charge that they were divorced from the active, physical life. They succumbed to the "mystique of the proletariat" because "its appeal lies partly in the intellectual's sense of guilt over living pleasantly by his wits instead of unpleasantly by his hands, partly in the intellectual's somewhat feminine fascination with the rude and muscular power of the proletariat, partly in the intellectual's desire to compensate for his own sense of alienation by immersing himself in the broad maternal expanse of the masses."[23] Yet in turning his fire against intellectuals, Schlesinger—anticipating conservatives like Irving Kristol—aimed, ironically, at the very category to which he belonged. Schlesinger's attacks on intellectuals burnished his own manly credentials. In criticizing those seduced by the siren's call of the "mystique of the proletariat," Schlesinger showed that he was strapped to the mast. He was not alone. Manliness, action, and patriotism walked shoulder to shoulder in Cold War rhetoric.[24]

Christopher Lasch would later describe this embrace of action-oriented bravado as "the anti-intellectualism of the intellectuals." Schlesinger's liberalism "became in time the official creed of the intellectual establishment" because such liberals were able to "present themselves as hard-boiled and 'pragmatic,' and thus to appeal convincingly to the American intellectual's need to see himself as a 'tough-minded' man of the world, not a mere spectator, but an active participant in the great events of the day."[25] The desire to be in the action rather than on the sidelines was a questing after both relevance and manliness—the two thoroughly imbricated.

Intellectuals could demonstrate their manliness through action that took the form of commitment: in the battle between America and the Soviet Union, there could be no neutrality; one must take sides. As anticommunist writer Arthur Koestler put it: "When man stands at a crossroads which only leaves the choice of this way or that, the difference between the very clever and the simple in mind narrows almost to the vanishing point." Those thinkers confronting "destiny's challenge" and failing to choose were "victims of a professional disease—the intellectual's estrangement from reality."[26]

Schlesinger's attacks on left intellectuals competed for ink with his criticism of Republicans. These agendas could undercut each other. His swipes at intellectuals resembled the scorn they received from the likes of Joseph McCarthy—scorn leveled against Schlesinger's political hero of the 1950s: Adlai Stevenson. By 1953 Schlesinger was lamenting that intellectuals were "on the run today in American society" and that Stevenson's defeat had turned the White House over to Republicans.[27] Schlesinger's aim as a loyal Democrat was to win it back. He did so not by firing at the Eisenhower administration from the left, but by moving to its right.

The 1960 Kennedy campaign accused Republicans of military weakness, making the apocryphal "missile gap" a major issue. On the campaign trail, Schlesinger warned that the Soviets had "three times as many intercontinental missiles" as the United States and were "outstripping us in the stratosphere." Nevertheless, "the Eisenhower-Nixon answer is that the United States can't 'afford' to do more than it is doing." Republicans' fiscal qualms became a glaring lack of toughness, and the consequence was "a shocking decline of the United States . . . as a world power."[28] The 1960 campaign was not a contest between Nixon's anti-communist bravado and Kennedy's brains—it was a contest between two forms of bravado, and Schlesinger's brand won.

In the Kennedy brand, Schlesinger saw a synthesis of intellect and action, glamour and toughness. In verses for Kennedy's inauguration, Robert Frost looked forward to the new administration as "a golden age of poetry and power." Schlesinger found this pairing within the president himself. "One cannot be sure what an intellectual is," he wrote, "but let us define it as a person whose primary habitat is the realm of ideas. In this sense, exceedingly few political leaders are authentic intellectuals, because the primary habitat of the political leader is the world of power." Kennedy, however, was no ordinary political leader. "He was a man of action who could pass easily over to the realm of ideas and confront intellectuals with perfect confidence." Schlesinger pressed this description into a distinction, saying the Kennedy years "were not ideological, though they could perhaps be termed intellectual."[29]

Kennedy could fly with intellectuals, but he did not carry the baggage that Schlesinger had heaped upon them. For Kennedy's "mind was not prophetic, impassioned, mystical, ontological, utopian or ideological"—those characteristics that made intellectuals susceptible to "the mystique of the proletariat." Instead, Kennedy was "objective, practical, ironic, skeptical, unfettered and insatiable."[30] These two sets of attributes show the line Schlesinger drew between two types of intellectual. When the term "intellectual" was applied to the first set, it was derisive. When applied to the second it was—to borrow a phrase from Schlesinger's Exeter essay—"a term of respect." In the Kennedy White House, Schlesinger saw an opportunity to define intellectuals by this second set of attributes, to win for them a respect rooted in the union of action and ideas, poetry and power.

The initial challenge for Kennedy was not to gain respect for intellectualism but to gain the allegiance of intellectuals. At Harvard's 1956 commencement ceremony, he had told his audience that politics "needs to have its temperature lowered in the cooling waters of the scholastic pool. We need both the technical judgment and the disinterested viewpoint of the scholar, to prevent us from becoming imprisoned by our own slogans." Kennedy suggested that the situations of politicians and intellectuals were surprisingly similar: neither of them enjoyed much public respect. Yet the two groups were deeply suspicious of each other. "Let us not emphasize all on which we differ," Kennedy advised, "but all we have in common"—including shared ancestors: "Our nation's first great politicians were also among the Nation's first great scholars." He called for this link between scholarship and politics to be restored, admonishing those who contented themselves with "the mysteries of pure scholarship or the delights of abstract discourse" to take a more active role:

> "Would you have counted him a friend of ancient Greece," as George William Curtis asked a century ago during the Kansas-Nebraska controversy, "who quietly discussed patriotism on that Greek summer day through whose hopeless and immortal hours Leonidas and his 300 stood at Thermopylae for liberty? Was John Milton to conjugate Greek verbs in his library or talk of the liberty of the ancient Shunamites when the liberty of Englishmen was imperiled?" No, the duty of the scholar, particularly in a republic such as ours, is to contribute his objective views and his sense of liberty to the affairs of his State and Nation.

Five years before telling Americans to ask what they could do for their country, Kennedy was summoning intellectuals with a similar call. "I do not say that our political and public life should be turned over to experts who ignore public opinion"; he was calling for scholarship to serve politics, not to replace it. In service to government, intellectuals would not only make "a tremendous contribution to their society" but also gain "new respect for their own group." Such respect might be needed, Kennedy implied, for "politicians have questioned the discernment with which intellectuals have reacted to the siren call of the extreme left."[31]

Kennedy's speech may have aimed at gaining him a measure of recognition *from* intellectuals, but his call to government service held out the larger prospect of a path to recognition *for* intellectuals. Schlesinger was at the center of this traffic, carrying the opinions of intellectuals to Kennedy and the good news of Kennedy to intellectuals. Schlesinger, like Hughes, looked upon the coming 1960s as an opening for intellectuals in American politics. Hughes saw an opportunity for intellectuals to infuse new ideas, new thinking into public affairs. The Kennedy campaign also trumpeted new thinking—expediently rendering the Eisenhower administration as moribund. While Hughes saw the position from which intellectuals might best contribute new thinking as a dissenting one, Schlesinger believed that the surest opportunities lay within the circle of power—particularly the executive branch.

That branch appeared open to intellectuals. Louis B. Wright, director of the Folger Shakespeare Library, found the invitation of artists, writers, and thinkers to Kennedy's inauguration "encouraging and heartening evidence of a desire by the head of our nation to enlist the whole of the intellectual resources of the country in a common effort to maintain the United States in a position of world leadership."[32] Intellectuals were not only invited to the inauguration; they were given positions in the administration.

"A new breed had come to town," Schlesinger wrote. They esteemed themselves, and were seen by the public, as a new brain trust, aspiring, "like their President, to the world of ideas as well as to the world of power." The Kennedy officials were a scholarly group, but not abstractly so: "The mood of the new Washington was more to do things because they were rational than because they were just and right."[33]

Already a public persona, Schlesinger became a visible figure in the new administration. His eyeglasses, high brow, and bow tie made him look an intellectual out of central casting. Schlesinger might thus serve Kennedy as a symbol as well as an adviser, and he recognized this potential. Schlesinger's visit to Latin America would "help persuade the Latinos that the new U.S. Government is not run by money-grubbing materialists," he told Kennedy in the first weeks of the administration. Schlesinger's presence in it was only one basis upon which the Kennedy White House could "launch a new image of America as a land which deeply values artistic and cultural achievement." Kennedy had "appointed intellectuals to positions within [his] administration" and given "the intellectual community of the United States a sense of being important to the country once again." Schlesinger was not immediately concerned with whether this new image corresponded to underlying reality; the image itself was instrumentally valuable for waging cold war, as "it would confound Communist propaganda and increase our appeal to the intellectuals of both old and new nations." Schlesinger would work "with Ed Murrow and Pierre Salinger to consider ways in which the White House could communicate a sense of genuine cultural concern."[34] He was eager to put the propaganda value of American intellectuals, including himself, to work.[35]

Intellectuals had more to offer the president than symbolic power; they were also adept at manipulating symbols—as Schlesinger would in making the case for Kennedy's Cuba policy in early 1961. His subsequent role in the Bay of Pigs affair raised significant questions about the relationship between intellectuals and power. Schlesinger crafted the public rationale for a disastrous covert operation that he ultimately opposed. He willfully misled the press. Rather than using intellectual capacities to craft good policy, he was in the position of using those capacities to legitimate bad policy. Instead of curbing an untoward use of power, he clothed power in poetry so that it might pass unnoticed.

In a memorandum following a March 1961 meeting on Cuba, National Security Advisor McGeorge Bundy wrote that the "President expects to authorize U.S. support for an appropriate number of patriotic Cubans to return to their homeland." In preparation, the "Government must have ready a white paper on Cuba, and should also be ready to give appropriate assistance to Cuban patriots in a similar effort. Action: Arthur Schlesinger in cooperation with the Department of State." Schlesinger recalled the "intimidating group" at that meeting: Kennedy, Dean Rusk, Robert McNamara, three of the Joint Chiefs of Staff, and the CIA director. Schlesinger later said he "shrank into a chair at the far end of the table and listened in silence." Yet he had written to Kennedy the day before urging "a comprehensive campaign to acquaint the hemisphere with the facts of the Castro situation." Indeed, Schlesinger wrote, "the time is ripe for a propaganda counteroffensive." One day later, Schlesinger had a commanding role to play in that strike.[36]

A month earlier, Schlesinger had expressed misgivings about the operation. "However well disguised any action might be," he warned Kennedy, "it will be ascribed to the United States" and trigger "a wave of massive protest" at home and abroad.[37] Yet planning for the invasion gained momentum, and Schlesinger's white paper on Cuba was soon circulating among high-level officials. It conveyed "the United States attitude toward the Cuban Revolution and the Castro regime," arguing "that the first had been betrayed by the second, and that the result offered 'a clear and present danger to the authentic and autonomous revolution of the Americas.'" The paper suggested that freedom-loving Cubans would take action unless

Castro renounced international communism. US Information Agency Assistant Director for Latin America John P. McKnight thought the paper would "do an especially good job of bringing closer to our way of thinking people on the fence," but when it went "on to say that the 'people of Cuba remain our brothers' and that we 'acknowledge our own past omissions and errors,'" it strayed from the threat Castro posed and, McKnight concluded, "I don't think this is good propaganda."[38]

When the document was released to the public, the *Christian Science Monitor* reported that it "minces no words. It is a blunt, briskly written, 36-page pamphlet . . . fashioned largely by Prof. Arthur M. Schlesinger, Jr." According to columnist Max Lerner, this "analysis and manifesto . . . is an important event in the technique of American foreign policy." It showed that "the key to Castro's future is with the intellectuals in his own country and—perhaps even more—in the other Latin American countries" who, persuaded by Schlesinger, might press for change. Lerner hailed this "new diplomacy of the intellectuals." The *Chicago Daily News*, however, doubted that "Dr. Castro's wrath" would "abate in the face of the Schlesinger-Kennedy intellectual-historical onslaught." The document was unlikely to "reach through [Castro's] censorship to the Cuban people," and "the unlettered masses who are controlled by emotion" would not "respond to the intellectual reasoning if it did."[39]

More than the white paper's usefulness, the *Gazette and Daily* of York, Pennsylvania, questioned its integrity. The document lacked "the intelligence and careful consideration that the Kennedy Administration seems to be devoting to other problems." The *Gazette* editors' disappointment was heightened "when we read that it was prepared mostly by a White House aide, Arthur Schlesinger, Jr.," for the document did not sustain his scholarly reputation. "It is smoothly written, to be sure. But the scholarship, the evidences of really honest research, are lacking. It is not a work in which one can have confidence that its author sought only for truth." The *Gazette* did not specify Schlesinger's other motives. Instead, it asked: "What forces govern the corruption of scholarship?"[40]

These responses to Schlesinger's white paper capture three views of intellectuals' political power. Lerner had a sense of bright possibility. The *Gazette* had a sense of dark betrayal. The *Daily News* suggested that the document was full of sound and fury, signifying nothing. Lerner and the *Gazette* believed that intellectuals in politics *could* matter, while the *Daily News* dismissed that proposition entirely. The widely held opinion that

THE MORALIST AND THE MANDARIN

intellectuals were superfluous raised the stakes for those who felt otherwise, for they had something to prove. Debate about the role of intellectuals tended toward the messianic ("an important event in . . . American foreign policy") and the apocalyptic ("the corruption of scholarship") precisely because some questioned whether such debate was worth having at all.

For Lerner, the "diplomacy of the intellectuals" was an alternative to "armed showdown."[41] Part of intellectuals' promise was the belief that moral force or the force of argument could forestall physical force. Shifts from hopefulness to disappointment to feelings of betrayal occurred when intellectuals proved not only unable to replace violence with reason but ultimately became, either wittingly or not, midwives of war.

In "Washington Opens Fire on Fidel Castro," *Newsweek* made Schlesinger's writing sound like warfare. His document was "a massive salvo" that "launched a direct attack on the Castro regime." Explaining Schlesinger's role, *Newsweek* hit upon both the symbolic and the symbol-manipulating value of the intellectual to the administration. "The reasons for asking Schlesinger to write the report seem to be these: First, literary—'There's no reason why these documents have to be turgid and unreadable,' said a New Frontiersman." An adroit wordsmith, Schlesinger presented the administration's policy in a cogent, forceful manner. "The other reason may be political. By asking a well-known liberal to put his imprimatur on this devastating attack on Castro," *Newsweek* surmised, "the Administration is suggesting that there is considerable unanimity of opinion in America as to what Castro stands for."[42] Attaching Schlesinger's name to the policy legitimated it.

Yet Schlesinger continued to express concerns about an actual invasion to topple the regime. "If we could achieve this by a swift, surgical stroke, I would be for it," he told Kennedy. "But in present circumstances the operation seems to me to involve many hazards; and on balance—and despite the intelligence and responsibility with which the case for the action has been presented—I am against it." An invasion could undo many of the gains Kennedy had made in changing "(to use that repellent word) the 'image' of the United States before the world." The new president's "soberness of style" and "tough-minded idealism of purpose" had eclipsed "the muddling and moralizing conservatism of the Eisenhower period with surprising speed." These gains were all jeopardized by the Cuba plan, which would suggest that despite the style of the New Frontier, its substance was the same as the Eisenhower administration's. Moreover, since "the alleged threat to our national security" posed by Castro appeared slight, observers "will assume that our action is provoked by a threat to something other than our security," namely, business interests.[43]

Schlesinger offered "countermeasures" to mitigate potential harm to the administration's image. These included diversions to "counteract the Soviet claim that we are unregenerate imperialists," such as taking an anti-imperialist stance at the United Nations. Other measures should be in place to protect Kennedy's reputation, which was an "invaluable asset. When lies must be told, they should be told by subordinate officials." Schlesinger emphatically advised that "at no point should the President be asked to lend himself to the cover operation." In fact, "someone other than the President [should] make the final decision and do so in his absence—someone whose head can later be placed in the block if things go terribly wrong."[44]

In the run-up to the Bay of Pigs, Schlesinger went beyond suggesting countermeasures to implementing them. The operation's planners worried that media reports on the training of Cuban exiles might expose the role of the American government, a role they intended to deny. Schlesinger was therefore alarmed to read "a devastating account of CIA activities among the refugees" slated to appear in the *New Republic*. Schlesinger wrote Kennedy that Gilbert Harrison, the publisher and chief editor of the *New Republic*, "would withdraw the article if we asked him to do so." Kennedy pressed Schlesinger to stop the article, and later that day Schlesinger reported: "Gil Harrison came through like a gentleman and a patriot. He asked no questions and said he would drop the piece, though it must have done violence to his journalistic instinct." Schlesinger wished "there were some way we might acknowledge his sense of responsibility in the matter."[45] In this case, acting responsibly meant unquestioning acquiescence to the wishes of the White House.

At dawn on April 15, airstrikes from bases in Nicaragua hit Cuban airfields. The official story was that rebels in Castro's air force conducted these strikes, and one of the pilots thus landed in Miami, proclaiming that he was a defector. The next night, a force of exiles began landing on Cuban beaches, coming under fire almost immediately. That day, Schlesinger "told the [New York] Times's Washington Bureau, for publication on a background basis, that the landing force numbered no more than 200 to 300 men. He said then that the operation was not an 'invasion' but was designed to get supplies to the Cuban underground, which had recently been augmented by six small landing[s] of guerillas."[46] Schlesinger knew this was a lie. The invasion force stood at roughly 1,400 men, and by April 20 its defeat was clear. The next day, President Kennedy took responsibility for the failed operation.

In the wake of the debacle, questions arose within the government about how such a catastrophe could have occurred. Questions also arose among the public, many of them focused on the role of intellectuals and Schlesinger in particular. For Schlesinger, the criticism fell into two categories: legitimate and illegitimate. Legitimate, responsible criticism took place within the administration, where the president "set quietly to work to make sure that nothing like the Bay of Pigs could happen to him again." According to Schlesinger, "The first lesson was never to rely on experts. [Kennedy] now knew that he would have to broaden his range of advice, make greater use of generalists in whom he had personal confidence."[47]

Schlesinger was such a generalist, and he regretted not opposing the operation more strongly. "I can only explain my failure to do more than raise a few timid questions by reporting that one's impulse to blow the whistle on this nonsense was simply undone by the circumstances of the discussion," he wrote in his carefully sculpted account of events, published four years later. "It is one thing for a Special Assistant to talk frankly in private to a President at his request and another for a college professor, fresh to the government, to interpose his unassisted judgment in open meeting against that of such august figures as the Secretaries of State and Defense and the Joint Chiefs of Staff."[48] These reflections ironically suggest a certain contempt for academic intellectuals in policymaking. Was Schlesinger self-conscious about his background, and did this self-consciousness halt him from speaking out?

Schlesinger indicated that the invasion's proponents "had a rhetorical advantage. They could strike virile poses and talk of tangible things—fire power, air strikes, landing craft and so on." Opponents "had to invoke intangibles," such as "the moral position of the United States, the reputation of the President, the response of the United Nations, 'world public opinion' and other such odious concepts." Indeed, "the desire to prove to the CIA and the Joint Chiefs that they were not soft-headed idealists but were really tough guys, too, influenced State's representatives at the cabinet table."[49] Though he believed intellectuals' presence in the halls of power would ultimately encourage "debate, . . . a heightened interest in ideas, [and] a growing commitment to analysis and thinking ahead,"

Schlesinger recognized that "some intellectuals, anxious to blend with their new environment, prove themselves . . . more belligerent than the soldiers."[50] Here was the posture of toughness and its attendant vulgar pragmatism fostering a disposition toward war.

Schlesinger depicted himself as cowed by this tough posture and overpowered by the momentum toward invasion. He not only felt inhibited by the seemingly abstract nature of his objections to the operation but also unable to question military expertise. Schlesinger later wrote that he assumed the military brass knew things he did not, and he mistakenly deferred to them as a result. He did not consider his own culpability in creating such dynamics. In the preceding two decades, Schlesinger had expended a great deal of ink castigating soft-minded idealism, the failure to take an uncompromisingly militant attitude toward dictators and tyrants, and the moralistic preference for intangible rather than tangible considerations. He had therefore stood in the same relation to those who questioned anti-communism or sought a reduction of tensions with the Soviet Union as the Joint Chiefs stood to him in those fateful meetings leading up to the Bay of Pigs. There, Schlesinger was rendered silent by his own brand of posturing.

And yet, when Schlesinger turned from culpable parties in the administration to critics outside it, he relied on the very attributes of the former to silence the latter. For he found those outsider critics illegitimate. They were not vested with the responsibility for policy; they were not apprised of inside information. Schlesinger characterized them as "some on the left"— "impassioned liberals" who had "convinced themselves that the cult of toughness, the determination to win at any cost or something else they supposed to characterize Kennedy, would now lead him to throw the book at Castro." H. Stuart Hughes had "led seventy academicians"—including Chomsky—"in an open letter to Kennedy," which, in Schlesinger's view, "imprudently" suggested "that the United States had driven Castro into the arms of the Soviet Union." Schlesinger reported on C. Wright Mills's message to a Fair Play for Cuba rally, which read: "'Kennedy and company have returned us to barbarism. Schlesinger and company have disgraced us intellectually and morally.'" After surveying these wild critics on the left, Schlesinger claimed that "most Americans of course rallied to their President in the moment of national crisis."[51]

It may have been easy to dismiss Mills—the motorcycle-riding, power-elite-exposing Texan—as a radical, but much of the criticism of the Bay of

THE MORALIST AND THE MANDARIN

Pigs had come from Harvard, Schlesinger's erstwhile home, which could not so easily be painted with the brush of radicalism.[52] Instead, Schlesinger told his Harvard critics that their stance was uninformed. "My dear colleagues . . . ," he began a draft letter to signers of the Cuba statement, "I feel that your argument exhibits undue ignorance about the recent history and the present circumstances of the Cuban Revolution." Schlesinger professed incredulity: "Do you not know that over two-thirds of the faculty of the University of Habana is today in exile?" Schlesinger did have allies at Harvard. The economist Seymour E. Harris assured him and McGeorge Bundy that their "status" on campus was "undiminished." "For every Harvard professor who signed" the open letter, Harris "would guess 10 refused." Harvard's dissidents were, in short, outsiders at the institution from which so many administration insiders had emerged.[53]

Others were not so sure. Hughes observed a "vehement reaction to the landings among intellectuals in the United States." Not since McCarthyism had there been "such wide-spread mobilization of writers and professors against the policy of our government. It has broken up old friendships, it has divided 'liberals' from 'radicals' the way no previous issue has done. Feeling has run particularly high here in Cambridge."[54] It ran high in newspaper columns as well, where writers targeted Kennedy's intellectual advisers for special blame and, occasionally, special dispensation.

In "How Cambridge Flunked the First Test," James Reston wrote that "the saddest men in Washington these days are the intellectuals on the White House staff who helped deal with the Cuban issue," including Schlesinger. According to Reston, these men "have left the impression that the Cuban decision was reached . . . without that larger perspective of history which places specific decisions in proper relation to the commitments and objectives of the nation." Thus, Reston concluded, "part of the policy miscalculation was due to a lack of precisely those qualities which the intellectuals were expected to bring to bear." As a result, "the intellectuals who arrived here as critics are now the objects of criticism themselves."[55]

Writing in the *New York Times*, Ronald Hilton, director of the Institute of Hispanic American and Luso-Brazilian Studies, questioned the expertise of Kennedy's advisers: "He may be a perfectly honorable professor of United States history or of law, but this does not make him competent in the highly technical field of inter-American affairs." On the copy of this letter to the editor in Schlesinger's files, someone wrote: "Arthur, resign!"[56]

Max Lerner, who had written hopefully about "a new diplomacy of the intellectuals," now asked, only a few weeks later, whether the Bay of Pigs revealed a "new Treason of the Intellectuals." Schlesinger had proclaimed, Lerner noted, that Kennedy "would force a break from the old, tired, ineffectual policies." Instead, they continued.[57]

Amid these criticisms, Peter Lisagor defended Schlesinger in the *New York Post.* "In the Cuban misadventure that stirred up a latent anti-intellectualism in the country, the Ivy League advisers to the President were perhaps the least implicated group." Those most culpable were "the same military and intelligence professionals who handled it in the Eisenhower Administration, which was not noted for its affinity with the academic community." In fact, "President Kennedy's respect for the scholars around him has, if anything, been increased." Instead, "the chief criticism of the professors . . . has come from their former colleagues on the campus, motivated either by frustration or by envy or by an inbred passion for dissent." Schlesinger, for instance, "was burned in effigy at Cambridge in protest over the Cuban episode—a doubly ironic twist inasmuch as Schlesinger opposed the invasion attempt and won the President's admiration for saying so in advance and then lining up like a good soldier to take his lumps with the rest." Lisagor defended such cerebral soldiers, claiming that "since the Roosevelt era, the so-called braintruster has been in bad odor, often pictured as an impractical visionary, a pipe-smoking exile from the ivy towers, a bumbler and a fool. It was patent nonsense then; it still is, only more so." After all, "the men who built the atomic bomb were college professors."[58] Lisagor's approach resembled Schlesinger's dismissal of critics to the left as wild men and those to the right as anti-intellectuals. What remained, then, were the hardheaded intellectuals in the center who strove to enlarge American power in a complex and dangerous world.

Schlesinger pursued this theme in 1963 with "The Administration and the Left." He identified "two strains . . . in American progressivism." One was "pragmatic," which "accepts, without approving, the given structure of society and strives to change it by action from within." The other was "utopian," which "rejects the given structure of society, root and branch, and strives to change it by exhortation and example from without." Both strains were interested in a better future, "but the actuality of power splits them. The pragmatists accept the temptations of responsibility—and thereby invite the risk of corruption. The utopians refuse the temptations of complicity—and thereby invite the risks of irrelevance." By "offering intellectuals an access to decision," Kennedy offered relevance.[59]

In the fifties, "the traditional division between the pragmatists and the utopians" had run "between those intellectuals, like Galbraith and Rostow, who worked with Stevenson and Kennedy and the Democratic Advisory Council and those, like David Riesman and Paul Goodman, who explicitly renounced pragmatism." Schlesinger placed Hughes in the latter camp: "The mission of the American intellectual, as Professor Hughes sees it, is to do what the Asians and Africans have thus far failed to do and define neutralism 'as a faith and a way of life.'" Schlesinger declared this view "fatuous."[60] His own preference was clear and consistent: thought directed toward action, a commitment to toughness in foreign policy, and a belief that the intellectual's place was in the melee of politics and events. "Those who acquiesce in the idea," he later wrote, "more characteristically propagated by anti-intellectuals, that intelligence has no role in public affairs, voluntarily resign power to . . . diplomats and soldiers—as if the ordinary course of things had not given diplomats and soldiers enough power already."[61]

Schlesinger's outlook remained constant, but a great deal around him had changed. Critics like Hughes were raising serious questions about the Cold War amid growing stockpiles of nuclear weapons. They added questions about the moral orientation (or lack thereof) of intellectuals in government to concerns about their effectiveness at and expertise in crafting policy. The Bay of Pigs fueled these questions, and Schlesinger pondered them too. "I do not know anybody, except [Senator J. William] Fulbright, who was bothered about the morality of the operation," he told JFK. "In retrospect, we would have been better off if more people had worried about" it; that "may be one of the lessons of Cuba."[62] As Cuban concerns gave way to matters in Southeast Asia, however, it was unclear how such lessons were being applied. Schlesinger himself largely continued to exclude moral considerations from his appraisal of policy.

Schlesinger predicted that "pragmatists and utopians will continue in their accustomed state of symbiosis tempered by mutual disdain." As "the utopians do their job of maintaining ideals in their purity, the pragmatists will do their job of trying to fulfill ideals in the obstinacies and complexities of democratic society."[63] Schlesinger aimed these words at Hughes in the fallout over Cuba, but they also describe how Schlesinger would move forward into debate about Vietnam. His adversary in that debate would be

Noam Chomsky, whom Schlesinger would characterize after 1967 in the same dichotomous terms he used in 1963: pragmatists and utopians.

* * *

Like Schlesinger, Avram Noam Chomsky followed in the academic footsteps of his father, who wrote books on Hebrew grammar. Young Chomsky was raised in Philadelphia but often took the train to New York to visit relatives. There he had his "first experience with radical intellectuals—though they wouldn't be called 'intellectuals' as the term is standardly used, applying to people with status and privilege who are in a position to reach the public with thoughts about human affairs and concerns." Rather, they were working class and largely unschooled. His uncle ran a newsstand, which Chomsky found to be "one of the most lively intellectual circles I have ever been part of." Chomsky encountered other "radical intellectuals" at "small bookstores . . . run by refugees from the Spanish revolution of 1936" and at "the office of the Anarchist *Freie Arbeiter Stimme* in Union Square." These people "didn't fit the standard formula for intellectuals," yet they thought "seriously about life and society, their problems and possible solutions, against a background of knowledge and understanding," making them "indeed intellectuals, impressive ones."[64]

Though lacking formal education, Chomsky's uncle explained the work of Sigmund Freud to him. "My uncle was not so unusual" among working people in the 1930s and early 1940s, Chomsky said. "At that time there were leftist intellectuals, mostly Communist Party, who were writing for the mass of the population," and "people like A. J. Muste, the great anarchist thinker, were involved in workers' education," which unions sponsored. For Chomsky, his uncle's newsstand was only one outpost in a wider intellectual world of city streets, factory floors, and family dinner tables.[65]

Chomsky, like Schlesinger, began college at age sixteen. At the University of Pennsylvania, he joined a circle around Professor Zellig Harris, who created the first Department of Linguistics in the United States. Chomsky's 1949 honors thesis is considered "the first example of modern generative grammar"—his signal contribution to linguistics.[66] In 1951 Chomsky followed Schlesinger into Harvard's Society of Fellows. There Chomsky had his "first extensive experience with the elite intellectual world." He recalled being "regaled by a very distinguished philosopher with an account of the Depression—which, he assured me, had not taken place. . . . A few businessmen might have suffered, but there was nothing beyond that." Most of the faculty "were Stevenson liberals."[67]

Chomsky found that intellectualism as practiced at Harvard was deeply embedded in social class, with its norms of dress, speech, and manner. He "discovered that a large part of the education was simply refinement, social graces, what kinds of clothes to wear, how to have polite conversation that isn't too serious, all the other things that an intellectual is supposed to do." He came to believe that "a large part of what is called education" involves "teaching conformity to certain norms that keeps you from interfering with those in power." Chomsky would ultimately describe this kind of education as "indoctrination."[68]

In Chomsky's Harvard years, the McCarthyite surge in American political culture was reaching its crest. While Hofstadter was documenting evidence of anti-intellectualism in American life, the working-class scene that sustained intellectualism at Chomsky's uncle's newsstand had changed. "Hofstadter wasn't wrong," Chomsky said. "There's an anti-intellectual stream that runs through American culture that shows up all the time." But whereas Hofstadter saw anti-intellectualism as the manifestation of a perennial conflict between intellectuals and the masses, Chomsky saw anti-intellectualism as a result of the rug being pulled out from beneath the thriving intellectual culture he knew. "When you break up unions, you take away the left intellectuals, ostracize them and so on, you break up the working-class culture and institutional programs . . . you're going to get Masscult."[69] If, as Hofstadter argued, anti-intellectualism is the default position of the general public, then intellectualism has to be imposed upon them through education from the top down. But if intellectualism is integral to significant segments of the general public, then *anti*-intellectualism is imposed upon them from the top down, through assaults on their institutions. Chomsky was influenced in this view by the work of Friedrich Wilhelm von Humboldt (1767–1835), who created Prussia's system of public education. "Let no one believe . . . that the many are so exhausted by activities dictated by the need for earning a living," Humboldt wrote, "that freedom of thought is useless to them, or even disturbing." Nor can people "best be activated by the diffusion of principles handed down from on high, while their freedom to think and to investigate is restricted."[70] State power could either develop humans' innate intellectual and creative capacities through education or repress them.[71] Where Hofstadter saw the life of the

109

mind threatened by the crowd, Chomsky found living minds among the crowd—or at least the potential for them.

These were not the prevailing ideas, Chomsky believed, in the Society of Fellows, which he left for a spot at MIT's Research Laboratory of Electronics (RLE). Its director was Jerome Wiesner, who would become JFK's science adviser, having met the president-elect at Schlesinger's home in January 1961.[72] At RLE Chomsky worked on *Aspects of the Theory of Syntax* (1965) and earned a National Science Foundation Fellowship leading to the Institute for Advanced Study in Princeton. Schlesinger would follow Chomsky there in 1966.

Chomsky's dispute with Schlesinger had roots in Chomsky's running battle, begun in the late 1950s, with B. F. Skinner's behaviorism.[73] Chomsky argued, contra behaviorist theory, that "humans are not merely dull mechanisms formed by a history of reinforcement." He found behaviorism scientifically empty but ideologically significant, allowing techniques of social control to "look benign and scientific."[74] Critiquing Skinner's ideas on their intellectual merits, Chomsky also challenged the instrumental uses to which those ideas were put, finding that intellectually flawed concepts often served morally objectionable agendas. That link explains why Chomsky would later say: "My contempt for the intellectual world reaches such heights that I have no interest in pursuing them in their gutters, unless there are serious human interests involved, as [there often are] in the political realm."[75] Chomsky published his 1959 critique of Skinner in the journal *Language*, but he published his 1971 "Case against B. F. Skinner" in the much more widely read *New York Review of Books*. Between these articles, Chomsky's politics—and his increasing efforts to engage a wider public—found their sharpest expression in the realm of American foreign policy, particularly the intensifying involvement in Vietnam.

After Vietnam-wide elections to be held in 1956 were scuttled by South Vietnamese leader Ngo Dinh Diem, Communist insurgents in the south opposed to his regime sparked a crackdown that roiled the country. In 1960 the National Liberation Front formed to organize guerrilla operations against the Saigon government. Though Kennedy refused to send combat troops to bolster South Vietnamese forces, he dramatically increased the number of American military advisers in the country from 2,000 when he took office to 16,000 at the close of 1963.

In 1964 the Gulf of Tonkin Resolution gave President Johnson a broad mandate to expand American military action in Vietnam. Despite statements in the 1964 presidential campaign suggesting that he would not send more troops to Vietnam, Johnson did just that. In February 1965, the US Air Force began an escalating bombardment of North Vietnam, and in March, American combat troops arrived in South Vietnam. By 1966 there were 385,000 US troops "in country."

At home, opposition to the war took shape. Draft resistance began in 1964, when a dozen young men publicly burned their draft cards in New York. "Teach-ins," started at the University of Michigan in 1965, spread to other campuses. "I decided that it was just too intolerably self-indulgent merely to take a passive role in the struggles that were then going on," Chomsky said. "And I knew that signing petitions, sending money, and showing up now and then at a meeting was not enough. I thought it was critically necessary to take a more active role. . . . And I knew that I would be following a course that would confront privilege and authority." Ultimately, it was a course that would lead him to confront Schlesinger.[76]

* * *

Chomsky and Schlesinger intensified their public engagement with Vietnam between 1967 and 1969. Each published a book on the war: Schlesinger's *The Bitter Heritage: Vietnam and American Democracy, 1941–1966* (1967) and Chomsky's *American Power and the New Mandarins* (1969). Chomsky's book was dedicated "To the brave young men who refuse to serve in a criminal war," while Schlesinger's was "For those fighting in Vietnam."[77] Chomsky condemned the war in moral terms and stood with those who defied it. Schlesinger was less willing to evaluate the justice of American involvement. Instead, he questioned the wisdom of the war from a strategic standpoint even as he struggled with the moral dimensions of its conduct.

Schlesinger's doubts flowed from the military and political mess that Vietnam had become, rather than from concerns about America's initial involvement. "Why we are in Vietnam is today a question of mainly historical interest," he wrote. "We *are* there, for better or for worse, and we must deal with the situation that exists." Escalation in Vietnam was "a triumph of the politics of inadvertence. We have achieved our present entanglement, not after due and deliberate consideration, but through a series of small decisions." Vietnam was "a tragedy without villains."[78]

Schlesinger, who located himself among "moderate critics of the administration's Vietnam policy," did "not question its proclaimed purposes"—

"self-determination for South Vietnam" and checking "Communist aggression"—but did "question, with the greatest urgency, the theory that the way to achieve these objectives is to intensify the war." In a 1966 article for *Look* magazine, Schlesinger asserted that "the more we Americanize the war . . . the more we make the war unwinnable."[79] These were recommendations for fixing a war that had gone wrong, not stopping a war that was wrong.

Schlesinger did "not see that our original involvement in Vietnam was per se immoral"; it was, rather, the "misapplication of valid principles." The tagline to his 1971 *Harper's* article, "The Necessary Amorality of Foreign Affairs," framed those principles: "Saints can be pure, but statesmen, alas, must be responsible." Only "extreme cases" called upon moral reasoning; otherwise, "attempts to determine the national interest" were "the safest" guide for policymakers. This view reaffirmed his statement at the Air War College in 1953 that foreign policy aims "not . . . to express subjective feelings, but to affect objective facts in ways which will benefit the nation." It was "not an instrument of our moral idealism or indignation, but a means of affecting power in the world so as to give one's own nation a better chance of self-fulfillment."[80]

But was Vietnam one of those rare cases when moral judgment applied? Schlesinger asked whether "even those quite satisfied to oppose the war as contrary to our national interest [were] still obliged to face the question of whether it may not be an immoral as well as a stupid war? I think they are, if we are ever to extract the full and awful lesson from this catastrophe." The moral threshold was, for Schlesinger, tied to the war's conduct rather than its causes. Vietnam "became . . . what can properly be called an immoral war when the means employed and destruction wrought grew out of any conceivable proportion to the interests involved."[81]

Chomsky also objected to these excesses but focused his criticism on how the war began. "American intervention in a civil war in Vietnam was converted into a colonial war of the classic type," he wrote, one where a powerful nation sought to control the internal affairs of a less powerful one. American troops had entered Vietnam not to aid an ally but "to enforce our will." Chomsky characterized military escalation not as a product of "the politics of inadvertence," but as "the decision of a liberal American administration" supported by "leading political figures, intellectuals, and academic experts, many of whom now oppose the war because they do not believe that American repression can succeed in Vietnam and therefore urge, on pragmatic grounds, that we 'take our stand' where the prospects are more hopeful"—as they had been, he suggested, in Thailand, Guatemala, and Greece. Chomsky rejected these experts' and intellectuals' premises: "By entering into the arena of argument and counterargument, of technical feasibility and tactics, of footnotes and citations, by accepting the presumption of legitimacy of debate on certain issues, one has already lost one's humanity." There was no question of practical national interest: "The war is simply an obscenity, a depraved act by weak and miserable men, including all of us, who have allowed it to go on and on with endless fury and destruction—all of us who would have remained silent had stability and order been secured."[82]

Chomsky saw Schlesinger as one who would have remained silent—or been satisfied—if resistance to American forces had collapsed. In *Bitter Heritage*, Schlesinger relayed columnist Joseph Alsop's impression that the Communists would soon buckle under American military pressure. "We all pray," Schlesinger wrote, "that Mr. Alsop will be right." If force prevailed, then "in another year or two we may all be saluting the wisdom and statesmanship of the American government"—an outcome Schlesinger thought highly unlikely. Citing these comments, Chomsky labeled Schlesinger a "spokesman" of the "liberal ideologists" who "continue to urge that we organize and control as extensive a dominion as is feasible." The emphasis that intellectuals like Schlesinger placed on whether the war was working ignored the prior question of whether it was just.[83]

Chomsky argued that such emphasis promoted unjust wars, because it placed the national interest—tantamount in his eyes to maximal domination—above moral reasoning. "American politics is a politics of accommodation that successfully excludes moral considerations," he wrote; "only pragmatic considerations of cost and utility guide our actions."[84] To place the national interest at the center of the table was to push moral matters off of it.

Chomsky and Schlesinger both sought an end to military escalation, but for completely different reasons. What Chomsky derided as "the 'responsible' attitude" would have urged continuation or even intensification of the war had the costs been acceptable. Instead, he called for "a change of policy caused by recognition that what we have done in Vietnam is wrong, a criminal act."[85] Rather than judge the costs and benefits of intervention, Chomsky held "that 'we have no authority and no competence to make such judgments about Vietnam or any other country and to use our mil-

itary power to act on these judgments.'"[86] He challenged his opponents'
Skinnerian focus not "on 'intentions and objectives' but rather on 'behavior and results.'" To Chomsky, intentions and objectives were exactly why
America's war in Vietnam was "criminal," lacking any "legitimate interest
or principle" behind it.[87]

Not only had policymakers acted without "legitimate" principle, but
the climate of thought in America tended to condone such action. "Much
more dangerous than the falsification and cynicism of the American government," Chomsky wrote, was "the tolerance by even enlightened American opinion of the notion that we have a perfect right to intervene in the
internal affairs of Vietnam."[88] The "hardheaded and pragmatic liberals"—
like Schlesinger—"were never divided on the issue of our right to violate
international frontiers." Their rationale for intervention amounted to "the
classical rhetoric of long-decayed imperialism."[89]

Imperial policies abroad provoked little resistance at home due, in
part, to intellectuals who normalized such policy. "Arthur Schlesinger has
recently characterized our Vietnamese policies of 1954 as 'part of our general program of international goodwill,'" Chomsky wrote. That year saw
both the creation of the Southeast Asia Treaty Organization, which the
United States later invoked to justify its intervention in Vietnam, and
the Geneva Accords, which partitioned Vietnam and shifted American
support in the region from the French colonial regime—whose unsuccessful military campaign it had been funding—to what ultimately became,
under the anti-communist leadership of Diem, the state of South Vietnam.
"Unless intended as irony, this remark shows either a colossal cynicism"
or a gross misreading "of contemporary history." Chomsky found it "startling to see how easily the rhetoric of imperialism comes to American lips,
sometimes muted, sometimes overt." For Chomsky there was no possibility of debating intellectuals like Schlesinger, for their terms were incom-
mensurable with his. "It is because argument fails us when we come to deal
with pure questions of value, as distinct from questions of fact," A. J. Ayer
observed, "that we finally resort to mere abuse."[90] And, indeed, that is what
the two men did.

In April 1970, Reuben Eisenstein of Lincolnwood, Illinois, responded
to a Chomsky-Schlesinger exchange that had appeared in *Commentary*
over the preceding five months. "Apart from the sad but entertaining spectacle of two scholars calling each other names in public," Eisenstein wrote,
"I have learned two things. Dr. Schlesinger thinks Dr. Chomsky is either

a faker or is putting us on, while Chomsky regards Schlesinger as either a liar or insane." The substance of their engagement was out of all proportion to its tone. In a review of *New Mandarins*, Schlesinger had pointed to a passage in which Chomsky attributed a quote to Truman that was "not from Truman at all but from a book by J. P. Warburg in which Warburg was giving his own theory as to what was in Truman's mind."[91] The thrust of Warburg's comment was that American freedom depended upon capitalism spreading around the globe. Schlesinger attacked Chomsky for his error, launching "interminable controversies" between the two across several periodicals.[92]

There was a "self-righteousness in which people become so suffused with the virtue of their cause that they cease to care about intellectual honesty," Schlesinger wrote. "Dr. Chomsky, I fear, has succumbed to this malady of moralism. . . . He begins as a preacher to the world and ends as an intellectual crook." Chomsky was a "phoney" who in moving beyond linguistics was out of his league. Schlesinger suspected that, having "read superficially in American history," Chomsky had "no idea what he is talking about."[93]

Chomsky characterized Schlesinger's attack as part of his "efforts to come to grips with material which, not surprisingly, he finds outrageous." That material was Chomsky's argument in *New Mandarins* that intervention in Vietnam was driven by an ideology that justified imperial power at the expense of moral norms. Claiming that Schlesinger's *Bitter Heritage* eschewed "any effort at historical or political analysis that goes beyond his 'politics of inadvertence,'" Chomsky accused him of "regression to the technique and style of a Stalinist hack attempting to shore up a discredited ideology." *Bitter Heritage* was "a shade to the hawkish side of the Pentagon."[94]

Was it? Perhaps Chomsky had in mind Schlesinger's conclusion that "strategy directed to the physical destruction of North Vietnam would seem on balance less likely to lead to negotiation than a strategy of determined long-run defense." For Chomsky, destroying North Vietnam was not a strategy but rather an outrage. Yet Schlesinger also wrote passages that Chomsky might have otherwise endorsed. "There is a deeper question," Schlesinger wrote,

> a question which already haunts the American conscience. Are we really carrying out this policy, as we constantly proclaim, to save the

people we are methodically destroying, or are we doing it for less exalted purposes of our own? Are we treating the Vietnamese as ends in themselves, or as a means to our own objectives?[95]

For Chomsky, whose moral logic has been described as "that of a Kantian categorical imperative," Schlesinger's invocation of means versus ends would seem a welcome one. But Chomsky did not approach Schlesinger's writings with an eye toward their Kantian qualities. He instead viewed Schlesinger as defending "the most extreme pro-war position that was at all tolerable among American liberals."[96] For Chomsky, a Schlesinger book was "a specimen" of "American ideology," part of "a certain mainstream of political thought (which is, illegitimately, designated 'responsible thought') that stays within the rather narrow bounds of the prevailing ideology and does not challenge the conceptions, or the rationalizations, of those who have direct influence over decision making."[97] Schlesinger and his books were prime examples of the intellectual climate that, for Chomsky, sustained the war in Vietnam.

Schlesinger became for Chomsky a "new mandarin," an intellectual who abetted imperial wars. "In no small measure," Chomsky wrote, "the Vietnam war was designed and executed by these new mandarins." He quoted Zbigniew Brzezinski to describe these intellectuals as "experts and specialists," or "generalists-integrators, who become in effect house-ideologues for those in power, providing overall intellectual integration for disparate actions."[98] New mandarins had replaced "free-floating intellectuals"—Karl Mannheim's conception of an intelligentsia independent of any social stratum or power structure. They occupied prestigious, often lucrative positions in government, academia, and foundations—and thus, Chomsky claimed, "are strongly tempted . . . to take what is now called a 'pragmatic attitude' . . . that is, an attitude that one must 'accept,' not critically analyze or struggle to change, the existing distribution of power."[99]

New mandarins—not political or military leaders—were the prime target of Chomsky's criticism.[100] His article titles from the period bear out this aim: "Objectivity and Liberal Scholarship," "Some Thoughts on Intellectuals and the Schools," "The Responsibility of Intellectuals," "Scholarship and Ideology: American Historians as 'Experts in Legitimation,'" "Philosophers and Public Policy," and "The Menace of Liberal Scholarship." Chomsky criticized intellectuals because he set high standards for them: those operating within the bounds of "responsible thought" were, in fact, outside the bounds of what Chomsky considered the actual, crucial responsibility of intellectuals. "Intellectuals are in a position," he wrote, "to expose the lies of governments, to analyze actions according to their causes and motives and often hidden intentions." In democracies, citizens are responsible for investigating these same matters and for holding their governments accountable. Yet ordinary citizens are usually not at leisure to undertake research. "For a privileged minority, Western democracy provides the leisure, the facilities, and the training to seek the truth lying hidden behind the veil of distortion and misrepresentation, ideology, and class interest through which the events of current history are presented to us. The responsibilities of intellectuals" were therefore "much deeper than" those of ordinary people.[101] Their unique opportunity to find and speak truth is what made it so damning, in Chomsky's eyes, for new mandarins to serve power.

Schlesinger's service in the Kennedy White House made him the prototypical new mandarin. "When Arthur Schlesinger was asked by the *New York Times*, in November 1965, to explain the contradiction between his published account of the Bay of Pigs incident and the story he had given to the press at the time of the attack," Chomsky wrote, "he simply remarked that he had lied" and applauded "the *Times* for also having suppressed information on the planned invasion, in 'the national interest.'"[102] Instead of speaking truth, an exemplary new mandarin concealed it, on behalf of imperial policy.

Schlesinger did not see it that way. While he apologized for conveying the cover story[103] and wondered whether "he should have resigned from the Government 'rather than mislead' the *New York Times*," he later wrote that, having "confidence in President Kennedy and his essential purposes, I did not choose to resign. In retrospect I believe that confidence—and that choice—to have been fully justified."[104] Schlesinger noted that the *Times* itself had "'suppressed a story . . . from Miami, giving a fairly accurate account of the invasion plans.'" He defended these actions by arguing that "'the *Times* and I were actuated by the same motives: that is, a sense, mistaken or not, that this was in the national interest.'"[105]

Yorick Wilks's 1969 review of *New Mandarins* sparked a further exchange between Chomsky and Schlesinger. Wilks described Chomsky as measuring "the effect of the war at home, and in particular its effect on American intellectuals." *Mandarins* was "particularly good when savaging the Administration spokesmen, not only for their moral blindness, but for their lies, their cheap arguments, their behavioural science clap-trap, and the obvious contempt they have for their audience." Schlesinger, vigorous in defense, pointed out that "neither of these righteous apostles of the truth, Dr. Chomsky or Mr. Wilks, cares to mention the fact that I strongly opposed the Bay of Pigs expedition and argued in vain against it," animated by "a deep conviction that such clandestine undertakings were incompatible with a democratic society." Chomsky countered that in Schlesinger's *A Thousand Days*, "there is nothing . . . about his deep conviction that such clandestine undertakings were incompatible with a democratic society. Rather, he felt that we probably just couldn't get away with it."[106] In a memorandum to JFK after the Bay of Pigs, Schlesinger had "suggest[ed] that any secret operation whose success is dependent on the suppression of news, on the lying to Congressmen and journalists and on the deception of the electorate should be undertaken only when the crisis is so considerable that the gains really seem to outweigh the disadvantages." Size mattered: "Small operations can be done with a minimum of accompanying corruption. The greater the visibility of the operation, the more its success depends on thwarting the impulses and denying the values of an open society, the riskier it becomes, and the more urgent it is that an overwhelming case be made for its necessity."[107]

Schlesinger's view was not that clandestine operations are inherently incompatible with democracy but that imperfectly clandestine operations—those likely to generate questions from reporters and legislators—are problematic. The vital distinction is not between secret and open actions, with the former always being corrupt and undemocratic; it is between secret actions likely to require lies and those less likely to do so because they are more fully in the shadows. Indeed, Schlesinger's role in suppressing the *New Republic* story and his misleading of the *New York Times* suggest a bounded regard for democratic oversight. While Schlesinger was prepared to voice dissent inside the White House, he was not prepared to provide the American public with information it would need to voice dissent outside it. When the requirements of democratic oversight conflicted with the national interest as he saw it, Schlesinger prioritized the latter.

Schlesinger sought to make Chomsky's misattributed Truman quote the focus of their dispute. "When Dr. Chomsky tells us in his sententious way that 'it is the responsibility of intellectuals to speak the truth' one can only conclude that he must be kidding," he wrote. Schlesinger suggested that his dishonesty had been in service to President Kennedy and, therefore, the nation. Chomsky, by contrast, had been dishonest in the service of no cause higher than his desire to score ideological points. An incorrect footnote for a speech and a lie to the press about an invasion are not commensurable, however; neither are their implications for the relationship of intellectuals to truth. Benda's *La Trahison des clercs* (1927), a lodestone for debate about the role of intellectuals in this period, made plain that whatever other commitments intellectuals might have, their commitment to the truth could not be subordinated.[108]

Chomsky's ultimate concern was not Schlesinger's truthfulness, however, but the climate of opinion that he and intellectuals like him created around American foreign policy. "Schlesinger's personal difficulties with the world of fact are of little interest," Chomsky wrote, but his "political position" was "significant." That position was "a perverse 'pragmatism': in practice, the doctrine that if the United States can get away with something—say, an invasion of Cuba, or the transformation of Vietnam into 'a land of ruin and wreck,' in Schlesinger's apt phrase—then it is quite all right." Should such ventures fail, "the apologist can summon up Schlesinger's 'politics of inadvertence.'" The location of this "ideology within the mainstream of American opinion" underwrote the ongoing use of American military force.[109] Chomsky was not a Benda accusing Schlesinger of intellectual apostasy. He was intent, rather, on exposing the worldview that Schlesinger represented, for the deeper problem with new mandarins lying on behalf of those in power was that such lies flowed from a larger ideology that legitimated egregious uses of that power.

In 1969 the arch new mandarin fired back. He described Chomsky as someone who

> sees American intellectuals as divided into two main groups: the Mandarins (bad) and the Resistance (good). The Mandarins are . . . elitist, reformist, pragmatic, managerial, manipulative, technocratic, counterrevolutionary, opposed to popular movements and mass participation in decision making, addicted to the behavioral sciences, contemptuous of principles, moral issues and human rights.

Such views were a caricature that "purports to be political analysis. But Dr. Chomsky, it soon becomes evident, does not understand the rudiments of political analysis."[110] Where Chomsky indicted Schlesinger for abrogating intellectual honesty for imperial ideology, Schlesinger accused Chomsky of ditching analysis for dogmatism.

Chomsky stood, in Schlesinger's mind, for the fanatical moralist. "Dr. Chomsky's idea of the responsibility of intellectuals," Schlesinger wrote, "is to foreswear reasoned analysis, indulge in moralistic declamation, fabricate evidence when necessary and shout always at the top of one's voice."[111] As one of "Seven Heroes of the New Left," Chomsky was, moreover, a figure-head for the radical movement.[112] The arch moralist, he "settled every issue with ecclesiastical certitude. His sermons covered interminable pages in the *New York Review of Books.* He was cited with reverence by the young. It was rah, rah, rah for Prof. Dr. Chomsky."[113] Just as Chomsky identified the threat posed by Schlesinger and the new mandarins as paramount, Schlesinger regarded the danger of Chomsky and the moralists as extreme.

Schlesinger's brand of liberalism was suspicious of fundamental doc-trines and their moralizing exponents. "As one supposed Reinhold Niebuhr had demonstrated long since," he wrote, "most secular questions intermin-gle good and evil in problematic proportions and are more usefully handled in other than moralistic categories."[114] The world's complexity and the elusive character of ultimate truth resisted moral judgments, which relied upon blunt terms like good and evil. Schlesinger understood Vietnam this way, calling it "one of the most complex and difficult issues our country has faced for a long time." Chomsky, by contrast, thought it "part of the self-defense of intellectuals to say . . . the world is so complex that we're the only ones who we can understand it." In practice, "nobody believes" the world so inscrutable as to render moral judgment impossible. "I don't think any of the New Frontiersmen hesitated to criticize communism" by saying: "I'm sorry, I can't criticize Stalin, the world's too complicated. Besides, he knew things I didn't know."[115] In Chomsky's view, neither the purported complexity of the world nor a lack of expertise should prevent people from forming moral judgments about political decisions.[116]

For Schlesinger, moral principles were not only an inappropriate frame-work for political decisions, they were downright dangerous: "Those who rush around ladling out moral judgments quickly arrogate to themselves an alarming and repellent sense of their own moral infallibility."[117] Such certitude fuels fanaticism, and thus "the compulsion to see foreign pol-icy in moral terms may have, with the noblest of intentions, the most ghastly of consequences." In fact, it was moralists who fueled the violence in Vietnam: "The moralistic cant of Presidents Johnson and Nixon helped delude a lot of pilots into supposing they were doing God's work." Amer-icans might have recoiled from destruction wrought in the name of facile morals, looking instead to the nation's interests. "Unfortunately, instead of strengthening the national-interest wing of the opposition to the war," Schlesinger observed, "Vietnam seems to have incited an equally moralistic outburst on the part of the war's most clamorous critics. Too many people on both sides of the Indochina debate feel they know exactly what the Lord would do."[118] Moralists threatened the vital center from both sides of the political spectrum.

Schlesinger compared Chomsky to the cold warriors who cast the fight against communism in Manichean terms. "Both regard foreign policy as a branch of ethics." They are "mirror images of each other. In the process of moral self-aggrandizement, each loses the humility which is the heart of human restraint." For Schlesinger, the threat posed by Chomsky loomed large because he was a moralist masquerading as an intellectual—injecting absolutism into debate that should be rooted in political realities. Such absolutism was a species of the thinking that had, in the form of crusading anti-communism, promoted the war itself. "An intelligent regard for one's own national interest . . . seems more likely than the invocation of moral absolutes to bring about greater restraint, justice, and peace among nations," Schlesinger wrote. "One must hope that the Indochina experience will inoculate the nation against the perversion of policy by moralism in the future."[119]

H. Stuart Hughes was no stranger to this debate on morality and the national interest. He told a 1966 "Speak-Out on Vietnam" that "those who defend the Administration's conduct of the war—or who demand further escalation of it—are accustomed to accuse us in the opposition of being soft-minded, of introducing moral criticisms into a world of tough power-politics where they don't apply." Hughes, like Chomsky, observed: "Of course we make moral statements. Most of us are convinced that it is impossible to conduct the foreign policy of our country . . . with total disregard for human values." Hughes concluded that "on no stretch of the imagination can the present war be called a just war. It is time to end it— and fast."[120]

The war did not end fast. It persisted until 1975, widening to include Cambodia and Laos. Publication of the Pentagon Papers in 1971 revived discussion of how American involvement in Vietnam had begun. In 1972 the Senate Committee on Foreign Relations held hearings on the origins of the war. On May 10, two witnesses testified: Arthur M. Schlesinger Jr. and Noam Chomsky. It was the only time they ever met.

Schlesinger's testimony emphasized errors in judgment, insufficiencies of information, and incorrect assumptions. "I am conscious that I myself at earlier times have shared some of the illusions that I will discuss today," he began. "I only wish that I had understood earlier what I think I understand now; and I certainly do not seek to exempt myself from a share, however trivial, of personal responsibility for going along with directions of policy whose implications did not become evident to me until the summer of 1965."[121] Illusion was a category central to Schlesinger's thought. A *Thousand Days* is shot through with the term, whether reporting on JFK urging "listeners to distinguish between hopes and illusions" or worrying that the president was himself susceptible "to the illusion . . . that he . . . could achieve his purposes without pain or trauma."[122] Foggy thinking flowed from imbibing illusions and losing track of sober realities, and this fogginess went a long way, Schlesinger claimed, toward explaining Vietnam. "Both as a historian and as occasional participant in Government, I have concluded that very much of what takes place in Government is a product of ignorance, improvisation, and mindlessness. I think that stupidity is a more helpful factor in interpreting our policy than conspiracy." ("We talked afterwards," Chomsky remembered. "[Schlesinger] said one thing he really disagreed with me about . . . is that I underestimated the role of stupidity in decision-making.")[123]

Schlesinger pitted this account against Chomsky's: in viewing American policy as calculated, "Mr. Chomsky may be too much of a rationalist." Though he had previously accused Chomsky of favoring moral declamation over rational analysis, Schlesinger likely intended no irony in now calling him "a rationalist." In order to condemn actions, moralists must believe in the rational character of those actions. Crimes are not accidents. And, indeed, Chomsky did find a kind of rationality behind what Schlesinger called illusions. "The Pentagon Papers give an extremely rational, also an extremely cynical justification, up to about 1960, for an immoral or illegal intervention [in Vietnam] that would have supported long-term American interests," Chomsky testified. He suggested that after American intelligence in the 1940s had failed to find evidence that Ho Chi Minh was a pawn of Moscow or Beijing, this claim was nevertheless "taken as doctrine, and stated, formulated." When Senator J. William Fulbright asked whether his account supported Schlesinger's claim about policymakers' stupidity, Chomsky said that it showed, rather, "a very rational approach toward developing a technique of propaganda which will enlist the American population behind the opposition to indigenous communism."[124]

Whereas Schlesinger saw the task of intellectuals as thinking without illusions, Chomsky held that intellectuals perpetuated illusions—in the service of elite interests. Foreign policy "is determined by a commitment to the national interest as that is defined by the dominant groups in the society," Chomsky testified. "Of course . . . imperial powers state that their concerns are noble, they are interested in self-determination or development or one thing or another," but these stated concerns were the actual illusions—consciously crafted for public legitimation.[125]

Schlesinger had proposed not that the national interest was noble so much as that it was concrete, even self-evident. This construction foreclosed policy debate, for who could argue against the national interest when stated as a given, seemingly making the costs and benefits of a policy clear? Yet "in the absence of any other effective agency," Chomsky objected, "it is we who determine the costs."[126] The national interest should be determined through public debate, not invoked to stop it.

Instead, intellectuals framed a narrow policy discussion that rendered alternatives invisible. Beyond those who believed the United States could win in Vietnam and those who believed the costs were too high, Chomsky testified, "there is a third position which, unfortunately, is barely represented in policy making . . . namely, that the US executive should abide by the supreme law of the land and refrain from forceful intervention in the internal affairs of others."[127] Both Chomsky and Schlesinger suggested that intellectuals' role was to frame important questions. For Schlesinger, intellectuals resisted false frames generated by moralists or ideologues; they looked beyond these "banalities of the present."[128] For Chomsky, intellectuals qua mandarins were the ones imposing false frames, not seeing beyond them.

After a time, Chomsky claimed, the frameworks that intellectuals imposed became simply the frameworks they used. The result was not stupidity, as Schlesinger held, but skewed vision—an inability to see inconvenient facts or alternative interpretations. "What struck me was the ignorance of the senators," Chomsky recalled. They were "people who were supposed to know something and knew nothing. They were asking me questions, raising points that were so simple-minded it was embarrassing." This ignorance marked "something significant about intellectuals," among whom Chomsky classed the senators. "Quite possibly they know less than other people. And the reason is because of the level of indoctrination." A constitutive feature of Chomsky's mandarins—as opposed to the "radical intellectuals" of his youth—was their exposure to indoctrination and "certainly to propaganda." Throughout a long apprenticeship and credentialing process, intellectuals in the making were exposed to more indoctrinating propaganda than any other group in society. "And furthermore, they're the purveyors of it. And it's very natural when you put forth views to end up believing them." The longer an intellectual acts as a mandarin, the more an intellectual thinks like one—though ultimately not, Chomsky would acknowledge, in Schlesinger's case. "When it got to the [2003] Iraq War," Chomsky recalled, Schlesinger

> took the same position I had taken on Vietnam. . . . When the bombing started, first day, he had an op-ed, a very powerful op-ed. . . . He said FDR talked about the "date which will live in infamy"—Pearl Harbor Day—he says now as Americans we live in infamy because we're following the policies of Imperial Japan. That's pretty strong.[129]

CRITIC, COUNSELOR, CRITIC

Three linked questions sparked debates about the role of intellectuals in American political life in the 1960s. Chomsky's dispute with Schlesinger raised the question of intellectuals' relationship to power. While Chomsky envisioned intellectuals as adversaries of regnant powers, Schlesinger believed that intellect could partner with power. The question of intellectuals' vantage point sought the grounds from which they addressed American life. Did they speak from the standpoint of universal values or from within a particular tradition of American thought? Schlesinger invoked an intellectual tradition in which JFK was descended from William James. Chomsky conjured an innate moral sense.

The third question—that of intellectuals' work—rested, in part, on the other two. Serving power is different work than opposing it, and different vantage points lead to different duties as well. Since work was seen as constitutive of the intellectual, this question was pivotal. Debates did not turn so much on what work an intellectual *should* do as on what work an individual *could* do and still be considered an intellectual. What boundaries existed in the world of work such that, when persons crossed them, they could no longer be said to be acting as—or even to *be*—intellectuals?

A look at Christopher Lasch in the late 1960s and early '70s illustrates these concerns. In his thought, writing, and more directly political activity, Lasch struggled to identify and inhabit the role of the intellectual in American politics. His struggle took the form of changing vantage points—from heights of Olympian detachment to grounding in American populism— and changing work—from social commentary to programmatic political organizing and back. As for any person, political, cultural, and social shifts make for changing terrain beneath an intellectual's feet. Moreover, the self-consciousness of intellectual life—ongoing debates about intellectuals' role and responsibilities—continually reshapes that role.

For those engaged in social criticism, there is an additional dynamic—one embedded in the practice itself. Lasch has been remembered as "the most important American social critic of the late twentieth century." Richard Fox recalled that when he first read Lasch's *The New Radicalism in America, 1889–1963* (1965) the "prose . . . felt like revelation."[1] Lasch the critic was, for many readers, also Lasch the seer. Those who felt the force of his criticism looked to him for guidance: could he translate the insights of an incisive observer into the work of social change?

After *The New Radicalism*, Lasch combined social criticism with projects highly programmatic in nature. He joined planning for a new political party that would provide an alternative to conventional partisanship and what he considered the flawed New Left. His interventions culminated in a partnership with historian Eugene Genovese that sought a blueprint for a new, more effective politics. Their manuscript, called "Beyond the New Left," was never published.

Deploying the analytical rigor that made him a trenchant critic, Lasch came to see where his designs for a new politics misfired. By the mid-1970s, he had withdrawn from overt political involvements and turned his attention to psychoanalytic theory—starting down the path that led to the most popular of his books, *The Culture of Narcissism*.

Lasch's arc demonstrates the logic of social criticism. The more influential his criticism became, the more he was tempted to translate it into a program. The very qualities, however, that define effective social criticism—thorough and insistent challenging of assumptions, values, and priorities—complicate more direct forms of political intervention. This logic describes Lasch's path in the decade after *The New Radicalism*, and it offers an alternative to his argument in that book—a way of understanding the process by which intellectuals are drawn from social criticism into more immediate and programmatic political action. Unlike his new radicals, Lasch undertook political work seeking neither romance nor power; he did it because he felt that the conditions and people around him demanded it.

* * *

Christopher Lasch was born in Omaha in 1932. Zora Schaupp Lasch had earned her doctorate in philosophy at Bryn Mawr. She taught logic and did professional social work. Robert Lasch was a journalist and Rhodes Scholar. The family moved with his newspaper jobs, going from Nebraska to Chicago to St. Louis, where Robert became editor of the *Post-Dispatch*'s editorial page.[2]

Lasch entered Harvard in 1950 and in 1952 volunteered for Adlai Stevenson. Two years later, he became a graduate student in that hotbed of Stevensonian liberalism, the Columbia University history department, home of Richard Hofstadter and William Leuchtenburg.[3] Lasch worked most closely with Leuchtenburg, but he later said that Hofstadter "was and remained the dominant figure on my intellectual horizon." Like Hofstadter, Lasch was interested in intellectuals' place in American society. He initially proposed a dissertation on that theme, which Hofstadter encouraged. "I am inclined to be very high on the idea of a dissertation on the [FDR] brain trust," he told Lasch. It might illuminate "the developing role of expertise in our society, policy formation on many specific issues, and the whole problem of the role and function of the expert and the intellectual in our society, which I would think would include some account of the public reputation of the brain trusters."[4]

Though Lasch shared Hofstadter's interest in intellectuals, he would draw different conclusions about them. Near the end of his life, Lasch said that Hofstadter's "work regrettably reinforced a tendency of American liberals to regard themselves as a civilized minority, an enlightened elite in a society dominated by rednecks and other 'anti-intellectuals.'" He pointed to Hofstadter's "disdain for the hopelessly muddled thinking of ordinary Americans," especially "their insatiable appetite for symbolic actions that provide the illusion that something is being done when in fact nothing is happening, their absolute dedication to a kind of entrepreneurial view of life, and above all their racism, xenophobia, anti-Semitism." Hofstadter could not credit Americans' ability "to think straight about politics."[5]

Yet Lasch did see Hofstadter as a model for using the past to engage the present. Lasch looked to scholars writing with "a fairly high political charge" and "some fairly obvious current reference" on topics "of interest to general readers." He "admired" historians who did such work, including Hofstadter and Arthur M. Schlesinger Jr.[6]

In 1956 Lasch married Nell Commager, and they had two children before settling in Iowa City, with Lasch at the University of Iowa. Throughout this period, Lasch struggled to understand the academy, the historical profession, and American political life. In "the political atmosphere of the late fifties," he recalled, there was a "widespread feeling of helplessness in the face of impersonal forces." That feeling "made some people activists and organiz-

ers." It made Lasch "redouble my efforts to write in such a way that somebody would hear it, so that it might have some influence, however small, on
the course of events that otherwise just seemed inexorably to unfold." Lasch
sought influence through writing, yet there can be a tension between writing that aims to influence and that which aims to illuminate. For historians
intent upon producing influential writing that was also good scholarship,
the balance could be difficult to find. "There is a kind of opinionatedness
to try to avoid, and a kind of superimposed *Weltanschauung* to avoid too,"
Leuchtenburg had told Lasch, "but you certainly don't avoid either danger, or avoid it at an overwhelming cost, by being a eunuch." Between pon-
tification and emasculation—if it was possible to be both a scholar and a
publicly influential presence, it was possible only within a certain space.[7]

For his next book, Lasch stepped into that space. In the summer of
1961, he informed Leuchtenburg that he wanted to interpret progressivism
"as a stage in the history of the alienation of the intellectuals."[8] His argument challenged Hofstadter's *The Age of Reform*, but Lasch looked beyond
historiography. He was rethinking American liberalism and assessing the
place of liberal intellectuals in particular.

Indeed, "liberals" and "intellectuals" were often interchangeable in
Lasch's writing. In early 1960s book reviews for his father's *St. Louis Post-
Dispatch*, Lasch challenged liberals. Instead of "ridiculing" a "discredited"
conservatism, they "should concentrate on offering a better explanation"
of social and cultural problems than conservatives did.[9] His assignment for
liberalism was an intellectual one: a "better explanation," a clearer understanding of issues, a more insightful social criticism.

Lasch also thought about why liberals had failed, thus far, to perform
this intellectual work. He looked, first, to little-known critic Benjamin
Ginzburg who in 1931 had written:

> In no country of the world is there such a tremendous gap between the
> values recognized by intellectuals and the values that actually govern
> political and economic realities. And yet in no country is the intellec-
> tual so preoccupied with affecting the course of politics to the exclusion
> of his intellectual interests. . . . Pragmatism has been wrongly called
> the philosophy of the practical man. It represents rather the anti-
> intellectualism of the American intellectual.[10]

Ginzburg etched a boundary between intellectual life and political action;
to cross it was to subordinate intellect in some crucial way. As Lasch inter-

preted it, the trouble was putting intellect to the test of politics rather than politics to the test of intellect. Intellectuals embraced politics as a way of overcoming alienation, fleeing austere chambers of the mind for the crowded halls of public affairs. The communism some writers adopted in the thirties "did not exhaust the possibilities open to intellectuals whose besetting concern was to escape the responsibility of being intellectuals," Lasch wrote. It "was one phase in a general retreat—a retreat which in our own day, far from having been arrested, threatens to become a rout."[11] He had in mind liberals.

Lasch applied Ginzburg's ideas to a well-known contemporary liberal in a 1963 series for the *Iowa Defender*, "Arthur Schlesinger and 'Pragmatic Liberalism.'" At Harvard, Schlesinger had read Lasch's thesis and presided over his oral exams. Months before his critical profile, Lasch sent clippings to his former teacher at the White House. "You have done so much, from time to time, to make it possible for me to persist in a scholarly career," Lasch wrote, "that I wish I could reward you other than by sending you reprints."[12]

The *Defender* series was no reward. In "The Cult of the Hard Boiled," Lasch highlighted the irony of Schlesinger charging "the 'utopian' Left"— particularly H. Stuart Hughes—with being soft on communism. "Not only intellectuals like Stuart Hughes" had "to suffer" such accusations; "the most eminently practical, responsible men—men who hold office, men of the 'pragmatic' Left" were also tarred. "Adlai Stevenson was an appeaser because he wanted to suspend nuclear tests." As a Stevenson adviser, Schlesinger "was an appeaser too. In fact he was the classic case of an egg-head, and the object, on that account, of endless abuse." Lasch explained Schlesinger's hard-boiled exterior by locating its internal source: "This very abuse now accounts for Schlesinger's eagerness to show that he can be as tough as anyone else." Ginzburg's influence here was clear: intellectuals' "estrangement from the American scene, their sense that they and the values they hold are under more or less continuous attack," Lasch wrote, "drives" them "to demonstrate their toughness and practicality, drives them to attach themselves to men of action, drives them in this way to attempt to reestablish connection with the common life around them."[13]

In his second installment, Lasch pushed this analysis all the way back to childhood. "Most people who grow up to be intellectuals tend even as children to display characteristics which distinguish them from most of their contemporaries and which expose them, therefore, to ridicule—

bookishness, sensitivity, and so forth." Reaching adulthood, the intellectual tries to show "that he was, all along, one of the gang—a regular fellow and as quick with his fists as the best of them." Lasch assumed that intellectuals were necessarily male and proceeded to assess the special burdens that masculinity placed upon the cerebral child. Parents' eagerness "that their sons be sufficiently masculine" could be behind "the bellicosity of American intellectuals," which was "one of the most dangerous developments of the recent past."[14]

Throughout this period, Lasch had been collaborating haltingly with William Taylor on a study of women and families.[15] While his thinking about gender and family clearly informed his ideas about intellectuals, Lasch failed to draw one seemingly obvious conclusion: if the "cult of the hard-boiled" arose from the conditioning experiences of men, then why not look to women intellectuals and the different outlook they might bring to policy debates? Reviewing Lasch's body of work in 1979, Berenice M. Fisher, professor of educational philosophy at New York University, noted that while he etched "a biting portrait of the sixties version of the academic-intellectual complete with Ivy League suit and advanced opinions," Lasch "significantly forgets the academic's wife." Such "blinders to the relation between women and intellectual work" had endured, Fisher wrote, "perhaps even longer than blindness to that between women and politics or the arts." As a result, "standards for . . . intellectual work have remained firmly masculine." While the gendering of some roles had changed, "the intellectual is still male, working safely cloistered in his study while his wife fixes everything from electrical appliances to his most recent *faux pas*." Not only did these blinders and the standards they perpetuated mean that debates about the role of intellectuals were conducted as debates about men, but they also indicated "why women have had such difficulties in becoming intellectuals themselves." Women's work "keeping the male intellectual role afloat has entailed their own exclusion from intellectual life." Fisher challenged the gendered assumptions with which Lasch wrote while highlighting the importance of gender analysis to the topic on which he wrote: "the inquiry concerning the character of the intellectual's role."[16]

In his final *Defender* piece, Lasch examined intellectuals' vantage point and their work, using Schlesinger as a foil. Locked "in the windowless room of present preoccupations," Schlesinger, the political operative, had no proper vantage point, no detachment. "Faced with the example of Mr. Schlesinger," Lasch wrote, "one might easily conclude that monastic seclusion, after all, was the best course for scholars to follow," but that "would be a great pity." The "real question" was not whether intellectuals "ought to assume political commitments but what form the commitments ought to take." The work an "intellectual can do best—as scholar, as agitator—is to encourage people to imagine other alternatives besides the ones whose timeless truth they take for granted." Intellectuals ought not only to adopt a vantage point beyond "the prison of the present," but also cultivate it among others, fostering "perspectives—notably the perspective of the past—from which the irrationality of contemporary society might be clearly perceived." Since this work was open-ended, "the political potency of intellectuals" remained an open question.[17]

On the eve of *The New Radicalism*, Lasch's effort was twofold: to identify vantage points from which intellectuals could engage politics as intellectuals, and to indict intellectuals who abandoned these vantage points for other kinds of political work. Over the next decade, the second effort would prove more successful than the first.

* * *

In 1964 Richard Hofstadter's *Anti-Intellectualism in American Life* won the Pulitzer Prize. That year, Lasch labored to complete his book on progressivism. These two books marked a turning point in debates about the role of intellectuals in American political culture. The former looked back to the 1950s, locating the sources of anti-intellectualism in "American life." The latter located the sources of anti-intellectualism within intellectuals themselves.

Lasch's interpretation of progressivism developed in correspondence with Staughton Lynd, son of *Middletown* authors Helen and Robert Lynd and a historian at Spelman College. Lynd celebrated Progressive Era intellectuals like Jane Addams as radicals who saw themselves "not as a persecuted minority but as the voice of the people." In contrast, Lasch neither celebrated progressive intellectuals nor conceded that they were, in fact, intellectuals. Having abandoned "the real function of the intellectual"— "criticizing"—they embraced the pragmatism that Ginzburg had condemned. "The mystique of action, of 'doing something about it,' the cult of experience, of 'life,' and of the working class—these things made the progressives impatient with mere criticism," Lasch told Lynd. Wary of "academic cloisters," progressive intellectuals were "impatient with intellectual activity itself." When "they got involved with what they liked to think of as 'life,'" they "surrendered the only point of view from which they could successfully criticize society"—"detachment." Progressives' support for World War One "was the final capitulation," the ultimate relinquishing of detachment in favor of participation.[18]

Addams, however, had not supported World War One. She was a pacifist who paid a price for dissent. Yet Lasch saw in her claim that education had "the power to adjust [people] in healthful relations to nature and their fellow men" another disturbing tendency: the drive toward manipulation and social control. "Isn't she here describing," he asked Lynd, "what has . . . come to pass: a society in which knowledge is used, all right, for social ends, the ends, however, being defined, as they always will be, by the people with power: in our society, by the so-called military-industrial complex."[19] In this scheme, intellectuals not only served power, but they also accommodated the powerless to it. In neither case did they forge a root-and-branch critique of the distribution of power.

Lasch and Lynd's correspondence turned from the lives of others to their own. Unlike Lynd—who asked: "Is there . . . no longer a place for the totally committed life?"—Lasch did not believe the intellectual's "advantage lies in the commitment he makes to radicalism, as opposed to the lack of commitment of the ordinary professor."[20] Indeed, Lasch contended, the professor's problem is "not that he lives in an ivory tower but that he is so pathetically far from living in one, because he is committed, often in a very immediate way, to the current consensus." Increasingly, the professor was "working for the government as a technical advisor," identifying "new ways of blowing people up, or . . . of persuading Africans to be on our side." One had "to become a radical and an activist to avoid being drawn into this miserable academic routine." Yet the "trouble with the radical movement" was "that it so often seems to impose a conformity of its own."[21] Hofstadter had arrived at the same conclusion in the 1930s.

Practicing politics, radical or otherwise, imposed constraints that undermined intellectuals, who "had some sort of obligation to maintain a certain independence and detachment." They could "best serve their purpose by being critical rather than 'constructive,'" Lasch wrote; "someone has got to be critical, and intellectuals are probably in a better position to give it than other people." Intellectuals in the mold of Schlesinger "abdicate their function when they throw themselves into political causes which by their very nature rest on an implicit acceptance of the status quo—like become advisers to Presidents. The delusion that they can decisively influence politicians, which is the excuse always given for this particular kind of activism, has proved . . . fatuous on innumerable occasions."[22]

Lasch was formulating his ideas about the limited way that intellectuals might act politically through a process of elimination. "Obviously some kinds of activism are more eloquent criticism of the status quo than any amount of words," he conceded to Lynd. "But even this kind of criticism may eventually be unavailing unless it is properly interpreted by the people involved, or by someone in a position to interpret it properly. Actions can be . . . misunderstood." Lasch cited Addams as an instance, suggesting that her ideas became lost among her deeds. "Perhaps . . . Addams was too intent on practical results to take the time to understand and explain what she was doing," Lasch wrote. "Perhaps . . . there was too much working for good causes . . . and too little real social criticism."[23]

Lynd wrote of the "relentless desire that the radical impulse shall find its outlet in action." Lasch demurred. "Maybe I am callow. But I can't help feeling that practical action has . . . limitations, that it is not in the long run much good without theory to support it, and that it is too bad, in this . . . case, that the energies of the movement that Jane Addams was involved in should eventually have been drained off into bland and harmless dogoodism."[24] Were all the Hull Houses in the world less important than a theory of social change? It was one thing to criticize intellectuals for failing to be critical; it was another to diminish Addams's settlement work as "bland and harmless" compared to criticism.[25] Lasch's critique of intellectuals who sought too much after "real life" sounded as though it came from one who preferred the realm of the forms instead.

Lasch sent his manuscript for *The New Radicalism* to a reader who appreciated the platonic qualities of "the life of the mind," which he had made it his own political work to defend: Hofstadter. One of the manuscript's preliminary titles, "The Anti-Intellectualism of the Intellectuals: Studies in American Progressivism," made clear the extent to which the themes of Hofstadter's recent volume reverberated in Lasch's work. "You are accusing certain intellectuals of treason to the intellectual life, or of unduly subordinating it to other commitments," Hofstadter wrote, and that was "not quite the same thing as anti-intellectualism," which was more "sociological than philosophical." Hostile social forces, rather than abstract distinctions between detachment and commitment, were still the most dangerous source of anti-intellectualism for Hofstadter.[26]

Lasch's correspondence with Hofstadter, as with Lynd, turned to personal reflection. Considering the place of intellectuals in American life, they considered themselves. Lasch was not "throwing myself into the [1964 Lyndon] Johnson campaign, though I know perfectly well that it is essential that he should win." Unprepared to plunge into ordinary electoral politics, he was "still less" interested in "'radical' causes, led by 'radicals' whose thinking has stopped dead at the political ideology of a generation ago"—perhaps he had Lynd and Addams in mind.[27] Elections were unappealing, reform work became "harmless do-goodism," radicals were stuck in fossilized thinking, the academy was implicated in the military-industrial complex, and the cloistered life was no alternative. What was left for a Lasch to do?

Hofstadter had no firm answers. Unlike in 1952, he did not "get enlisted in practical politics." Nor did he "get enlisted in the ideologies—indeed, at times I feel even more detached from them." Temperamentally, Hofstadter was not prepared to devote his mind entirely to politics, unlike his old colleague C. Wright Mills, whose "whole intellect was, in the last dozen years of his life, simply consumed by politics." That Mills "did not ring doorbells or write party pamphlets does not seem to constitute an important qualification upon the generalization that he politicized everything."[28] Both Hofstadter and Mills were interested in political ideas, but Hofstadter emphasized the second word in that term, while Mills focused on the first. Lasch was casting about somewhere in between. Unlike Hofstadter, who feared the political fires burning without, Lasch still had a strong political fire burning within. But he was determined, like Hofstadter, not to let politics crowd out ideas.

The New Radicalism emerged from this tension. "I've invented as a working title *Sources of the New Radicalism: Studies in the Social History of the American Intellectual*," Lasch told publisher Alfred Knopf. "The subtitle shows where my real interest lies: there, more than in progressivism or radicalism itself."[29] Lasch was writing to take intellectuals to task for subordinating intellectual work—identified with uncompromising and uncompromised social criticism—to other idols. As social criticism, *The New Radicalism* was itself a model of the work that Lasch called upon intellectuals to do. Yet the book formed a closed circuit. Lasch was urging intellectuals to act as intellectuals by engaging in social criticism, but his own critical project turned out to be largely a criticism of intellectuals. He was in danger of inhabiting a sealed world, one where intellectuals criticized other intellectuals while failing to comment on the broader world and its problems. In the years after the book's publication in 1965, Lasch would try to break out of this circuit.

The New Radicalism reprised Lasch's interest in Ginzburg's ideas and Schlesinger's sins. American radicals, failing to remain true to the critical thinking constitutive of the intellectual life, had over the course of the twentieth century been drawn into either the Scylla of bohemian romanticism or the Charybdis of bureaucratic power. These outcomes were consequential beyond the boundaries of intellectual history, for Lasch saw intellectuals as key figures in shaping—or, rather, delimiting—the political possibilities of Cold War America.

Intellectuals' "presumed capacity to comment upon [society] with greater detachment than those more caught up in the practical business of production and power" required social distance, making their "relation to the rest of society . . . never entirely comfortable," though "not always . . . as uncomfortable as it is today." Whereas Hofstadter traced that discomfort to anti-intellectual impulses rumbling just beneath the surface of mass democracy, Lasch found that "'anti-intellectualism' offers only a partial explanation of the present tension." American "intellectuals' own sense of themselves . . . as members of a beleaguered minority" was also a cause. This "class-consciousness of the intellectuals" made them more sensitive to their status than conscious of their vocation, leading them to "agonize endlessly over 'the role of the intellectuals.'"[30] He left unexplored whether intellectuals' "sense of themselves" as a "beleaguered minority" was merely a "sense" or, indeed, accurate.

Lasch traced his story from the America of the military-industrial complex back to that of the robber barons, finding in progressivism the roots of the "new radicalism." He pointed to the "pervasiveness of the ideal of 'service'" among progressive intellectuals. By idealizing service, he suggested, intellectuals abandoned their inquiry into which values might be worth serving. Some "could find comfort and meaning, it appeared, only in large, encompassing movements of masses of people, of which they could imagine themselves a part."[31]

Though intellectuals might imagine themselves part of mass movements, their relationship to the masses was a fraught one. They "were torn between their wish to liberate the unused energies of the submerged portions of society and their enthusiasm for social planning," which Lasch equated to social control. "The rage for planning reflected the planners'

confidence in themselves as a disinterested elite, unbound by the preju-
dices either of the middle class or of the proletariat." In a line of reasoning
that would be reprised by neoconservatives like Irving Kristol, Lasch saw
behind intellectuals' interest in social policy a darker motive than the
humane ones professed. Foreshadowing Michel Foucault's critique of the
human sciences as a technology of power, Lasch raised concerns over progressive intellectuals' emphases on education and psychological adjust-
ment, their effort to bring the individual into "healthful relations" with
the community, as Addams put it.[32]

Even the new radicals' desire to replace force with reason had a manip-
ulative side. Intellectuals, "having no resources of their own to throw
into the social struggle—no resources, as a class, except argument and
exposition—had a class interest in nonviolence for its own sake. In a struggle of force against force the intellectuals, possessing neither property nor
the force of numbers, had everything to lose." They therefore held "that
the way of progress was necessarily the way of peace."[33] Like Nietzsche arguing that the Judeo-Christian credo of love and forgiveness was in fact an
expression of the *ressentiment* of the powerless, Lasch was turning professed
values on their head by exposing their origins. New radicals did not prefer
peace and reason for their own sakes; they preferred them as a terrain upon
which they enjoyed a comparative class advantage.[34] "Their confidence
that 'education' could take the place of force" at times seemed "to rationalize a crude will to power." Fortunately, ordinary people turned their backs
on this program. Among "'the people,' in whose interests [they] so often
professed to speak," intellectuals "aroused indifference at best and resentment at worst, not merely because they flew in the face of accepted orthodoxies but because they were irrelevant to the conditions under which
most people continued to live."[35]

Whether the new radicalism proved helpful or harmful to the American people, it was, without doubt, an abrogation of the responsibility of
intellectuals. Once again, Lasch turned to Ginzburg's argument "that the
principal obligation of the intellectuals was not to any political program
but to the intellectual life itself." Yet Lasch was groping toward some course
for intellectuals that avoided both monastic seclusion and immersion in
a particular political agenda. For Lasch, Ginzburg "was not urging intellectuals to leave politics to the politicians; he was asking them to make
a more realistic estimate of their potential influence." Recognizing "that
they could seldom hope to influence politics directly," intellectuals should

embrace the fact that they "had more influence over politics as *intellectuals* than as political activists in their own right."[36] As the political climate of the sixties grew more tumultuous, Lasch would wrestle with translating this formula into work.

In the "hard-boiled and 'pragmatic'" posture of contemporary liberal intellectuals like Schlesinger, Lasch saw once again the new radical's desire to be "not a mere spectator but an active participant in the great events of the day."[37] Lasch had traveled a long road in his book—from Addams's progressivism to Schlesinger's liberalism. Addams served the people and Schlesinger the president, but both, in Lasch's eyes, sought to overcome alienation by engaging current events.

The current event for liberal intellectuals was Kennedy's presidency, which represented not only a coming to power but also a cultural vindication. Intellectuals saw in Kennedy's style a reflection of themselves, or at least what they aspired to be. Whereas Hofstadter emphasized the tension between mind and masses, Lasch saw substantial agreement between them on this question of style. "The intellectuals' self-image" in the glow of the Kennedy presidency "had come to coincide with the popular stereotype of the intellectual." While Kennedy intellectuals thought this image flattering, "the picture could be reversed, as it was in the days of [Joseph] McCarthy." In McCarthyism's eye, the "intellectual's cosmopolitanism became un-American, his sophistication snobbery, his accent affectation, his clothes and his manner the badge, obscurely, of sexual deviation." Indeed, Lasch pointed out, "even as a subversive, the intellectual was still an Ivy League aristocrat." Intellectuals who opposed "McCarthyism did not question the essential accuracy of the popular image of themselves; they merely objected to the ugliness and unseemliness of organized envy."[38] The clash between intellectuals and anti-intellectuals did not come down to substance versus style, Lasch suggested; on both sides, it was always a question of style.

And style was, at bottom, a question of class. Anti-intellectuals' targets were, for the intellectuals themselves, markers of their own distinctive class identity. With the ascendance of Camelot, research showing intellectuals' "unexpectedly high degree of social status was pointed to as proof that intellectual *values* were held in high esteem. The confusion, in the mind of the intellectuals, between intellect itself and the interests of the intellectuals as a class had become almost complete, though the two . . . had never been more hopelessly at odds." Their positions as corporate technicians and presidential advisers signaled "the rise of the intellectuals to the status of a privileged class." Even the academic was "indistinguishable both in his social function (to lobby for patronage) and in his style of life (expense-account affluence) from his counterpart in industry." Forfeiting social criticism, this new brand of intellectual attended instead to the imperatives "of a mature class jealous of its recognized position in the social order."[39] These were not the responsibilities of intellectuals that Ginzburg had in mind.

As intellectualism became conflated with the prerogatives and status of intellectuals, the very concept of the intellectual became attenuated. "Neither the academic statesmen nor the academic technicians were any longer intellectuals at all," Lasch wrote. They qualified "only by Reinhold Niebuhr's definition of intellectuals as 'the more articulate members of the community,' and the technicians did not qualify even under a definition as broad as that."[40]

Publication of The New Radicalism in 1965 had a threefold yield for Lasch: it raised his public profile; led to his being misread—or, in spite of Lasch's insistence to the contrary, read accurately—as a new Julien Benda; and generated calls for him to lead a movement, to point the way forward. As biographer Eric Miller put it, "Lasch went from being a slightly heterodox, little-known academic to a literary commodity—and a beacon to many both in his generation and the one that followed." Leuchtenburg told Lasch that The New Radicalism left him "wandering around in a daze and thinking about my megalomania and that of my old ADA associates and that of my intellectual friends and back to myself again. You make reading the book not something to be commented upon at a distance but something to be lived through and experienced." Lasch greeted this reception with surprise, telling his parents, "The book has been praised beyond its real merits."[41]

Criticism of the book addressed not its historiographical claims but, rather, its comment on the role of intellectuals in American politics. This element had struck a nerve that, in the spring of 1965, was particularly raw. In the first days of March, civil rights marchers en route from Selma to Montgomery, Alabama, clashed with a white mob, including state troopers, on the Edmund Pettus Bridge. The next day, 3,500 Marines landed in Vietnam, marking the overt beginning of American combat missions. In late March, Martin Luther King and 25,000 civil rights activists completed the march to Montgomery. In early April, Students for a Democratic Society

organized 25,000 marchers on Washington for an antiwar protest. At the
close of April, President Johnson sent troops to intervene in the Domin-
ican civil war. In May, the University of California at Berkeley witnessed
a mass teach-in and the widespread burning of draft cards. "Suddenly,"
Michael Harrington wrote that fall, "everybody is talking about radicalism."[42] Many were talking and writing about *The New Radicalism*, too.

"It was about time that someone made a categorical definition of the
stake that so many intellectuals now have in the inequalities of our society," Alfred Kazin wrote in the *New York Review of Books*. It was "time that
someone held the mirror up to American intellectuals and showed us the
extent to which we are implicated in our wars as in our prosperity—for it
is also us, and not just President Johnson and General [Maxwell] Taylor,
that other people are thinking of when they level the charge that is unin-
telligible to most American intellectuals—'American imperialism.'"[43] For
Kazin, Lasch's book called intellectuals to account at a moment when their
complicity in troubling features of American society and policy could no
longer be ignored.

For others, Lasch simply sounded the familiar refrain that intellectuals must remain aloof from this world. "I have not wished to write a tract,
another *Trahison des Clercs*," Lasch asserted. Many of his readers did not see
it that way. Edward T. Chase was characteristic of reviewers who found in
Lasch the Benda-like "theme of the betrayal of the life of reason" and the
"abdication of intellect." According to Daniel Aaron, "It would be inac-
curate to say that Mr. Lasch has written a new 'Trahison des Clercs'; he is
ironical and speculative rather than hortatory. But his book can be read as
a treatise on the fate of intellectuals who forsake the role of criticism and
who sacrifice present moral and intellectual imperatives to the hopes of the
future." As Peter Filene saw it, "The only tenable position for intellectuals,
Lasch concludes, is alienation. From the fringe of American society they
can perform their essential role as critics without sacrificing their rationality or integrity to the inevitably hostile and more powerful society." He
found Lasch "dogmatic" on the "claim that public involvement corrupts
intellectuals."[44]

Some critics—like Kennedy cultural adviser August Heckscher II—
took that claim head-on. "It is easy to say that these newer radicals, of
whom Arthur Schlesinger is characterized as typical, confused 'style' with
intellect," Heckscher wrote. "But what would have been the judgment
upon the intellectuals had they said in 1960 that they were sorry but they

were too busy, and too pure, to heed the call of a President who seemed ready to put all things in a new light?"[45] Heckscher was not the only New Frontiersman to take on Lasch.

"The Lasch book is amazingly bad, and I am baffled at the favorable press it received," Schlesinger wrote Sidney Hook in March 1966, shortly after publishing his own review in the *London Sunday Times*, where he began "by declaring an interest. In the course of this spirited polemic against the pragmatic intellectual in the United States, disguised as a scholarly essay in American intellectual history, Mr. Lasch lists me as among the attending minor villains." Schlesinger criticized Lasch's psychological analysis of the new radicals' politics, arguing that its "deprecation of the idea that a political position might be, in addition, a rational response to the real world, conceals a subtle anti-intellectualism." Schlesinger asked whether Lasch's "characters might have been striving to cope with external reality as well as with themselves."[46]

Schlesinger also hit Lasch's Benda-like flank: "His ostensible position is that it is wrong to mix politics and culture" and that "the role of the intellectual must be disinterested inquiry and speculation." Schlesinger found it "excessive to demand that every intellectual conform at every moment to this single model." He suggested that Lasch's contradictory book left readers with the impression that "an intellectual who rejects society has surrendered to one form of neurosis, one who takes part, another."[47]

While Schlesinger found neuroses in *The New Radicalism*, others found hints of a new way forward. Could intellectuals like Lasch now fulfill the promise of social criticism that he accused prior generations of abandoning? Benjamin DeMott found that Lasch neither joined "faculty club optouts who claim that social, economic, moral, even national causes and interests are beneath the notice of a true gent of the mind," nor indulged "the opposite illusion . . . that brains well-applied can easily smooth or redirect the historical wave." Instead, "a sound politics for an intellectual, a well-judged commitment, reserves high places for academic and cultural values—for truth, not policy; liberty, not license; thinking, not willing." *The New Radicalism*, DeMott contended, "points a way, indirect but legible, toward an adequate radical politics—in which 'social awareness' nourishes the sense of intellectual responsibility instead of cancelling it." It also pointed a way for Lasch himself: "It would be neither surprising, nor unhelpful to those whose political choices are still to be made, nor unlucky for the country as a whole, if, as a result of the response to this book, Christopher Lasch awoke one morning this summer to find himself accepted as a spokesman."[48]

* * *

In September 1965, Fred Rue Jacobs of Inglewood, California, wrote Lasch to say that *The New Radicalism* "is about the best thing I have ever come across in U.S. history." Jacobs claimed that reviewers "seem to think you will become the center of a cult and so do I." "There is no danger that I will become the center of a cult," Lasch replied. But Lasch would at least be a focus of hope for those seeking intellectual and political change. "Your manifesto—for it is being accepted as just that and will be more and more—lays down some lines that will be battle lines among intellectuals in this country," historian William Stanton wrote Lasch, "and now having read it, I put myself down as a Lasch Man."[49]

The New Radicalism touched a nerve among historians. At the Organization of American Historians' (OAH) annual meeting in the spring of 1966, Berkeley's Samuel Haber characterized the book as "overrun" with the idea "that an intellectual who is true to his calling will be 'above the battle.'" Yet, Haber suggested, "surely" intellectuals cannot be "above all battles." Finding Lasch "too limited . . . in fact, in thought, and in sympathy," Haber counseled greater understanding for those, like Schlesinger, who took part in political battles. "We live, understandably enough, with a sense of urgency, and the desire of an intellectual to establish the responsibility of the intellectual certainly deserves our respect," Haber observed. "It is only to be regretted that in order to endorse being above the battle, Professor Lasch was . . . condescending and sometimes captious to those who were not."[50]

Lasch attempted to clarify what he meant by "intellectuals" and what he proposed that they should do. "All I meant was that intellectuals are people who think about contemporary society from the perspective of general ideas." Their authority "derives not from the material power they command but from whatever wisdom comes from their preoccupation with values," and "also from their specialized skills." While intellectuals' "wisdom often amounts to folly," they are nonetheless "assumed to have accumulated a fund of useful and edifying knowledge. This definition includes both social philosophers, as we might call them—'intellectuals in the classic sense'—and experts."[51] It excluded "scholars who don't comment on contemporary issues at all, from any perspective, expert or philosophical."

Scholars, however, were under no "obligation to be intellectuals." Nor did "choosing to be an intellectual somehow preclude[] scholarship—a suspicion which mysteriously persists in academic circles."[52]

Haber had suggested that, in writing a book critical of intellectuals who had not been above the fray, Lasch wholeheartedly entered the fray himself—drawing his sword against intellectuals whom he denounced for drawing theirs. Lasch made no excuses for his critical tone. "Whether intellectuals ought to see themselves as philosophers or as experts—these cannot possibly be regarded as dead issues, to be discussed with elegant neutrality," he said. "Detachment" was "a valuable quality of mind" not to be confused with "the pretense of neutrality." It was possible to be detached but not neutral, to be analytical while at the same time taking a stand. And yet, Lasch seemed to suggest that intellectuals ought to resist taking stands, or at least those that might too easily be taken. "The world is full of instant ideologies and ready-made radicalisms," he said. "As scholars, as radicals if you like, we can have nothing to do with them. We can't become believers. Our job, as Lincoln Steffens once said, is to doubt."[53]

Lasch's readers, like the OAH panel, asked him to clarify what he thought the intellectual's job *was*. *The New Radicalism* dwelt upon what that job *was not*. His claim that intellectuals should doubt was insufficient for those who wondered what intellectuals should do. Amid the strong response to his book, Lasch attempted to work out a more robust answer to that question. He also attempted to put his provisional answers into practice. Even as he offered ambiguous prescriptions for the role of the intellectual, audiences nonetheless felt that Lasch was worth listening to.

"The current crop of graduate students discusses [your book] avidly," Leuchtenburg wrote Lasch."[54] Though "more sanguine" about intellectuals' government service, without which "20th century reform would be quite thin of achievement," Leuchtenburg was also "bothered . . . by the atrophying of the critical function when the intellectual engages in politics." On balance, he thought intellectuals should expand their role in public life. "If what is wrong in America is the barrenness of culture, the lack of community, and if it is utopian to expect from the ordinary politician any awareness of these problems, is it not the function of the intellectual to find 'solutions'?" Perhaps "the real fault of the liberal intellectual" was not political involvement per se, but "that he was too preoccupied with . . . minimum wages or federal highways." For Leuchtenburg, it was neither "just megalomania to feel a responsibility" toward the broadest social issues, nor "just a fear of aloneness that would lead an intellectual to feel that there was something futile in a role that was wholly 'critical.'" He wanted space for intellectuals to act affirmatively and constructively, space for which he thought Lasch made little allowance. "Given your pessimistic view of the nature of modern society . . . is there anything in your view that the intellectual can/should do to alter it?" Lasch's work could lead "to the conclusion that it doesn't matter what the intellectual does—yet your book demonstrates that you care deeply about what he does."[55] Leuchtenburg, like others, saw *The New Radicalism* pointing to a role for intellectuals other than the spiritual isolation that Benda had counseled yet leaving readers with precious little of a guide to it.

Lasch responded that he did not think intellectuals "should do nothing." He "only ask[ed] that they act like intellectuals." Just what constraints that placed on their work was unclear. "It isn't really a matter . . . of whether or not to engage in practical politics," he wrote. The key question was that of their proper vantage point: if work was compatible with being a rigorous, doubting critic, Lasch abided it. If, however, the dynamics of certain kinds of work might undermine that vantage point, he raised concerns. "I don't think one automatically ceases to be an intellectual when he gets on the inside of things," he wrote, but "intellectuals who try to speak for intellectual values in the seat of power" are often warped by the effort, for "when they try to speak a language which powerful people can understand, they soon forget that there is any other language."[56]

Lasch countered the persistent perception that in pointing out this problem he was "advocating a fashionable cult of 'alienation'" or "symbolic gestures of withdrawal and rejection." He called instead for "what the new radicals promised but drew back from, trying to see middle-class society from the outside in, and then using this perspective to analyze, criticize, argue, persuade, in one's 'work' or in one's polemics, it makes no difference." As he told Leuchtenburg, "Some perspectives seem . . . more fruitful for intellectual work than others, and I would like to see more people cultivate those perspectives."[57] One means of cultivating them might be to work, as Addams had, among those on the margins of society. Such work could provide the opportunity to behold middle-class culture from a critical distance.

Lasch was inclined, however, to see any work but the mental labor of criticism and the craft of critical writing as potentially hostile, rather than beneficial, to the cultivation of intellectual perspectives. The "only good thing," he told Leuchtenburg, that might come from activism "is that it helps to produce the perspective I mentioned, but unfortunately . . . it often does so at the price of intellectual effectiveness; one forsakes the language of criticism, the Western tradition of rational discourse for the obscurantist jargon of 'the movement,'" which was "as bad in its way as the language of power."[58] The most important consideration when assessing intellectuals' work was its effect on their perspective, since the latter, not the former, defined them.

Yet Lasch did not think that intellectuals were *only* a perspective—floating eyeballs untethered to the things of this world. "I am far from saying that it doesn't matter what intellectuals do," he told Leuchtenburg. "It seems to me to matter plenty," except "when you think your function is to change government policy, or . . . to make a revolution." Since these were at bottom not intellectual tasks, intellectuals did them poorly. In other areas, however, "intellectuals have indisputable and immediate influence. Many of them, for instance, are teachers." But even promising developments like the teach-in movement that began at the University of Michigan in the spring of 1965 disappointed Lasch. Teach-in faculty revealed, in his view, that "they really hanker for the status of government advisers" and are "just sore because no one is listening to their advice."[59] Here, again, extra-intellectual impulses pulled intellectuals away from the critical perspective that defined them. Lasch thought there was a better path for intellectuals' work, but it was a narrow and dimly lit one. It was perhaps no wonder that he stumbled repeatedly in his attempts to tread it himself.

In a series of essays published mostly in the *New York Review of Books* between 1965 and 1967, Lasch blended criticism of intellectuals with thinking about the politically relevant work they might do. Expert and alienated intellectuals were "powerless to change anything," he wrote, "but as members of a community of scholars they represent a fund of moral and intellectual power, the withdrawal of which, from the governments it now justifies and supports, would be difficult for those governments to ignore." For Lasch, "withdrawal" did not mean "retreat into an absolute pacifism or a utopian internationalism, still less into hip, but a refusal to put intellect—and the moral and philosophical values of which intellectuals are the guardians—at the disposal of nations and nationalisms, whose purposes have nothing to do with those values." The need, Lasch concluded, "is neither [for] expert advice nor empty moral protests but better thinking, better scholarship: scholarship which will be itself informed with moral passion, and which will express itself with deliberate disregard for the conventional distinction between 'education' and political agitation."[60]

For E. Jeffrey Ludwig, writing to the *New York Review*, Lasch sowed confusion. He found it unclear how "better *scholarship* will build to an understanding that is at once sound and *inexpert*." Ludwig's letter demonstrated, Lasch replied, how "scholarship has become so closely bound up with expertise that it is hard for people to imagine one without the other." He claimed that "the highest act of scholarship isn't making a 'contribution' to one's field, it is the application of scholarship to experience itself, the willingness to let one's critical judgment inform one's life—one's political life in particular—instead of suspending it at the water's edge of moral commitment."[61]

For English professor John F. Withey of Nacogdoches, Texas, also writing to the *Review*, lack of moral commitment was the problem. In fact, he attacked Lasch for favoring too much criticism and not enough commitment. Withey held that "criticism accomplishes too little too late, and . . . words, spent upon the ears of those who cannot or will not participate in a reasoned dialogue, avail us almost nothing, and that, much too slowly." Scholars "have talked to *each other* too long," making "a cult of erudite repetitiousness and call[ed] it intellectualism. . . . It is time for the intellectual to do and to initiate—to become, much more than he already is—the performing expert Mr. Lasch deprecates." Lasch tried to "clear things up" by noting that "some of the best scholars . . . are people who don't even hold advanced degrees. Some of the activists in the civil rights movement, for instance—people who *do* things, Professor Withey—are capable of analytical flights that would be incomprehensible to most of our sociologists and political scientists." The latter "think like experts" by adopting "the posture of scholarly detachment" and "confin[ing] themselves to small suggestions within the framework of an overriding assumption about American benevolence, without examining the assumption itself." The new scholarship Lasch called for would presumably question just such assumptions.[62]

Yet readers had trouble imagining what that scholarly work might look like. In *The New Radicalism*, Lasch had pitted detached criticism against something like what he now called "committed scholarship"—scholarship bounded by certain antecedent commitments that went beyond the commitment to criticism itself.[63] Whether he was now modifying that position depended upon the meaning of "detachment." In criticizing experts who took "the posture of . . . detachment" while working on problems defined for them by the government, Lasch was claiming that they were not detached from the assumptions handed to them. These experts might be performing "value-free" analysis, but they were firmly attached to the status quo, which they did not interrogate. Committed scholarship, by contrast, was not "value-free"; it was scholarship informed by a set of values, not detached from them.[64] It was, however, detached from the assumptions that governed what Lasch saw as the prevailing consensus. In advocating for committed scholarship, Lasch was still urging detachment, not from moral values—as the experts claimed to be—but from unquestioned assumptions.

Berenice Fisher of NYU pointed to Lasch's own unexamined assumptions, which lay at the heart of the intellectual life he was sketching. "Given the criteria of intellectual life he offers," Fisher wrote, "it is hard to see how such a life can be maintained without also maintaining a set of social assumptions that are themselves deeply undemocratic." Detached, critical intellectuals ate meals, lived in homes, and had children cared for while they wrote, argued, and thought. Rather than account for this work, Fisher observed, Lasch and other male intellectuals simply assumed it was women's domain. This "division of mental and physical labor cannot be just," Fisher wrote, "for the cardinal intellectual virtues of craft, distance, and integrity are predicated on the exploitative use of someone else's manual labor." Feminist criticism held, further, "that the labor which makes possible intellectual life is psychological (or emotional) as well as physical, and that a disproportionate amount of both kinds is done by women."[65] If the role of the detached intellectual was to be a democratic one, open to all and built upon the oppression of none, then the gendered assumptions about work on which it rested had to be addressed.

The feminism taking shape as Lasch wrote—New York Radical Women published *Notes from the First Year* in June 1968—grappled with this issue. Turning "an eye to the distinct features of contemporary feminism, with its struggle to respond to unjust realities," Fisher wrote, one "might well discover new attempts to define intellectuality and new modes and arenas for cultivating and sharing intellectual resources." Within feminist organizations, the division of intellectual and other forms of labor became the subject of debate and, ultimately, experimentation. Two radical groups in New York, the Redstockings and the Feminists, used a system that distinguished intellectual from routine labor and assigned tasks among themselves by lot in an effort to avoid the creation of a permanent intellectual caste resting upon a base of typists and mimeograph-machine operators.[66]

Feminists challenged assumptions not only about intellectual labor, but also about intellectual detachment. "We . . . have to contend with the widespread assumption that women's concerns in general are 'personal,' 'subjective,'" critic Ellen Willis wrote in her journal in 1969. "The very idea of male-female relations as a political question confounds most people: politics takes place between groups of men, in the 'world.'" Such a conception exiled women's experiences and concerns, and the idea of detachment reinforced that exclusion: intellectuals thought in a detached manner about politics; women's issues were personal rather than political, and personal matters were attachments rather than the objects of critical detachment. "It is because of this prejudice," Willis wrote, that feminists' "consciousness raising method—an attempt to define our political reality that has had its analogues in the black movement and the Chinese revolution—is so often dismissed as 'group therapy.'"[67] Feminists saw ideas rising not from the detached contemplation of single intellectuals, but from the shared circumstances of women and their collective endeavor to become critically conscious of those circumstances.[68] In the crucible of the feminist movement, women were renovating notions of intellect and the role of the intellectual by exposing gendered assumptions and developing new modes of intellectual activity that took democratic equality seriously. "Sometimes," Fisher wrote, "it is even hard for those involved to see the importance of such feminist redefinitions because they seem 'natural' to women too, or because we too see the world through prevailing cliches about what is valuable human activity." It was, however, "the job of intellectuals . . . to challenge cliches as well as . . . more abstract assumptions. Parlors do not always breed parlor politics. Tempests do not always stay in teapots."[69]

The tempest of the 1960s was growing, intensified by radicalism developed within social movements like feminism. As Lasch elaborated his notion of the intellectual's role—and wrestled with readers who could not make sense of it—his writing took on a tone of heightened urgency. His calls for "committed scholarship" were not only theoretical claims; they were invitations for intellectuals to undertake a certain type of work—work that seemed to him increasingly needed. He believed that the peace and civil rights movements, along with burgeoning student activism, were reaching a critical phase.[70] While Lasch saw social and political movements as promising, he also believed that their paths were fraught with peril. They seemed to lack direction—either not having programs that, stepwise, might bring about structural change or missing the theoretical framework to generate such programs.

The growing calls for change were up against a political culture that Lasch saw as deeply invested in quashing change. "The structure of American society makes it almost impossible for criticism of existing policies to become part of political discourse," he wrote. Moreover, he believed that the growing agitation might bring on the worst kind of repression. "There is a small but growing public outcry in these parts, to the effect that it is up to the government to make foreign policy and nobody else has a right to criticize it," Lasch wrote to *New York Review of Books* editor Robert Silvers from Iowa City, where he had acquired some notoriety as a dissenting voice. "I'm feeling pretty grim. The other day someone sent me a dead animal wrapped in a box." Grim, indeed.[71]

This sense of the moment's perils as much as its prospects joined the list of factors pulling Lasch toward making his ideas about committed scholarship, intellectual work, and social criticism not only theoretical but also operational. Yet his work continued to focus on criticism of intellectuals rather than the broader social criticism his work called intellectuals to do. His most prominent article of 1967, "The Cultural Cold War," might easily have been another chapter in *The New Radicalism*. In the Congress for Cultural Freedom, an international organization of anti-communist intellectuals formed in 1950 whose CIA backing had recently been reported, Lasch saw the familiar themes of intellectuals guarding their interests as a newfound class and, in so doing, growing cozy with the state. "In all of this," Lasch wrote, "the cold-war intellectuals revealed themselves as the servants of bureaucratic power."[72]

Noam Chomsky had drawn similar conclusions months earlier. He saw widespread support for American policy "among intellectuals who have already achieved power and affluence, or who sense that they can achieve them by 'accepting society' as it is and promoting the values that are 'being honored' in this society." This consensus was "most noticeable among the scholar-experts who are replacing the free-floating intellectuals of the past." Both Chomsky and Lasch saw any esteem, power, and privilege that intellectuals enjoyed not as the hard-won fruits of their confrontation with a society hostile to freedom of thought and speech but, rather, as the result of their almost total concession to that society. "The university is free,"

Lasch wrote, "but it has purged itself of ideas. The literary intellectuals are free, but they use their freedom to propagandize for the state."[73]

Intellectuals had become respectable to the extent that they had become tame, and they confused respectability with influence. Both Chomsky and Lasch believed that intellectuals had forsaken, not gained, influence by drawing closer to state power. Intellectuals' skills served the agenda of powerful actors rather than determining it. Moreover, they legitimated the policies of the state by lending them the moral credibility and technical authority associated with intellectuals. That is why Lasch had urged intellectuals to withdraw their "fund of moral and intellectual power."[74]

By the close of 1967, Chomsky and Lasch had done much to ignite and shape discussion on the political and moral responsibilities of intellectuals. More accurately, they had focused almost entirely on the irresponsibility of intellectuals. Their writing offered detailed, scathing indictments of policy intellectuals and, in Lasch's case, revolutionaries. They deplored the idea of the intellectual as expert, exposed the values behind "value-free" analysis, and drew attention to the delimited character of policy debate. Though they did each outline a normative role for intellectuals, their criticisms— relentless, researched, almost encyclopedic—far surpassed the few lines they devoted to the way forward.

On the cusp of 1968—and the sense of crisis that the Tet Offensive, political assassinations, street demonstrations, and a tumultuous presidential election would bring—Lasch found that events and the logic of his own position were calling him to action. Could he model in his own work the kind of contributions he was calling intellectuals to make? Could he become a counterexample to the dereliction he did so much to expose? As he wrestled with these questions, Lasch heard the voices of others asking him to act.

* * *

"If you could see your way clear to being our candidate," wrote Isabel Condit, chair of the Thirteenth Congressional District Politics for Peace group in Morton Grove, Illinois, "there's no question in my mind that . . . it would be a marvelous thing for our district."[75] Lasch had moved to Evanston in 1966 for a job at Northwestern. Had he run in Illinois's Thirteenth Congressional District in 1968, he would have faced the young Republican incumbent Donald Rumsfeld.[76] Lasch told his parents that he felt "sort of bad about declining, knowing how desperate they must be if they're considering me, but I don't really believe in campaigns of this kind as a long-range strategy and I'm not willing to make such sacrifices for a policy I have so many doubts about, even though I can see that independent campaigns may have some short-range educative effects." That had been H. Stuart Hughes's hope six years earlier. "Instead," Lasch was "trying to finish another essay, this one on the New Left and other current matters. Knopf has agreed to publish it and three others as a book. That will have to be my contribution for the moment."[77]

Hughes had run for Congress *and* published a book with contemporary political relevance in 1962; Lasch chose only the latter in 1968. *The Agony of the American Left* came out in 1969, and it reprinted many of Lasch's recent essays. Just as he had taken intellectuals to task in *The New Radicalism* for their failure to practice social criticism while eschewing both the seduction of power and the romance of alienation, Lasch indicted New Left intellectuals in *Agony* for "the substitution of revolutionary rhetoric for programs that speak to people's needs."[78]

As the *Harvard Crimson*'s reviewer put it, "Lasch makes no apologies for his emphasis on the importance of intellectuals in producing social change. He sees intellectuals as essential catalysts in the restructuring of societies, and believes that the history of major periods in American history is in large measure the history of its intellectual elite." Indeed, "the elitist bent of Lasch's argument" was "apparent." That approach was "not . . . very fashionable . . . for an American leftist today. The Movement is characterized by anti-intellectualism; the cult of direct action . . . leaves little legitimacy among radicals for intellectual concerns." Moreover, an "activist proves his worth by 'doing' rather than by 'talking.' Such theory as will be needed, the argument goes, can be developed as the Movement progresses: a program can work itself out."[79]

Reflecting on the history of radicalism in his postscript to *Agony*, Lasch claimed that "struggle itself leads only to more struggle." A vision—social theory—must guide struggle, but in America, "a society for which no kind of precedent exists, the problems of which, accordingly, are almost entirely novel, a theory of social change can develop only if radicals—particularly radical intellectuals—cultivate it systematically." The *Crimson* reviewer agreed: "The most pressing task is to develop a coherent program for social change, based on actual American experience and conditions." It was time for intellectuals to create strategies that addressed the challenges and opportunities attending the American Left.[80]

This position pitted Lasch against those on the left who, like his old friend Staughton Lynd, argued for the primacy of direct political action. The New Left "rebelled precisely against Old Left parties which began by formulating 'analysis, plans, program, theory,'" Lynd noted. "Our alternative style of work has been for individuals to engage themselves in specific direct actions which influenced others by example." In response, Lasch said that "Lynd confuses tactics with strategy, forgetting that neither the tactics of nonviolent confrontation nor any other tactics can be effective except as part of a general strategy for social change." Lasch called for the formation of a new party, because "only a party can unite diverse types of protest and give them a common purpose, develop an ideology and a program, and engage people not simply as demonstrators but, for instance, as intellectuals, thereby making it possible for people to commit not only their bodies but their brains and talents to radical action." Lasch was beginning to outline the tangible political role that intellectuals could play.[81]

Scholars and non-scholars alike would respond to his call. David Marr of Bradley University told Lasch that "critics like you . . . give us all hope for a politics of reason and, by extension, a humane social order in this country. . . . If, as you have argued for so many months and even years, American intellectuals would just do their job—provide the very best social analysis—then and only then will a politics committed to radical principles arise to meet American needs commensurate with American conditions." Ed Trory wrote Lasch that "your voice and a few others are making others think and the small spark must ignite other[s]." Robert Brustein wrote Lasch that he made "a very strong case . . . for our desperate need for new political ideas; now I hope you will think them. Nobody seems better qualified." Tom Blandy echoed this sentiment: "I devoutly hope you get your political ventures going. You make more sense than anyone else I have read." B. Hal Eskesen was "troubled, however, by the absence" in Lasch's work "of prescriptive ideas for application of what are brilliant descriptions of our predicament"—the proposal for a new party evidently seemed too amorphous to him.[82]

In early 1969, J. T. Gault of Skokie, Illinois, wrote to Lasch expressing his desire for a new socialist movement. He closed by saying, "I know that you can become a leader in such a movement. I urge you to do so."

In another letter, David Jones offered what he called "a one-man, grass-roots, proletarian expression of cordial gratitude" for a Lasch essay in the *New York Review*. "My pulse rose with each of your sentences stating what Democratic Socialists have to do to be effective, no kidding. . . . We need to break off inertia and we need a stirring manifesto." He urged Lasch and other radical intellectuals to "get together and get into it." Peter Israel expressed frustration with those same intellectuals' squabbling. "I feel like knocking your heads" and "saying: Look, the ones who need weeding out (or educating) are the one-issue people who can't make the connections, they're the ones who need you, stop bickering or they'll be long gone. . . . Stop talking to yourselves, organize!"[83]

Activist Paul Lauter was doing just that, and he invited Lasch—along with Harvard historian Gar Alperovitz, Chomsky, and others—to formulate a "Working party paper (Why Johnny drops bombs and what you can do about it)." Lauter envisioned a pamphlet containing the group's analysis of American policy and "some general strategies for the movement, particularly with respect to the problems of militarism and its control." Alperovitz had invited Lasch to Harvard to discuss "how radical organizing efforts in the here and now may be related functionally (as experiments and prototypes) to the longer term evolution of a specific set of political objectives." The invitation was a welcome one. "I'm working directly on the kinds of questions you raise," Lasch replied, "but I don't seem to be making much progress; partly because I'm working in isolation." The lone social critic was ready to become part of a team, and that team had ambitions of redirecting what many were simply calling by the summer of 1968 "the movement."[84]

Before the Lauter group could gain momentum, however, Lasch's attention turned to another circle forming around Marxist scholar Eugene Genovese and *Studies on the Left* editor James Weinstein, which was meeting in Chicago to formulate "a statement calling for a new socialist party."[85] It "seems to me an urgent necessity," Lasch wrote Alperovitz, "that the few of us who seem to be thinking along the same lines try as hard as we can to get ourselves together in one place." Lasch reflected on the demands of the moment: "While I am unsure of what action to take, I do find my isolation out here increasingly dispiriting, and apart from these personal considerations there is the larger question of whether we can work very effectively scattered around the country."[86]

For Lasch, the "larger questions" were increasingly those raised by the political climate. "It is no longer a question with me as to whether to sac-rifice a certain portion of my scholarly work to other work," he wrote. "As a matter of fact I have been doing that for some time now . . . and the question is what practical arrangements to make so that I can devote myself more effectively to political work."[87] At the urging of readers and admirers like J. T. Gault, Isabel Condit, and David Jones; after the exhor-tation of "tremendous[ly] impatien[t]" radicals like Peter Israel; and, finally, in response to the invitation of sympathetic intellectuals like Alperovitz, Lasch had determined to move from prophecy to political intervention.[88] For a critic who had so often placed the blame for lost political oppor-tunities on "the failure of intellectuals" to show "a capacity for critical thought," here was a determined attempt not to do the same.[89] "The next few years are going to be rough," he told Genovese in late 1968, "but if we can survive them we'll have achieved something very valuable."[90]

Much of what was rough for him in those years, it turned out, came from the problems confronting a group of scholars trying to hammer out a single position, let alone a single document. As a social critic writing books and essays, Lasch had been able to formulate his thinking independently. Crit-icism need not be a group undertaking, but political work is inherently so. Joining the Weinstein group's work of drafting "pre-party papers," Lasch encountered the messiness of collaborative action. Though he found flaws in the group's draft—"the document is the product of group-think and shows most of the weaknesses associated with group-think"—Lasch did not lose interest in the larger enterprise: "The statement is certainly disap-pointing, and falls short of what I had hoped would emerge out of a series of discussions and earlier drafts. But that makes it all the more important to try to understand where its weaknesses and failures lie."[91]

It remained to be seen how Lasch would square the imperatives of intel-lectual life with those of doing programmatic political work among a team of radicals. He sought resolution in swapping the team for a duo. Geno-vese shared Lasch's criticism of the New Left, and the two formed what looked to be a serviceable partnership. They were offered a contract by Harold Strauss of Knopf for a manuscript entitled "Beyond the New Left." Genovese and Lasch aimed to press forward with the salvageable ideas emerging from the Weinstein group, formulating the "preface to a social-ist program that must evolve slowly through the collective efforts of men and women."[92]

Their early drafts spared nothing in indicting the New Left for its "evils," which included "self-defeating violence" and "adolescent assaults on national sensibilities."[93] "I don't regret our decision to burn certain bridges to the left," Lasch told Genovese. "In this sense I feel better than I have for a long time."[94] The two sought to lay the theoretical foundations "for a new course—for a third road between a discredited social democratic reformism and a quixotic Leninism." Addressing themselves "directly to those much-abused people over thirty," they offered their analysis "in the hope that it can serve as a basis for fruitful discussion among those who would build a new socialist movement in America."[95]

But how should intellectuals relate to such political movements? As Lasch increasingly engaged in political work, he struggled with this question. If in 1965 he explained that intellectuals should not withdraw into "monasteries of the mind," in 1969 he explained why they should not become street-level leaders of revolutionary groups either.[96] Between these two poles, however, stretched a poorly charted middle ground. How could intellectuals take part in social movements without undermining the democratic character of those movements? Lasch castigated the anti-democratic reliance on experts that he found characteristic of Cold War America, but how could intellectuals play a role in social movements other than by setting themselves up as expert advisers to them? As Lasch correspondent and Ohio State political theorist David Kettler put it: "The question is not simply about the place of theory and reason in the doctrine and utterances of the radical movement . . . it is also about the place of intellectuals and their institutions within the structure of whatever political movements unfold and in their visions of the future."[97]

Whatever else their role in radical politics, Kettler argued, intellectuals must "fight for the distinction between theory and ideology." Letting it go would empower "those who defend contentions about the way the world is and what it means on the grounds that such contentions make them feel good or make the bastards feel bad"—thus abandoning rational discourse.[98] Lasch, Kettler, and Chomsky were all committed to maintaining such discourse; for Lasch and Kettler, it was essential to the critical enterprise; for Chomsky, in particular, it was also democratic.[99] Yet Lasch and Chomsky had also claimed that some modes of reasoning—appeals to "realism" or to rationality defined as expert judgment—in fact functioned as an ideology underwriting disastrous American policies. For many on the New Left, rationality was not the antidote to repressive ideology—it was complicit in it. As Lasch and others struggled to formulate a program for the Left in rationalist terms, they had to fight a two-front battle: First, they wrestled with the elusive quality of such a program; second, they had to justify their rationalist approach to that endeavor.

Lasch was in a position relative to the New Left akin to that of Schlesinger relative to the hawkish, "hard-boiled" elements of the Kennedy administration in the run-up to the Bay of Pigs. Schlesinger had done much before 1961 to advance the standing of the tough-minded over the tender. When he found himself in opposition to the tough-minded call for moving forward with the Cuban landings, he faced a wolf that he had fed. When Lasch decried how "much of the New Left is resolutely anti-intellectual," he, too, was facing a creature of his own making. If his work had not been anti-intellectual in the strict sense—Hofstadter's concept of a contempt for the life of the mind—it had nonetheless been anti-*intellectuals*. If many in the New Left discarded the trappings of intellectualism, they were rejecting the style and methods of the policy intellectuals that Lasch depicted as so worthy of rejection. If they failed to replace bankrupt intellectuals and blinkered thinking with a more thoroughgoing form of rational social criticism, perhaps it was because influential writers like Lasch had done more to demonstrate how bad intellectuals were than how necessary a renewed intellectualism was.[100]

At the very least, Lasch's work had called into question the authority that policy analysts and experts invoked. When intellectuals like Lasch, Genovese, and Kettler turned to the social and political movements gaining momentum around them, however, they faced the challenge of contributing to these movements without relying on the same forms of authority that they had questioned.

Ellen Willis's New York feminist group, soon to name itself Redstockings, was confronting expertise at this moment too—not by overturning the concept but, rather, by changing the relationship between expertise and its objects. "The state is holding another of its 'expert' hearings on abortion reform," she wrote in February 1969, "in which (mostly male) doctors, lawyers, politicians and clergymen go before an all-male legislative committee to decide whether in certain special circumstances the government should stop forcing women to have babies." Willis and others protested the hearing, challenging "these phony experts [who] have no right to control our bodies and our lives." They "demand[ed] that the forum be turned over to women, the only experts on abortion." Following this protest, the Redstockings arranged their own hearing on abortion at which the authority of expert testimony was rooted in lived experience. The expert witnesses "will not talk theory," Willis wrote. "They will talk about themselves."[101]

African American women intellectuals were drawing similar conclusions. When experts are men, Toni Cade Bambara wrote in *The Black Woman* (1970), their "images of the woman are . . . derived from their needs, their fantasies, their secondhand knowledge, their agreement with other 'experts.'" Bambara further questioned whether emerging white women scholars' "priorities" or "concerns and methods are the same" as African American women's, "or even similar enough so that we can afford to depend on this new field of experts (white, female)." African American women had, therefore, to develop their own self-knowledge, and they were doing so, Bambara reported, in cooperative settings outside the academy. These included "work-study groups, discussion clubs, cooperative nurseries, cooperative businesses." In *The Black Woman*, Bambara gathered a sampling of thought and writing from this world of conversations, organizations, and analyses. The contributors included professional writers and those who "never before put pen to paper with publication in mind." They were mothers, students, and both at once. "All are alive, are Black, are women. And that," Bambara concluded, "is credentials enough to address themselves to issues that seem to be relevant to the sisterhood."[102] Pushing back against flawed expert analyses, African American and other women were the producers, not objects of knowledge, approaching it not only as the result of detached contemplation, but through the work of cooperative consideration of their own experiences.

While Willis, Bambara, and other feminist intellectuals undertook democratizing renovations of expertise, Lasch and Kettler sought alternatives to it. Kettler argued that "what is required in radical theory and practice is an adequate conception of the politics of counsel." For Kettler, the role "of a counselor is by no means identical with that of the 'expert,' who presumably makes available instrumental knowledge which can effectively implement any value specified by his principal." Nor was the counselor a veiled "way of presenting the Mandarin or the Platonic philosopher-king." It was, instead, "closely related to the role of teacher." Such counsel was something "we encounter in our practice but whose explication has been relegated to literature, largely because it presupposes the possibility of 'wisdom.'" Kettler enumerated the "norms defining counselors to the radical democratic movement":

1. The theorist gives advice, not commands.
2. The content of his advice will likely be an assessment of what has been done, an interpretive statement of where things stand, and then some projection of what is to be done.
3. The form of his advice will be reasoned argument and explication.
4. The occasion and forum of his advice will be appropriate to his relationship to the political movement: it is not proper to say all things in all places and at all times.

Not only did Kettler contrast counsel with expertise, but he also distinguished it from leadership. "Political leadership will always distrust demanding counselors and prefer the more convenient ones," he noted. "Given the temptations of Platonism"—the ambition of counselors to become philosopher kings—"political leadership should be suspicious; given the temptations of excessive accommodation to power (even 'our own'), intellectuals ought not be too cozy."[103] Lasch told Kettler that his work was "one of the best essays on the subject I have ever read" and that "the idea of 'counsel' seems most helpful."[104]

In "Beyond the New Left," Lasch and Genovese tried to provide something akin to Kettler's second norm of counsel: "an assessment of what has been done, an interpretive statement of where things stand, and then some projection of what is to be done." Their proposals rejected both the revolutionary rhetoric of the New Left and the patchwork approach of the Democratic Party. The latter's "traditional reforms [only] serve to rationalize the existing system and to enable it to function more efficiently," while immediate revolution threatened both a descent into chaos and a reaction that could end in American fascism. Their alternative was something they called—following Austro-French social theorist André Gorz—"structural reform." Such "reform 'is . . . implemented or controlled by those who demand it.' It leads to decentralization of decision-making, an infringement of corporate or state power, and the growth of new centers of democratic power." Concrete control of decisions affecting their lives would be in the hands of workers, wrested from the grip of economic elites. Steps toward this change would "dramatize the social consequences of corporate power which masks itself as 'economic' decision-making and . . . involve the working class in political action (not in the usual sense of the passive consumption of pre-packaged political candidates)."[105]

Genovese and Lasch offered a program for achieving structural reform

---

that advanced along three axes: a new political coalition, a new unionism, and changes at all levels of education. The coalition would be "[a] new party recruited from various sections of the Left and Center," including "those engaged in responsible manual, technical, and intellectual labor."[106] It would exclude those of the New Left whom Lasch and Genovese invidiously characterized as romantic revolutionaries likely to alienate more moderate people.

A critical piece of the coalition would be "a new kind of unionism in the industrial working class." The New Left had been wrong, they argued, to focus on the revolutionary potential of students or the *lumpenproletariat*. In Lasch and Genovese's view, the industrial workers traditionally at the heart of organized labor were still the key to structural change, but "the existing state of working-class consciousness, embodied in the unions, is so narrowly interest-oriented" as to ignore broader questions of the distribution of power and its implications for democracy.[107] Unions must become vehicles not simply for collective bargaining but for transformation of the entire society.

To bring about this shift, fundamental changes in education were necessary. The school system functioned merely to replicate the status quo, "train[ing] people for consumption and work" and producing "a passive, ignorant, and demoralized labor force." Community control of schools—often mistaken, Genovese and Lasch contended, for an end in itself—could be a valuable tool in "the broader fight to humanize technical and scientific education as a central prerequisite of the cultural and political self-emancipation of the working class."[108]

Movement building called for writing and thinking of a different kind than Lasch had been used to as a social critic. "One thing we have not succeeded in doing," he wrote Kettler, "is in bringing about an accommodation between the socialist mode of discourse and the one to which we're accustomed."[109] Lasch struggled to find the appropriate tone: "Parts sound too manifesto-like, almost official. This is understandable when you consider that we were starting, in effect, from a manifesto (the old Weinstein statement), but the tone is nonetheless deplorable." Lasch lamented the "too free . . . use of terms like ruling class, working class, etc.," so why did he go along with it? Perhaps he found the Marxist lexicon necessary for movement building even though the critic within him sensed that it weakened the document. Lasch also wrestled with the content appropriate to programmatic work. "Most of the book is too abstract in quality and needs much more concrete illustration and even demonstration," he confessed to Kettler.[110]

Though their project foundered, Genovese wanted Lasch to join him at the University of Rochester, where they could begin a journal to carry forward the work outlined in the manuscript. Lasch did move to Rochester, but he was becoming wary. He had received highly "critical reactions" from those to whom he had sent the manuscript. Backing away from the idea that their work could become "a public rallying-point for a new political movement," Lasch was returning, he told Genovese, to "what we said in our books, that intellectuals cannot organize political movements, that their job is to clarify issues, and that unless we can clarify them somewhat more than we seem to have done in this book we will have failed in our own self-imposed task." Readers' responses, Lasch reported, "clearly indicate that the book needs to be rewritten."[111] It would ultimately be neither rewritten nor published.

If the manuscript for "Beyond the New Left" marked the crest of Lasch's attempts to formulate a radical political strategy, its failure signaled the beginning of his withdrawal from such work. "The only form of political action that seems to make much sense right now, for people in our position," he told Genovese, "is a holding action in the university. I mean a movement of faculty to reassert academic standards in the face of all kinds of demands for their abandonment."[112] Genovese's efforts, as the newly minted chair of the history department, to bring Lasch and other like-minded scholars to the University of Rochester, where he aimed to start a new journal, appeared to hold out that hope.

But even this less ambitious form of intervention seemed to recede as Genovese made what Lasch considered increasingly disturbing moves. At the American Historical Association conference in December 1969, Genovese, over Lasch's objections, attacked Staughton Lynd's candidacy for the association's presidency. This episode built on Lasch's frustrations from the preceding summer when, he reminded Genovese, "you wanted to rush out to Chicago with bodyguards and put down SDS 'once and for all.'" Lasch reminded Genovese that their political strategy, rooted in a belief in rational, critical discourse, "requires qualities of tact and discretion and good judgment that I am bound to say are the opposite of what came out so strongly at Washington."[113] Lasch feared that Genovese was engaging in the sort of conduct that had soured Lasch on the New Left and aligned him with Genovese in the first place. No one, it seemed to Lasch—not Lynd, not the Weinstein group, and now not Genovese—could join a commitment to level-headed criticism with political intervention in the way that Lasch, wrestling with Benjamin Ginzburg's constraints, was trying to do.

In the early spring of 1970, Lasch looked back. "Surveying the wreckage of the sixties," he told his parents, "one is amazed at how little has been accomplished"—a conclusion with which other observers of the decade, right and left, would disagree. Just as he could have written in the pages of *The New Radicalism* in 1965, the *New York Review of Books* in 1967 or 1968, and "Beyond the New Left" in 1969, he told his parents: "I don't see any hope at all unless people who want change get down to some serious, patient thought." He had been such a person; he had applied himself to such thought, "and nothing has changed." "In my own case," he wrote, "the occasion seems to call for an abandonment of political writing and an effort to get down to fundamentals, and I hope to provide myself with an interval of study and reflection undistracted by political alarums and excursions. I think others would be wise to do the same."[114]

As part of his taking stock, Lasch reached out to his old teacher Richard Hofstadter, writing to him about his efforts at Rochester to uphold the academic standards they shared. This work appeared "both more plausible generally and better suited to our own abilities than a number of other projects, all abortive, that I've been involved with during the last couple of years—new political parties (which turned out to consist of about fifteen people, none of whom could agree on anything), a proposed journal that would be purely political (and would immediately rally the whole country behind it), and others of a similarly fantastic nature."[115]

The letter returned to Lasch unopened. On its top he scribbled: "probably received in the hospital by Saturday, the day of Hofstadter's death." Among handwritten notes that may have served as the basis for his 1973 introduction to Hofstadter's *American Political Tradition*, Lasch recorded posthumous praise for its author: "He was extremely suspicious of big theories," which was "infuriating to those who . . . spent much of the 60s ransacking 19th-c European social theory. He relied on cool common sense."[116] As he reflected on his "fantastic" but "abortive" projects of the last several years, Lasch may have concluded that he was among those caught up in "big theories" rather than maintaining the "cool common sense" appropriate to, as Ginzburg or Hofstadter might remind him, "the intellectual life."

* * *

In 1965 Lasch had reported Ginzburg's view that "instead of trying to save culture through politics . . . intellectuals should first reform culture itself, over which, in any case, they had more power than they had over politics."[117] After years of work on no less a political project than the formation of a new party and a blueprint for the Left, Lasch returned in the 1970s to the kind of work he had been doing before—writing history as social criticism.

To be sure, Lasch had other brushes with practical politics. His work with the journals *Marxist Perspectives* and *democracy* represented the continuation of his ambition for a journal that had contemporary political heft. Most famously, Lasch was called to the White House in 1979 to meet with President Jimmy Carter on the basis of having diagnosed what he called "the culture of narcissism" in his surprising hit book of the same name. The gathering, however, did not result in any substantial exchange.[118] These ventures, in short, were not the kind of programmatic political work that Lasch had engaged in during the late 1960s, culminating in "Beyond the New Left." Lasch would offer social criticism, but he would never again work as counselor to a movement—inchoate or otherwise.[119]

As the 1970s opened, Lasch pursued "a partial retirement . . . from public distractions."[120] He had gone from a being a detached social critic, to being a frustrated would-be counselor to social and political movements, to being a social critic once again, though ultimately a "connected" one rooted in American populism.[121] At the outset, Lasch had criticized intellectuals whose work compromised their critical vantage point while vigorously—if unconvincingly—claiming that he did not wish intellectuals to stay out of politics. When the time came for his own entry into programmatic political work, he could find neither his way nor—tellingly for a writer recognized for his literary and trenchant style—his voice.

Lasch returned from these ventures to writing books that sparked fierce debate about the state of American culture. Social criticism was both the vantage point and the mode of work that he came to inhabit; it was the role of the intellectual. The effects of criticism can be constructive, but criticism itself is not construction. When Lasch undertook to go "beyond the New Left," he was moving from criticism to construction. He was building an edifice rather than pointing to the structural flaws or plastered-over cracks in one. Yet even in his attempts to be constructive, he quickly reverted to criticism. When he gave counsel, advice, and guidance to the Left, it repeatedly took the form: you are lacking counsel, advice, and guidance. He was pointing to an absence rather than filling it in.

While Lasch was backing away from political action, other intellectuals were heading toward it. These were neoconservatives like Irving Kristol, who were moving from being critics to counselors. As the high tide of the New Left receded and the wave of the Reagan Revolution began to build, intellectuals like Kristol were increasingly finding that they had ever more corporate leaders, aspiring politicians, and elected officials eager to receive their advice.

THE INTELLECTUAL
AGAINST INTELLECTUALS

At New York University in 1970, Irving Kristol's "Colloquium on the Urban Intellectual" examined "the problematic relations . . . between philosophers, theologians, artists, scientists, etc. and their political communities," targeting "the role of intellectuals in sustaining or subverting Western civilization."[1] Much had changed since Richard Hofstadter anxiously watched Adlai Stevenson confront anti-intellectualism at the ballot box. Intellectuals were then threatened, Hofstadter believed, by well-nigh innate popular animus. Now, Kristol reversed that dynamic. No longer were intellectuals besieged by the people but the people by intellectuals. A New Class associated with media, government, nonprofits, and universities was gaining unprecedented influence in a post-industrial society where knowledge was becoming capital.[2] From powerful positions in the state, the culture, and the information economy, these intellectuals could subject Americans to increased regulation and even ideological conversion. They could transform the nation's politics and culture, "subverting" its civilization.

Hofstadter had viewed Joseph McCarthy and his adherents as radicals. For Kristol, the New Class was the vehicle of radicalism. Whereas Hofstadter saw the populist Right threatening the values underlying intellectual life, Kristol identified the "adversary culture" of the New Class as a threat to the sturdy virtues of Middle America. Both saw the bearers of time-tested ideals facing a powerful insurgent force.

Just as Hofstadter joined the fray in the 1950s, so did Kristol in the 1970s (not that he avoided battles before). Both deployed the dialectical and rhetorical tools at their disposal to steady their ranks and frame devastating attacks on the enemy. Hofstadter became a spokesman for intellect and scourge of "pseudo-conservatives"; Kristol became a champion of "the people"—or those Richard Nixon called in 1969 the "silent majority"—and adversary of the adversary culture.

Kristol contested the New Class on multiple fronts. One was "the war of ideas . . . now taking place," he wrote in 1976, "about the role of the individual, the corporation, and government in a democratic society." As the *Denver Post* put it: "America is engaged in a war of ideas which will shape the future of society, but the nation's businessman isn't taking it seriously."[3] Kristol and his allies were "taking ideas seriously" and urging others, especially businesspeople challenged by the New Class, to do so, for, as conservative intellectuals were fond of pointing out, "ideas have consequences."[4] "The political ideas that men have *always* help to shape the political reality they live in," Kristol wrote, "whether these be habitual opinions, tacit convictions or explicit ideologies." That ideas had consequences was overdetermined for Kristol, an inheritance both from his Marxist origins (as a Trotskyist at City College) and later affiliation with conservatives. These strands joined in Kristol's neoconservatism; and "if the rise of neoconservatism in our day means anything at all," journalist Peter Steinfels wrote, "it is this: Ideas matter, even in America, where we often don't take intellectuals very seriously."[5]

Ideas mattered, but so did power. Schooled in Marxist materialism, Kristol was no outright idealist. He waged a war of ideas but may have asked: "How many divisions do the intellectuals have?" Kristol sought tangible alliances between his ideas, corporate America, and the Republican Party. V. I. Lenin had described three political actors: bourgeoisie, proletariat, and vanguard. Kristol mapped them onto the 1970s United States. The New Class, occupying post-industrial society's seats of power in the information sectors, were the bourgeoisie. Businesspeople, ironically, were now among the proletariat. They and working-class Americans were a potential majority, but both groups lacked the political consciousness to see that they were locked in a war of ideas with the New Class, let alone to perceive that they were losing that war. Kristol and conservative intellectuals were a new vanguard—raising business's political consciousness and supplying it with the strategies necessary for toppling the New Class.

If corporate America needed intellectuals, what did intellectuals need from it? Confronting the New Class required resources: a "counterestablishment" of think tanks, journals, and academic posts.[6] Kristol was at the center of this effort—a founder of *Public Interest* and the Institute for Educational Affairs. He fought the New Class on the intellectual plane and the solid ground of institution building.

Kristol aimed to check the New Class and to sustain the social order threatened by the modernity that spawned it. No society could "cope with the spiritual turbulence engendered by . . . modernity," he wrote. While he waged the "war of ideas" on political battlefields, Kristol's deeper effort addressed "the spiritual history of modern man."[7] Businesspeople may be allies in the political clash, but in the spiritual struggle, intellectuals stood alone. He evoked the Grand Inquisitor from Dostoevsky's *Brothers Kara-mazov*, which he assigned as a professor at NYU, who held a spiritual screen between the emptiness of the cosmos and the hearts and minds of ordinary people.[8] Such intellectuals prevented nihilism from damaging the social edifice, even though they knew it was an edifice absent foundations. The alternative was chaos.

"To evolve a set of values, insofar as it is at all susceptible to conscious effort, is a question not of expertise but of moral example and spiritual leadership," critic Josiah Lee Auspitz observed in 1973; "it is in this context that Kristol focuses on the American intellectual." The intellectual's "ability with general ideas . . . enables him to be a 'moral guide'" and "a 'writing cleric,' a leader of opinion, a shaper of ideals. Kristol's polemics against 'the intellectuals' and 'the intellectual class' should not obscure the fact that he believes their role to be crucial."[9] Auspitz captured the contradictory nature of Kristol's endeavors. Characterizing the New Class as intellectuals, Kristol railed against them. Between business and intellectuals, he sided with business. Yet Kristol was himself an intellectual—one who assigned a lofty, almost cosmically significant role to them. Was Kristol for intellectuals or against them?

That he was both points to the uncertain place of intellectuals in American political culture. Kristol pitted intellectuals as ethically authoritative individuals against intellectuals as a uniquely dangerous class. The New Class contested or called into question a range of assumptions—from the inevitability of economic inequality to the virtue of conventional morality—upholding the status quo. Alert to this "slow draining away of legitimacy from existing institutions and prevailing traditions," the individual intellectual fashioned a plug.[10] The intellectual class thus gave individual intellectuals their purpose: generating a crisis that they first detected and to which they best responded.

The New Class was, in one sense, the product of neoconservatism's polemical imagination. It may be more an idea than a social fact—but ideas have consequences. One consequence of the New Class idea is that it set Kristol to work. He elaborated and publicized New Class theory while responding to the situation it posited, building the network of publications, institutions, and people that earned him the title "Godfather of neoconservatism." Kristol opposed the intellectual class, which could be menacing, elitist, or hapless, but never heroic. That was the role of the singular intellectual, holding the thread of Western civilization as it threatened to snap.

* * *

Irving Kristol was born to a Brooklyn Jewish family in 1920. His father sought a secure foothold in the garment industry, and his mother died of cancer when Kristol was sixteen. The family was nominally orthodox but not particularly observant.[11]

At City College in 1936, Kristol entered the fabled "New York Intellectuals" story. There he encountered "people and ideas that prompted me to read and think and argue with a furious energy." The non-Stalinist Left in cafeteria Alcove No. 1 debated sectarian rivals in Alcove No. 2. Several from Alcove No. 1 became notable intellectuals: Kristol, Irving Howe, Daniel Bell, and Seymour Martin Lipset. Though the fires of debate burned brightly, they did not engulf the college. "Politics were a minority affair, and what the passive majority thought really did not matter," Kristol observed. "What 'happened' on campus was determined by . . . the denizens of Alcove No. 2 or us."[12]

After college, Kristol joined his wife, the subsequently eminent historian Gertrude Himmelfarb, in Chicago.[13] Drafted into the army, he fought with the Twelfth Armored Division, which liberated concentration camps as it drove into Germany. The war provided manifold evidence of inhumanity. In Kristol's "opinion, his fellow GI's were inclined to loot, rape and murder, and only Army discipline held them in check," journalist Barry Gewen wrote. "It was a perception about human nature that would stay with him for the rest of his life, creating a tension with his alternative view that ordinary people were to be trusted more than intellectuals to do the right thing."[14]

After the war, Kristol became an editor at *Commentary*. His essay "'Civil Liberties,' 1952—A Study in Confusion" dropped like a grenade into the politics of that year. Kristol's most inflammatory lines—"there is one thing that the American people know about Senator McCarthy: he, like them, is unequivocally anti-Communist. About the spokesmen for American liberalism, they feel they know no such thing. And with some justification"—overshadow other strands of his argument.[15]

Intellectuals who opposed McCarthyism were anxious for comfort, Kristol claimed, not liberty. "These 'intellectuals' of Hollywood and radio who are outraged at a Congressman's insistence that they say what they actually believe, and who wail that they are in danger of—being excluded from well-paying jobs! Is this the vibrant voice of 'nonconformity' and 'dissent'?" Kristol anticipated Lasch's claim that intellectuals constituted "a mature class jealous of its recognized position in the social order." Like Lasch, Chomsky, or Hughes, Kristol held that "the responsibility for the mind's freedom in a democracy lies with the intransigent thinker, with his courage to shout the truth in the face of the mob, with his faith that truth will win out, and with his maddening commitment to the truth, win or lose." Citing William James's "mournful conviction that 'the prevalent fear of poverty among our educated classes is the worst moral disease from which our civilization suffers,'" Kristol questioned intellectuals' commitment to truth.[16]

He distinguished intellectuals as a group from individual intellectuals. The "spokesmen for American liberalism," "'intellectuals' of Hollywood and radio," and "'educated classes'" figured in stark contrast to "the intransigent thinker, with his courage to shout the truth."[17] Before Kristol thought explicitly of the New Class, he had already begun to think, like Lasch, in terms of intellectuals as a class, and he had already begun to agitate against them.

In 1953 Kristol helped found the journal *Encounter*, publishing writers from the United States and Europe outside the Iron Curtain. Displays of Western intellectual unity pleased *Encounter*'s sponsoring organization, the Congress for Cultural Freedom (CCF); they also pleased the CIA. When in 1967 the public became widely aware that the CCF had received CIA funds that were then used to support *Encounter*, critics descended upon Kristol, who had left the periodical in 1958.[18] "Had I known what has since been revealed," he later wrote, "I would not have taken the job."[19]

Lasch become one of *Encounter*'s fiercest critics. "For a group of intellectuals who prided themselves on their realism, skepticism, and detachment," he wrote, "the editors of *Encounter* and their contributors showed an unshakable faith in the good intentions of the American government." In "'Civil Liberties,' 1952," Kristol had quipped that historian Henry Steele Commager's "critical faculties are less alert when he looks out of the left corner of his eye." Lasch found Kristol less alert when he looked out the western corner of his eye, as *Encounter* "consistently approved the broad lines and even the details of American policy." It did so, Lasch claimed, for reasons not purely intellectual.[20]

American intellectuals "had achieved both autonomy and affluence" by becoming "indispensable to society and to the state," as "the cold war seemed to demand that the United States compete with communism in the culture sphere as well as in every other."[21] Lasch suggested a tacit arrangement: intellectuals attained prestige and comfort; the state garnered cultural legitimacy in its global struggle for hearts and minds.

Kristol's 1968 "Memoirs of a 'Cold Warrior'" made light of the charge that "a mass *trahison des clercs* by the liberal anti-communist intellectuals" was "suitably rewarded with money, honors and privileges of all kinds." He quipped that "it was generally assumed by everyone (including, apparently, the CIA) that being an intellectual was not a way to make money." No member "of an intellectual class living high off the hog" or part of "the 'ruling elite,'" Kristol said he lived without luxuries and had "practically no influence at all outside the hermetic universe of New York literary politics." He joked that his "most intimate contact with . . . national power came when I was introduced to Arthur Schlesinger Jr., who . . . was reported to know some very important people within the Democratic Party." Kristol's real offense for critics, he claimed, was not being "chic at all." Unlike "the literary left and café society," he did not "think homosexuality is normal; I distrust drugs, and I don't find pornography all that readable."[22]

In 1952 Kristol accused intellectuals of caring more for perquisites than truth. Now on the receiving end of that charge, Kristol turned the tables. Even as he lampooned characterizations of CCF intellectuals as the "ruling elite," he accused the intellectual Left of elitism. He was "bewildered by a highbrow left-wing magazine which proudly advertises that it is 'cliquish' and 'snobbish.'"[23] An unapologetic "cold warrior" who stood for capitalism and democracy, Kristol drew lines placing him on the side of ordinary Americans and opposite intellectuals. The seeds of his assault on the New Class were planted early.

"'Civil Liberties'" was not the only early writing to anticipate Kristol's later work. Reviewing Leo Strauss's *Persecution and the Art of Writing*, which told of premodern philosophers veiling ultimate truth from the public, Kristol wrote: "Popular opinions had to be accepted in order that the unenlightened might be slowly moved toward an approximation of the truth, in the measure that they could tolerate it."[24] Philosophers admitted a modicum of truth's rays while blocking its stronger beams, which might cause cancer on the body politic.

Philosophical truth seems an odd threat to social order. As Kristol explained it, Strauss believed "no civil order can be stable or enduring unless it is founded on a common assent to a revealed religion; for society needs a code of morality, and reason (that is, philosophy) cannot provide any such specific code." If the Enlightenment had aimed to refound society on a rational basis, Strauss suggested that rationality could provide no basis at all. Philosophers nevertheless persisted as moral beings beyond religion while morality for others *relied* upon it. As Kristol put it, Strauss "assumes the superiority of the contemplative life," believing "that most men are not capable of ascending from the cave of the commonplace to the sunlight of the *vita contemplativa*."[25] Philosophers were a breed apart.

Three years earlier, in 1949, Kristol had walked a Freudian path to Straussian conclusions. There were "few men, very few, who are willing to look at life" as Freud did: "a bleak prelude to death" with "civilization as an enormous distraction from self-extinction." These few "submit to the truths of Reason, because in them Reason is the master of the instincts. . . . But in the great mass of men it is the opposite: Reason is the toy of instinct and happiness and untruth is preferred to truth." Religion veiled the awful truth, creating a separation between "philosophers and the common men" that required the former's "atheism [to] become[] a guarded, esoteric doctrine—for if the illusions of religion were to be discredited, there is no telling with what madness men would be seized." It was therefore "the duty of the wise publicly to defend and support religion, even to call the police power to its aid, while reserving the truth for themselves and their chosen disciples."[26]

This schema separates philosophers from the crowd, but among philosophers there is a further division. Some uphold social order while others court danger—by philosophizing in public. Each may pejoratively label the other "elite." The public philosophers challenge tradition. By contrast, those veiling philosophy may claim to be respecting it; far from being an "elite," they uphold common beliefs. These same philosophers, however, are an elite insofar as they are anti-democratic. As Kristol put it, their conduct is "definitely opposed to democratic, or liberal, ideologies,"[27] which do not abide the indelible distinction between the philosophic few and the unthinking many, upon which the concealment of philosophy rests.

Indeed, philosophers publicly speaking truth could locate themselves on the popular side, opposed to an elite that misleads the people. While each philosophical faction may brand the other "elite" as an epithet, they may reserve it for themselves as an honorific. Those speaking truth are a vanguard, raising the consciousness of their fellows. Those concealing it are guardians, protecting the public from corrosive thought.

In 1952 Kristol suggested that "responsible political thinking" required turning "to sources more deep than the Enlightenment and its adoration of human innocence, its impatience with human limitation, its lust for redemption." For many conservatives, Strauss illuminated these sources. "The two contemporary thinkers who have most shaped my own thought, not necessarily in ways they would always approve of," Kristol wrote in 1972, "are Lionel Trilling and Leo Strauss."[28]

In New York after 1958, Kristol found an intellectual scene where Trilling loomed large. Kristol pitched *Public Interest* to him as a prospective contributor in 1963 and later invited him to jointly interview Hubert Humphrey, who was "unhappy at the way the intellectual community seems to be regarding him."[29] Trilling's *Beyond Culture* (1965) exerted significant influence on Kristol. It highlighted "the adversary intention, the actually subversive intention, that characterizes modern writing." Such literature aimed at "detaching the reader from the habits of thought and feeling that the larger culture imposes, of giving him a ground and a vantage point from which to judge and condemn, and perhaps to revise, the culture that produced him."[30] It prompted readers to think beyond their culture.

Those readers were growing in number. In the 1960s, "a great many more people . . . adopt the adversary program than" before, and it was now "possible to think of [them] as a class." A "class" constituted on the basis of its "adversary culture" shaped Kristol's understanding of the New Class. Trilling saw among them not only "common interests and presuppositions" but also "a considerable efficiency of organization, even of an institutional kind." This class was, therefore, "not without power, and . . . as we can say of any other class with a degree of power . . . it seeks to aggrandize and perpetuate itself."[31]

The adversary class gained power, Trilling wrote, at the expense "of its old antagonist, the middle class," from which "it has detached a considerable force" and "captivated its allegiance."[32] Combining this thinking with Strauss's suggests a tug-of-war for the soul of the middle class. As subversive philosophers—the adversary culture—pull more people to their side, the momentum becomes almost irresistible. Opposite them are guardian philosophers turned into activists by a new mission: no longer simply to uphold the social order by concealing philosophy, but to restore that order by combating philosophy. The "middle" class sits between not rich and poor but two bands of intellectuals, each trying to "captivate its allegiance."

Kristol considered intellectuals' role in the policymaking tug-of-war as well as the cultural one, with the Kennedy administration a baseline for his views. Conservatives "were . . . alarmed at the thought of a horde of liberal professors clustering around the centre of national power," he wrote in January 1962. "But their apprehensions were baseless," for the professors were consumed by "the sheer, routine exercise of this power."[33] Intellectuals gathered no praise, but their presence seemed harmless.

By November, however, having "been fortunate enough to acquire some friends in the business and financial community," Kristol "gained an appreciation of their problems" under the Kennedy administration. He learned of the "personal animus toward businessmen" at the Internal Revenue Service, fueled by resentful bureaucrats who "exercise power—direct, personal power—over those who are more successful." Similarly, housing programs were "administered with a routine stupidity by thousands of little men who, far from being able to cope with the housing problem, are swallowed up by it." Indeed, "the major intellectual problem facing the American polity in the decades to come might well be: How can we realize the potentialities of big government without surrendering ourselves and our goals to the mercies of little men?"[34] Government workers had devolved from harmless and overwhelmed to malicious and overwhelmed.

Intellect was not the answer. The Kennedy administration's "sophistication and wide-ranging thoughtfulness" made it "intellectually attractive" but "practically ineffectual," Kristol wrote. "In politics, intelligence and imagination are qualities to be desired, but it is a misfortune when they are not subordinated to a readiness to look reality in the face."[35] Kristol increasingly saw a sprawling state administered by "little men" and visionaries, a volatile blend of envy and ideas.

The academy was little better. "Not only are some of my best friends professors," Kristol quipped, "*most* of them are professors, and more are becoming so with each passing year." They were "gently sustained by a half-million dollar research grant from The National Institute for Mental Health, consulting fees, textbook royalties and other interesting perquisites." Their fields of study "retreat behind prickly barricades of technical expertise—technical knowledge, after all, is the most expensive knowledge, justifies the highest salaries and the largest research grants, is most impervious to outside meddling and inspection." This trend was ominous. "Professors are riding high these days. But unless they pause to take their bearings in the real world about them, they may well be riding for a fall," he wrote. "Unhappily, if and when such a fall occurs, all of us will be hurt. Anti-intellectualism is so indigenous in American life, and its appetite is so insatiable, that one is reluctant to see any victim fattening himself for the feast—no matter how much the victim may have provoked his fate."[36] Did Kristol foresee that when roast intellectuals were served a decade later, he would hold the carving knife?

Before Kristol would characterize academic, government, and other professionals as a dangerous New Class, his editorial instincts told him to publish for them. "There has clearly emerged in this country a class of sophisticated and educated readers," he and journalist Joseph Kraft wrote in a 1960 proposal for a new magazine. They were "the college and high-school teachers, the journalists, the civic-minded business executives, the social workers, the lawyers (some of them, anyway), the scientists (some of them too, anyway), the higher levels of the civil service." Having, "as never before, an identity," they were "a community—and, with the 'education bulge' still swelling, one that will grow."[37]

Kristol ultimately launched *Public Interest* with fellow City College alumnus Daniel Bell in 1965. It sought to "provide politicians with the latest insights of the intellectual community, while giving intellectuals an understanding of the process of government."[38] Kristol believed it would satisfy the "need for a post-ideological journal," a concept drawn from Bell's *The End of Ideology* (1960), which declared the "exhaustion of political ideas" such that "the radical intellectual who had articulated the revolutionary impulses of the past century and a half" now faced "an end to chiliastic hopes, to millenarianism, to apocalyptic thinking." Ideology gave way to "a rough consensus among intellectuals on political issues: the acceptance of a Welfare State; the desirability of decentralized power; a system of mixed economy and of political pluralism." Technical and managerial questions supplanted debate about ultimate ends. In his readership, Kristol saw a post-ideology cohort coming of age. "Among younger people," he wrote, "there are large numbers who are willing to think with a disinterested professionalism . . . and who will inherit the posts as economists, public administrators, civil servants, professors, etc. The professionalization of intellectual life in this country is a mixed blessing . . . but the blessing part can be too easily overlooked."[39]

Kristol was ambivalent about those he would soon condemn as the New Class. He worried about their "adversary culture" but could be sanguine about their technical prowess: the "professionalization of intellectual life" held promise. *Public Interest* proposed to survey policy without ideological blinkers, relying upon disinterestedness, empiricism, and analysis. What were these traits, if not the markers of the emerging New Class?

Kristol's unsettled thinking reflected ambiguity in the idea of the New Class itself. Was the rising professional, post-ideological cohort the New Class, or were those who participated in the adversary culture the New Class? Were these two groups one and the same? With such questions subject to a variety of answers, the New Class was, Bell later concluded, "a muddled concept."[40]

* * *

The New Class was also not new; its genealogy extended to the nineteenth century. In contrast to the idea that intellectuals espoused universal claims, New Class theorists investigated the extent to which intellectuals pursued interests of their own.[41] Lasch and Chomsky fit this tradition when they wrote about how the needs—psychic, economic, or otherwise—of intellectuals as a group determined the content of their thought and the conduct of their political involvement.

Russian anarchist Mikhail Bakunin used "new class" in the 1870s, warning that a state controlled by intellectuals would be as tyrannical as one ruled by any other group.[42] Highly trained administrators could consolidate power on the basis of expertise, making "the reign of scientific intelligence the most aristocratic, despotic, arrogant and elitist of all regimes." Bakunin predicted "a new class, a new hierarchy of real and counterfeit scientists and scholars," with society "divided into a minority ruling in the name of knowledge, and an immense ignorant majority. And then woe unto the mass of ignorant ones!"[43]

New Class thought in the United States addressed structural changes in capitalism.[44] Thorstein Veblen looked to engineers as a transformative new group.[45] Adolf Berle and Gardiner Means's *The Modern Corporation and Private Property* (1932) pointed to the rise of a corporate managerial class to a significant position of power. James Burnham built upon their work with *The Managerial Revolution* (1941), positing a "managerial society" in which industrial bureaucrats supplanted capitalists as the dominant class.[46]

Austrian-born Harvard economist Joseph Schumpeter despaired about the future of capitalism, which he saw succumbing to a socialism nourished by intellectuals. In *Capitalism, Socialism, and Democracy* (1942), Schumpeter, like Marx, found in capitalism the seeds of its own destruction, emphasizing their intellectual rather than material germination. "Capitalism creates a critical frame of mind which, after having destroyed the moral authority of so many other institutions, in the end turns against its own," he wrote. "The rationalist attitude does not stop at the credentials of kings and popes but goes on to attack private property and the whole scheme of bourgeois values." The danger of such rational criticism was that it was not ultimately rational. Behind it Schumpeter found frustrations and resentments, and while counterarguments "may tear the rational garb of attack," they could "never reach the extra-rational driving power that always lurks behind it." Worse still, "capitalist rationality does not do away with sub- or super-rational impulses. It merely makes them get out of hand by removing the restraint of sacred or semi-sacred tradition." The "utilitarian reason" that justified capitalism was no "match for the extra-rational determinants of conduct."[47]

Capitalism nurtured the critical mentality and those imbued with it. It "creates, educates, and subsidizes a vested interest in social unrest"—a growing class of intellectuals. Since free speech was a corollary of free markets, capitalism provided the "freedom to nibble at the foundations of capitalist society," and "the intellectual group cannot help nibbling, because it lives on criticism and its whole position depends on criticism that stings."[48] In capitalist society, intellectual termites had their ideal home.

Capitalism indulged intellectuals but fanned their discontent. Higher education produced more people "who wield the power of the spoken and the written word" than employment for them. Intellectuals' "hostility" thus intensified, "instead of diminishing, with every achievement of capitalist evolution." Their discontent influenced government. Though they "rarely enter professional politics and still more rarely conquer responsible office," intellectuals "write party pamphlets and speeches, [and] act as secretaries and advisers," stamping "their mentality on almost everything that is being done." They pushed policy changes that Schumpeter compared to surgeries upon the social body, hubristically acting "with information and technique so inadequate that . . . an observer of a later period" would find their measures, "even from a purely intellectual standpoint, inferior to the actions and anti-surgical propensities associated with attitudes that at the time most people felt inclined to attribute to a low I.Q."[49]

Intellectuals were also the blasting cap for the dynamite of the working class—"stimulating, energizing, verbalizing and organizing" the "hostile atmosphere which surrounds the capitalist engine." Their alliance with workers was unstable, however, for "having no genuine authority and feeling always in danger of being unceremoniously told to mind his own business, [the intellectual] must flatter, promise and incite, nurse left wings and scowling minorities, sponsor doubtful or submarginal cases, appeal to fringe ends, profess himself ready to obey."[50] The result was often extremism.

Three decades after *Capitalism, Socialism, and Democracy*, critics deemed Kristol's work "hardly more than an up-dating of Schumpeter's argument" with "no mention" of its influence. "Kristol's New Class echoes J.A. Schumpeter's speculations," wrote Robert Lekachman. William Wolman, *Business Week*'s chief economist, found "nothing new about Kristol's observation that capitalism, by its very success in raising standards of living . . . is breeding a new class of intellectuals that perceives that its self-interest lies in undermining the system." While "Schumpeter's book was marked by a generosity of spirit and grandeur of vision that impressed many intellectuals who did not share his love of capitalism's creative energy," Kristol's work was "an amalgam of innuendo and banality that could easily do damage to the capitalist cause."[51]

Kristol was one of several to reprise the idea of a new class after World War Two. New patterns of employment and education seemed to erode the simple binary of proletariat and bourgeoisie. C. Wright Mills's *White Collar* (1951), William H. Whyte's *The Organization Man* (1956), and John Kenneth Galbraith's *The Affluent Society* (1958) assessed the phenomenon. Postwar "affluent" society was manifest culturally as well as economically. The "embourgeoisement" of working-class Americans altered the style of homes they inhabited, cars they drove, and books they read. These changes accelerated as ever more students entered college.

Law professor David T. Bazelon characterized the New Class as the "educated masses." Lasch summarized this argument in his chilly review of Bazelon's *Power in America: The Politics of the New Class* (1967): "Whereas the feudal nobility ruled through 'aristocratic status and tenure' and the bourgeoisie through 'entrepreneurial use of property,' the new class relies on its all-important educational advantage, which in turn secures the organizational leverage—the tenured positions at critical points in bureau-cracies." As this group "becomes conscious of itself, it will make over the country in its own image—friendly, tolerant, noncompetitive." In *The New Radicalism*, Lasch had argued that intellectuals were already conscious of and acting upon their class interests. The results were not "friendly, toler-ant, and noncompetitive"; they were new techniques of social control and imperial domination.[52]

Lasch criticized the idea of social change organized from above, claim-ing that Bazelon viewed "radicalism based on or addressed to the dis-possessed [as] futile and irrelevant." Racial progress, for instance, would come not from the African American grassroots but "through the efforts of liberals—the 'forward-looking intellectual types' who represent the flower of the new class and the vanguard of social change." This approach overlooked "the protest of people who insist that they do not wish to be 'raised.'"[53] Lasch was trying to determine for himself what role, if not uplift engineered from above, intellectuals might play in the process of social change.

Galbraith's *The New Industrial State* (1967) grappled with the strange bedfellows of the New Class—technical experts and humanistic scholars. Galbraith referred to the first as the "Technostructure" and the second as the "Educational and Scientific Estate." The latter were transformative, for they might set a new agenda for American policy at home and abroad, replacing power politics with human values. The "new industrial state" could only be built in what Galbraith had earlier deemed "the affluent soci-ety": while the "Technostructure" still operated under a politics of material scarcity, the "Educational and Scientific Estate" prepared to transcend it.[54]

Michael Harrington, whose *The Other America* (1962) warned that society was not so affluent after all, seemed unlikely to envision a politics transcending economics. His *Toward a Democratic Left* (1968), however, embraced the New Class: "a new social stratum . . . formed by modern tech-nology which could well have a non-material interest in basic change." Like Galbraith's "Educational and Scientific Estate," this stratum was not an interest group but a "conscience constituency" made up of "politically and socially unprecedented types of human beings."[55]

A "conscience constituency" of old—including abolitionists and tem-perance crusaders—had been forged in the furnace of millennial Chris-tian faith. The New Class was tutored in the lecture halls of the modern university. This distinction mattered for Kristol, who would embrace the

Republican coalition's evangelical Christians.[56] While abiding conscience emanating from religion, Kristol criticized conscience founded in secular moral aspirations. Utopianism was more dangerous than millennialism.

Kristol ultimately cleaved to an analysis of the New Class more Marxist than that of Harrington, who was chair of the Democratic Socialists of America. As one reviewer put it: Kristol "subjects the present conflict between the private and public sectors to rigorous class-interest analysis," unpacking the "struggle for power and moral influence between corporate business and the 'New Class'—that educated elite which has carried the anti-capitalist and anti-bourgeois values of the campus-based adversary culture into our society's dominant bureaucratic power centers."[57] The cultural superstructure of the New Class was, for Kristol, set upon a material base.

Harrington, Galbraith, Bazelon, Schumpeter, and others stretching back to Bakunin formed the contours of New Class thought when Kristol took it up.[58] He made it more polemical, wove it into cultural and political elements unfolding in the Nixon years, linked it with postwar American conservatism, and, finally, responded to it with a potent program of intellectual activism.

* * *

The February 6, 1966, *New York Times* carried an interesting mix of news. "A bipartisan panel" concluded "that most state income taxes should be raised and that the Federal Government should give the states an incentive to raise them." In Manhattan, "750 antiwar demonstrators marched outside the United States Mission to the United Nations." They carried American flags with skulls and dollar signs in place of stars, facing "seven angry counterpickets who screamed such epithets as 'Red traitors' and 'yellow Red rats.'" Meanwhile, "a rally in support of American military action in Vietnam drew 200 persons to Union Square" with signs reading: "'Don't Be Left, Be Right in Our Foreign Policy' and 'Bomb Hanoi.'" At the airport, "Staughton Lynd, the Yale history professor who visited Hanoi last December in defiance of a State Department ban," had his passport revoked. Lynd protested the violation of his "'elementary and constitutional right'" to travel.[59]

"A Band of New York Intellectuals Meets with Prof. Schlesinger for a Talk-In on Vietnam," the magazine section reported. At the studio of Shirley Broughton, a choreographer and dancer who hosted the Theater for Ideas, panelists included Michael Walzer, Arthur M. Schlesinger Jr., Lynd, Elizabeth Hardwick, and Kristol. Among the audience were Norman Mailer, Susan Sontag, Irving Howe, Dwight Macdonald, Helen Lynd, and Muriel Rukeyser. Kristol opened by arguing that since World War Two, "the definition of our national security involved the United States as a world power." Prewar isolationism was simply no longer an option. Lynd quickly charged Kristol with falsely equating Communism to Nazism.[60]

Another panelist defended Kristol: "I don't think Mr. Kristol meant to compare the situation in Southeast Asia with the Nazi threat," Schlesinger said. "Obviously these are very different things." Schlesinger, characteristically, positioned himself in the sensible center, between a hotheaded Left and a foggy-thinking Right. But this evening his tack failed. Walzer and Lynd criticized him from the panel, as did Macdonald and Howe from the floor, which booed Schlesinger after he disparaged antiwar street protest. So great was opposition to Schlesinger that Sontag reminded everyone who the most objectionable panelist really was: "I'm very concerned that Mr. Kristol—whose views I don't share and I doubt a majority of the people in this audience share them—that he not be submerged in a kind of general left-wing consensus."[61]

The February 6, 1966, *New York Times* gathered elements that would animate Kristol's New Class thought: higher taxes and bigger government; division on foreign policy and doubts about the moral status of the nation; dissenting intellectuals; and the dynamics of debate over Vietnam, which lumped Schlesinger with Kristol in the face of a critical Left.

Kristol thought 1966 was a plastic moment for intellectuals. He forecast that "involvement of intellectuals in American politics" would "be a most useful educational experience." It would challenge the "ingrained philistinism and anti-intellectualism that has been the cause of infinite mischief" if intellectuals could effectively shape and administer policy. "We *need* the best efforts of the best minds to make our cities inhabitable, our schools educational, our economy workable"; and "our best minds *need* to be chastened by some first-hand experience in . . . governing." Policy intellectuals were not the only ones needing a lesson: "Too many literary intellectuals" opined on policy rather than conducting "critical examination [of American life] from the perspectives of moral and political philosophy."[62] Those at Broughton's studio were likely guilty of such misdirected efforts.

By 1967 the plasticity had passed, and intellectuals generated more peril than possibility. In *Foreign Affairs*, Kristol contended with a "new intellectual class." Unlike prophets of old, the contemporary "intellectual, lacking in other-worldly interests, is committed to the pursuit of temporal status, temporal influence and temporal power." Indeed, American life was marked by their striving. Understanding "what is happening in the United States today" required putting "the sociological condition and political ambitions of the intellectual class very much in the forefront of one's mind." Looking beyond intellectuals' opposition to Vietnam, Kristol examined "the highly problematic relationship of the modern intellectual to foreign affairs, the basic self-definition of the American intellectual, the tortured connections between American liberal ideology and the American imperial republic, and the role of the newly established academic classes in an affluent society."[63]

Intellectuals constituted a "community" because they shared both an ideology and an interest in perpetuating ideological politics. The alternative to ideological politics was the application of "value-free" expertise to public affairs—but who, if not intellectuals, would apply such expertise? Kristol addressed this contradiction by emphasizing the distinction between two kinds of intellectuals. "A small section of the American intellectual class has become a kind of permanent brain trust to the political, the military, the economic authorities." Lacking practical experience, they were at worst ineffective—not subversive. Alongside them, however, "a whole new intellectual class has emerged as a result of the explosive growth, in these past decades, of higher education in the United States. And these 'new men,' so far from being any kind of elite, are a mass—and have engendered their own mass movement."[64] They were the community of ideologues.

With their ideology, these intellectuals interpreted society and defined their identity. On his copy of Chomsky's "The Responsibility of Intellectuals," published five months earlier, Kristol scribbled: "Transcendentalism plus populism—the marriage that has made the American mind." He pursued this idea in *Foreign Affairs*: "The American intellectual sees himself as being in perpetual 'prophetic confrontation' with principalities and powers." This "*transcendentalist populism*" mingled "disrespect for tradition, a suspicion of all institutionalized authority, an unshakable faith in the 'natural' (what once was called 'divine') wisdom of the sincere individual, [and] an incorruptible allegiance to one's own 'inner light.'" Such intellectuals were "humble toward an idealized and mythical prototype of the common man" while "arrogant toward existing authority." These attitudes generated a "transcendentalist politics" focused "less on the reform of the polity than on the perfection and purification of self in opposition to the polity."[65]

Intellectuals' idealism had origins, however, other than ideals. "It is not that intellectuals actually believe—though they often assert it—that the heavy reliance upon expediency in foreign affairs is intrinsically immoral." Rather, it "renders intellectuals as a class so much the less indispensable." Ideological politics afforded intellectuals "a pivotal social and political role," while for "coping with expediential situations you don't have to be an intellectual—and it may even be a handicap."[66] Excluding ideology from policymaking empowered technical intellectuals, but infusing policy with ideology served the new "mass" born of the academy.

That mass opposed American foreign policy. While "polls generally reveal that the overwhelming majority of ordinary citizens" endorse "their government's foreign policy," Kristol wrote, "among intellectuals, this majority tends to be skimpy at best, and will frequently not exist at all. It is reasonable to suppose that there is an instinctive bias at work here, favorable to government among the common people, unfavorable among the intellectuals." That bias hampered the "imperial role" that "the United States, as the world's mightiest power," had no alternative but to play. Lacking "the endorsement of its intellectual class," the United States faced "a domestic climate of ideological dissent that will enfeeble the resolution of our statesmen and diminish the credibility of their policies abroad."[67] Kristol made no room for the proposition that intellectuals' dissent may harm the credibility of the empire but uphold the culture of democracy.

Kristol had called upon literary intellectuals to shift from debating policies to examining values. How was that examination different from their moral criticism of foreign policy that he now denounced as mere ideology? Kristol hoped the "intellectual class" would stop "the shrill enunciation of pieties and principles that have little relevance to the particular cases our statesmen now confront" and instead "formulate a new set of more specific principles that will relate the ideals which sustain American democracy to the harsh and nasty imperatives of imperial power." The distinction was no longer between technical intellectuals who worked on policy and literary intellectuals who focused on values. It now ran between intellectuals who accepted American imperialism and crafted its values, and those who recklessly persisted in opposing it. Kristol saluted the former. "For their efforts and pains, they have been subjected to the scorn and contempt of the intellectual community as a whole. (Arthur Schlesinger . . . could provide us with eloquent testimony on this score.)" Imperial policymakers found their "responsibility a terrible burden. The intellectuals, in contrast, are bemused by dreams of power without responsibility, even as they complain of moral responsibility without power."[68] At Shirley Broughton's studio, Sontag had reminded the crowd not to elide Kristol's and Schlesinger's views. Now, Kristol sympathized with Schlesinger's position as an imperial adviser, if not his positions as a liberal.

Foreign policy was one site of a looming, larger conflict. "Our intellectuals are moving toward a significant 'confrontation' with the American 'establishment,'" Kristol predicted. Despite the deference of the American people, who "have always had a superstitious, if touching, faith in the importance of education," the academic mass was "full of grievance and resentment." It was "a new class . . . 'alienated' from the established order because it feels that this order has not conceded to it sufficient power and recognition." Their confrontation with the establishment gave intellectuals "an interest in thwarting . . . any kind of responsible and coherent imperial policy. Just what this interest is, and what this confrontation involves, we are only now beginning to discern." Kristol was in the crow's nest, peering into the mist with a hand on the bell. "Behind the general fog that the ideology of dissent generates, the outlines of a very material sociological and political problem are emerging."[69] He saw the dark, hulking shape of a New Class steadily approaching.

Kristol contested that class on a variety of fronts as the decade closed. His earlier suspended judgment about "professional intellectuals" gave way to thorough skepticism about the federal policies he associated with them. *Public Interest* criticized those policies, finding fault with intellectuals and bureaucrats. Kristol described the Model Cities Program—a subset of the War on Poverty that emphasized local planning encompassing a range of services rather than top-down urban renewal focused on physical infrastructure—as "a typical social welfare program that threatens to metamorphose into one controversial shambles after another." It was administered by experts but "very few . . . expert enough to avoid major miscalculations."[70]

In 1968 Kristol joined "Citizens for Humphrey," though he sensed that party alignments were shifting.[71] "Incredibly enough," he told his son William, "Humphrey does best among people earning less than $5,000 a year, among Negroes, and among Jews. [Eugene] McCarthy makes his best showing among those Democrats earning above $10,000 a year, the very young voters, and the females." The Democratic Party's "'right wing' . . . is appealing primarily to the 'underprivileged,' while the 'left' gets its support from all those whom one used to count on to be more conservative. It does look as if some kind of basic change is taking place in American politics."[72] The "academic mass" was becoming a visible political bloc.

On the personal front, Kristol faced a classmate's criticism. Irving Howe attributed his alcove mate's rightward migration to "the cajolements of the *Zeitgeist.*" At the risk of "idealizing in an absurd way what the intellectual calling amounts to," Howe believed intellectuals "not worth a minute's notice" unless they "try to live by some value or ideal" rather than "run in packs." Kristol rejected "transcendental admonitions" that "because people like me have ceased being radical or socialist, we have somehow descended from the kingdom of intellectual responsibility to the realm of mindless and spiritless 'conformity.'"[73]

Howe's was not the only criticism from the Left. The *Encounter* exposé brought opprobrium upon Kristol, who defended himself with "Memoirs of a 'Cold Warrior.'" That defense turned into an offensive against his critics, whom he characterized as pampered yet subversive intellectuals. The day after "Memoirs" appeared, Jason Epstein, a vice president at Random House and co-founder of the *New York Review of Books*, wrote Kristol in alarm. "You say that the problem is . . . an assortment of evils including the literary left in league with café society, homosexuals, madmen, neo-Castroite journals, drug takers, literary celebrities and pornographers." Kristol had stoked fears of communism in the 1950s, and his new "coalition of devils," Epstein wrote, "offered up by a future demagogue to a confused and frustrated public, is likely to inspire—in a country already predisposed to paranoia—such panic as to make McCarthy's or even Hitler's cultural revolutions seem to have been ordinary. I fear that, once again, you are playing with fire."[74] If Epstein thought Kristol in danger of igniting anti-intellectualism, Kristol thought intellectuals endangered the timbers beneath Western civilization.

Like Schumpeter, Kristol saw intellectuals nibbling at the foundations. America's "civic-bourgeois culture is not being overwhelmed from without, but is rather being casually and almost contemptuously subverted from within." For a veteran of the Second Red Scare, charges of internal subversion carried echoes of Alger Hiss. While in 1948 Hiss symbolized a communist underground, by 1968 Kristol saw subversion being visibly enacted by an entire intellectual class. It took the form not of espionage, but "the slow draining away of legitimacy from existing institutions and prevailing traditions."[75]

Intellectuals were no longer a peripheral bohemia. They were an ascendant generation representing the triumph of Trilling's adversary culture, "contemptuous of capitalism, liberalism, democracy, materialism, organized religion, and all the familiar domestic virtues." Kristol believed that "militant New Deal liberals and exponents of 'modernist' culture" had been "able to change the entire academic temper of the university." That new temper coincided with the growth of the university system such that higher education could convert the bacillus of intellectual modernism into an epidemic. Adversary culture had become "popular culture." Kristol questioned whether "bourgeois society" could "survive" this "cultural ambiance that derides every traditional bourgeois virtue." At such moments, he sounded like a Victorian moralist. At others, he sounded like Marx: "Our world is being emptied of its ideal content, and the imposing institutional façade sways in the wind."[76] All that is solid melts into air, indeed.

In 1969 Kristol joined a fairly solid institution: NYU. The irony was not lost on him: "I am on the verge of becoming a professor, so help me God."[77] His Henry Luce Professorship of Urban Values had been endowed by the media potentate of Time Incorporated and was the result of "vigorous lobbying" by longtime NYU professor Sidney Hook.[78] "The Urban Intellectual," Kristol's graduate course, examined "the 'crisis of modernity' in terms of the historical relations between intellectuals and artists on the one hand, and the body politic on the other."[79] Teaching allowed Kristol to further explore ideas animating his commentary.

It also allowed him to assemble a reading list, including Matthew Arnold's *Culture and Anarchy*, Sigmund Freud's *Civilization and Its Discontents*, Norman Podhoretz's *Making It*, Theodore Roszak's *The Making of a Counter Culture*, and, unsurprisingly, Lionel Trilling's *Beyond Culture*. Also on the list was Martin Green's *The Problem of Boston*, which Hofstadter had reviewed in *Public Interest*. According to Hofstadter, Green highlighted how modernism's "romantic" passions were not easy to reconcile with "the demands of the responsible society." Instead, Hofstadter concluded, "we are really confronted with two cultures" in conflict: "a massive adversary culture on the one side, and the realm of socially responsible criticism on the other." Kristol saw a trend: "An awful lot of people are thinking about this subject and are writing about the problem of culture, counter-culture, and what Lionel Trilling has called 'adversary culture.'"[80]

Trilling wrote of "the dark and bloody crossroads where literature and politics meet." Kristol articulated in piecemeal a theory of politics and culture based upon the premise that ideas, whether from political philosophy or literature, mattered. Ideas shaped "in men's minds the categories of the politically possible and the politically impossible, the desirable and the undesirable, the tolerable and the intolerable. And what is more ultimately real, politically," Kristol asked, deploying a Trillingesque formulation, "than the structure of man's political imagination?"[81]

Though he still wrote about policy, Kristol increasingly focused on the basic outlooks from which policies emerged. Characteristic of this effort was his "Urban Civilization and Its Discontents," from 1970. "Classical political philosophy" doubted whether an "urban mentality"—"irreverent, speculative, pleasure-loving, self-serving, belligerent toward all conventional pieties"—could be "compatible with republican survival."[82] "Urban mentality" joined "adversary culture" in Kristol's lexicon for corrosive attitudes taking on new and dangerous proportions.

Just as the "academic mass" was the metastasized adversary culture, so the urban mentality was becoming the American mentality—a development not all bad. "No one, after all, can sincerely mourn the passing of the *Saturday Evening Post* and of that superficial, provincial, and, above all, philistine popular culture it so smugly affirmed." Such provincialism "may have contributed to political stability—but it also represented a spiritual torpor that, in the end, could only be self-defeating because it was so thin in its sense of humanity." The urgent task was to shore up or reconstruct a political culture that could produce stability *and* be philosophically, even aesthetically thick enough to endure the corrosive character of modernity; it was "to evolve a set of values and a conception of democracy that can function as the equivalent of the 'republican morality' of yesteryear."[83] Taking up that task, Kristol would build an alliance of intellectuals and the *Saturday Evening Post* set.

Kristol's professorship was, appropriately, in "urban values," for he saw values at the heart of cities' problems, just as he saw cities at the heart of American life. Against those who said that inadequate housing, underfunded schools, racism, unemployment, or depressed wages were to blame for conflagrations engulfing American cities during the "long, hot sum-

THE INTELLECTUAL AGAINST INTELLECTUALS

mers" of the era, Kristol claimed that it was a "startling absence of values that represents the authentic 'urban crisis' of our democratic, urban
nation." His preoccupation with values was not simply a reaction to hip-
pies, uprisings, and dissent. "The twentieth century is experiencing a crisis
of values—not simply a conflict between values, but a crisis in the very idea
of value," he had written in 1961. While his thinking about the importance
of values became more central to Kristol's work after the events of the late
1960s, it was not caused by them.[84]

So serious was Kristol about a crisis of values that he criticized even
capitalism's role in it, pulling anti-capitalist conservatism from an unlikely
source for a New York intellectual: the antebellum South. In an essay entitled "'When Virtue Loses All Her Loveliness'"—a phrase from George
Fitzhugh, proponent of slave-based agrarian societies as against urban
industrial ones—Kristol claimed that "the inner spiritual chaos of the
times, so powerfully created by the dynamics of capitalism itself . . . make[s]
nihilism an easy temptation." In early capitalism, the "correlation between
certain personal virtues," like "frugality, industry, sobriety, reliability,
piety," and the distribution of "power, privilege, and property" signaled
"a just society, not merely of a free one." That correlation was unraveling,
"subverted by the dynamics of capitalism," which spawned "affluence and
liberty" but not justice and thus enjoyed only "questionable legitimacy."
His concern for moral legitimacy separated Kristol from libertarian champions of capitalism for whom liberty and prosperity were sufficiently justifying. Kristol believed, however, "that men cannot accept the historical accidents of the marketplace" as the basis for distributing social goods. They
needed to see "power, privilege, and property . . . distributed according to
some morally meaningful criteria."[85] The adversary culture expanded in
place of a capitalism that no longer claimed Americans' moral allegiance.

To regain that allegiance, Kristol believed, a "combination of the
reforming spirit with the conservative ideal" was "most desperately
wanted." The "reforming spirit" he associated with Progressive Era intellectual Herbert Croly, who suggested that a good society could not be left
to the anarchy of individual actions but must become the object of coor-
dinated efforts. The "conservative ideal" was a standpoint from which to
criticize the mantra of modern life (that, ironically, named Croly's ethos):
progress. "The idea of progress" suggested "that the quality of life would
inevitably be improved by material enrichment," Kristol wrote. "To doubt
this is to doubt the political metaphysics of modernity and to start the

long trek back to pre-modern political philosophy."[86] The combination
of reforming spirit and conservative ideal pointed toward a powerful role
for intellectuals. Who but intellectuals would make the "long trek back"
to premodern ideas? Who but intellectuals would undertake the conscious direction of social forces that defined the reforming spirit? The figure called for is not simply a literary conservative nor a technocrat; it is a
politically engaged intellectual armed with the Western canon. Sounds
like Irving Kristol.

In essays from 1971, Kristol demonstrated more conservative ideal
than reforming spirit, urging less government intervention in the economy and more in the media. Extending the welfare state was an act of
hubris that would "surely end up making our world worse than it need
have been." "Pornography, Obscenity and the Case for Censorship," by
contrast, encouraged state action—to limit adult media—for "civilization
and humanity, nothing less" were "at stake" with pornography. Under "an
older idea of democracy" that emphasized "the character of the people who
govern," there was "an obligation to educate [citizens] into what used to
be called 'republican virtue.'" Censors inculcated virtue by the judicious
imposition of restraints upon public discourse. Kristol left unexplained
how those entrusted with virtue education had themselves become virtuous. The hidden premise was Straussian—censors had a special relation to
the good that common persons did not.[87]

By the election year of 1972, Kristol was reaching new audiences. That
fall he joined the *Wall Street Journal*'s board of contributors, opening a
direct line to the business community. Meanwhile, *Public Interest* was "the
most-cited single source when talking . . . with policy-oriented White
House aides, or assistant secretaries of Cabinet departments or assistant
directors of the Office of Management and Budget."[88] Kristol's collected
essays, *On the Democratic Idea in America*, also won well-placed readers. A
Washington, DC, bookstore shopper could not get it despite seeing "a stack
of some 20 copies behind the clerk's desk. 'They have all been ordered by
the White House, no less,' the clerk explained." Another report claimed
that "President Nixon urged his staff to read it. Vice President Agnew
touted it to his friends. Its author, Irving Kristol, was invited to dine pri-
vately with the President."[89]

Kristol was building a circuit between the intellectual world, the business community, and the center of political power. It was a circuit through
which a current of ideas and ideologues would flow, powering a rightward

surge that culminated in the presidency of Ronald Reagan and in a legacy of neoconservative institutions, outlooks, and policies.

Critic Damon Linker calls this process "Irving Kristol's other journey." While moving from left to right on the political spectrum, Kristol also became "frustrated with the political and cultural drift of the country . . . and . . . tempted by the prospect of using political power and cultural influence to reverse it." He shifted "from a dispassionate analyst of American politics and culture to a fully engaged advocate for a comprehensive political ideology."[90] Linker attributes Kristol's migration to the push of frustration and the pull of temptation—extra-intellectual reasons for reshaping his role as a politically active intellectual. Kristol's moves, however, flowed from the current of his philosophical analysis, not against it.

His writings before 1972 pointed to a mission that Kristol could undertake as a publicly engaged intellectual after it. He was not the only observer to see an influential cohort of educated Americans emerging after World War Two, and strands of New Class thought stretched from Bazelon back to Bakunin. Kristol came to see the rising class in terms of Trilling's adversary culture. Indeed he came to see it as an epoch in the dialectic of modernity, in which capitalism spawned the very intellectuals who could be its downfall. Following Schumpeter and Strauss, Kristol believed the perennial antagonism between intellectuals and the social order had reached a new, critical phase.

He responded by rhetorically transforming the rising new class into the polemically useful New Class. If intellectuals' adversary culture shook bourgeois society's fragile underpinnings, Kristol resolved to reinforce them. He did so at the level of ideas, but he also did so by attaching his ideas to social forces that might counteract the power of the New Class—business, the Republican Party, religion. He waged a "war of ideas" on multiple fronts not because he wearied of analysis but because his analysis led him to it. A few years earlier, Lasch had also determined to shift from social criticism to social movement. Kristol's move was considerably more effective. As Wall Street Journal editor Robert L. Bartley put it in 1972, "When the intellectual history of the 1960s is ultimately written, we may find that the event of most lasting significance was not the advent of a new radicalism but the evolution of a new and newly relevant conservatism."[91]

* * *

As Kristol took aim at the New Class, in 1972 it provided a target: the "New Politics." Norman Podhoretz characterized the New Politics as "the insurgency within the Democratic party which came out of the antiwar movement," was bolstered by the McGovern-Fraser Commission's reforms, and was ultimately embodied in "the candidacy of [George] McGovern himself."[92] Among its slate of measures aimed at opening up the presidential nominating process, the commission called for increasing the number of women, minority, and young delegates to the Democratic National Convention, offsetting unions and urban machines. McGovern became the first nominee under this system, beating out more conservative contenders Hubert Humphrey and Henry "Scoop" Jackson as well as Shirley Chisholm, the first African American woman to seek a major-party presidential nomination.

The New Politics demonstrated, for Podhoretz, the New Class's "consciousness of itself as a class and as a potential political force." It included "educated, prosperous people, members of the professional and technical intelligentsia and their wives and children, academics and their students." They held in "contempt . . . the ordinary workingman and the 'racism' and vulgar materialism which allegedly define his character."[93] Though he identified the New Politics with the McGovern-Fraser measures to make the Democratic Party better reflect the population, Podhoretz characterized it as anti-populist. Kristol had criticized intellectuals' "transcendentalist populism" with its faith in "the common man." He now claimed that ordinary Americans' common sense upheld basic values that intellectuals' uncommon sense threatened. To Kristol and Podhoretz, the New Politics seemed another wedge between the New Class and "the people."

Eyeing the 1972 election, sociologist Edward Shils assessed this phenomenon. "The anticipated supporters of the Republicans are populistic; they see a virtuous, industrious and respectable people misused and exploited by bureaucrats and radical intellectuals," he wrote. "The Democratic Party, which the radical intellectuals (except for the small Maoist and Trotskyite sects) are now supporting, is permeated by populism; both the new Democrats and the old machine Democrats are populistic in their idiom, although they differ in their conception of just who are 'the people.'" As Shils saw it, "The newer radical intellectuals, more comprehensively and more vehemently hostile to American society than their forerunners, have concentrated . . . on . . . the most peripheral elements of American society, the *Lumpenproletariat*." When Republicans conjured "the people" they "invoke the spirit of 'middle America'—meaning the more or less respectable working classes."[94] Battle lines were drawn between populist-sounding Republicans and "respectable" people on one side and populist-sounding intellectuals and "peripheral" people on the other.

Shils opposed the intellectuals for their "populist denigration of institutions." By stoking demands for government services, especially "welfare and . . . education," they forced politicians "to keep a vast bureaucracy going" that, in turn, relied upon "intellectuals . . . as experts, advisers, administrators, research workers, technologists, etc."[95] A juggernaut of popular clamor and intellectuals' activism overwhelmed elected officials, expanding technocratic government.

"The country," however, "has not gone entirely to the dogs; not even its intellectuals have." Shils cited "Mr. Kristol himself as an example." Kristol and *Public Interest* "stood out against the ravages of the oppositional radical populism of the progressivist intellectuals, academics, publicists, literary men and student leaders." Opposing these foes without triggering a new McCarthyism, Kristol could help politicians "demand a better accounting from" experts in their service "while avoiding the anti-intellectual brutishness which has cropped up recurrently in America for nearly a century." As Shils put it, "not everyone, either in the intellectual stratum or in the laity, need espouse and practice the 'virtues' needed by a republic for those virtues to be decisively influential. A 'saving remnant'" sufficed "to steady the minds of rulers, publicists, and teachers and the more numerous minds which are ruled, informed and taught by them." There was "hope for the country. Mr. Kristol and his collaborators might themselves be the answer."[96]

Kristol steadied the ruler's mind by endorsing Nixon, providing "an opportunity for the Republicans to break the Democratic strangle-hold on intellectual talent."[97] As Kristol went, so did the electorate: Nixon resoundingly defeated McGovern. Speculation grew about a "Nixon-Kristol partnership" for the new term, with reports that "Nixon . . . tentatively decided" to make Kristol "a high-level White House aide." According to the *Evening Standard*, "Nixon likes to keep at least one thoroughbred egghead in his stable of advisers." Kristol—"a deadly polemicist, an excellent writer and a skilled deflator of modish liberal ideas"—would be a fitting choice.[98] Though Kristol saw his writings "regularly included in President

Nixon's week-end reading list," he would not become "the next White House intellectual in residence" but, rather, a director of the Corporation for Public Broadcasting.[99]

The *National Observer* thought Kristol and Nixon natural allies. Kristol was "point man of a small but growing band of writers and scholars who are a centrist—conservative may be too strong a term—counterpoint to what they consider the anti-Americanism, self-hatred, and utopianism of many American intellectuals." Nixon, criticizing "programs aimed at lifting the poor—particularly urban blacks—out of squalor and into the middle-class life of education and affluence with one mighty bound," deflated utopianism in the policy realm. Kristol aimed to "restore values" challenged by it in the moral domain. "To Kristol, 'Religion is the only source, with rituals, a moral code, that's the only way it can come.'" But Kristol's more sociological than theological conception of religion made it a field for intellectuals. The problem, he said, was that intellectuals "want to be only prophets, like Isaiah. We need prophets, but not so many. We also need the rabbinical function of telling us what to do and keeping things together, so we can weld change into the traditions and past and not destroy continuity.'"[100] With Kristol the rabbi and Nixon the ruler, the work of welding was set to begin.

Outside the administration, Kristol continued rallying the silent majority against the growing, vocal intellectual minority. Podhoretz forecast that "a catastrophic McGovern defeat" would show that the adversary culture was "still confined to an ideologically passionate minority" while "most other people, if they are really infected with disgust, are disgusted not with the 'Establishment' in general but precisely with that wing of it dominated by the New Class and the New Politics."[101] Momentum seemed to be shifting. As Bartley put it, "After years of demoralization, a pro-American type of intellectual is starting to speak up, to launch vigorous counterattacks on the chic radicalism, to debunk the debunkers." These counterblows signaled "a reawakening of . . . the clerisy, intellectuals who despite a certain necessary detachment from society are close enough to it to act as its spokesmen." They were crucial, for "in defending [American] society [intellectuals] can do some things politicians cannot. If it is threatened by an imbalance of cultural power, intellectuals can see to it that fashionable but airy ideas do not go unchallenged."[102]

Posing such a challenge, Kristol's "About Equality" became the *locus classicus* for his opposition to the New Class.[103] "Some Americans," he wrote, "are profoundly and sincerely agitated by the existing distribution of income in this country, and these same Americans—they are mostly professors, of course—are constantly insisting that a more equal distribution of income is a matter of considerable urgency." Philosopher John Rawls's *A Theory of Justice* had recently proposed a "difference principle": just societies countenance only those inequalities that work to the advantage of the least well-off. Rawls's work provided Kristol an occasion not only to contest the value of equality, but to examine what he took to be the ulterior motives of intellectuals advocating it.[104]

As Kristol saw it, theories of equality were characteristic of the modern period, when intellectuals translated utopian visions into blueprints for social change or, at least, standards against which the present society could be found wanting. In response, "political regimes" upheld "their legitimacy either by claiming an ideal character which in obvious truth they did not possess, or . . . making what were taken to be 'damaging admissions' as to their inability to transform the real into the ideal." The status quo was perennially on the defensive. "The only corrective to this shadow of illegitimacy . . . was the 'common sense' of the majority of the population, which had an intimate and enduring relation to mundane realities that was relatively immune to speculative enthusiasm."[105]

The stability produced by the preponderance of "common sense" dissolved as society began "breeding more and more 'intellectuals' and fewer common men and women." Expanding higher education created "a large class of people . . . who, though lacking intellectual distinction (and frequently lacking even intellectual competence), nevertheless believe themselves to be intellectuals." There was now "a mass of several millions of 'intellectuals' who are looking at their society in a highly critical way and are quick to adopt an adversary posture toward it."[106]

Rising material comfort did nothing to diminish intellectuals' calls for economic equality, as their real concern was "almost embarrassingly vulgar in its substance"—power. "The simple truth," Kristol declared, "is that the professional classes of our modern bureaucratized societies are engaged in a class struggle with the business community for status and power." Intellectuals believed they could "do a better job of running our society and feel entitled to have the opportunity. This is what *they* mean by 'equality.'"[107]

Will to power mingled with "authentic moral passion" in intellectuals' rejection of middle-class values. "The class of people we call intellectuals—poets, novelists, painters, men of letters—has never accepted the bourgeois notion of the common good," scoffing at "personal security under the law, personal liberty under the law, and a steadily increasing material prosperity for those who apply themselves to that end." Such humble goods deprived "the intellectual of his traditional prerogative—which was to celebrate high nobility of purpose, selfless devotion to transcendental ends, and awe-inspiring heroism."[108] Intellectuals' opposition to bourgeois values was both immanent and transcendent.

It was also "quite explicitly 'elitist.'" Intellectuals objected to the prosaic character of capitalism because they believed "that common men could only find true happiness when their lives were subordinated to and governed by uncommon ideals, as conceived and articulated by intellectuals." This view was "highly presumptuous and self-serving," but Kristol was "not so certain that it was or is altogether false."[109] Subordinating common people to higher ideals was, after all, a vision not unlike Strauss's, which Kristol admired. How was philosophers' maintenance of an orderly untruth any less objectionable than the New Class's promulgation of an egalitarian ideal? Would not both, by Kristol's logic, accord unusual power to the intellectual few at the expense of the many?

Kristol's view of the many was changeable. He had accused intellectuals of making a cult of the common people. Now, he championed those people as a bulwark against intellectuals. As the New Class reevaluated traditional values, "only the common people . . . remain loyal to the bourgeois ethos." Those "familiar with the American working class" know "they are far less consumed with egalitarian bitterness or envy than are college professors or affluent journalists."[110] Working people had been gunpowder into which intellectuals might toss a match; now they were wet blankets on the smoldering heap of New Class resentment.

While such "ordinary people are not significantly impressed by the assertions and indignations of egalitarian rhetoric," Kristol warned, "they cannot help but be impressed by the fact that the ideological response to this accusatory rhetoric is so feeble." As the New Class articulated grievances and utopian visions, the status quo mounted little intellectual defense. "Somehow, bourgeois society seems incapable of explaining and justifying its inequalities" in terms of "the common good." There was a need for intellectuals like Kristol to equip it with that justification, which ordinary people wanted. As he put it more boldly a decade later: "It is the self-imposed assignment of neoconservatism to explain to the American people why they are right, and to the intellectuals why they are wrong."[111]

This assignment was crucial, for Kristol believed the American people's allegiance hung in the balance. The years 1968–80 were a "realigning" period when voters upended established electoral coalitions, creating volatility in the distribution of political power. Working-class and southern whites drifted from the Democratic Party. Michael Novak's *The Rise of the Unmeltable Ethnics* (1972) foresaw that "white ethnic Catholics, especially from Eastern and Southern Europe," would give Republicans a decisive advantage if Democrats embraced the New Class.[112]

While political scientists saw voters swinging between two parties, Kristol saw them swaying between intellectual groups. One was "an intelligentsia which so despises the ethos of bourgeois society, and which is so guilt-ridden at being implicated in the life of this society, that it is inclined to find even collective suicide preferable to the status quo." They were seconded by "a 'new class' of self-designated 'intellectuals' who share much of this basic attitude—but who, rather than committing suicide, pursue power in the name of equality." Opposing them were intellectuals, like Kristol, upholding bourgeois society. In the middle were "ordinary people, working-class and lower-middle-class, basically loyal to the bourgeois order but confused and apprehensive at the lack of clear meaning in this order."[113]

Electoral realignment went beyond structural changes—migration from unionized Rust Belt to anti-union Sun Belt states, racialized suburbanization, the decline of manufacturing—to strike at the spiritual roots of modern society. "The real trouble is not sociological or economic at all," Kristol wrote. "It is that the 'middling' nature of a bourgeois society falls short of corresponding adequately to the full range of man's spiritual nature, which makes more than middling demands upon the universe, and demands more than middling answers. This weakness . . . has been highlighted by . . . intellectual critics from the very beginning." Such a problem was not for parsing by political science but intervention by moral philosophy. "It is not too much to say that it is the death of God . . . that haunts bourgeois society. And *this* problem is far beyond the competence of politics to cope with."[114]

Responding to "About Equality," Michael Walzer tried to bring debate about economic inequality back down to material conditions. Kristol's attempt "to expose egalitarianism as the ideology of envious and resentful intellectuals," Walzer wrote, ignored that economic inequality was a concrete problem for ordinary Americans. "The distribution of medical care actually follows closely the lines of the income graph," he observed. "It's not how a man feels, but how much money he has that determines how often he visits a doctor." This was not a philosophical point but a "demonstrable fact! Does it require envious intellectuals to see that something is wrong?"[115]

Kristol, however, was looking beyond debates with *Dissent*. He was building ties to political and business leaders, using perches at the *Wall Street Journal*, *Public Interest*, and American Enterprise Institute (AEI)—a fiscally conservative think tank headquartered in Washington—to bolster these relationships. Geoffrey Norman suggested that becoming a senior fellow at AEI "completed [Kristol's] network of interlocking directorates." Profiling him in *Esquire*, Norman was one of several who saw Kristol at the center of an increasingly powerful intellectual-institutional web. "At precisely the right time, he had everything he needed to advance his ideas and the ideas of people who thought like he did," Norman wrote. "Kristol had become, in every way, a real American force."[116] That force pursued the assignment Kristol gave counter–New Class intellectuals: shoring up bourgeois society by pairing an intellectual justification of it with the institutional power of the Republican Party and American business. Kristol offered the latter a potent set of arguments; they offered him the resources to not only broadcast those arguments, but embed them in new think tanks, periodicals, and professorships. Vice President Spiro T. Agnew, who began corresponding with Kristol in 1973, understood the moment thus: "I believe you are correct in emphasizing the power of ideas and the potential for rapid change which ideas unleash. If you are correct, and ideas are more powerful than institutions, then those of us who fear utopianism had better get at the business of providing better ideas to the major institutions of American society."[117]

Kristol's intellectual and institutional work proceeded in mutually reinforcing fashion. Writing in the *Wall Street Journal*, *Public Interest*, and elsewhere gave him a platform for describing what he saw as the underlying problems facing American society, for laying out the weaknesses of corporations and the Republican Party in addressing those problems, and for indicating how intellectuals like him could help. In turn, Kristol was appointed to corporate and foundation boards, developed strong ties to Republican leaders like Jack Kemp and David Stockman, and leveraged these relationships to carry his message to broader audiences and small influential ones as well.[118]

The first link in Kristol's logic was his premise that *the* conflict of the

1970s—a decade, he believed, of peril but also plasticity—would occur on the plane of ideas. "The crisis of modernity we are now experiencing, was created by ideas and by the passions which these ideas unleashed," he wrote in 1973. "To surmount this crisis . . . will require new ideas—or new versions of old ideas—that will regulate these passions and bring them into a more fruitful and harmonious relation with reality." Against the charge that institutions trumped ideas, Kristol claimed that "the leverage of ideas is so immense that a slight change in the intellectual climate can and will—perhaps slowly, but nevertheless inexorably—twist a familiar institution into an unrecognizable shape." Against the charge that economics trumped ideas, Kristol claimed that it was "the ethos of capitalism . . . in gross disrepair, not the economics of capitalism—which is, indeed, its saving grace. But salvation through this grace alone will not suffice."[119]

If ideas were the crucial front, then exponents of ideas, the New Class, were the crucial people. "We are talking," Kristol wrote, "about scientists, teachers and educational administrators, journalists and others in the communication industries, psychologists, social workers, those lawyers and doctors who make their careers in the expanding public sector, city planners, the staffs of the larger foundations, the upper levels of the government bureaucracy, and so on." They not only carried corrosive ideas, but also represented the loss of ballast traditionally provided by educated professionals. "If one cannot count on these people to provide a political, social, and moral stability—if they do not have a good opinion of our society—how long . . . can that stability and good opinion survive?"[120]

The New Class had not simply withdrawn support from bourgeois society but become its enemy. Since the market reflected the "appetites and preferences" of ordinary people, the New Class "tries always to supersede economics by politics—an activity in which *it* is the most competent—since it has the talents and the implicit authority to shape public opinion on all larger issues." Its aim was "both material and ideological. It is a question of jobs and status and power. But it is also a question of using the state for the purpose of 'realizing one's ideals.'" The result, Kristol warned, would be statist rule.[121]

Kristol's New Class operated at the level of the nation if only to capture its state. Lasch, by contrast, came to see "elites"—he preferred that term to "class"—as defined not by desire to rule the nation but by having slipped the bonds of it. "Their loyalties . . . are international rather than regional, national, or local. They have more in common with their counterparts in Brussels or Hong Kong than with the masses of Americans not yet plugged into the network of global communications." These elites' cosmopolitanism was a mark, therefore, not only of their cultural tastes, but also their abandonment—even "betrayal"—of other Americans.[122] When, years after Lasch and Kristol had written their last, opposition to a still seemingly new class of elites took shape, it carried neither the banner of Lasch's "populism" nor Kristol's "virtue" but, rather, nationalism. In the early 1970s, however, the threat Kristol envisioned came from Naderites more than globalists.

Those who might contest this threat were either blind to it or bumbling in response. "For two centuries," Kristol wrote, "the very important people who managed the affairs of this society could not believe in the importance of ideas—until one day they were shocked to discover that their children, having been captured and shaped by certain ideas, were . . . rebelling against their authority."[123] Corporate executives were a telling example. Kristol had visited "many conferences of businessmen" where "someone will . . . inquire plaintively: 'What can we do to make the profit motive respectable once again?' Or: 'Why, in view of the general prosperity which the free exercise of the profit motive has brought to our society, is it held in such low esteem—indeed, in contempt—by intellectuals, academics, students, the media, politicians, even our very own children?'"[124] Corporate America "is in serious trouble," Kristol told *Wall Street Journal* readers, but "it is reacting in a largely frivolous way." In order "to avoid socialization and burdensome government regulation" and to seek "the good opinion of the American public," executives "had on occasion to think politically rather than economically."[125] Corporate and other leaders hapless in responding to the New Class had to confront ideas, and they needed the counsel of friendly intellectuals to do so. It was "within the power of the large corporations to do something for their own survival," Kristol wrote. "So the question," echoing Lenin, "is: What is to be done?"[126]

Kristol had answers. As "just about the only major institution in our society which does not have . . . a constituency," he claimed, "the corporation today is largely defenseless." To cultivate a constituency, executives had to break out of the balance sheet and consider the role their enterprises played in society, a role that—given the scale of corporations—was public. Executives should "learn to govern, not simply to execute or administer." Governing meant creating incentives for long-term shareholding (as opposed to short-term speculation), which could build a constituency of investors to bolster business politically.[127]

Kristol also suggested that executives think strategically about philanthropy. Too much corporate money went to "foundations and universities . . . populated by those members of the 'new class' who sincerely believe that the larger portion of human virtue is to be found in the public sector, and the larger portion of human vice in the private." These institutions were "the idea-germinating and idea-legitimizing institutions of our society," and corporations had no "obligation to give money to institutions whose views or attitudes they disapprove of." Indeed, corporate philanthropy "ought to include as one of its goals the survival of the corporation itself," which "inevitably involves efforts to shape or reshape the climate of public opinion, a climate that is created by our scholars, our teachers, our intellectuals, our publicists: in short, by the New Class." Corporate foundations must shift their "support to those elements of the 'new class' . . . which do believe in the preservation of a strong private sector." These members of the New Class "may not be much interested in business at all, but [they] *are* interested in individual liberty and limited government," concerned "about the collectivist tendencies in the society."[128] Kristol was promoting a looser conception of the New Class that still included education but left open the possibility that members had not become infected by the adversary culture while obtaining it.

How would corporate dollars locate such people? "Well, if you decide to go exploring for oil, you find a competent geologist," Kristol noted. "Similarly, if you wish to make a productive investment in the intellectual and educational worlds, you find competent intellectuals and scholars— 'dissident' members as it were, of the 'new class'—to offer guidance." Corporations had blundered in this arena: "How many large corporations make use of academic advisory committees?"[129] Here Kristol's intellectual work bolstered his institutional work, for the institutions he participated in, like AEI and, as of 1978, the Institute for Educational Affairs (IEA), benefited from the redirection of corporate funds that he counseled as part of his broader strategy for business.

That strategy envisioned a campaign of public persuasion, but first corporate complicity in the adversary culture had to cease. Daniel Bell's *The Cultural Contradictions of Capitalism* (1976) described how an abstemious producer ethos made possible an indulgent consumer one. The culture of capitalism undid the personal traits that had spawned capitalism. Kristol offered his own warning to large companies whose businesses were hurting business: they unthinkingly "publish books and magazines, or press and sell records, or make and distribute movies, or sponsor television shows which celebrate pornography, denounce the institution of the family, revile the 'ethics of acquisitiveness,' justify civil insurrection, and generally argue in favor of the expropriation of private industry." Having advocated censorship to uphold virtue, Kristol now encouraged corporations to curtail activities, however profitable, which encouraged the adversary culture.[130]

Public persuasion had to go beyond the case made for the market by economists like Milton Friedman and Friedrich Hayek, who emphasized growth and efficiency.[131] Capitalism had become "a system for the impersonal liberation and satisfaction of appetites—an engine for the creation of affluence. And such a system, governed by purely materialistic conceptions and infused with a purely acquisitive ethos, is defenseless before the critique of its intellectuals." The roots of anti-business attitudes were planted not in economics but in values, and the "process of 'value formation' is one in which intellectuals and academicians and artists are sovereign. For corporations it is an alien territory . . . into which they had best not intrude."[132] They were, however, welcome to provide financial support for intellectuals who did.

Only a certain type of counterforce could truly meet the New Class threat. "Businessmen who cannot persuade their own children that business is a morally legitimate activity are not going to succeed, on their own, in persuading the world of it. You can only beat an idea with another idea." In "the war of ideas and ideologies," exponents of ideas, like members of the New Class, were those most capable of confronting that class. Friedman and Hayek were such exponents, but they were not the right intellectuals for the job because "it is becoming clear that religion, and a moral philosophy associated with religion, is far more important politically than the philosophy of liberal individualism" favored by the economists.[133] For Kristol, "the moral authority of tradition, and some public support for this authority, seems to be needed." That was "an authentically 'conservative' thought, a pre-capitalist thought, and how it can be assimilated into a liberal-capitalist society is perhaps the major intellectual question of our age."[134] The true paladins of bourgeois capitalism, then, were not the libertarian defenders of the market; they were the Straussian bearers of premodern wisdom.

The next link in Kristol's logic was that ideas and governing should be joined, which is not to say that intellectuals should always govern. Instead, there were times when "fundamental questions of political philosophy emerge into the public forum and demand consideration. The life of politics then becomes enmeshed with the life of the mind." In such times, "intellectuals, who are marginal to a healthy society, suddenly become important political spokesmen." This was a problem for Republicans because, Kristol claimed, they lacked intellectual heft. That absence was typically an advantage, since it inoculated Republicans from ideology, but when debate about fundamental political ideas resurfaced, "'the stupid party'—which is always the less articulate party—finds itself at an immense disadvantage." There was "a possible conservative majority out there," but it had to "be welded together out of disparate parts; it has to be created, not just assumed. And it can only be created through the unifying power of political ideas." The old chestnut of a balanced budget was not enough. Republicans had "to 'stand for' a perceived vision of a decent society" and "articulate the elements and rationale of this vision." That intellectual work was now "indispensable to effective conservative government."[135] Intellectuals like Kristol could help corporations blindsided by the New Class, and they were needed to formulate the vision around which a Republican electoral majority could coalesce.

The changing character of American populism was vital to gaining that majority. In 1976 it was not novel to observe, as Kristol did, that "if you want to find a radical, go to the nearest college, not the nearest factory." Nor was Kristol's the only voice saying that "the common man has always preferred bourgeois capitalism to its intellectual critics; in the United States, for the most part, he still does." Kristol pushed these ideas further, however, flipping the picture of populism. Whereas Hofstadter had argued that elites—particularly intellectuals—were threatened by populism, Kristol found that "intellectuals are now more consistently populist than the populace itself." They were populist in the same way that Hofstadter had described populism: resentful, anxious, and prone to imagine conspiracies—of imperial mandarins or military-industrial complexes. "Indeed, when the American people sensibly resist the populist temptation—when they exhibit a preference for a politics of calm deliberation over a politics of passionate resentment—they are likely to be rebuked by their intellectuals for their disgusting 'apathy.'"[136] Hofstadter's conception of populism held, but the groups to which it applied were switched.

Now the people were calmly deliberative and intellectuals were dangerous hotheads.

If intellectuals had become "populist" in the Hofstadterian sense, ordinary people were populist in resisting the encroachment of the state and its New Class operatives. "It is the middle class that manages our welfare state, whereas our working class is managed by it—and it is a lot more fun to manage than to be managed," Kristol observed. "Middle-class reformers will find, to their surprise, that the populace is going to be quick to bite the hand that aims to feed it. The populace doesn't want to be fed; it wants more freedom to graze on its own." The populace also wanted a morally coherent social order. While ideas might disrupt that order and "alienate us from our world, so it is ideas which can make us at home in the world"—a place for "the practice of ordinary virtues in the course of our ordinary lives." The people could do without the interference of New Class intellectuals in their economic lives, but they needed the intervention of Straussian intellectuals in their moral ones. A renewed moral order was "the intellectual enterprise that most needs encouragement and support today."[137]

The links of Kristol's logic created not so much a chain as chain mail—each part connecting to and reinforcing the others. Clothed in this armor of ideas, intellectuals like Kristol could sally forth in support of corporate capitalism and the Republican Party, jousting with the New Class on the tournament grounds of culture and values. As steel is an alloy of iron and carbon, Kristol's armor was forged from the fusion of intellect and institutions.

The Institute for Educational Affairs, which Kristol founded in 1978 with former treasury secretary William E. Simon, embodied this fusion. Corporations had "become increasingly concerned about the efficacy of their contributions" to higher education, reported a committee that Simon chaired. "They have been made aware of the need to devote a portion of their efforts to reinvigorating the intellectual climate that nourished them, the 'cultural capital of capitalism' to use Irving Kristol's phrase." Kristol's work had indeed been "a frequent topic of discussion at meetings of businessmen, educators, and others committed to a free society." They sought an organization whose "mission would be to channel grants to those who are engaged in preserving (and refining) that intellectual and cultural atmosphere without which a free society and economy cannot long survive."[138] What would become the Institute for Educational Affairs was born.[139]

IEA's initial slate of directors brought together intellectuals, corporate executives, and political leaders. In addition to Kristol and Simon, it included UC San Diego literature professor Ronald Berman, University of Toronto government professor Walter Berns, former United States solicitor general Robert Bork, San Jose State University president John Bunzel, Kmart's Harry Cunningham, SmithKline's Robert Dee, Motorola's Robert Galvin, Mellon Bank's James Higgins, Republican fundraiser Jeremiah Milbank, writer Michael Novak, Hewlett-Packard's David Packard, education scholar Diane Ravitch, RKO's Frank Shakespeare, and W. Allen Wallis, chancellor of the University of Rochester and chairman of the Corporation for Public Broadcasting.[140] It was their "profound belief that this new Institute can have a significant effect on the climate of opinion in which we live, think, and work."[141]

Though IEA was the work of many hands, Kristol was the animating force. The "Statement of Purpose" in IEA's 1980 annual report described how the organization arose in response to the troubling cultural landscape that Kristol had been mapping for more than a decade. "No sooner did the late Lionel Trilling coin the phrase 'adversary culture,' than it became increasingly the common term capturing events that all of us, vaguely or acutely, had found intruding into our lives." IEA "exists because our culture . . . had become disjointed and infused with adversary sentiments and with utopian expectations." The adversary culture "rose on the strength of ideas hostile to many of the fundamental values of our society, and it is with ideas that the adversary culture must be combated." Through its educational and grant-making activities, IEA sought to foster "a culture that fulfills its traditional role as sustainer and guardian of our civilization." In 1980 IEA had a budget of $883,150, with more than "74 corporations, foundations, and individuals" as donors.[142]

That year Kristol's and IEA's efforts to oppose the New Class, promote conservative ideas, and build a Republican majority bore fruit: Ronald Reagan was elected president. The Reagan campaign appointed Kristol to a group giving "advice and counsel on a broad range of key national policy issues." By July 1980, he was head of Reagan's "task force on social policy." Critics saw Kristol providing the Reagan Revolution's intellectual underpinnings. As the U.S. News & World Report put it, Kristol "sowed the ideological seeds for Reagan's 1980 presidential victory, paving the way for such new-fangled ideas as supply-side economics." The Village Voice reported that "like no other conservative, Irving Kristol ties the Reagan administration to its intellectual moorings." According to journalist Walter Goodman, "The ideas that Kristol purveys can be felt today in tax cuts and budget cuts, in the movement toward deregulation and away from social programs, in breaks for the well-to-do and aches for the poor. The ideas that inspire the Reagan Administration are hardly the invention of Irving Kristol, as he would be the first to concede, but he has turned an assortment of academic propositions into justifications for a set of White House policies." After Reagan's reelection, Phillip Marcus of IEA quipped that "the media, when trying to find beyond the President's popularity causes for his electoral success, have rediscovered our work. It seems to some in the national media that IEA must be part of the explanation for a nation enthralled."[143]

Reagan himself acknowledged Kristol's role, observing "that the political revolutions we've seen in America in domestic and international policy are only a reflection of a deeper trend" in "the world of ideas." Reagan saw a "dramatic turnabout among the intellectuals. For most of my adult life, the intelligentsia has been entranced and enamored with the idea of state power, the notion that enough centralized authority concentrated in the hands of the right-minded people can reform mankind and usher in a brave new world." Now, however, "the trend in America and the democracies has been just the other way. In the political world, the cult of the state is dying; so too the romance of the intellectual world is focused these days on the concerns of human freedom, on the importance of transcendent and enduring values." This change had "been spearheaded for 30 years by intellectual presences like William F. Buckley's *National Review*. It's been supplemented recently by what's called the 'neo-conservative' revolution led by Irving Kristol."[144]

In 1973 Kristol had asked: "What medicine does one prescribe for a social order that is sick because it has lost its soul?" If a decade later America was taking the prescription written by Dr. Reagan, not everyone welcomed the pill. Irving Howe was among them, but he marveled at Kristol's pharmacology. He had "'persuaded the bourgeois managers that ideology matters, that they have a body of thought, a morality on their side,'" Howe said. "'That's a new thing for corporation people—that they, too, have an idea and aren't just greedy and selfish. Everybody needs a fix.'"[145]

On the eve of the Reagan Revolution, Schlesinger also doubted Kristol's diagnosis of America's ills. The two discussed the Department of Health, Education, and Welfare. "Arthur," Kristol said, "you know from your own university experience a lot of the really absurd regulations that are imposed on our economy and society. And since I don't think the people who foster such regulations are stupid and I don't think they really believe in an absurd world, I can only assume that this is part of a general strategy of involving government more and more in the economic and social life of the country." Schlesinger did not "believe that for a moment. It may be a dream of some, but I think, Irving, one can never underestimate the power of mindlessness in human affairs"—a line that echoed the one he used years earlier in response to Noam Chomsky. New mandarins and the New Class were both to be shrugged off as conspiratorial fiction. "I must confess a skepticism," Schlesinger remarked, "on the existence of the 'New Class.' The New Class has been predicted forever. Veblen wrote about the soviet of engineers. . . . I am reminded of that old Chinese proverb: 'There's a lot of noise on the stairs, but no one comes into the room.'" Kristol persisted: "There are a great many people in this society, particularly people who are now called liberals and are members of this New Class, who think redistribution on moral grounds is the most important political necessity, and that if you have to frustrate economic growth to achieve that redistribution, that's the way to do it." Schlesinger was unconvinced. "I think that's a bizarre and unduly conspiratorial reading," he replied. "No one is going to succeed in making a political appeal on those grounds."[146]

The ensuing years proved Schlesinger wrong. Political appeals on the grounds that a New Class of intellectuals sought the apparatus of government to stifle economic growth and thereby enhance its own power did succeed, and marvelously so. This was the backdrop against which Reagan's well-known 1986 statement resounded: "The nine most terrifying words in the English language are 'I'm from the government, and I'm here to help.'"[147]

* * *

Kristol's career spans heated moments of debate about the role of intellectuals in American political culture after World War Two. He entered the fray in 1952, that year of Stevenson and McCarthyism, when embattled intellectuals like Hofstadter defended the life of the mind. Thirty years later, intellectuals were again embattled. This time, however, their antagonist was not a senator from Wisconsin but an intellectual from New York. Kristol had become the scourge of the New Class, head of a neoconservative movement that he helped build, intellectually and institutionally.

This surge on the right contained elements of intellectual activism on the left. Both camps regarded American political culture as a stage upon which a cast of intellectuals, good and bad, participated in a morality play. The villains were intellectuals—not lone actors but a whole faceless chorus of them, whether new mandarins or a New Class. The saviors were single intellectuals, voices of protest and dissent who delivered soliloquies on the threat posed by intellectuals as a group and lamentations over how the very heart of intellectual life, its concern for non-material things, had been warped and broken by the practices of this group. The players, playwrights, stagehands, and directors were mostly white men. The audience was the American people. A significant difference between Kristol's performance and that of intellectuals on the left was that he could better elicit an ovation.

As the curtain descended on this drama, a pressing question remained: Was the relation between people and intellectuals always going to be a spectatorial one? In the next decade, even as commentators like Russell Jacoby and Allan Bloom mourned the passing of certain intellectuals from the stage, another set of thinkers, including Cornel West and bell hooks, sought to break the fourth wall. They took up the problem of democratizing the interplay of intellectuals and others by emphasizing the concept of community.

CRITICAL ORGANIC CATALYST,
PROPHETIC PRAGMATIST,
AND PUBLIC INTELLECTUAL

Racialized and gendered blinkers and barriers produced a narrowed, simpli-fied view of American intellectual life. Theodore White's 1967 *Life* maga-zine series on "Action Intellectuals" described a "brotherhood of scholars" who were "the most provocative and propelling influence on all American government and politics." Among members of the "brotherhood" receiv-ing sustained coverage and, crucially for *Life*, a photograph, only one—Kenneth Clark—was African American. None were women. In *Ebony* the year before, by contrast, Ponchitta Pierce's "Problems of the Negro Woman Intellectual" featured *Life*-like portraits of poet Gwendolyn Brooks, civil rights leader Pauli Murray, US Ambassador to Luxembourg Patricia Rob-erts Harris, ACLU legal theorist and future congresswoman Eleanor Holmes Norton, and several other African American women intellectuals. Pierce's piece proved more prescient than White's, for during the 1960s, a wider panorama was replacing the incomplete picture given in *Life*.[1]

Shattered was the illusion that intellectual opinion could be canvassed over cocktails at Schlesinger's Manhattan apartment. There had always been intellectuals excluded from that world, yet intellectual life, especially as it bore upon politics, nonetheless had in venues like *Life* a perceived center of gravity located between Boston and Washington, composed mostly of Anglo-American and, especially after World War Two, Jewish men. As more voices historically barred from this center occupied it, and as competing centers of intellectual activity gained visibility, American intellectual life changed.

The social movements of the 1960s highlighted women, African Amer-ican, Latin American, Native American, lesbian, and gay intellectuals. They also amplified radical voices and those, like Irving Kristol, counter to them. These developments multiplied the grounds on which one might speak as an intellectual in American public life. They exploded the con-ventional image of who an intellectual might be.

If *Life's* 1967 stock intellectual had horn-rimmed glasses, an Ivy League affiliation, and a white male body, by 1995 there was no such image. In the *Atlantic* and the *New Yorker* that year was Cornel West—a philosopher who swapped the fustian tone of Schlesinger for the homiletics of the Baptist Church, wore an Afro, and would appear in a blockbuster science-fiction film. There were, in short, breaks from the past sparking new debates about the role of intellectuals in American political culture.

Yet there were also continuities. Despite breaking parts of the mold in which intellectuals had been cast, West was a man who had Ivy League addresses and grappled with familiar debates. Against Richard Hofstadter's counsel of safe distance between intellectuals and a populace inclined to anti-intellectualism, West sought to remove barriers between intellectuals and everyday life. Kristol lauded the virtues and values of the middle class against the new one; West saw a rich cultural tradition in the "doings and sufferings" of ordinary people. Like H. Stuart Hughes and Christopher Lasch, West undertook political work, struggling to engage as an intellectual while upholding democratic norms. Like C. Wright Mills, Hughes, and Lasch, he sketched broad blueprints and programmatic plans for political formations he hoped would emerge.

Beyond these postwar debates, West entered a longer conversation that, taking W. E. B. Du Bois's 1903 "Talented Tenth" essay as a touchstone, weighed the particular responsibilities of African American intellectuals, especially to their race.[2] Not only policy but also literary intellectuals—from Frances Ellen Watkins Harper to Langston Hughes to Ralph Ellison to Toni Morrison—addressed and were confronted by this question.[3] On either side of West's rise to prominence, James Baldwin and Ta-Nehisi Coates transmitted their insights in the form of letters to young men—a nephew and a son. Baldwin's *The Fire Next Time* (1963) and Coates's *Between the World and Me* (2015) are meditations upon and indictments of the color line that both spoke to African American experiences and reached white audiences. Like Frederick Douglass's 1852 "What to the Slave Is the Fourth of July?" speech, they are searing appraisals of American society delivered by intellectuals positioned to see it from without as well as within.[4] In the long African American intellectual tradition, responsibility to the race ran alongside critical perspectives for the entire culture.

West's career came at a moment when uniting two strands—debates about the role of African American intellectuals and those about intellectuals overall—seemed possible. He was called both an important African American intellectual and an important American one. This double distinction followed the perceived retreat of intellectuals from public life. In the 1980s, critics Russell Jacoby and Allan Bloom sparked debate about intellectual decline by claiming that academicizing intellectuals and their stultifying postmodern discourse left the public sphere impoverished. These lamentations suggested a nostalgia for the heyday of the New York Intellectuals (Russell Jacoby), the pre-1968 version of collegiate life (Allan Bloom), and the palpable presence of intellectuals as a beacon in the cultural night (both).[5] In this moment of attending to the absence of intellectuals, West and a cohort of African American scholars—bell hooks, Henry Louis Gates Jr., and others—became a visible presence: the representatives of a new and potentially improved public intellectualism. West emerged, therefore, as new conceptions of the intellectual's role did too. He exhibited the tensions and contradictions among these roles even as he self-consciously attempted to manipulate and negotiate them. West figured as an "organic intellectual" and a public intellectual, a celebrity intellectual and an academic intellectual, an African American intellectual and a left intellectual, a Christian intellectual and a neo-pragmatist. He was a lightning rod for debate about the role of intellectuals and an instance of the ongoing indeterminacy, multiplicity, and importance of that role.

* * *

Cornel West's parents met at Fisk University before moving to Oklahoma, where his grandfather had been a minister and where West was born in 1953. The family moved to Sacramento, which, despite its segregation, West remembered as a place where African American humanity was assumed rather than questioned. He cultivated Christian faith at Shiloh Baptist Church while reading via bookmobile European philosophy that doubted such faith. Next door to Shiloh was the Black Panther Party, and West read its newspaper "all the time." Though feeling "'called' to be someone who spoke with and for a larger group," West—idolizing Willie Mays and James Brown—"wanted to be either an athlete or an entertainer." He "didn't think of the life of the mind or an intellectual vocation until . . . college."[6]

At Harvard, West studied intellectual history with H. Stuart Hughes and discovered *Dissent* through Michael Walzer.[7] His degree in Near Eastern languages and literature reflected sustained engagement with scripture. Going on to graduate school in philosophy at Princeton, West encountered Richard Rorty, whose neo-pragmatism—a revival of the American philosophy concerned with the uses rather than a priori foundations of thinking—"had a tremendous impact" on him.[8] His philosophy nurtured by Rorty, West's conception of political theory was shaped by Sheldon Wolin.[9] In "Political Theory as a Vocation" (1969), Wolin formulated an ideal of the theorist that began with a concern for public problems, not—as in much social science of the day—a research question. "For us, Wolin-influenced intellectuals," West wrote, "to be a political theorist is to make a choice to be a certain kind of human being—one who . . . pursue[s] fundamental criticisms of power-laden circumstances" on behalf of "ordinary people."[10] West sought to weave Rorty's philosophy into Wolin's theory on behalf of a democratic movement from below, which he would serve as an intellectual from some position other than above.

Despite his training, West "never became a philosopher, professionally speaking."[11] Union Theological Seminary in Manhattan offered a more public-facing alternative—"the perfect place to become a broadly engaged cultural critic."[12] A center of religious thought once home to Reinhold Niebuhr and Paul Tillich, Union had long engaged its community, including with a settlement house modeled after Hull House. In 1969 James H. Cone arrived as one of Union's first African American professors. His *Black Theology and Black Power*, published that year, viewed Christianity in the light of African American liberation and self-determination.[13]

West arrived at Union in 1977, after a fellowship at Harvard's W. E. B. Du Bois Institute and some thoughts of becoming a novelist. His writing in this period—from "Socialism and the Black Church" (1979) to *Prophesy Deliverance!* (1982)—placed Marxism into conversation with African American religious tradition. In 1984 West moved to Yale Divinity School, where he advocated for divestment from apartheid South Africa and on behalf of employees seeking living wages. After being arrested during a protest, West left Yale and returned briefly to Union in time for his second book, *Prophetic Fragments* (1988). Ruth Simmons and Toni Morrison recruited him to direct Princeton's African American Studies Program, and his next book, *The American Evasion of Philosophy: A Genealogy of Pragmatism* (1989), garnered academic acclaim.[14]

West's star was soaring. On April 1, 1990, he appeared on PBS with Bill Moyers. "For many Black Americans," bell hooks wrote, "watching Cornel West on the Bill Moyers show broadcast from Riverside Church was a major cultural event signifying a change in who is allowed to speak for and about Black experience."[15] In a voice-over accompanying images of West teaching at a chalkboard and walking in New York, Moyers described him as someone who "moves in many worlds. He writes about everything from postmodern architecture and rap music to teenage suicide and black politicians. You will find him often speaking to community groups and to kids in public schools and, as a lay preacher, in the pulpits of various denominations." West sat facing Moyers and framed by the church—a cross and Bible visible over his shoulder. Their conversation ranged from electoral politics to Prince and Public Enemy, from Christianity to urban poverty.[16]

A week later, Duke University philosopher Kwame Anthony Appiah noted that West "bridges cultural theory and the black community," bringing "the black church, for example, into debates about the politics of postmodernity, while transforming discussions in the black community with his sharp sense of the relevance of theory to its concerns."[17] Different threads in American culture were joining, and West seemed to hold the sewing kit. He wrote about philosophy that was transforming the epistemological foundations of authority, leaving many wondering what a new basis for truth—moral and even empirical—could be. He was part of an African American community—so diverse that "community" seemed more aspirational than real—for which the early 1990s were a pregnant moment, shaped by Rodney King, Clarence Thomas, Oprah Winfrey, Michael Jordan, Toni Morrison, Dr. Dre, Louis Farrakhan, and others. In the midst of it all, West fashioned a public presence as an intellectual who contained—if he could not reconcile—contradictions and cultural forces within himself, representing Du Bois's "two-ness" anew. Between the academy and the public, the Christian tradition and the philosophical one, Michael Jackson and Michel Foucault, West held "warring ideals in one dark body, whose dogged strength alone keeps it from being torn asunder."[18]

* * *

"Struggles over the intellectual construction of reality," historian Daniel T. Rodgers writes, "took on new breadth and intensity in the last quarter of the twentieth century." Noting how "assumptions that had defined the common sense of public intellectual life since the Second World War were challenged, dismantled, formulated anew," Rodgers calls this period the "age of fracture." In 1967 Noam Chomsky asserted: "It is the responsibility

of intellectuals to speak the truth and to expose lies." Although his state‑
ment seemed like "a truism," Chomsky believed it necessary since intel‑
lectuals were perpetuating lies, not exposing them. In the age of fracture,
Chomsky's statement was no truism either: not because intellectuals were
failing to tell the truth, but because the notion of truth itself had become
problematic.[19]

Thomas Kuhn's *The Structure of Scientific Revolutions* (1962) rattled
notions of objectivity by introducing paradigm shifts as the basis for chang‑
ing scientific knowledge. Paradigms are the theoretical backdrops against
which scientific research is conducted. Kuhn's work suggested that social
forces—not rational method—kept paradigms in place, prompting dis‑
missal of data that did not fit current theories. As anomalous data accumu‑
lated, however, some would question the dominant paradigm and begin
formulating a new one, but why these particular individuals made the leap
from one paradigm to another while others tenaciously refused to do so was
a subjective matter—a black box of individual personality and proclivity
sitting at the heart of a scientific enterprise supposed to open such boxes
to the light of objectivity.[20]

Physical science was not the only bastion of truth under assault. Cri‑
tiques of Enlightenment ideas about knowledge, rationality, and the indi‑
vidual as knowing subject arrived under the heading "postmodernism." Its
prominent exponents were French intellectuals whose American recep‑
tion traces to a 1966 conference at Johns Hopkins, "The Language of Crit‑
icism and the Sciences of Man," that included Roland Barthes, Jacques
Derrida, and Jacques Lacan.[21] Though he was not present in Baltimore,
no French theorist shook the foundations of American social thought
more than Michel Foucault. He challenged the simple idea of intellectu‑
als speaking truth to power by arguing that power actually speaks through
intellectuals. The very concepts of "truth" and "the intellectual" were
themselves products of discourses infused with power relations. Foucault
was a wrecking ball swinging toward the platform upon which intellectuals
like Chomsky spoke.

Something of this moment was captured when in 1971 Chomsky
appeared with Foucault on a Dutch television show that hosted philosoph‑
ical debate.[22] Foucault challenged the notion of an autonomous human
being, giving "very little room to what you might call the creativity of
individuals, . . . to their aptitude for inventing by themselves, for origi‑
nating concepts, theories or scientific truths by themselves." The truth‑

discovering individual was a character produced by "a certain 'romanticism' about the history of science." Toppling premodern, communal forms of understanding, scientific culture celebrated "the solitude of the man of truth." Truth and the truth-seeker therefore had genealogies; they were products of history rather than standing, objectively, outside it. Having unmasked its past, Foucault suggested that in the future truth may be supplanted by "understanding"—replacing "individuals and their 'knowledge'" with "knowledge as a collective practice" that "functions according to certain rules which one can register and describe." Where Chomsky highlighted the creative capacities of individuals as demonstrated by their ability to produce language, Foucault wanted to remove the creative individual from center stage. "For me it is a matter of effacing the dilemma of the knowing subject," he said.[23]

These ideas shaped the two thinkers' politics. Humans, Chomsky observed, "don't know enough and we're too limited and too biased" to "create a system of ideal justice." With their innate reason, however, people could nonetheless evaluate the world and "must act as sensitive and responsible human beings . . . to imagine and move towards the creation of a better society and also a better system of justice." The very concept of political struggle relied upon this prospect. It differed dramatically from Foucault's picture of people entangled in modes of knowledge and power that acted upon them rather than at their direction. Indeed, Foucault said, "justice in itself is an idea which in effect has been invented and put to work in different types of societies as an instrument of a certain political and economic power or as a weapon against that power." Justice had a genealogy. Chomsky, however, thought there was "an absolute basis—if you press me too hard I'll be in trouble, because I can't sketch it out— ultimately residing in fundamental human qualities, in terms of which a 'real' notion of justice is grounded." Foucault was unimpressed. "However regrettable it may be," he replied, there were no ahistorical ideals that could "describe or justify a fight" for social change. There was neither a knowing subject nor an absolute justice to which Foucault would allow Chomsky to appeal; there was only power and its serpentine trail through history.[24]

The Chomsky-Foucault debate framed the uncertain role of intellectuals as the age of fracture dawned. Intellectuals' authority flowed from a presumption that they trafficked in truth. The expert dealt in empirical truth and the social critic in moral truth. Chomsky put the dogged exposure of facts—the number of dead beneath American bombs—in the service of moral judgments: the conclusion that such bombing was a crime. Calling into question the epistemological grounds upon which Chomsky or any intellectual claimed to know such truths undermined this effort. With truth claims disrupted, so was any authority intellectuals enjoyed on the basis of them.

While epistemological uncertainty posed a challenge, it also contained an opportunity. "The grand quest for truth is a thoroughly historical one," West wrote in 1984, siding with Foucault. There were "standards of adjudication, but such historically constituted standards include multiple viewpoints worthy of adoption."[25] If a singular conception of truth had been toppled, then so had a singular platform for intellectual authority. If this singular conception could be replaced by a multiplicity of modes of knowing plural truths, however, then the age of fracture might see not the erosion of platforms for intellectual authority, but their proliferation: "multiple viewpoints worthy of adoption." There may be space for more voices to speak—if not to converse.

As Foucault debated Chomsky on the heights of abstraction, changes on the ground occurred that enabled other voices to speak and be heard. These developments were linked. Changing demographics in higher education provided a broader public for the critical questions that postmodernists and others were asking about the nature of knowledge and the role of intellectuals. The percentage of women college students climbed from 29 percent in 1947 to over 50 percent by 1979. By 1980, 16 percent of college students were people of color.[26] At Harvard in 1970, West "became part of the first generation of young black people to attend prestigious lily-white institutions of higher learning in significant numbers."[27] Increased diversity on campuses stemmed from social movements aimed at capturing a fuller measure of equality and power for marginalized groups. Higher education, West wrote, felt "the tide of decolonizing sensibilities," which created "unprecedented opportunities—discursive, political, ideological, existential"—for African Americans and "for Latinos and Latinas, for Native Americans, and for American women."[28]

Historians Joyce Appleby, Lynn Hunt, and Margaret Jacob—who had been students at the time—linked changing campus populations to intellectual shifts. "It is as if higher education was opened to us—women, minorities, working people—at the same time that we lost the philosophical foundation that had underpinned the confidence of educated people," they wrote. Students who a generation earlier would have been excluded from college arrived there with "little confidence in . . . prevailing intellectual assumptions" and "less impressed by the model of objective knowledge."[29]

These new undergraduate students became graduate students who rewrote history "from the bottom up." Their work engaged swaths of historical experience previously neglected: the realm of everyday life; the histories of working people, enslaved labor, and women; the experiences of immigrants and people of color. This scholarship mined new sources and crossed disciplinary boundaries, deploying the insights of anthropology, ethnography, sociology, geography, economics, linguistics, and psychology.[30]

These interdisciplinary angles influenced West. Trained as a philosopher, he taught in theology schools and African American studies programs, deploying literary and social scientific sources to analyze politics, culture, and economics. This ecumenical approach pulls away from the specialization that enables intellectuals to speak as experts. West did not eschew expertise, however, so much as demand that intellectuals attain it in multiple fields. The image of intellectuals ranging across varied domains of knowledge evokes eighteenth-century polymaths like Thomas Jefferson or Benjamin Franklin. West pointed out that disciplines in their time were limited, however, built upon but not accounting for "social structural constraints . . . that reinforce and reproduce hierarchies based on class, race, gender, and sexual orientation."[31] Having eschewed specialization and critiqued the polymathic tradition's simplification, West faced the daunting prospect of being an intellectual who could achieve both interdisciplinarity and mastery. He risked being jack of all trades but master of none—and mastery had been a crucial feature of the authority that intellectuals invoked in the public sphere.

The new historical scholarship's impact on West was manifold. He deemed it "the most important" of the "crucial processes that have affected the life and the mind of the country." It was the steering column for his "historicist turn"—an attempt to generate knowledge, understanding, and political consciousness by shifting from abstract philosophical reasoning toward historical experience. As the new historiography focused on popular religion and culture, folklore, and everyday life, it demonstrated the presence of intellectual traditions where it had been assumed none existed, revealing for West "the impact of forms of popular culture, on highbrow literate culture." Academics were "usually running from" non-elite cultural practices, "because we know that popular culture has been associated with anti-intellectualism that tends to suffocate the life of the mind." The histories of ordinary people revealed, however, that the contents of their cultures were a rich set of intellectual resources in their own right. The implications were profound. An intellectual could now speak from a multiplicity of sophisticated intellectual and cultural traditions that, while previously overlooked, could take their place not in opposition to, but in the ranks of what Matthew Arnold called "the best which has been thought and said in the world." It was not a matter of relaxing standards for "the best"; it was about expanding the scope of "the world."[32]

The new social historians wrote of "ordinary people and everyday life," and West borrowed their vocabulary. He saw politics, for instance, "rooted in the everyday lives of ordinary people" and applauded intellectuals who took "the life of the mind seriously enough to relate ideas to the everyday life of ordinary folk." He described poet and scholar Sterling Brown as "a highbrow intellectual . . . humble enough to recognize that there's a sense of the tragic and majestic and problematic shot through the lives of what Sly Stone calls 'everyday people'—James Cleveland calls 'ordinary people.'" Where Hofstadter saw the popular and quotidian as breeding grounds for anti-intellectualism, West found in them the site of and source for intellectuals' work.[33]

As new scholars opened the academy, new publications broadened the print culture of American intellectual life. In African American studies alone, several important journals started between 1967 and 1977, including *Black Scholar*, *Callaloo*, and the *Journal of Black Studies*. Similar growth occurred in women's studies with *Signs*, *Frontiers*, and *Feminist Review*; and conservative circles, with *American Spectator*, *Imprimis*, and *Policy Review*.

Beyond academia, media of all types multiplied. "We are now a culture whose information, ideas, and epistemology are given form by television, not by the printed word," Neil Postman proclaimed in 1985. New modes of transmission met new audiences for reception. "There are now a plurality of audiences within a public culture that is essentially cosmopolitan and contested," Thomas Bender observed in 1993. The white middle class that had long masqueraded as "the public" no longer could. "Today, the public is at once increasingly representative, and more fragmented," Bender wrote, "making it harder to find, to reach, and to define." This transformation posed challenges for intellectuals seeking to reach a wider public. As Bender put it, the "public and the intellectual's relation to it can no longer be assumed in the way that [Lionel] Trilling assumed his public." West suggested that the "intellectual space Trilling had helped create—the space of liberal bourgeois humanist conversation and civil intercourse in which the cult of complexity reigned supreme, above political polemics and mass culture—had been eclipsed by an intensely polarized intellectual life in America."[34]

Yet this same fragmentation, multiplication, and polarization that made it difficult for Trilling-like intellectuals to locate "the public," allowed others to locate *a public*. Questioning the epistemic foundations of intellectuals' authority undermined that authority but also created space for new authorities rooted in alternative modes of knowing. Even as new audio and visual media seemed cacophonous, they increased communication between intellectuals and publics. Fracture and opportunity, it turned out, could be two faces of the same age, one in which the role of the intellectual was redefined and contested, not destroyed.

The age produced another element that framed intellectual life: retrospection. Some critics were looking backward, and a wave of books recounted the American intellectual scene of the 1930s through the 1960s. Alexander Bloom's *Prodigal Sons: The New York Intellectuals and Their World*, Howard Brick's *Daniel Bell and the Decline of Intellectual Radicalism*, and Terry A. Cooney's *The Rise of the New York Intellectuals* came out in 1986. Alan Wald's *The New York Intellectuals* was released the following year. Preceding these studies were two Irvings' biographies: Kristol's *Reflections of a Neoconservative: Looking Back, Looking Ahead* (1983) and Howe's *A Margin of Hope: An Intellectual Autobiography* (1982).

Two 1987 books invidiously compared present to past: Allan Bloom's *The Closing of the American Mind*, written from the right, and Russell Jacoby's *The Last Intellectuals*, written from the left. Both were surprisingly popular. They focused on intellectuals' migration from the public sphere into academia. Jacoby worried about its implications for the public sphere, Bloom about its portents for the academy. West characterized Bloom's book as "a nostalgic and, for some, seductive depiction of the decline and decay of the highbrow, classical, humanist tradition," and Jacoby's as "a premature requiem for left public intellectuals." Both were "emblematic symptoms of the crisis in vocation of contemporary intellectuals."[35] They lamented the relocation not so much of intellectuals as the political controversy that intellectuals generated.

For Bloom, the problem was not that intellectuals had deprived the public of their political criticism but that they had politicized higher education. The result was a "crisis of liberal education," producing "incoherence and incompatibility among the first principles with which we interpret the world." The politicized university ceased to be a site of intellectual freedom for developing the souls of the young. Hofstadter had advanced a similar claim in 1968: "If an attempt is made to politicize completely our primary centers of free argument and inquiry, they will only in the end be forced to lose their character and be reduced to centers of vocational training, nothing more." Two decades later, Bloom read like a damage report from an academy unmoved by Hofstadter's warning.[36]

For Jacoby, intellectuals abandoned the public sphere and the social criticism that was their calling there. In the academy, they dilated upon esoteric discourse over narrow disciplinary turf. "Younger intellectuals no longer need or want a larger public," Jacoby wrote. "Campuses are their homes; colleagues their audience; monographs and specialized journals their media." They compared unfavorably with the "'last' generation of American intellectuals," who "mastered a public prose" by writing "to and for the educated public." Trilling, Mills, and Schlesinger were Jacoby's "benchmark." Lasch emerged after them, but was "neither young nor unestablished." Seeing no rising generation, Jacoby concluded that intellectuals "had surrendered the vernacular, sacrificing a public identity." An audience for their work had "dwindled" but not disappeared; it was therefore "less . . . the eclipse of a public" that concerned Jacoby "than . . . the eclipse of public intellectuals."[37]

And yet, Jacoby's book itself vivified the term "public intellectual."[38] He offered a simple definition: "Writers and thinkers who address a general and educated audience," not "intellectuals whose works are too technical or difficult to engage a public."[39] Yet "public intellectual" was less a taxonomical category than an ideal and a notation of its absence. It applied retroactively to the New York Intellectuals and highlighted, for Jacoby, the lack of contemporary figures like them. Rather than deconstructing "intellectual," a term that could already imply a public presence, Jacoby appended the adjective "public" and valorized the role thus described.

The Last Intellectuals "touched a nerve," Jacoby later wrote, "a widespread feeling that intellectual life had shifted, perhaps contracted." Critics called it "The Left Intellectuals" because it followed the arc of 1960s radicals. Dick Flacks of Students for a Democratic Society recalled that many from the New Left "opted for vocations in the university and the

professions" but "experienced such moves as an abandonment of their earlier commitment, a form of retreat." Jacoby's tale of intellectuals entering academe mapped onto the New Left's feelings of diminished engagement. But critics charged that in focusing on the left, Jacoby overlooked
other important developments, such as the rise of conservative intellectuals writing for a general audience. Jacoby approved their public idiom
while doubting their standing as intellectuals: they were neither generalists nor critics. (The conservative Bloom, however, was notably general—
ranging from Plato to the 1969 takeover of Cornell's student union—and
critical, targeting leftist professors.) More precisely, Jacoby held that conservatives were *ideologically* opposed to public intellectualism even when
they fit that bill. Rather than criticize the status quo, they tended to celebrate it. Rather than fostering generalists, they attacked academics who
spoke about political matters beyond their disciplinary expertise. Conservatives leaned "toward anti-intellectualism" rather than exemplifying
public intellectualism.[40]

Another species of intellectual that critics said Jacoby overlooked were
those operating behind the scenes—in organizations like Kristol's American Enterprise Institute. Jacoby "missed . . . fundamental changes in the
public sphere that shape the possibility of intellectual life outside the academy," reviewer Jeffrey Escoffier observed, especially "the growing influence . . . of 'think tank' intellectuals, predominantly neoconservatives."[41]
These intellectuals were not "public" in the sense of writing for a broad
audience—indeed, their audience was quite narrow: policymakers. But
that made them public in another sense: they influenced the formation of
public policy. Their audience was smaller, but their role in public affairs
was perhaps far greater, and certainly more direct, than that of Jacoby's
pantheon.

Escoffier charged Jacoby with missing something else: "the fragile intellectual life that has emerged from social movements and within minority
communities over the past twenty years." Writing in 1988, Escoffier noted
that "intellectuals in the black community, the women's movement, the
lesbian and gay communities, or the environmental movement participate in the internal intellectual and political debates within these communities, and frequently represent them externally." The Center for Third
World Organizing in Oakland, for example, "has a publishing program and
puts on conferences that bring together academics and activists." Escoffier concluded, however, that such "community intellectuals" were not

Jacoby's "public intellectuals." Lacking "resources to establish stable, long-lived institutions which can support intellectual work," they "play important roles in their own communities," but "few get the chance to address a broader public."[42]

The Last Intellectuals launched more arguments than it resolved, but it did have one shared result: people began looking for intellectuals. They wondered who was an intellectual and what an intellectual should be. The debates spilled into more popular periodicals. "The public intellectual's death knell was sounded by Russell Jacoby," Robert Boynton wrote in the *Atlantic* in 1995, and "a consensus soon formed that the era of the public intellectual was indeed over." The dirges, however, were premature. "No sooner had the last opinion piece about Jacoby's book been written than another group of intellectuals began getting quite a bit of attention," Boynton observed: "an impressive group of African-American writers and thinkers . . . bringing moral imagination and critical intelligence to bear on the definingly American matter of race—and reaching beyond race to voice what one calls 'the commonality of American concern.'"[43] Prominent among them were hooks and West.

* * *

Postmodern theory, new social history, proliferating media, a diversifying academy, and controversy around Jacoby's book and Bloom's framed debates about the role of American intellectuals. Further context informed debates about the role, specifically, of African American intellectuals. Behind West lay a conversation stretching beyond Du Bois to Alexander Crummell and Frances Ellen Watkins Harper about the relationship between education and leadership in the African American community.[44] It canvassed the need for autonomous African American intellectual life and the importance of African American thinkers to the life of the nation. Black Power, African American studies programs, and the rise of liberation theology within the African American church extended that conversation while West was a student. The precarious economic position of many African Americans in the 1980s sharpened the divide between the educated middle class and the "underclass" into a razor's edge. When West's *Race Matters* arrived in 1993, this sense of crisis had been concentrated by the Los Angeles riots. It was a moment when an African American intellectual might reach crossover audiences—African Americans looking for a voice within their community, white Americans looking for a voice from it, and

Americans in general looking for an assessment of the prospects and perils facing the country.

Henry Louis Gates Jr. suggested that he and West indeed belonged to a "crossover generation," the first "to attend integrated schools" after *Brown* and "to enter and integrate the elite" universities "just as the most expansive notions of radical democracy" arrived. For this generation, Du Bois's idea of a "Talented Tenth" leading the African American community was less intellectual history than live possibility. It "exerted unmistakable sway on us," Gates recalled. That idea had come under strain in books like E. Franklin Frazier's *Black Bourgeoisie* (1957) and Nathan Hare's *The Black Anglo-Saxons* (1965): "Where Du Bois saw saviors," Gates wrote, "a new generation saw only sellouts." Gates and West nonetheless sought "to think through—and critique—Du Bois's challenge of commitment to service that, we deeply believe, the formally educated owe to all those who have not benefited from . . . expanded opportunities." Their generation's reckoning with Du Bois was shaped by the advent of African American studies. University students entered preprofessional programs while also seeking "knowledge about their cultural and their ethnic heritages."[45] With prospects for upward mobility joined by a deepened sense of African American history, feelings of opportunity accompanied those of responsibility.

Gates was thrice assigned in college Du Bois's "The Talented Tenth" and Harold Cruse's *The Crisis of the Negro Intellectual* (1967)—"the two signal works in the black tradition meant to help us find our way through the abyss of integration."[46] Cruse's book appeared the same year as Chomsky's "The Responsibility of Intellectuals," underlining the double debate facing young scholars like Gates and West: the responsibility of intellectuals and the responsibility of African American intellectuals specifically.

Du Bois's essay proclaimed that "the Negro race, like all races, is going to be saved by its exceptional men." The Talented Tenth, as "the Best," could "guide the Mass away from the contamination and death of the Worst." The Tenth were not to be vocational instructors but "leaders of thought and missionaries of culture among their people." The masses—"so mystified and befuddled by the hard necessary toil of earning a living, as to have no aims higher than their bellies"—needed "the college-bred . . . man who sets the ideals of the community where he lives, directs its thoughts and heads it social movements."[47]

Du Bois revisited this idea in 1948, faulting himself for assuming the commitment of those tasked with executing it. The problem was as old as

Plato: why, having attained knowledge, would philosophers reenter the cave to aid those still in the shadows? Du Bois contemplated something more sinister. "Training a talented tenth might put in control and power, a group of selfish, self-indulgent, well-to-do men, whose basic interest in solving the Negro Problem was personal; personal freedom and unhampered enjoyment and use of the world, without any real care . . . as to what became of the mass of American Negroes." This realization and his engagement with Marxism led Du Bois to augment his old idea with two new features: "expert knowledge of modern economics as it affected American Negroes" and the "willingness to sacrifice and plan for such economic revolution in industry and just distribution of wealth, as would make the rise of our group possible." The new goal, he said, was "organized scientific leadership of the American Negro."[48]

Though modeling his own distinctive attire on Du Bois's, West criticized the Talented Tenth and its progenitor as deeply elitist.[49] While Du Bois "saw, analyzed, and empathized with black sadness, sorrow, and suffering," West wrote, "he didn't feel it in his bones deeply enough, nor was he intellectually open enough to position himself alongside the sorrowful, suffering yet striving ordinary black folk." Had he been, Du Bois might have noticed a great deal the Talented Tenth could learn from the other nine-tenths. "Such lessons would have required" Du Bois to "believe that they were or might be as wise, insightful, and 'advanced' as he; and this he could not do."[50]

While Du Bois lionized intellectuals, West elevated "ordinary black folk"—calling the Tenth the "educated and chattering class." He rejected the notion that "self-appointed agents of Enlightenment constitute a sacrificial cultural elite engaged in service on behalf of the impulsive and irrational masses," a service rendered by "molding the values and viewpoints of the masses." West argued that intellectuals had not, in fact, guided the African American community. The "most effective political forms of organizing and mobilizing" in Du Bois's time included "the black women's club movement led by Ida B. Wells." Not specifying why Wells, a powerful thinker and writer, was not considered an intellectual, West simply suggested that momentum arose from strong "black civic associations like churches, lodges, fraternal orders, and sororities," rather than intellectuals' direction.[51] The cultural tastes of the Tenth, moreover, did not equate to higher character, for "people who delight in the works of . . . Mozart and Beethoven or Goethe and Wordsworth" were not "any more

or less humane than those who dance in the barnyards to the banjo pluck-
ing of nameless rural folk in Tennessee." Indeed, "white supremacists who
worship the Greek and Roman classics and revel in the plays of . . . Shakespeare weaken [that] case."[52]

West admired the scope of the intellectualism that Du Bois represented:
it "elevates the role of public intellectuals who put forward overarching
visions and broad analyses." But he urged moving "beyond any notions of
free-floating elites, suspicious of the tainted masses—elites who worship at
the altar of highbrow culture while ignoring the barbarity . . . in their own
ranks."[53] In keeping with the new historiography's identification of intellectual traditions among those who did not necessarily write them down,
West argued for a shift in the locus of intellectual life—from the rarified air
of the Tenth to the everyday environs of ordinary people.

Retaining the distinct role of the intellectual, however, West faced the
problem of locating it on social terrain other than Du Bois's high ground.
He had to sail between the Scylla of Du Boisian elitism and the Charybdis of popular anti-intellectualism. In *The Future of the Race* (1996), he
and Gates did not skirt these perils so much as float into them. "We, the
members of Du Bois's Talented Tenth, must accept our historical responsibility," they wrote.[54] West assumed the mantle while resisting the pit-
falls of the Tenth by pointing to the "role of the public intellectual." This
role—"distinct from, yet building on, the indispensable work of academics, experts, analysts, and pundits"—was to "create and sustain high-
quality public discourse addressing urgent public problems," discourse that
"enlightens and energizes fellow citizens, prompting them to take public
action." It had the scope laudable in Du Bois and "requires a deep commitment to the life of the mind—a perennial attempt to clear our minds
of cant (to use Samuel Johnson's famous formulation)—which serves to
shape the public destiny of a people." Intellectuals' mental clarity shaping
people's destiny sounds rather elitist, however, alongside West's populist
critique of the Tenth. He navigated this contradiction by asserting that
"intellectual and political leadership is neither elitist nor populist; rather
it is democratic, in that each of us stands in public space, without humiliation, to put forward our best visions and views for the sake of the public
interest."[55]

If Du Bois framed the relationship of African American intellectuals
to the African American community, Cruse's *Crisis of the Negro Intellectual* framed their relationship to whites. Like Kristol, Cruse attended City

College and served in Europe during World War Two. A playwright, he cofounded Harlem's Black Arts Repertory Theatre.[56] By 1967 Cruse could look back upon the gathering strength of the civil rights movement. From the 1955–56 Montgomery, Alabama, bus boycott to the 1963 March on Washington, local successes joined rising national attention. This momentum spurred passage of the Civil Rights Act of 1964 and the Voting Rights Act of 1965—years marked, however, by more than legislative victories. Residential segregation, employment discrimination, and police brutality fueled uprisings in Rochester, Harlem, Philadelphia, and Chicago. Thirty-four died in Watts. In these cities outside the South, African Americans' frustration with the contrast between putative de jure equality and glaring de facto inequality mounted.

As the sites of protest shifted, so did debate about its aims: was the goal integration or something else? "Black Power"—emphasizing African American autonomy rather than integration—gained traction in the Student Nonviolent Coordinating Committee (SNCC). When Stokely Carmichael succeeded John Lewis as head of SNCC in 1966, he steered it toward Black Power, and this new goal brought new methods. Nonviolent protest sought integration; Black Power called for confrontation. SNCC was succeeded by groups, like the Black Panther Party, fitted to that approach.

The changing African American freedom struggle was Cruse's occasion to assess African American intellectuals from the Harlem Renaissance on, and he criticized those of both the integrationist and Black Power orientations. The former "are still geared to piddling intellectual civil writism and racial integrationism," and the latter "have not advanced one whit in their thinking, beyond the 1919 writers of A. Phillip Randolph's *Messenger* magazine"—radical socialists who emphasized economic and political power rather than culture, which they thought Du Bois had wrongly prioritized.[57]

African American intellectuals were, Cruse argued, undermined by their social location: "not fully integrated into the intellectual class" but "socially detached from" their "own Negro ethnic world." Any integration among African American and white intellectuals had not altered the subordination of the former, who "plays second and third fiddle to white intellectuals in all the establishments—Left, Center, and Right." White intellectuals "do not recognize the Negro intellectual as a man who can speak both for himself and for the best interests of the nation, but only as someone who must be spoken for and on behalf of."[58]

During the Harlem Renaissance, African American intellectuals might have developed control over a portion of "the cultural apparatus."[59] Not doing so meant operating within the institutions and frameworks of white intellectuals—including the Marxist and Communist organizations and ideologies that many African American leaders turned to as the Renaissance twenties gave way to the Depression thirties. Having "failed to grasp the radical potential of their own movement" in Harlem, "they remained under the tutelage of irrelevant white radical ideas."[60]

Black Power seemed to overcome Cruse's strictures, for rather than enfolding African American efforts in white radicalism, it rejected any coalition in which whites were not the junior partners. "Behind the brave verbalizations of Black Power," however, "lay a muddled intellectual world of vague ideas and conceptual confusion." Cruse questioned Black Power's emphasis on African heritage rather than "Afro-American history, which is of more immediate political significance than how many black Africans sat on the throne of Egypt." In the absence of "social theory based on the living ingredients of Afro-American history," white intellectuals' ideas still governed public policy on the ground that Black Power claimed: cities. "New Deal economics . . . decides how Anti-Poverty funds are allotted to black ghettoes, but people in the ghettoes have no say" over basic elements of their distribution. "Is *this* economic Black Power?"[61] For Cruse, the answer was obviously no.

Cruse, like Mills, had high hopes for intellectuals. "With a few perceptive and original thinkers," he wrote, "the Negro movement conceivably could long ago have aided in reversing the backsliding of the United States toward the moral negation of its great promise as a new nation of nations."[62] In the depth of its disappointment, *Crisis* was akin to Lasch's *Agony of the American Left*. Indeed, it inspired a portion of it. "Cruse's book . . . is first-rate and is giving me lots of ideas," Lasch told *New York Review of Books* editor Robert Silvers.[63] With intellectuals seen as "the very symbol of futility" or urged to become street radicals, Lasch wrote in his review, "Cruse feels no need to apologize for the intellectual's work, which is to clarify issues." His account of African American intellectuals' shortfalls "applies without much modification to white intellectuals, now as in the recent past."[64] Cruse hoped Lasch's "review would break the 'Establishment' freeze and force them to discuss the book," but "the New York intellectual crowd . . . has . . . refused . . . a critical rejoinder." Lasch was "disgusted by the silence." On the cusp of the "age of fracture," intellectual life looked monolithic and closed to Harold Cruse. "If it's any consolation," Lasch told him, "many of my students have . . . found it more exciting than anything that has come out in a long time. I suspect the same thing is happening at many other schools."[65] It certainly was happening for Gates and West.

Religion was not an overriding concern for Cruse, but it was for many of the African American students assigned his book. The year before Cruse's *Crisis*, a full-page statement signed by fifty-one members of the National Committee of Negro Churchmen appeared in the *New York Times*. "Too often the Negro church has stirred its members away from the reign of God in *this world* to a distorted and complacent view of *an other worldly* conception of God's power." The signers pledged instead to devote their churches to "working for human justice in the places of social change and upheaval where our Master is already at work." As James Cone put it, "The biblical God is the God who is involved in the historical process for the purpose of human liberation."[66]

This African American religious thought joined currents of liberation theology flowing through Latin America. Amid revolutionary Marxism and Catholic openness after Vatican II, theologians like Gustavo Gutiér-rez, Juan Luis Segundo, and Rubem Alves espoused a Christianity rooted in the quest for social justice. Since the content of their ideas—a call to see society from the bottom up—made intellectuals' traditional top-down approach problematic, liberation theologians were "conscious of this distance between themselves and the ordinary people."[67] Liberation theologians grew closer to communities, and communities, in turn, shaped them. They closed the distance between intellectuals and the people.

Cone became a leading voice in African American liberation theology, providing a Christian interpretation of Black Power. Cone's "Black Theology" meant identification with African Americans and their history, "casting one's mental and emotional faculties with the lot of the oppressed" to "learn the cause and the cure of their humiliation." To adopt this perspective was to look from a place of suffering toward a day of liberation—the essential Bible story. Black theology was an intellectual's effort to place himself in relation to African American protest and to place that protest in the guiding light of religious tradition. West found Cone's work "an intellectually creative . . . response to the spontaneous rebellion of black people in the streets, the more disciplined political praxis of Black Power groups and the paralysis of most white North American theologians."[68]

West came of age at a moment when he and others of the "crossover generation" could root themselves in ancestors and antecedents surveyed by newly established African American studies programs. This experience shaped their identities as intellectuals—reckoning with, rejecting, and reformulating the ideas of Du Bois and the criticisms of Cruse. Their intellectual formation and sense of privilege-derived duty were two effects of the same cause: the freedom struggle whose achievements led to West going to Harvard and Gates to Yale. Emerging from college, this generation encountered a manifold African American social movement. As they searched for ways to engage this movement, realize their responsibilities to the community, and ground themselves in a usable African American past, Cone's liberation theology offered one mode of being an African American intellectual that might satisfy all of these requirements.

* * *

African American intellectuals were not the only ones rethinking the tropes and meanings of the figure of the intellectual in the 1970s. "We are at present experiencing the disappearance of . . . the 'great writer,'" Foucault announced in 1977.[69] Ten years later, The Last Intellectuals surveyed a landscape in which disappearance had become absence. If the decade between Foucault's last rites and Jacoby's requiem saw a kind of intellectual passing from view, it did not see the end of intellectuals in toto, for the forces destructive to the "great writer" turned out to be constructive of a new intellectual.

In the wake of postmodernism's interrogation—some would say demolition—of epistemological foundations, grounding intellectuals' authority in objective or universal truth was problematic. There was no such truth, Foucaultians claimed; there were only genealogies. If intellectuals could not stand on truth, what would it mean to stand within a genealogy? It meant, first, not claiming to stand outside history, evaluating it with rational, external standards. Intellectuals were in the stream of events, for there was no shore. Thinking, writing, and arguing were historical creatures. Intellectuals would operate from traditions, not from truth.

Two renderings of this historically and socially situated version of the intellectual sparked debate: Antonio Gramsci's "organic intellectual" and Foucault's "specific intellectual." Their foils were those who claimed to occupy a purely rational standpoint—Gramsci called them "traditional intellectuals" and Foucault "universal intellectuals." By 1977 Foucault noted a departure from this role. "Intellectuals have got used to working, not in the modality of the 'universal,' the 'exemplary,' the 'just-and-true-for-all,' but within specific sectors, at the precise points where their own conditions of life or work situate them." Intellectual work was increasingly "conducted alongside those who struggle for power," rather than "their illumination from a safe distance."[70] "Specific intellectuals" operated in specific clusters of ideas, vocabularies, institutions, and people.

Gramsci similarly placed intellectuals in their social locations. Each class, he wrote, "creates with itself, organically, one or more groups of intellectuals who give it homogeneity and consciousness of its function not only in the economic field but in the social and political field as well." These organic intellectuals were members of their social stratum. Intellectuals who claimed no class affiliation, who "put themselves forward as autonomous and independent of the dominant social group," were "traditional intellectuals." In reality, however, they were little more than the organic intellectuals of the ruling class, their claim of autonomy only obscuring their links to particular interests. There were *only* organic intellectuals; some just professed otherwise.[71]

Gramsci and Foucault gained American readers starting in the late 1960s. Their writing had to be translated for most readers, and so did their ideas. To what social formations might American intellectuals be organic? Could specific intellectuals address matters of national significance? If intellectuals were localized and linked rather than universal and detached, to where would such intellectuals be local and to what would they be linked? As these questions reverberated, a rising cohort of African American intellectuals visibly answered.

* * *

For West in particular, this was a moment of convergence. He straddled forces shaping African American intellectual life and those destabilizing the concept of the intellectual itself, ultimately proposing figures like himself as the intellectuals for this juncture.[72] West conceptualized and played the role of the intellectual as an act of synthesis between the foundationless realm of contemporary philosophy and the rooted world of African American ministry.

In the early 1980s, West underwrote his commitment to a historically

rooted African American "prophetic voice" with philosophical pragmatism's historicist turn. In so doing, he envisioned an intellectual at once
postmodern and tradition-bound. Identifying intellectual traditions within
the African American past, he put them in service to African Americans'
struggles in the present. Like Foucault, he suggested that there was no universal philosophy, only specific modes of it. Like Gramsci, he suggested
that these modes of thought inherently served the social group to which
they were organic. "As . . . Gramsci has shown," West wrote, "any political
consciousness of an oppressed group is shaped and molded by the group's
cultural resources and resiliency as perceived by individuals therein."[73]
West's aim was to encourage African Americans to perceive the resources
and resiliency immanent in their own experiences as a people.

His early term for this endeavor was "Afro-American philosophy." It
sought "to make theoretically explicit what is implicit in Afro-American
history," highlighting "cultural and social practices" that offered "solutions
to urgent problems." History furnished the materials that West now fashioned into a philosophy. That history showed African Americans making
their way in a world of racist oppression by dint of varied means, including
"prudential acquiescence plus courageous revolt[,] . . . institution-building
and violent rebellion," and "cautious reformist strategies." West's "philosophical inquiry into history" aimed not to establish an authoritative interpretation of the past, but to use "historical phenomena in order to unearth,
reject and endorse norms" that applied to present "existential and political
dilemmas."[74] The Afro-American philosopher mined history not in search
of objective truth but in service to contemporary people.

West unearthed norms of democracy and "unconstrained individuality"
in an African American "humanist tradition." In the manner of an academic philosopher, he appended a footnote: "Endorsement of the humanist tradition and its norms is not a justification of them." Justification was
"necessary if people are to be convinced." West had implied, however,
that no justification beyond a tradition's potential as a resource for contemporary African American communities was needed. That he felt compelled to temporize signaled West's uncertain academic agenda. His essay
positioned Afro-American philosophy vis-à-vis "the metaphilosophical
insights of Heidegger, Wittgenstein and Dewey" and appeared in *Philosophical Forum*.[75] He was using academic philosophy to point to something
beyond academic philosophy. He was attempting simultaneously to establish scholarly authority and serve the African American community.

While other African Americans did philosophy, West claimed, they lacked the valence he gave it. They, "like most Afro-American intellectuals," had attempted "to convince the black middle class that the world of ideas should be taken seriously," become "ideologue[s] for a particular political or cultural movement," or sought "acceptance in the predominantly white Academy." They were "effective propagandists and insecure academicians" but not Afro-American philosophers.[76]

The imperative of Afro-American philosophy was connecting the resources of tradition to contemporary people. How could an Ivy League philosopher writing in academic journals reach them?—by aiming not for "the" public but a particular one: West would "accent the prophetic voice in the black church tradition." He had no "illusion" of "reaching a majority of black parishioners," seeking instead a "humble vanguard." Rather than starting from a universal standpoint and addressing all rational beings, West would start, specifically, at "Union Seminary, where potential black and white leaders of the church come and will pass through my classes."[77]

Accenting the prophetic tradition required West to inhabit it— organically, as Gramsci held. The term suggested inheritance; one cannot synthesize organic ties—or at least not easily.[78] Being "organic" is a birthright. West highlighted this distinction by contrasting Latin American liberation theologians with African American clergy. The former, part of "the dominant cultural group," were "intellectuals educated in either European schools or Europeanized Latin American universities and seminaries" with "cosmopolitan habits and outlooks." This orientation blocked "their capacity to see the existential richness and radical potential of popular culture and religion." Their efforts to make common cause with parishioners were insufficient; they had to dwell within churchgoers' experience, feeling it in their bones—the same thing West said of Du Bois. "Black theologians," by contrast, "belong to the degraded cultural group in the United States," and "as intellectuals trained in American colleges, universities and seminaries," had "first-hand experiences of cultural condescension, arrogance and haughtiness." In facing this struggle, they incurred "personal debts to Black culture and religion."[79] West's standards for being organic were stringent, indeed.

So were his for being an intellectual. Though sufficiently organic, African American theologians were, West claimed, insufficiently theoretical. "Gramsci's conception of organic intellectuals" envisioned thinkers who "combine theory and action," connecting "popular culture and religion to structural social change."[80] Organic intellectuals were anchored to a social group, but they had to have broader theoretical horizons. To resist oppression, they had to understand it in theory.

West's description of organic intellectuals evokes—though differing in important ways from—Martin Kilson's "paraintellectuals." Writing in 1969, Kilson characterized paraintellectuals as potent communicators who, though lacking formal education, politicized "the urban black masses . . . by formulating descriptions of black-white relations, past and present, and policies for altering these relations that the Negro lower class finds meaningful." Their greater popular credibility than "established elements in the Negro intelligentsia" derived from "cultural experience similar to that of the black lower classes," including "brutalizing experience with the coercive arm of white-controlled cities, especially the police power." Paraintellectuals like Malcolm X and Eldridge Cleaver "came onto the scene," Kilson observed, "as legitimate and *natural* leaders." Those in the Black Panther Party could steer black nationalist momentum, he hoped, "into viable political channels." The Panthers were part of West's milieu growing up, and Kilson—the first African American tenured professor at Harvard—had been an important teacher of his.[81] Whereas Kilson found paraintellectuals in city streets, West looked for organic intellectuals in the pulpit and the lecture hall.

While preaching Gramsci to church leaders, West evangelized to academics about participation in political struggle—participation he saw flowing with, not against, the current of academic philosophy. "My idea of philosophy," Angela Davis had told her UCLA students in 1969, "is that if it is not relevant to human problems, if it does not tell us how we can go about eradicating some of the misery in this world, then it is not worth the name of philosophy."[82] A decade later, West endorsed Rorty's *Philosophy and the Mirror of Nature* for rejecting philosophy as "a tribunal of pure reason" and seeing the philosopher as "but one voice . . . among others in a grand Conversation." Yet West found Rorty reluctant to go where his thought pointed. Arguing that philosophy was necessarily embedded in its time and place rather than floating in a realm of abstract reason, Rorty "leads philosophy to the complex world of politics and culture, but does not permit it to get its hands dirty." Rorty's critique of academic philosophy remained academic—tacitly approving "the existing order."[83] To West, Rorty stayed above the fray while arguing that there was no such thing as being above it or anywhere but in it.

West urged philosophers to make plain that they were always already in the fray. They should own "that when we say we 'know' that a particular scientific or religious description, version, or theory of the self, world, and God is true, we are actually identifying ourselves with a particular group of people, community of believers, or tradition of social practices." Under this theory of knowledge, West could "cast off" his "dispassionate philosophical disposition and openly acknowledge . . . membership in the Christian community," rejecting any "conception of philosophy which does not permit one openly to acknowledge the particular tradition and community from which one speaks."[84] Rorty critiqued detachment, West charged, without acknowledging his own attachments or acting as an intellectual organic to them.[85]

Though he maintained that Rorty's work had no "ethical and political consequences," West aimed less at goading Rorty into activism than at using his ideas to underwrite new possibilities for "intellectuals from marginal groups and subaltern classes." Rorty's work challenged a philosophy profession that excluded culturally grounded modes of thought. Reimagined, philosophy could "enhance the capacity of men and women to create new and better self-images and vocabularies." When West urged neopragmatists to "not settle simply for . . . breaking out of professional modes" but to "contribute to the making of a new and better global civilization," he was describing his own aims.[86] He was moving from neo-pragmatism the philosophy to "prophetic pragmatism," the role he cast for himself.

* * *

West increasingly shifted from articulating a special kind of role for intellectuals to operating, more visibly, in that role. This period was bookended by *The American Evasion of Philosophy: A Genealogy of Pragmatism* (1989) and *Race Matters* (1993). While the former heightened West's academic reputation, the latter established him as a prominent voice in contemporary debates. In *Evasion*, West located his own "prophetic pragmatism" at the end of a genealogy of pragmatism. If "prophetic pragmatism" was the job description West wrote for himself, then *Race Matters* was him at work.

The road to *Evasion* was marked by a series of fault-findings. West stood at a pivot point from which to view academic intellectuals, largely in the humanities, and African American intellectuals, largely in the church, and he found both wanting. Academics' "philosophically critical yet culturally lifeless rhetoric" had "failed to project a new worldview, a countermovement." Church leaders had cultural resonance, but their "lack of a clear-cut social theory prevents the emergence of any substantive political program or social vision." An intellectual mode was needed that would combine the strengths and overcome the flaws of each—"a rapprochement" between Rorty's "philosophical historicism" and liberation theology's "moral vision, social analysis and political engagement."[87]

Before labeling that rapprochement "prophetic pragmatism," West formulated it as the role of the "critical organic catalyst" in 1985's "The Dilemma of the Black Intellectual." "Critical organic catalyst" was the hard-won role that "the African American who takes seriously the life of the mind" might attain after struggling through the "grim predicament" of being "caught between an insolent American society and an insouciant black community."[88]

Intellectual life was fraught for African Americans. Amid "vulgar (racist) perceptions fueled by affirmative action programs which pollute many black student-white professor relations," it was "difficult for black students . . . to be taken seriously as *potential scholars and intellectuals*." In intellectual periodicals the "black presence" was "negligible"—whether in "liberal journals like the *New York Review of Books* and the *New York Times Book Review*" or more radical outlets. Such "racially separatist publishing" highlighted "the chasm between black and white intellectuals." Finally, "rightward ideological drift" and the "politicization of American intellectual life (in the academy and outside)" created "a hostile climate for the making of black intellectuals." In the face of these obstacles, "the black infrastructure for intellectual discourse and dialogue is nearly nonexistent," with "not even a major black newspaper of national scope." As a result, "black intellectual exchange is at its worst since the Civil War."[89]

There were other predicaments as well. Beside "the general antiintellectual tenor of American society," West wrote, there was "deep distrust and suspicion of black intellectuals within the black community." Beyond "the usual arrogant and haughty disposition of intellectuals toward ordinary folk" was the "widespread refusal of black intellectuals to remain, in some visible way, organically linked with African American cultural life." This fraying of bonds was evident in their "preoccupation with Euro-American intellectual products." Moreover, "the minimal immediate impact of black intellectual activity" fanned "common perceptions" of its "uselessness." As members of the "status-hungry black middle class," intellectuals focused on "material gain and cultural prestige" for themselves.

Their quest came at a price, for it required "addressing oneself to the very culture and society which degrade and devalue the black community from whence one comes." Choices that "loom large in the lives of black intellectuals" were "meretricious pseudo-cosmopolitanism" or "tendentious, cathartic provincialism"—either selling out or being locked in.[90]

Looking beyond these alternatives, West rejected three conceptions of the intellectual's role: the bourgeois (i.e., academic), Marxist, and Foucaultian. The first was "existentially and intellectually stultifying," as African American academics faced racist doubt about their abilities and were channeled into "legitimate" rather than radical work. On "Marxist privileging of black intellectuals," West resembled Cruse: it "often reeks of condescension that confines black prophetic roles to spokespersons and organizers" rather than "creative thinkers who warrant serious critical attention."[91]

The Foucaultian "postmodern skeptic" held more promise. Exposing "rhetorics" that "authorize and legitimate . . . the privileged status of intellectuals," Foucaultians disrupted the "self-authorizing" stance of the universal intellectual. This disruption had special significance for "African American intellectual history," where "self-authorizing claims such as the 'talented tenth' . . . are widespread."[92] The Foucaultian model was inadequate, however, in the manner of Rorty's neo-pragmatism: encouraging "the kind of revolt enacted by intellectuals," it did not touch the struggles of ordinary people. Criticism was not an end in itself, and "making a fetish of critical consciousness . . . encapsulates black intellectual activity within the comfortable bourgeois academy of postmodern America."[93] The Foucaultian intellectual turned out to be a more self-conscious version of the bourgeois one.

West preferred what he called an "Insurgency Model: Black Intellectual as Critical Organic Catalyst." It embraced "the uniqueness of the black intellectual predicament," which might in time call forth "a new 'regime of truth'"—nothing less than "the emergence of . . . a post-Western civilization"—but applied to "the first step" within the oppressive conditions of that civilization: "black insurgency." The model emphasized "human will and heroic effort" but not "in individualistic and elitist terms." It replaced "the solitary hero, embattled exile and isolated genius—the intellectual as star, celebrity, commodity"—with "collective intellectual work that contributes to communal resistance and struggle."[94] It incorporated Marxist emphasis on economic structures, but not at the expense of

CRITICAL CATALYST, PROPHETIC PRAGMATIST, PUBLIC INTELLECTUAL

culture, as Marxists underestimated the emancipatory potential of religion and music—both essential to African American tradition.[95] Finally, it adopted Foucaultians' "illuminating oppositional descriptions," but not their "rejection of . . . utopianism and any positing of a telos," which were vital to insurgencies.[96] Foucaultians were critical without being hopeful, exposing every bind with no Jubilee.

West sounded a note of hope. "Despite the pervasive racism of American society and anti-intellectualism of the black community, critical space and insurgent activity can be expanded." African American intellectuals stood, advantageously, between prophetic churches and postmodern critiques. "One tries to root oneself organically in [churches] so that one can speak to a black constituency," West said, "while maintaining a conversation with the most engaging political and postmodernist debates on the outside so that the insights they provide can be brought in." Organic to their community, critical as a postmodern skeptic, and catalyzing for popular struggle, African American intellectuals were poised, West hoped, to lead the way toward social change.[97]

The requirements for being critical organic catalysts were, however, daunting. They had to reckon with "anthropology, sociology, philosophy, [and] history" as well as religion, without falling into "a debilitating dilettantism that obfuscates rather than illuminates."[98] They had to engage a variety of audiences, necessitating, in effect, multiple languages. West was "continually caught in a kind of 'heteroglossia,' speaking a number of English languages in radically different contexts"—using "Marx, Weber, Frankfurt theorists, [and] Foucault" for "theoretical reflection" and "Christian narratives and stories . . . filtered through and informed by intellectual developments from de Tocqueville to Derrida" for "speaking with the black masses." Critical organic catalysts also had to be critical of themselves, taking a "'self-inventory' that scrutinizes the social positions, class locations and cultural socializations of black intellectuals."[99] Finally, to be catalysts, they needed hope, which was hard to find. In African American life, "nondiscursive" manifestations of power—"forms of oppression like economic *exploitation* or state *repression* or bureaucratic *domination*"—operated every day. "We are not dancing on Nietzsche's texts here and *talking* about nihilism," West said; "we are in a nihilism that is *lived*." In that context, "anybody who takes hope seriously and possibility seriously is going to look like a fool."[100] That was another risk this intellectual had to run.

The difference between "critical organic catalyst" and West's later term, "prophetic pragmatist," was an instance of heteroglossia. The former's "historical forerunners" were "black preachers and black musical artists"; it was a model for young African American intellectuals.[101] "Prophetic pragmatist" targeted the philosophers, historians, and political theorists participating in the revival of American pragmatism then underway. Yet the messages of "critical organic catalyst" and "prophetic pragmatist" overlapped: "an intellectual calling to administer to a confused populace caught in the whirlwind of societal crisis . . . ideological polemics, and . . . class, racial, and gender conflicts," a calling "to be organic intellectuals" who connected "ideas to action by means of creating, constituting, or consolidating constituencies for moral aims and political purposes."[102]

Pragmatism suited these aims well. Regarding "thought as a weapon to enable more effective action," it was "less a philosophical tradition" addressed to "the Western philosophical conversation initiated by Plato"— hence its "evasion of philosophy"—than "a continuous cultural commentary or set of interpretations that attempt to explain America to itself." *Evasion* was West's genealogy of a pragmatist tradition rich in resources for the present. He canvassed it as a prelude to presenting his prophetic pragmatism as the next step. Part analytical work and part rallying cry, West considered *Evasion* "a political act."[103]

He began with Ralph Waldo Emerson. Appealing to "a significant segment of the educated classes," Emerson fashioned "a vocation and constituency for himself," carving "space in America for the organic intellectual." He undertook not the quest for truth but "a perennial experimental search . . . for the enhancement and expansion of the self (viz., America)." The individualist cast of Emerson's work, however, generated "neither social revolution nor cultural upheaval but rather moral transgression based on personal integrity and individual conscience."[104] Conscience was important, but so was social context.

Among classical pragmatists, William James also created "a constituency and . . . a public role for himself." His 1907 lecture "The Social Value of the College-Bred" specified pragmatism's "historical agent—the educated classes." A decade later, John Dewey reconstructed philosophy "in the name of critical intelligence and creative democracy," making it no longer "'a device for dealing with the problems of philosophers'" but "'a method, cultivated by philosophers, for dealing with the problems of men.'"[105]

After World War Two, "intellectuals in the pragmatist grain" faced the problem of upholding "human agency in a tragic world." West looked at Sidney Hook, Reinhold Niebuhr, Lionel Trilling, and W. E. B. Du Bois (who lived until 1963); but C. Wright Mills—who "views the vocation of being an intellectual as the only alternative to an emaciated liberalism, a traduced communism, and an impotent tragic viewpoint"—best carried the torch. In a confining Cold War political culture, Mills sought "to awaken the Promethean energies of the masses by means of critical intelligence and social action; . . . means most readily available to intellectuals whose cultural capital is, supposedly, critical intelligence." Mills's approach was cross-cutting, as it "promotes radical democracy yet focuses on intellectual elites as primary historical agents." Moreover, Mills and other pragmatists had not "grappled in a serious way" with the problem of racism.[106]

Nor was race their only blind spot. These intellectuals' "suspicion of working- and lower-class people with limited education" contradicted their "egalitarian and democratic sensibilities." They assumed "that bourgeois culture—its professors, writers, and artists—has a monopoly on critical intelligence." Not even Du Bois—"organically linked with one of the most deprived and despised people in America"—avoided this sense of "existential and cultural superiority over and distance from ordinary people."[107]

While overlooking the masses, midcentury pragmatists underwrote their own power. They were "personally empowered by pragmatism to overcome marginality" through "acts of intellectual will, i.e., writing." Their tone may have been tragic, but the subtext was heroic. Surveying American life from the viewpoint of those who, though often alienated, nonetheless felt efficacy, they lacked the perspective essential for West, that of "society's victims" and "those who suffer"—"the vantagepoint of the Cross," from which tragedy resided not in fate but in a historically contingent lack of power. "Pragmatism has not attracted significant numbers of women," West observed, because "its aggressive and self-confident stance toward the realities of the spheres of power has been virtually the possession of males in patriarchal America." Midcentury pragmatism was the preserve of male intellectuals who felt at least a modicum of power.[108]

Two upheavals ended the midcentury moment: the work of philosophers W. V. Quine and Richard Rorty, and the social movements of the 1960s. Together, they opened space for a new kind of pragmatism and a new kind of intellectual. Entry into academe of previously excluded groups "shattered male WASP cultural pretension and predominance." Conflicts along lines of race, sex, and class accompanying these changes "did not simply politicize American intellectual life; rather, they repoliticized in an explicit manner what had been political in an implicit manner": the academy's reproduction of social hierarchies. Intellect had never been outside politics. Social-movement upheaval on campuses showed that purportedly detached, neutral institutions were not set apart from historical struggles; the philosophers' work indicated that truth was not either. Everything had a history, and "it is impossible to historicize philosophy without partly politicizing . . . it."[109] As West saw it, developments in philosophy departments and on the streets pointed to the same thing: an intellectual life steeped in history and politics.

His genealogy complete, West capped it with his own conception of the pragmatist intellectual as "inextricably linked to oppositional analyses of class, race, and gender and oppositional movements for creative democracy and social freedom." Such opposition was grounded in traditions that "keep alive a sense of alternative ways of life and of struggle." West upended tradition as "solely" the site of anti-intellectualism, "ignorance and intolerance, prejudice and parochialism, dogmatism and docility." Tradition also contained "insight and intelligence, rationality and resistance, critique and contestation"—whether the African American traditions documented by historians or the American pragmatist tradition that West both assembled and invoked.[110] West built his pragmatist program not on unassailable philosophical foundations but on genealogical groundwork, presenting prophetic pragmatism as the next step in a distinctly American path of thought and action.

West renovated the resources of the pragmatic tradition for his purposes. He joined Mills's "tortuous grappling with the vocation of the intellectual" to Du Bois's emphasis on the oppressed to launch a "new kind of cultural criticism." This "prophetic pragmatism, with its roots in the American heritage and its hopes for the wretched of the earth, constitutes the best chance of promoting an Emersonian culture of creative democracy by means of critical intelligence and social action." Locating "politics in the everyday experiences of ordinary people," prophetic pragmatism was more than a role description for intellectuals; it was an outlook immanent in the lives of the American people themselves, a terrain where everyday folks and intellectuals could meet.[111]

To clear the way, prophetic pragmatism extended the "evasion" of philosophy, for "when philosophers 'substitute Reason for common sense, they tend to view the sense of commoners to be nonsense.'" Resisting a distinction between the world of intellect and that of ordinary people, pragmatism fostered what West, following Dewey, called "creative democracy."[112] The "rational deliberation" previously regarded as "the prerogative of philosophers" was "now that of the people—and the populace deliberating is creative democracy in the making." The result was "neither mob rule nor mass prejudice" but "the citizenry in action, with its civil consciousness molded by participation in public-interest-centered and individual-rights-regarding democracy." In creative democracy, a special role for designated "intellectuals" seemed obsolete, for all people acted as intellectuals. "Needless to say," West nevertheless wrote, there was no "license for eliminating or opposing all professional elites."[113]

It was not, however, "needless to say." West needed to explain how rapprochement between intellectuals and everyday people worked. To do so, he summoned familiar sources: Gramsci and Christianity. For Gramsci, West wrote, philosophy seeks not to "impos[e] its elite intellectual views upon the people, but to become part of a social movement by nourishing and being nourished by the philosophical views of oppressed people." Philosophy becomes a dialogue, not a lecture. Likewise, prophetic pragmatism refused "the arrogant scientistic self-privileging or haughty secular self-images of many modern philosophers and intellectuals." Intellectuals need not "surrender their critical intelligence," but nor should they "demand that all peoples mimic their version of" it.[114] Intellectuals would not wither away: creative democracy was a soundscape of many voices, intellectuals heard alongside, though not instead, of others.

Religion—hence "prophetic" pragmatism—facilitated this democratic relationship between intellectuals and other people.[115] Organic intellectuals were "entrenched in and affiliated with organizations, associations, and, possibly, movements of grass-roots folk." Similarly, a "prophetic religious person" emphasized "educating and being educated by struggling peoples, organizing and being organized by resisting groups." Religion connected West to everyday people, but organic intellectuals "need be neither religious nor linked to religious institutions. Trade unions, community groups, and political formations also suffice." West gave religion pride of place, however, because left intellectuals had often given religion no place at all. Their "antireligious strategy" was "political suicide," but adopting religion for other than genuinely felt spiritual reasons would be inorganic.[116] Other modes of organic intellectualism offered broader scope, for they had no test of faith.

The non-religious formations—unions, political organizations, and neighborhoods—that West cited as alternative sites of organic intellectualism were eroding as he wrote. Private-sector union membership had been declining since the mid-1950s, and public-sector unions had peaked in the 1970s. Enrollment in the Democratic and Republican parties fell sharply in the 1980s, with more voters identifying as "independent." As Robert Putnam's *Bowling Alone* put it: "We have been pulled apart from one another and from our communities over the last third of the century."[117] With these bases for being an organic intellectual dissolving, religion and race looked like comparatively stable categories.[118]

In this context, prophetic pragmatism pointed not so much to a new way of thinking as to a new kind of intellectual—one rooted in a community. As other formations fractured, prophetic pragmatism amplified the voices of those who still had communities to which they could be organic, as West did with the African American church.[119] The mantle of organic intellectualism was simply available to West in a way that it was not to Chomsky or Rorty.

Rorty thought himself poorly suited to intellectual activism, organic or otherwise. Noting West's contradictory "wish to evade philosophy and . . . hope that something rather like philosophy will be a powerful instrument of social change," Rorty wrote that it was "hard to feel that my professional services are just what victims of injustice need." Rorty's "professorial pragmatism" was not "a good place to look for prophecy, or for the sorts of rich possibilities which the prophetic imagination makes visible."[120] He proposed a division of labor between professors—who addressed philosophical problems inherited from the past—and prophets—who created visions for the future.

America's problem was not philosophical, Rorty wrote, but "a failure of nerve, a fairly sudden loss of generous instincts and of patriotic fellow-feeling." Intellectuals could address this issue without entanglement in academic philosophy. Yet West, "the closest thing to an 'organic intellectual' my country has these days, and . . . thus . . . (except for the feminists) as likely a source of specific, concrete, patriotic, prophetic vision as anybody else around," was still too professorial, "still enamored of the idea that his own academic discipline—philosophy—is somehow more closely linked to prophetic vision than" others.[121] Prophetic practice, Rorty claimed, had value independent of philosophical pragmatism.

For Kwame Anthony Appiah, however, philosophy was central to

West's project. Its foremost contribution lay precisely in building mutually fruitful relationships between academic theory and the African American community. *Evasion* was "a gentle rebuke to the pragmatism without consequences of Richard Rorty, and a powerful call for philosophy to play its role in building a radical democracy in alliance with the wretched of the earth."[122]

Howard Brick, reviewing *Evasion*, sidestepped the question of whether the philosophical, prophetic, and political aligned. Instead, he focused on "the spirit of the book as a whole," which made West's "pragmatist vision of a new kind of intellectual life inspiring"—it "would escape the caste consciousness of the academy without dismissing the worthy intellectual traditions or norms of scholarly rigor, and it would look outward as an ally of the oppressed to social and political life at large."[123]

Evasion served two purposes not usually joined in one book. It was received as scholarship, and it resounded as a manifesto. It engaged the academy on its own terms while calling for engagement beyond the academy. West took a formidable academic perch as head of Princeton's African American Studies program just months before *Evasion* was published. He also lectured and preached around the country. "For an intellectual, you've been sighted in some very unusual places," Bill Moyers noted in his 1990 interview: "the storefronts and streets of Harlem, the shantytowns of South Africa, one of the worst high schools in one of the worst districts in Brooklyn." Why go "so far from Princeton, so far from the ivory tower?" West replied that he understood "the vocation of the intellectual as trying to turn easy answers into critical questions, and ask these critical questions to those with power." That meant "allowing suffering to speak" and refusing a separation between "the life of the mind" and "struggle for those who have been dehumanized."[124] Straddling Princeton and the world outside it was West's way to "uphold the discipline of the life of the mind" while being connected to "other people's humanity, their predicaments and plights."[125]

West entered a prolific period of writing "in what I hoped might be a popular vein." A torrent of books flowed, though West "had low expectations" for their sales: "They were, after all, the books of an Ivy League professor." These expectations were defied by 1993's *Race Matters*—"the right book at the right time."[126] In April 1992, violent unrest had rocked Los Angeles after police officers who had been videotaped beating African American motorist Rodney King were acquitted by a largely white jury. The American economy was barely out of recession, heightening already significant pressures on the nation's poor. And 1992 was an election year, in which gangsta rap burst into political discussion with "Cop Killer" by Body Count.

Race Matters found a large audience looking for fresh insight. Taking on hot-button topics, West did not disappoint. He examined African American conservatives, "the taboo subject" of black sexuality, and affirmative action—all subject to intensified debate after the 1991 Supreme Court confirmation hearing of Clarence Thomas, an African American conservative who opposed affirmative action and had been accused of sexual harassment. West took on strained relations between African and Jewish Americans following violence in Brooklyn's Crown Heights neighborhood. He addressed "Malcolm X and Black Rage"—at the forefront of public consciousness amid gangsta rap, Los Angeles revolt, and the 1992 release of Spike Lee's film *Malcolm X*. West's take on "nihilism" in African American life straddled conservative and liberal positions, pairing claims about cultural decay to arguments about structural inequality.[127]

Identifying a "crisis of black leadership," West proclaimed that never "in the history of black people in this country" had "the quantity of politicians and intellectuals" been "so great, yet the quality of both . . . so low." In the vein of Jacoby, he asked: "Why hasn't black America produced intellectuals of the caliber of W. E. B. Du Bois, Anna Cooper, E. Franklin Frazier, Oliver Cox, and Ralph Ellison in the past few decades?" Toni Morrison was the only contemporary "race-transcending prophet." Others were "mere academicians . . . with little sense of the broader life of the mind and hardly any engagement with battles in the streets." More prophetic figures were needed, West told academics with *Evasion*; now, he told readers of a best seller the same. "The time is past for black political and intellectual leaders to pose as *the* voice for black America." Instead, "a serious black leader" would "be a race-transcending prophet who critiques the powers that be (including the Black component of the Establishment) and . . . puts forward a vision of . . . fundamental social change."[128] In *Race Matters*, West both called for such leadership and attempted it himself.

The year 1993 presented West the opportunity to be the intellectual whose role he had theorized. "I was asked to speak everywhere," he recalled. *Race Matters* "was used in classrooms around the world. President Clinton read it and gave it to his daughter and wife to read." At the White House, West and the president talked "far into the middle of the night." West also talked with Kuumba Ferrouillet Kazi of the *Black Colle-*

gian. "Cornel West speaks like a real 'down brother,'" using "the dialects of both academia and the proverbial street corner with equal deftness," Kazi said. West typified "the new, hip, 'public intellectuals,' academicians who step from behind the ivy-covered walls of academia to stand before the graffiti-covered walls of urban America." In 1993, Kazi reported, "the 'public intellectual' became a man in demand."[129]

* * *

In the years surrounding *Race Matters*, West loomed large in two overlapping conversations about the role of intellectuals in the United States. One, about "public intellectuals," gained steam following *The Last Intellectuals* as observers began to suggest that America's foremost public intellectuals were African Americans. The second focused on the distinct responsibilities of African American intellectuals. The emergence of West and others with strong-selling books and Ivy League addresses marked a shift in this long conversation. What did their new status portend for old debates about leadership, duty, education, and class within the African American community? What did it say about the role of white audiences for African American intellectuals?

Michael Eric Dyson celebrated West for taking "Afro-American intellectual and religious traditions, cultural products, and socio-political practices seriously," while showing "the Afro-American intellectual examining, debating, and criticizing ideas, events, and movements outside black life." West, Dyson wrote in 1989, demonstrated how African American life "grounds one's intellectual perspective" on a full range of issues. bell hooks, who had known West at Yale, offered a more critical appraisal in "Black Women Intellectuals," which was "a devastating critique" of West's "The Dilemma of Black Intellectuals."[130]

hooks's *Ain't I a Woman: Black Women and Feminism* (1981) had described African American women's "double bind": In the women's rights movement, race was submerged, and white women stood as the voice of all women; in the civil rights movement, gender was submerged, and African American men stood for all African Americans. In both contexts, poor women were rarely heard. Emphasizing the intersectionality of race, class, and gender, hooks analyzed African American women's struggle against oppression. She shared West's desire to let silences and sufferings speak, but she more clearly located this effort in everyday life—including her own. hooks and other feminist intellectuals showed the inseparability of the private and public realms while exposing the gendered thinking that feminized the former and masculinized the latter—crucial insights for the unfolding conversation about public intellectuals.[131]

Like West, hooks highlighted obstacles to becoming an African American intellectual. In addition, she addressed obstacles facing African American women. In a "fundamentally anti-intellectual" society, she wrote, intellectuals struggled "to affirm" their "meaningful impact." On the left, "work of the mind" was often overshadowed by "more visible expressions of concrete activism." Such "devaluation of intellectual work" made it especially "difficult for individuals from marginalized groups to feel that intellectual work is important." These feelings were amplified for African American women. One of six children raised by working-class parents in Hopkinsville, Kentucky, hooks wrote that "in underclass and poor Black communities, to ask too many questions, to talk about ideas that differed from the prevailing community world view, to say things grown Black folks relegated to the realm of the unspeakable was to invite punishment." In this context, hooks developed a powerful sense of intellectual vocation that, to modify Jane Addams's idea, underlined its subjective necessity. hooks's "lived recognition of how the mind engaged in critical thought could be used in the service of survival . . . enabled [her] to become an autonomous self." She embraced her intellect "not because it brought status or recognition but because it offered resources to enhance survival and [her] pleasure in living."[132]

hooks's personal pursuit of autonomy through intellectual development fit a larger pattern. "It . . . confirmed what Black leaders in the 19th century well knew—that intellectual work is a necessary part of liberation" for "oppressed and/or exploited people who would move from object to subject, who would decolonize and liberate their minds." Intellectual work was at the heart of African American experience: the ongoing freedom struggle. That struggle registered in "the politics of everyday life," such "that intellectual life need not lead one to be estranged from community but rather might enable one to participate more fully in the life of family and community."[133]

For African American women intellectuals, that participation was constrained by constructions of the intellectual—including West's— that favored men. "When Black scholars write about Black intellectual life, they usually focus solely on the lives and works of Black men," hooks observed. West, for example, overlooked "sexist notions of male/female

242

roles . . . that inform and shape . . . our sense of who the Black intellectual is or can be." Even in the face of "historical evidence that Black women have always played a major role as teachers, critical thinkers, and cultural theorists in Black life, particularly in segregated Black communities, there is very little written about Black female intellectuals. When most Black folks think about 'great minds,'" hooks observed, they "conjure up male images."[134]

African American women intellectuals' "invisibility" stemmed from "institutionalized racism, sexism, and class exploitation," and "the reality that large numbers of Black women do not choose intellectual work as their vocation." They were channeled into other occupations under gender norms amplified by intersecting racial and class constraints, including the "insistence that Black women be regarded as 'service workers' no matter our job or career status."[135] Since the stereotypical "intellectual is someone who is usually self-centeredly preoccupied with their ideas," intellectual labor was "not seen as 'selfless work.'" Women's "longing to read, contemplate, and talk about a broad range of ideas was discouraged, seen as frivolous activity, or as activity that indulged in too intensely would lead us to be selfish, cold, cut off from feeling and estranged from community." Overcoming these challenges, hooks wrote, "black women must re-vision notions of intellectual work that enable us to embrace a concern with the life of the mind and the welfare of community," for "it is only through active resistance that we claim our right to assert an intellectual presence"[136]

The "active resistance" necessary for African American women intellectuals was constitutive of the role of the intellectual itself. "An intellectual is not simply somebody who trades in ideas," hooks wrote. "An intellectual is somebody who trades in ideas by transgressing discursive frontiers."[137] By this definition, African American women were intellectuals par excellence, for their very presence in the public sphere signaled the breaking of boundaries.

Breaking Bread: Insurgent Black Intellectual Life (1991) was a dialogue between hooks and West. "Knowing that many folks, especially poor Black people, are not literate in this society," they asked how intellectuals could reach them. Engaging "a brother or sister on the block" meant thinking "in terms of mass culture, in terms of popular culture," West said. This approach underscored the need for "Black cultural workers within television, film, and video who are presenting alternative perspectives."[138] West later took this prescription himself, releasing several CDs and appearing in the blockbuster *Matrix* films.[139] As hooks put it: "Speaking at high schools, churches, at DSA [Democratic Socialists of America] meetings, Cornel does not limit himself to teaching in the academy, he goes wherever he is called." West became, biographer Rosemary Cowan writes, "a *multicontextual* public intellectual."[140]

hooks and West saw evidence that their outreach worked. After *Ain't I a Woman*, hooks received "dozens of letters a week, where, say, a Black woman from a small town, out in the middle of nowhere, would tell me that she read my book at the public library and it transformed her life." People in prison wrote to her. Such "affirmation . . . from individuals and locations . . . on the margins" debunked "the usual insistence that there can be no meaningful exchange, contact, influence, of intellectuals with everyday folks who may have no educational background." Though— two years before *Race Matters*—feeling on the margins of the major media themselves, hooks and West felt connected to a public. "African Americans struggling to make sense of the crisis we are facing as a people, economic assault, genocidal attacks, resurgence of overt racism and White supremacy, widespread drug addiction, and pervasive despair, are turning to intellectuals," hooks said, "to folks like Cornel West, for insight and guidance."[141]

For what were whites turning to them? The Moyers interview, hooks observed, perpetuated "this sense of White people coming to Black intellectuals to be informed, which is very different from us talking with one another about our situation as Black people." African American intellectuals might function as something akin to foreign correspondents for whites, but West did "not simply talk about race or commodify it for a White audience," hooks said; he resisted that role by working "to improve the lot of all Black people."[142]

The academy constrained African American intellectuals in other ways. While intellectuals "engaged in the public issues that affect large numbers of people," hooks felt that academic "professionalization . . . limits those of us who want to speak to broader audiences." Yet West and hooks were both academics and intellectuals nonetheless. hooks exhibited this tension, West said, by conveying "provocative arguments in an intelligible prose read by thousands of her literate fellow citizens" while being "a bonafide member of the academy—with a Stanford education, a highbrow Ph.D. and appointments at Yale and Oberlin." Scholars had faulted

Ain't I a Woman for lacking footnotes. Since "non-academic Black people" had told hooks "that when they open a book with footnotes they immediately think that book isn't for them," she eliminated notes—a decision "informed by questions of class, access, and literacy levels rather than a simple devaluation of footnotes, or 'shoddy, careless' scholarship." In the blowback she received, hooks felt the "pressure on people who are trying to speak to many audiences, trying to speak with the kind of poly-vocality and multi-vocality that allows us access to different audiences." Academics must "conform or be punished"—not promising options for prospective public intellectuals.[143]

Why, then, remain in the academy at all? "I tease you about giving up academe and becoming a prophet in the Black community," hooks told West.[144] Academe offered a living, however, and more: it conferred legitimacy. Positions at Princeton or Oberlin were shorthand that the person speaking from them was credible. They were also shorthand for social class. hooks and West worried about connections—or lack thereof—between the African American middle class, including intellectuals-cum-academics, and the poor. hooks fondly recalled West, "in his three-piece suit," stopping "in the wet streets of New York . . . to rap with a brother in a wheelchair, handing over a few dollars" and demonstrating a too-rare class-transcending "solidarity." Blinkered by a "middle-class mentality" that stunted "oppositional Black intellectuality," could African American intellectuals see a responsibility to the African American poor?[145]

Eugene Rivers, pastor at the Azusa Christian Community in Boston's Dorchester and Roxbury neighborhoods, raised this question in a 1992 letter to the *Boston Review*. Having read Chomsky's "The Responsibility of Intellectuals" as "a young Christian intellectual struggling to understand the role and the responsibility of the intelligentsia," Rivers now wrote "On the Responsibility of Intellectuals in the Age of Crack." In Rivers's Boston, "Chomsky's points . . . apply with particular force to the responsibility to tell the truth about the condition of the black poor. And that responsibility bears especially heavily on black intellectuals at elite universities." Like Chomsky, Rivers found intellectuals in dereliction of duty. "With political and domestic policy wars escalating against an entire generation of young black people in the cities," were African American intellectuals "not morally obligated to provide more than lecture circuit radicalism? How can we justify endless talk about Gramsci, Foucault, Derrida, Jameson, Bourdieu, Lukács, Habermas, and Marx—talk with no discernible bearing on the fact of social death in the cities?" Turning to West and hooks, Rivers suggested they "consider 'breaking bread' in ways that might benefit [a] black woman and her son in the Dorchester Court," deploying their "prestige and influence to promote cultural and economic development among the urban poor." For all West's talk about engagement outside the academy, Rivers saw solipsism in a three-piece suit; intellectual work had not produced concrete action. Without "a program or a mobilization of intellectuals around the needs of the poor," Rivers asked, "what is the functional, political difference between such conservatives as Alan Keyes or Thomas Sowell and such progressives as Henry Louis Gates or Cornel West?"[146] He called for a meeting to talk it out.

Two such meetings took place. The first included Rivers, hooks, West, Gates, Appiah, MIT law lecturer and former judge Margaret Burnham, and Boston University economist Glenn Loury. It revealed more agreement on the severity of "the age of crack" than on the responsibilities of African American intellectuals. Loury was "very uneasy" with his sense "that there is something special about blackness," some "peculiar responsibility" for African American intellectuals, "because it cuts against the universalistic principle that, as human beings, we all ought to be concerned about these things." West urged "progressive intellectuals . . . to talk a moral and spiritual language . . . of love, joy, communion, support, effective bonds." They had "to do more than talk," hooks replied. "People look at us and say: . . . we don't really see that love and communion taking place among *them*. We don't really see them living the anti-bourgeois life that would actually be against market forces." Speaking of market forces, Loury noted that "the other side of the black intellectual is the intellectual side," which "can reduce all of these questions to dialectical analyses of certain social processes." Perhaps they needed "to consider," instead, "being in relationship with the persons of concern," from whom they were detached. "I don't feel that I have been that kind of intellectual," hooks responded.[147]

If "the black intellectual" was a plural entity, so was the "black community" to which that intellectual was responsible. "There is a new black community—or new black communities—out there," Gates observed.[148] The African American community had seemed like a relatively cohesive basis for being an organic intellectual, but that notion papered over significant differences among African Americans, not least of which was the gap between those who had entered the middle class and those on the age of crack's sharp edge.

The ascension of some African American intellectuals to academic prominence and even public renown underscored that gap. "How do we mobilize your celebrity status," Rivers asked West, "so that those who live on the ground . . . have the kinds of resources they need"? Appiah wondered, however, why intellectuals should "use their celebrity any more than other black celebrities, who on the whole have a great deal more celebrity than most intellectuals." Why exceed "the obligation to act as an intellectual, to do the thinking that is necessary?" Everyone had responsibilities as persons, "but the idea of talking about the responsibilities of black intellectuals," Appiah noted, returning to something like Loury's earlier question, "is to talk about responsibilities *specific* to people as intellectuals."[149] The conversation was moving in a circle.

West reflected upon that circularity and the seemingly unresolvable tensions beneath it. "We all have been talking about this for twenty years—those of us who pursue truth-telling to the best of our ability, given the oppressed community that produced us and our interface and interaction with the academy." Cool intellect accompanied "boiling . . . urgency about all the hell that brothers and sisters are catching. How do you come to terms with that doubleness?" Despite his commitment to working in churches, prisons, and communities, West concluded: "As organically linked as you can be, and pursuing intellectual work as much as you do, that tension is just there. I think we are going to take it to the grave with us."[150]

The second discussion took place a year later. West's star had risen dramatically in the interval, and he was unable to attend. "Cornel has been in the mass-media in the last year," hooks said, "to use that vehicle, to reach a lot of black people who are not in universities, and who do now know who Cornel West is." On the cusp of a cultural moment in which African Americans would be considered the exemplary and, perhaps, the last public intellectuals, hooks predicted: "I think that you [will] see more black intellectuals utilizing those [mass-media] resources than ever before."[151]

* * *

"A few weeks ago, in a shopping mall somewhere on the American prairie," wrote Michael Bérubé in the *New Yorker* in early 1995, "I wandered into the local McBooks store to find fully half its 'Current Affairs' section occupied by the work of black intellectuals, chief among them Cornel West himself, peering back at me from the cover of 'Race Matters.'" hooks and Dyson books were nearby. "Something new is happening in American cultural history," Bérubé declared; "a new African-American intelligentsia has become part of this country's cultural landscape."[152]

In the *Atlantic* weeks later, Robert Boynton wrote that West and others were no "random blip on the screen of public intellectual culture"—they were the answer to Jacoby's missing intellectuals. "In addressing a large and attentive audience about today's most pressing issues, these thinkers have begun taking their places as the legitimate inheritors of the mantle of the New York Intellectuals." Indeed, Bérubé wrote, "the golden age of the American public intellectual" may describe not only "Trilling and Irving Howe but . . . the black intellectuals of the nineteen-nineties."[153]

Boynton linked African American intellectuals' prominence to the close of the Cold War, as America's focus turned, he claimed, "from ideological movements abroad to racial issues at home." Intellectuals with internal understandings of African American experience became more visible—to whites. As Bérubé put it, "black public intellectuals are legitimated by their sense of a constituency," that is, their "unprecedented opportunity to speak from, to, and for a public, since their professional bona fides depend not on their repudiation of vernacular African-American culture but on their engagement with it." They were public intellectuals not in spite of their race, but because of it.[154]

This basis for intellectuals' publicness also made it problematic. "Having distinguished themselves by their analysis of racial subjects, they must now widen their scope and address broader political questions," Boynton declared. Seth Forman of Commack, New York, echoed this idea in a letter to the *New Yorker*. The "nominally Jewish" New York Intellectuals, Forman wrote, "aspired to speak broadly about all topics as integrated Americans in a cosmopolitan intellectual environment." By contrast, African American intellectuals "speak almost exclusively about black issues, and particularly about the black underclass. In this sense, the new black intellectuals should be seen less as 'public intellectuals' than as black intellectuals who speak publicly." Forman's letter suggested that the very attributes of an organic intellectual prevented one from being a public intellectual.[155]

This claim had its mirror image: the more public the intellectuals, the less organic they were. Now "at the center of mainstream intellectual culture," Boynton observed, African American public intellectuals faced the criticism that they had "shed their 'authentic' minority identification." "Mainstream" connoted white audiences, arousing "the long-standing fear," Bérubé wrote, "that 'crossing over' must entail selling out." Intellectuals had since the days of Julien Benda faced charges of "selling out"—to power, status, ideology, or chic. African American public intellectuals faced the additional charge of selling out their race.[156]

Reprising another enduring theme, Boynton asked whether the new cohort "forfeited their claim on the public intellectual's traditional oppositional stance." While the New York Intellectuals "championed high culture in the romantic hope that the masses, once freed from their oppression, might demand the best," he wrote, the new public intellectuals had a "casual relationship to mass culture." Worse than embracing pop culture, they could end up commodities in it—"becoming mere pundits or intellectual celebrities." West expressed this concern himself. Part of the public intellectual phenomenon, he said, "is *celebrity*, which is part of the commodification of [the] academic star." African American intellectuals had "been commodified. There's no escape from commodification"; it had "to be looked at clearly and cautiously." As Boynton put it, "The quandary of the contemporary black intellectual" was "how to balance the requirements of truly independent thinking with the inherently coopting demands of mass public culture." The New York Intellectuals had faced this problem too—declaring a truce with America's political economy while maintaining a critical approach to its culture.[157]

Characterizations of hooks or West as insufficiently oppositional shrink before their writings, which vibrate between vivid renderings of injustice and lyrical calls to struggle against it. But was their force spent on cultural rather than electoral politics? Older African American intellectuals, Bérubé reported, "ridicule the members of the rising generation as being more concerned with hip-hop than with health care." The policy briefs of conservative African American economist Thomas Sowell were "a powerful reminder to his progressive counterparts that public intellectual work does not consist exclusively of deconstructing Spike Lee." West, hooks, and others "may take on matters of public concern," Bérubé wrote, but "they don't always take on matters of public policy." In the humanistic disciplines from which many of the intellectuals emerged, however, politics included the construction of individual subjectivities as well as affordable housing. "But not every kind of 'political' work has political effects," Bérubé wrote, "and at times it seems that you can redraw the map of cultural politics without touching the practical-political map of precincts, districts, policymakers, and appropriations committees."[158] The rarified air of cultural criticism might not produce a breeze in the halls of power.

Weeks after Bérubé's and Boynton's articles appeared, Leon Wieseltier of the *New Republic* amplified their criticism—specifically of West. Citing the "obscurity" of West's academic language, Wieseltier claimed the emperor had no clothes. "West's conception of the intellectual vocation is too complicated for clarity," he wrote, his "union of theory and practice . . . a union of pomposity and enthusiasm, a long saga of positioning." No "drug dealer in America . . . will give himself up to Deleuze and Guattari," Wieseltier wrote, mocking what he described as West's "confidence that the established order will eventually fall before" academic theory. West's writings, "undone by his own academicism," were "almost completely worthless."[159] The irony of this indictment was West's critique of academicism. He built his intellectual identity upon the idea of being something more (if not strictly other) than academic, and that drove his exhaustive public speaking schedule, television appearances, and radio interviews. That was why he engaged popular culture and deployed popular idiom. To charge West with being too academic was to contradict those who alleged that, being too publicly engaged, he was insufficiently academic.

Wieseltier's piece launched a thousand ships.[160] Some found West's rhetoric indeed too esoteric for a public intellectual. "To a dismaying extent," wrote Ellen Willis in the *Village Voice*, "West's oeuvre conveys muddled views in a jargon-ridden prose, a Zelig-like amalgam of mix-and-match personae (Christian moralist, economic determinist, poststructuralist pop critic)." "An Afro-American Studies concentrator at Harvard"—where West was then teaching—declared in a letter to the *New Republic* that "for all his good intentions, West embodies everything that is wrong with his argot-spewing generation of self-aggrandizing intellects." He "might claim to champion the black 'proletariat,' yet only a seventh-year graduate student could understand the majority of his work."[161]

Others found in these complaints at most a partial truth. Wieseltier failed "to account for West's presence as a speaker, his charisma as a teacher or his power as a preacher," Elizabeth Maguire wrote to the *New Republic*; "or for the fact that his speeches draw a standing-room-only crowd hungry for his message of change." West had tried to connect academic conversations with wider public ones, converting scholarly knowledge into usable insight for those outside the academy while showing those inside that "ordinary people" had valuable insights themselves. He sought common cause between academia and "the street" to better conduct the work of social change. West the academic could look phony, however, from the vantage point of the street, and West the street preacher could appear illegitimate in the eyes of the academy. West the public intellectual might then be just a concatenation of opposites—a danger he recognized: "The same folks who want you to be a public intellectual also want you to be an expert, a visionary, a technician and leader on the ground all at the same time. You can't do all those things and do them well," he said in 1993.[162]

The sharpest projectile in that early 1995 fusillade came not from Wieseltier, but from Adolph Reed Jr., professor of political science at Northwestern. As it had been for Booker T. Washington, Reed wrote, "the definitive role of the black public intellectual" continued to be "interpreting the opaquely black heart of darkness for whites." Washington assumed that role based "on designation by white elites rather than by any black electorate or social movement," becoming the template for "the Racial Voice accountable to no clearly identifiable constituency among the spoken for." The new public intellectuals had similarly become spokespeople, Reed argued, through white designation, not African American authorization. He questioned their rootedness in African American experience. They "claim to speak from the edges of convention, to infuse mainstream discourse with a particular 'counterhegemonic' perspective at least implicitly linked to one's connectedness to identifiably black sensibilities or interests," but if public intellectuals stood "on the metaphorical boundary" between black and white America, they did so "facing outward," toward whites. There was little "attention to flux, differentiation, contingency, or even analysis of social process in our public intellectuals' accounts of black life," Reed wrote, for "you don't see nuances with your back turned." Reed concluded that the "public intellectual pose" allowed West and others "to claim authority both as certified, world-class elite academics and as links to an extra-academic blackness," without meeting "the practical requirements of either role—to avoid both rigorous, careful intellectual work *and* protracted, committed political action."[163] Reed was not just charging that, in doing two things at once, West and others were doing neither well; he was suggesting that the public intellectual role itself was useless—the evasion of political work and scholarship.

Reed sounded criticisms heard elsewhere, but his most significant charge stood apart. A lively African American public sphere had once rendered a "Racial Voice" like Washington unnecessary. "The role was unthinkable, even for a figure as prominent and respected as [Frederick] Douglass, during the first three decades after the Civil War because a culture of broad, democratic political participation flourished among black citizens." What made Washington's role "possible, and credible, was black Americans' expulsion from civic life" under Jim Crow. A single, designated African American voice arose only in a context where a multiplicity of voices had been silenced. "The idea of the free-floating race spokesman was a pathological effect of the disfranchisement specific to the segregation era."[164]

A portion of Jacoby's golden age—the 1950s—was also a period of repression for both African Americans and intellectuals of all kinds. Amid crackdowns and restrictions both official and unofficial, public debate fell within narrowed parameters. Indeed, the period's youth have been called "the Silent Generation." To generalize Reed's argument: Do public intellectuals flourish when civil society is suppressed?

That question turns the view of public intellectuals as allied with democracy on its head. Rather than harbingers of democratic political culture, public intellectuals may be a symptom of its decline. Did obstacles to widespread African American civic participation pave the way for African American public intellectuals of the 1990s? In a political culture from Reagan through Clinton that emphasized the War on Drugs, the end of "big government," and the pathologizing of urban life, had space opened for public intellectuals as it narrowed for "everyday" African Americans?

West might agree that public intellectuals' prominence was no cause for celebration when it occurred amid stifled civic life. He often lamented the state of civic life himself. "To be an intellectual really means to speak a truth that allows suffering to speak," West said. It meant bringing "into the limelight the social misery that is usually hidden or concealed."[165] But when in that limelight suffering spoke, would it do so in its own voices, or would the critical organic catalyst, prophetic pragmatist, and public intellectual be its proxy?

CONCLUSION

In the fall of 2007, Cornel West embraced Barack Obama on stage at Harlem's Apollo Theater. "I will celebrate for one day," West said of a potential Obama victory. "But the next day, I'll become one of his major critics," which he did. "His calling is one of progressive governance," West said; "my calling is Socratic and prophetic."[1] For West and others on the left, Obama's presidency became a disappointingly centrist, even conservative, administration. For critics on the right, however, Obama's presidency required repudiation. It came in the form of Donald Trump.

West "aspire[d] to be the Frederick Douglass" to Obama's Lincoln—the voice pushing the politician toward progressive change.[2] The voice pushing Trump toward politics evoked not Lincoln's era but Eisenhower's: Roy Cohn. In the 1950s, Cohn was Joseph McCarthy's attorney at the high-water mark of the Second Red Scare. Three decades later, during "the formative years of Donald Trump's career," Michael Kruse wrote, Cohn suggested that Trump start holding forth about national political issues.[3] Cohn had been present at the creation of "the egghead"—part of the anti-communist undertow that raised suspicion about intellectuals in American public life and twice helped submerge Adlai Stevenson's presidential aspirations. After two terms of Obama—"the intellectual as president"—the White House became the weekday residence of Cohn's "prize pupil," who was, historian Walter Moss declared, "the opposite of the intellectual or 'egghead.'"[4]

But the opposite of eggheads has had a more ambiguous relationship to elites. At times, Trump rallied voters to cast them out along with the intellectuals: "I want you to imagine how much better our future can be if we declare independence from the elites," Trump told Pennsylvanians in the summer of 2016. Though the messenger—a Manhattan-based real-estate developer, celebrity, and luxury brand—was dissonant, the message that the cheated many must break the power of the elite few had deep roots in

American politics. At other times, Trump signaled his sense not only of the derisive but also the honorific meanings of "intellectual" and "elite." Those typically wearing these labels "are wrong so much," he said. "So don't call them the elite. Don't call them intellectuals. Call them establishment guys." The important distinction ran not between intellects and others, but between insiders and outsiders. Indeed, the injustice for Trump was that outsiders, including himself and his supporters, were more elite than those inside government, media, and other institutions who criticized and constrained him even after he became president. "I went to better schools than they did. I was a better student than they were," Trump told supporters in Arizona. "We've got more money and more brains and better houses and apartments and nicer boats," he told a rally in North Dakota. "We are smarter than they are. They say the elite. We are the elite. You are the elite." Indeed, he boomed: "Let's call ourselves the super elite."[5]

In Trump's rhetoric, the terms of decades-old debates—intellectuals, elites—were redefined once more. "Intellectuals" had, in fact, less-impressive brains. "Elites" were merely insiders. These charges evoked the contemptuous usage of "egghead" circa 1952, but they also went further—not only deprecating eggheads but proudly claiming the mantle of "elite" from them. Trump, scourge of so-called intellectuals, was now leading a mass movement of self-styled elites. If populist democracy has been a check on the pretensions and power of experts and elites, here was a populism that instead of checking those pretensions democratized them—in the name of aggrandizement or, as was Trump's watchword, greatness.

New York Times columnist David Brooks and network journalist Katie Couric may count among Trump's "establishment guys." In 2008 Brooks denounced Sarah Palin as "a fatal cancer to the Republican party" in Hofstadterian terms. Outside the conservative intellectual tradition, Palin represented "a counter, more populist tradition, which is not only to scorn liberal ideas but to scorn ideas entirely." Ten years later, Palin looked to Couric, who had notably exposed Palin's ignorance of current events in a televised interview during the 2008 campaign, like a "harbinger of things to come." Couric saw in her the germ of "a corrosive trend" that intensified: "contempt for experts and elites." This "disdain for the liberal intelligentsia morphed into a disdain for the highly educated." The result, Couric said, was "the current environment, where no matter what evidence the experts have brought to bear . . . it doesn't matter to many voters. These elites, and the arguments they make, are dismissed out of hand."[6]

In 2012 Brooks cast this confrontation between populists and elites as American political culture's "follower problem." While the nation once celebrated political leaders who were "embodiments of just authority," over time "fervent devotion to equality, to the notion that all people are equal and deserve equal recognition and respect," made it difficult "to define and celebrate greatness, to hold up others who are immeasurably superior to ourselves." Evoking Trilling and Kristol, Brooks argued that the "adversary culture of the intellectuals has turned into a mass adversarial cynicism." In the name of anti-elitism, earned elite status was cast away too. Intellectuals who challenged authority found their own gone. "You end up with movements like Occupy Wall Street and the Tea Parties," Brooks wrote, "that try to dispense with authority altogether." They resembled "the Internet—a disbursed semianarchy in which authority is suspect and each individual is king." Brooks urged "democratic followership" instead, a recognition that while "created equal," we "also elevate those who are extraordinary"; we "defer to them" and are thus "led by just authority."[7]

Trump exploded Brooks's "follower problem" by not only challenging elites' authority—just or otherwise—but conferring it upon himself. Trump did not dispense with greatness, superiority, or authority; he claimed them—including for his base: the newly minted "super elite." In the process, he exposed the political weakness of Brooks's call for deference and "followership." In American democracy, a rhetoric that elevates people over intellectual elites is more effective than one urging them to follow their superiors. That is the case even when, as Trump's rise also suggests, the anti-intellectual, anti-elite rhetoric ultimately serves a deference-demanding leader consolidating his own power.

Trump's is not, however, the only response to the problem of unequal cultural power and authority in American democracy. While Trump's rhetoric democratized for his followers the status of elite, that of his predecessor democratized the role of the intellectual. As one with "the great intellect," Obama may have claimed the "just authority" that Brooks conjured.[8] Instead, Obama spoke a language not of leaders and followers but, rather, civic participation: "Yes, we can."

Among the things "we" could do was originate, debate, and articulate political ideas. I remember a "platform meeting" at my friend Marlene's place in the summer of 2008. The Obama campaign had called upon people to gather ahead of the Democratic National Convention in order to discuss and submit items for the party platform. A dozen people of various political persuasions—many of whom were meeting for the first time—assembled at Marlene's table. For hours we debated foreign and domestic policy, ultimately writing thirteen "planks." We considered Obama not only an intellectual but also a community organizer, and small intellectual communities like ours—whether convened as a genuine attempt to canvass the grassroots or merely a clever party-building exercise—were among those organized around his 2008 campaign. Trump granted his supporters the status of elites; Obama asked his to shoulder the burden of intellectuals.

Participatory communities like that at Marlene's present a profoundly different model of democratic intellectual life than Brooks envisions. In his schema, intellectual excellence confers a rightful authority to which others should defer. Disruption of this deference is tantamount to the decline of authority itself. Anti-intellectual "semianarchy" is not, however, the only alternative to the presence in public life of authoritative intellectuals. Intellectual communities, groups of people thinking with one another, represent not the disintegration of authority, but its diffusion. Intellectual work as an ongoing collective endeavor is an alternative to the single individual—the expert, egghead, or elite—dispensing insight to an audience. The elaboration of ideas has happened in communal settings throughout the period examined here, from feminist consciousness-raising groups and radical experiments like the Combahee River Collective, to workers' education in the labor movement, to breakthrough research generated in ACT UP (AIDS Coalition to Unleash Power). These groups represent a displacement of the role(s) and responsibilities of the intellectual from the mind of a single individual to the ongoing process of encounter, dialogue, and action that is only possible with others.

Indeed, recent movements are embracing intellectualism while eschewing the figure of the intellectual. Black Lives Matter and Occupy Wall Street have been notable for their resistance to authorizing single individuals as spokespeople, theoreticians, or leaders. Instead, the formulation and articulation of ideas is decentralized—Occupy employed "general assemblies," and Black Lives Matter deploys social media. Critics question the effectiveness of these methods, and avoidance of "the intellectual" has been taken for anti-intellectualism.

I brought such doubts myself when visiting Zuccotti Park, epicenter of Occupy, in the fall of 2011. Alongside the food tent, medical tent, and assembly space, there was a sizable library, its paperback volumes dry beneath a canopy of blue tarps. I asked people at the library about

Occupy's much-maligned "lack of objectives." Pointing to the dog-eared books around me (I saw titles by Chomsky, hooks, and West) they said that refusal to distill Occupy into a few demands was their way of avoiding the orthodoxies and sectarianism that had historically divided the Left. What I saw was not a rejection of intellectualism or the role of the intellectual; it was an incipient community of intellectuals all.

Debates about the role of the intellectual in American political culture have been persistent and unresolved. They have persisted because the idealized contribution of the intellectual—bringing wisdom, insight, knowledge, and understanding to bear upon social and political life—has value. They are unresolved because the authority concentrated in individuals who would make such a contribution is dissonant to democratic politics. Democracies both need intellectual insights and resist the authority any individual wields in pronouncing these insights from a necessarily powerful, perhaps unaccountable position. Debates about the role of the intellectual may end their tortuous course not by finally specifying that role but by widening it.

The virtues and functions of the intellectual may shift from the shoulders of authoritative individuals to the hands of participatory groups, ranging from the Marblehead Town Meeting applauded by H. Stuart Hughes to the Occupy general assemblies. Such a shift could help to break the dead-end dichotomy between elitism and populism. A divided nation of smug intellects and resentful throngs might instead be a democracy of people in conversation and collaboration, intellectuals all.

That is a highly intellectualized and idealized conception of democracy. Indeed, it is a vision of deliberative democracy. The danger of deliberative democracy is that it packages the public sphere as a graduate seminar, privileging certain ways of speaking and arguing and thereby silencing far more citizens than it would empower.[9] But it need not be so. Debates about the role of intellectuals have for decades pointed to democratization of what counts as intellectual activity. While critics view this development as eroding standards of intellectualism, the efforts of bell hooks, West, and many others suggest that it is possible to have a rigorous discussion of public affairs without resorting to a single idiom, methodology, or mode of expression.

The profusion of voices in the public sphere is a necessary but not sufficient condition for fully realized democracy. Deliberative democracy must be supplemented and centered by participatory democracy—a theme that also emerges from debates about the role of intellectuals after World War Two. Not only were those aiming to play that role trying to speak, they were also searching for some kind of authority to be heard. In other words, they sought efficacy. Debates about their roles went more often to the question of *how* they could shape society than *whether* they should. They point toward a model of public intervention that emphasizes both deliberation and effective participation. This model aims not so much at an intellectualized, rarified version of democracy as one that radically centers people's role as citizens and political participants relative to other roles—family member, worker, consumer, etc.—that, though suffused with politics too, call upon their time and energies in different ways. Indeed, one way of characterizing the difference between intellectuals and other people is to say that intellectuals are those for whom citizens' work may be nearer the center of life. Chomsky has rightfully pointed to this gap between intellectuals and others as a privilege of the former, unequally distributed. In a fully realized democracy, this gap would close. Debates about the role of the intellectual and that of the citizen would merge.

The ideal constellation of qualities assigned the intellectual and that assigned the citizen turn out to have many of the same stars. Both citizen and intellectual are interested in and informed about matters of public concern. Both inhabit the public square, engaging in dialogues, exchanges, and arguments. Both are competent, but not narrowly so. There is no matter of civic importance beyond their ken. Their broad knowledge looks less like technical expertise than it does informed attention. They are concerned not only with themselves: in turning their minds and actions toward common problems, intellectuals and citizens express loyalties beyond the self.

This idealized version of the citizen has, for many, remained an ideal. Who among us can carve out space amid the rigors of daily life to fully meet the demands of democratic citizenship? Intellectuals are among the few who usually can. They have served not only as provocations to debate about the nature of democracy but as prototypes of citizenship to debate about. The roles they have tried to play—servants of and dissenters from the state, dedicated deliberators and invokers of expertise, voices in particular communities and seekers of the general good—are shining examples and cautionary tales in considering the possibilities and limitations of democratic citizenship. They also remind us that debates about the nature of American democracy and citizenship are ongoing, and that we have yet to realize either full democracy or full citizenship. As social critics, intellectuals call attention to this shortfall. As privileged participants in the public sphere, they are also creatures of it—for in a deliberative, participatory democracy, the role of the intellectual would be redundant; it would be that of every citizen.

Opposition to and, in smaller measure, support for Trump's presidency may have sparked a surge in civic education and participation.[10] This democratic energy is both fueled by and in spite of him, for whereas Trump's rhetoric democratizes the status of "elite," it narrows popular participation to one task: endorsing him. "I am your voice," he said at the 2016 Republican National Convention. "I alone can fix it."[11] The difference between Trump's "I alone" and Obama's "Yes, we can" is stark.

Trump aims to erase Obama—in policy and legacy. So large, indeed, does his version of populism loom that it overshadows what had not long before been Obama's own popular mobilization. Something of the latter's meaning can be learned not only in hindsight since 2016, but in comparing 1952 and 2008, elections when "egghead candidates" fared so differently. Adlai Stevenson promised a deliberative presidency, but he offered little in the way of participatory politics. He was more committed to intellectual impeccability than broader democracy. A biographer describes Stevenson's 1952 convention speech as "more appropriate to a Puritan preacher than to a presidential candidate." Stevenson's intellectualism, like that of Puritan divines, could appear distant, austere—a model easy to admire but daunting to emulate. In 2008, by contrast, Obama offset his occasional contemplative distance with a call for public participation. "Change," he said to a crowd in Chicago as the results from Super Tuesday primaries flowed in, "will not come if we wait for some other person or some other time. We are the ones we've been waiting for. We are the change that we seek."[12]

Obama's call to the American people in 2008 evokes C. Wright Mills's call to intellectuals in 1958. "Other men can feel that their power to reason, their skills to investigate, their ability to find out are inadequate to the situations they confront; they can feel that they are not expected to confront them," Mills wrote. "But intellectuals cannot. So long as they are intellectuals, they must reason and investigate and, with their passion to know, they must confront the situations of all men everywhere. That he expects this of himself is the mark of the intellectual as a type of social and moral creature."[13]

The rhetoric of 2008 may have included such lines, with "citizens in a democracy" wherever Mills placed "intellectuals." "It is our task to continually make the new beginning," Mills told intellectuals a half century before. "Maybe the voices of the American people can finally be heard again," Obama said in Chicago; "we have to write a new chapter in American history."[14] Indeed, we do.

ACKNOWLEDGMENTS

This book would not have been possible without the insights, generosity, and support of many others—more than I can name. Their contributions have enriched this work, and its remaining shortcomings are down to me.

In the history department at Rochester Institute of Technology (RIT), I am fortunate to have the best of colleagues: Tamar Carroll, Rebecca Edwards, Joe Henning (a fellow long-suffering Mets fan), Christine Keiner, Mary Beth Kitzel, Michael Laver, Rich Newman, Rebecca Scales, and Corinna Schlombs. Eric Nystrom was a very helpful reader and critic during his time at RIT and afterward. Museum studies colleagues Juilee Decker, Rebecca DeRoo, and Tina Lent have provided timely guidance and good cheer. Jamie Winebrake and his team in the dean's office gave invaluable support to this project, including from the College of Liberal Arts Publication Cost Grant Program. RIT students are an outstanding bunch, and I have benefited greatly from conversations with those in the museum studies program and in my history courses.

A few miles down the Genesee River, I had wonderful teachers and made good friends at the University of Rochester. Since the time I was a high school teacher considering doctoral studies, Robb Westbrook has encouraged my intellectual and moral interest in the possibilities of American democracy. I can think of no clearer critic or more careful reader than Robb. Conversation in American history at Rochester was vibrant, and I was also fortunate to have courses in the field with Dan Borus, Larry Hudson, Joan Rubin, Tom Slaughter, and the late Lynn Gordon. Jim Johnson and Jeff Tucker were helpful, critical readers from beyond the department. Among many brilliant classmates, Jeff Ludwig and Michael Fisher were particularly helpful conversation partners in the field of American intellectual history. Dean Wendi Heinzelman took an interest in my research and my progress, encouraging both with crucial fellowship funding.

The New York Public Library allowed me to spend wonderfully productive weeks in its reading rooms as a short-term research fellow, and I especially thank Thomas Lannon for his help. The John F. Kennedy Presidential Library and Museum generously made me a research fellow, and I pondered the archives while savoring the view from Columbia Point. The Friends of the University of Wisconsin–Madison Libraries provided me with a grant that led to weeks of good work along the shores of Lake Mendota. Jonathan Nelson was vital to my research there and has continued to offer advice and help. Archivists and library assistants at Columbia, Rochester, the University of Massachusetts Amherst, Yale, and elsewhere also provided valuable aid.

Among the most delightful gatherings in recent years were the Public Intellectuals Conferences (meetings of those who study them, rather than of such intellectuals themselves) championed by Larry Friedman, Pilar Damião de Medeiros, and Mark West, among others. The conversations at these small, international, and interdisciplinary conferences sharpened many of the ideas for this volume. Ron Doel and Kristine Harper were generous with their advice and time; Mark and Larry have been friends to this book and to me. Here in Rochester we are the beneficiaries of Alison Parker having launched RUSH—our United States history reading and writing group. I am thankful for the care with which members of the group responded to drafts of various portions of this book's manuscript.

Tim Mennel at the University of Chicago Press is a superb editor. His incisive questions, keen eye for clarity of expression, and encouragement made this book better. Susannah Engstrom and Erin DeWitt at the Press provided answers to my many questions, for which I am grateful. I would also like to thank the outside readers of the manuscript, whose thoughtful feedback was essential to improving the work.

Noam Chomsky and William Leuchtenburg generously obliged my requests for interviews. The book was greatly aided by the permissions and assistance granted to me by many of those who appear in its pages, or their families, estates, and/or executors. I thank, in particular, Sarah Hofstadter, Judith Hughes, William Kristol, Nik Mills, and Michael Riesman for corresponding with me regarding their late family members' materials. All of them have helped to make history accessible.

I first experienced history teaching as a vocation at the Harley School, and I wish to thank my colleagues and students from those three wonderful years. Harley is one of many Rochester institutions that contribute to the lively intellectual climate of the place, and I count myself lucky to participate in Flower City Philosophy, the John Dewey Group, the Twenty-Third Legislative District, and the coffee-shop conversation circuit.

Finally, I would like to thank my friends and family, whose contributions extend well beyond this volume. In Rochester, Ithaca, and London, I have found wonderful philosophical friends. At conclaves and convergences, over long emails and longer phone calls, we have exchanged thoughts, observations, and encouragement. Scott Belsky, Jack Kelley, Michael Schwalbe, and Kurt Zeller have been particularly important to my thinking about politics, culture, and writing over the years.

My mom, Barbara, made sure that I could visit cultural events and sites regularly, and I thank her for that hard-earned bounty of festivals, forts, concerts, plays, museums, and street musicians. While working in human services and caring for elderly parents, she found the strength to make memories, traditions, and a home for us. Talks with my father, Roger, about history, politics, and life have been vital to me. Since I was a kid, he has made history, whether our family's or the world's, feel vivid. Dad is a great autodidact—there was a small public library literally in his backyard when he was a teenager, and it shows. My grandparents—Agnes, Jeanette, James, and Victor—now gone, were the most loving connection to the past that one could hope to have. Thanks to Dick, Gary, Jim, Stella, and Sue, I have had a supportive wider family, at the center of which is very often earnest, frequently funny conversation about stories, ideas, news, and meals—just what I like.

Esther Arnold devoted an enormous amount of time, intellect, and energy to this book. She is a gifted writer, scholar, and editor, an exemplar of integrity and what it means to be considerate. We became partners not long before I started the process that now culminates in this book, which would not have come to be without her. We have shared hopes, anxieties, highs, lows, and the rhythms of day-to-day life. She is an exceptional person to whom I extend my deepest love and appreciation.

NOTES

Introduction

1. Adlai E. Stevenson, 1952, "I Love the Gov" (video courtesy of the John F. Kennedy Presidential Library), from Museum of the Moving Image, *The Living Room Candidate: Presidential Campaign Commercials 1952–2012*, www.livingroomcandidate.org /commercials/1952/i-love-the-gov. For the photo, see "Sparkman Derides G.O.P. Farm Plank," *New York Times*, September 3, 1952. For the "schoolboy" quotation, see "Here's a Footnote to Stevenson Tour," *New York Times*, September 6, 1952.

2. Richard Hofstadter, *Anti-Intellectualism in American Life* (New York: Vintage, 1963), 4.

3. For the Stevenson quote, see Robert North Roberts, Scott John Hammond, and Valerie A. Sulfaro, *Slogans, Issues, Programs, Personalities, and Strategies*, vol. 1 of *Presidential Campaigns, Slogans, Issues, and Platforms: The Complete Encyclopedia* (Santa Barbara, CA: Greenwood Books, 2012), 44.

4. On the term's origins and its application to Stevenson, see Aaron Lecklider, *Inventing the Egghead: The Battle over Brainpower in American Culture* (Philadelphia: University of Pennsylvania Press, 2013), 193.

5. See Hofstadter, *Anti-Intellectualism*, 227.

6. Plato, *Theaetetus*, 174a; *Shakespeare Jest-Books; Reprints of the Early and Very Rare Jest-Books Supposed to Have Been Used by Shakespeare*, ed. W. Carew Hazlitt (London: Willis & Sotheran, 1864), 38, http://www.gutenberg.org/files/29821/29821-h/29821 -h.htm#Page_ii38.

7. Thomas B. Edsall, "Barack Obama: Egghead?" *Huffington Post*, August 8, 2008, http://www.huffingtonpost.com/2008/08/20/barack-obama-egghead_n_120005.html; Michael Schaffer, "We're All Eggheads Now," *New Republic*, November 5, 2008, http:// www.newrepublic.com/blog/the-plank/were-all-eggheads-now.

8. Susan Jacoby, *The Age of American Unreason* (New York: Pantheon, 2008), xi. Jacoby updated this volume just after the 2008 election (Vintage, 2009) and again after the 2016 election (Vintage, 2018). In both updates, she affirms the basic thesis, noted above, of the original.

9. Louise Williams, letter to the editor, *Washington Post and Times Herald*, Decem-

ber 8, 1957; sanang, August 20, 2008, phughez, August 20, 2008, Redrover666, August 20, 2008, hippydippy, August 20, 2008, all comments on Edsall, "Barack Obama: Egghead?"

10. Conor Lynch, "Donald Trump's Glorious Victory for Anti-Intellectualism: 'Drain the Swamp' Just Meant the Eggheads," *Salon*, January 7, 2017, http://www .salon.com/2017/01/07/donald-trumps-glorious-victory-for-anti-intellectualism -drain-the-swamp-just-meant-the-eggheads/.

11. Scholars have traced the changing landscape of intellectual life in midcentury United States history by looking at how individuals attempted to construct, defend, and/or practice their own roles in particular settings and moments. Joy Rohde examines "the relationship between scholarship and the national security state" by studying those who "grappled with it daily in word and deed." Similarly, Robert Vanderlan eschews precise definition of "the intellectual" to allow for "greater fidelity to the complexity of the intellectual's experiences in particular historical and cultural contexts." Mark Lilla, writing about European intellectuals, also advises "studying intellectual and political lives in concrete historical situations." Rohde, *Armed with Expertise: The Militarization of American Social Research during the Cold War* (Ithaca, NY: Cornell University Press, 2013), 7; Vanderlan, *Intellectuals Incorporated: Politics, Art, and Ideas Inside Henry Luce's Media Empire* (Philadelphia: University of Pennsylvania Press, 2010), 10; Lilla, *The Reckless Mind: Intellectuals in Politics* (New York: New York Review Books, 2001), xi. See also David Paul Haney, *The Americanization of Social Science: Intellectuals and Public Responsibility in the Postwar United States* (Philadelphia: Temple University Press, 2008).

12. Stefan Collini, *Absent Minds: Intellectuals in Britain* (New York: Oxford University Press, 2006), 1 (emphasis in original).

13. Collini, 4.

14. Jeffrey C. Goldfarb wrote in 1998, for instance, "that the diminution of intellectual activity presents a major threat to democracy in our times. Intellectuals are central democratic actors, and when they leave the political stage, democratic performance ends in failure." Goldfarb, *Civility and Subversion: The Intellectual in Democratic Society* (Cambridge: Cambridge University Press, 1998), 1.

15. See Jamie Cohen-Cole, *The Open Mind: Cold War Politics and the Sciences of Human Nature* (Chicago: University of Chicago Press, 2014), and Lecklider, *Inventing the Egghead*.

16. Sociologists have been particularly attentive to such questions. See, for example, Barbara A. Misztal, *Intellectuals and the Public Good: Creativity and Civil Courage* (Cambridge: Cambridge University Press, 2007). Max Weber's work on power and authority, especially in *Economy and Society: An Outline of Interpretive Sociology* (1921– 22), ed. Guenther Roth and Claus Wittich (New York: Bedminster Press, 1968), is a foundational statement of these concepts and their relation to the role of intellectuals.

17. For Plato's discussion of philosopher kings, see Book VI of *The Republic*.

18. Walter Lippmann, *Drift and Mastery: An Attempt to Diagnose the Current Unrest*

(1914; repr., Madison: University of Wisconsin Press, 1985), 85. On America as a "business civilization," see, for instance, James Truslow Adams, *Our Business Civilization: Some Aspects of American Culture* (New York: Albert and Charles Boni, 1929). Lippmann was neither the first nor the last to use language that assumed an identity between intellectual and male. Both he and Adams were associated with Woodrow Wilson's Inquiry—a group of academics tasked with studying problems and possibilities for the post–World War One world and a notable instance in this period of intellectuals' enlistment by government. Leon Fink explores a range of intellectuals' attempts to serve American democracy in this era in *Progressive Intellectuals and the Dilemmas of Democratic Commitment* (Cambridge, MA: Harvard University Press, 1997).

19. "Harding to Consult Some 'Best Minds' after His Vacation," *New York Times*, November 6, 1920.

20. Walter Lippmann, *Public Opinion* (1922; repr., New York: BN Publishing, 2007), 115.

21. See Daniel Bessner, *Democracy in Exile: Hans Speier and the Rise of the Defense Intellectual* (Ithaca, NY: Cornell University Press, 2018); Paul Erickson, Judy L. Klein, Lorraine Daston, Rebecca Lemov, Thomas Sturm, and Michael D. Gordin, *How Reason Almost Lost Its Mind: The Strange Career of Cold War Rationality* (Chicago: University of Chicago Press, 2013); Rohde, *Armed with Expertise*; Mark Solovey and Hamilton Cravens, eds., *Cold War Social Science: Knowledge Production, Liberal Democracy, and Human Nature* (New York: Palgrave Macmillan, 2012); David C. Engerman, *Know Your Enemy: The Rise and Fall of America's Soviet Experts* (New York: Oxford University Press, 2009); Bruce Kuklick, *Blind Oracles: Intellectuals and War from Kennan to Kissinger* (Princeton, NJ: Princeton University Press, 2006); and Nils Gilman, *Mandarins of the Future: Modernization Theory in Cold War America* (Baltimore: Johns Hopkins University Press, 2003).

22. See Ellen W. Schrecker, *No Ivory Tower: McCarthyism and the Universities* (New York: Oxford University Press, 1986), and Landon R. Y. Storrs, *The Second Red Scare and the Unmaking of the New Deal Left* (Princeton, NJ: Princeton University Press, 2012). A foretaste came during World War One when, for example, Columbia University fired three professors for criticism of American policy, leading Charles Beard, chair of the political science department, to resign in protest. Rather than dashing Beard's reputation, however, his resignation burnished it. See David S. Brown, *Beyond the Frontier: The Midwestern Voice in American Historical Writing* (Chicago: University of Chicago Press, 2009), 58–59.

23. These questions famously arose on the cusp of the twentieth century, at the very birth of the term "intellectual." During the Dreyfus Affair, French intellectuals who rallied to Alfred Dreyfus's cause were deemed insufficiently loyal to the army and, by extension, the national state. See David Drake, *French Intellectuals and Politics from the Dreyfus Affair to the Occupation* (New York: Palgrave Macmillan, 2005).

24. Raymond Aron, *The Opium of the Intellectuals* (1955; repr., London: Secker &

Warburg, 1957). For versions of Aron's thesis appearing elsewhere, see Paul Holland-
er's *Political Pilgrims: Travels of Western Intellectuals to the Soviet Union, China and Cuba,
1928–1978* (New York: Oxford University Press, 1981) and *The End of Commitment:
Intellectuals, Revolutionaries, and Political Morality in the Twentieth Century* (Chicago:
Ivan R. Dee, 2006). On the phenomenon of some intellectuals accusing others of
being intellectuals, see Stefan Collini, "'Every Fruit-Juice Drinker, Nudist, Sandal-
Wearer . . .': Intellectuals as Other People," in *The Public Intellectual*, ed. Helen Small
(Malden, MA: Blackwell, 2002), 204.

25. Alvin W. Gouldner, *The Future of Intellectuals and the Rise of the New Class: A
Frame of Reference, Theses, Conjectures, Arguments, and an Historical Perspective on the
Role of Intellectuals and Intelligentsia in the International Class Contest of the Modern Era*
(New York: Seabury Press, 1979), 1.

26. See Sidney Blumenthal, *The Rise of the Counter-Establishment: From Conser-
vative Ideology to Political Power* (New York: Times Books, 1986); Kim Phillips-Fein,
*Invisible Hands: The Making of the Conservative Movement from the New Deal to Rea-
gan* (New York: W. W. Norton, 2009); and Jason Stahl, *Right Moves: The Conservative
Think Tank in American Political Culture since 1945* (Chapel Hill: University of North
Carolina Press, 2016).

27. Ian Tyrrell's work on the discipline of history provides an instructive counterpoint to declension narratives. Challenging the story that professional historians
turned their backs on the public over the course of the twentieth century, Tyrrell points
instead to a continually renewed debate about historians' public role and, over several generations of historians, varied attempts to meet that role. Tyrrell, *Historians in
Public: The Practice of American History, 1880–1970* (Chicago: University of Chicago
Press, 2005).

28. Edward W. Said, *Representations of the Intellectual* (New York: Pantheon,
1994), 13. George Scialabba took a pragmatic approach to the subject, in *What Are
Intellectuals Good For?* (Boston: Pressed Wafer Press, 2009).

29. Alexis de Tocqueville, *Democracy in America*, trans. George Lawrence, ed. J. P.
Mayer (Garden City, NY: Anchor Books, 1969), 641. The latter-day Tocquevillean
Allan Bloom suggested that "the deepest intellectual weakness of democracy is its lack
of taste or gift for the theoretical life. All our Nobel prizes . . . do nothing to gainsay
Tocqueville's appraisal. . . . The issue is not whether we possess intelligence but whether
we are adept at reflection of the broadest and deepest kind." Bloom, *The Closing of the
American Mind* (New York: Touchstone, 1988), 252.

30. Within the disciplines of history and philosophy, there have been extensive
debates about the detachment or engagement appropriate to the roles of historian and
philosopher. Several of the figures dealt with here participated in both these intra-
disciplinary discussions and the broader question of intellectuals. The border between
these domains of debate is not always clear, especially when participants use terms like
historian or philosopher, scholar, and intellectual interchangeably. At other moments,

NOTES TO PAGES 13-14

however, they draw explicit contrast between disciplinary roles and the role of the intellectual. On the discipline of history, see Peter Novick, *That Noble Dream: The "Objectivity Question" and the American Historical Profession* (New York: Cambridge University Press, 1988). As an example of the positions staked out within the discipline of philosophy, see Virginia Held, Kai Nielsen, and Charles Parsons, eds., *Philosophy and Political Action* (New York: Oxford University Press, 1972).

31. Zachery R. Williams has noted, for example, how coverage of this cohort in the 1990s largely elided their connection to a predecessor generation of African American academic and public intellectuals at Howard University who "operated from the late 1920s to about 1970 and paralleled and rivaled the activity and work of the New York Intellectuals," with whom the "new black intellectuals" of the 1990s were most frequently associated in mainstream media. Williams, *In Search of the Talented Tenth: Howard University Public Intellectuals and the Dilemmas of Race, 1926–1970* (Columbia: University of Missouri Press, 2009), 197.

32. On this point see, for example, Cornel West, "Horace Pippin's Challenge to Art Criticism," in *I Tell My Heart: The Art of Horace Pippin*, exhibition catalog by Judith E. Stein (Philadelphia: Pennsylvania Academy of Fine Arts and Universe Publishing, 1993), 44–53; and West, "The Dilemma of the Black Intellectual," *Cultural Critique* 1, no. 1 (1985), reprinted in his *Keeping Faith: Philosophy and Race in America* (New York: Routledge, 1993), 72–73. The phrase "doings and sufferings" appears in West, *Prophesy Deliverance! An Afro-American Revolutionary Christianity* (Philadelphia: Westminster Press, 1982), 15. Writing about "Black music, creativity, and experimentation in language," Robin D. G. Kelley cautions that "though they may . . . reflect and speak to the political and social world of inner city communities, expressive cultures are not simply mirrors of social life or expression of conflict, pathos, and anxieties"; they "must also be understood as sources of visceral and psychic pleasure." These are not the practices, moreover, of "an undifferentiated mass" but, rather, "a hybrid [culture] that draws on Afro-diasporic tradition, popular culture, the vernacular of previous generations of Southern and Northern black folk, new and old technologies, and a whole lot of imagination." Kelley, *Yo' Mama's DisFunktional: Fighting the Culture Wars in Urban America* (Boston: Beacon Press, 1997), 41–42.

33. Daniel Drezner has recently argued, for example, that the erosion of public intellectuals' and experts' authority opens space in the public sphere for a new kind of ideas merchant: "thought leaders" who pitch ideas often rooted in experience rather than analysis. Thought leaders receive a hearing because they speak not from an authoritative place but, rather, a perceived authentic one. Drezner, *The Ideas Industry: How Pessimists, Partisans, and Plutocrats Are Transforming the Marketplace of Ideas* (New York: Oxford University Press, 2017).

34. Debates about the meaning of democracy could become debates about its desirability, especially at moments when anti-intellectual populism and demagoguery were perceived as the result rather than the warping of democratic politics. On the long

history of this question, see, for example, Nancy Isenberg and Andrew Burstein, *The Problem of Democracy: The Presidents Adams Confront the Cult of Personality* (New York: Viking, 2019).

35. Richard Hofstadter, "The Development of Higher Education in America," in *The Development and Scope of Higher Education in the United States*, by Hofstadter and C. DeWitt Hardy (New York: Columbia University Press, 1952), 107; Hofstadter, "The Paranoid Style," in *The Paranoid Style and Other Essays* (New York: Knopf, 1965), 29–30.

36. H. Stuart Hughes, *Gentleman Rebel: The Memoirs of H. Stuart Hughes* (New York: Ticknor and Fields, 1990), 313; Lawrence Spivak, William Buckley, Richard Clurman, H. Stuart Hughes, Frank McGee, and Chalmers Roberts, *Meet the Press*, National Broadcasting Company, aired August 12, 1962, transcript, box 10, folder 15, Henry Stuart Hughes Papers (MS 1446), Manuscripts and Archives, Yale University Library.

Chapter One

1. "What You Need to Read Now: Rebels with a Cause," *Newsweek*, July 30, 2010, http://www.newsweek.com/2010/07/30/books-list-rebels-with-a-cause.html; Jon Meacham, "Meacham: Words Have Consequences," *Newsweek*, September 19, 2009, http://www.newsweek.com/2009/09/18/words-have-consequences.html; David Greenberg, "The Obama Haters: We Still Don't Understand How Fringe Conservatism Went Mainstream," *Slate*, September 23, 2009, http://www.slate.com/id/2229352/; Greenberg, "Richard Hofstadter: The Pundits' Favorite Historian," *Slate*, June 7, 2006, http://www.slate.com/id/2143217/; Evan Osnos, "The Fearful and the Frustrated," *New Yorker*, August 31, 2015, http://www.newyorker.com/magazine/2015/08/31/the-fearful-and-the-frustrated; Conor Lynch, "Paranoid Politics: Donald Trump's Style Perfectly Embodies the Theories of Renowned Historian," *Salon*, July 7, 2016, http://www.salon.com/2016/07/07/paranoid_politics_donald_trump. Alan Wolfe's *The Politics of Petulance: America in an Age of Immaturity* (Chicago: University of Chicago Press, 2018) applies Hofstadter's work on demagoguery and democracy to Trump's ascendency and sees in that work a model for public intellectuals today. For a critique of contemporary invocations of Hofstadter—and Hofstadter's work itself—see Jeet Heer, "Donald Trump Is Not a Populist. He's the Voice of Aggrieved Privilege," *New Republic*, August 24, 2015, http://www.newrepublic.com/article/122590/donald-trump-not-populist-hes-voice-aggrieved-privilege.

2. Sam Tanenhaus, "The Conservative Movement," *New Republic*, March 12, 2007, http://www.tnr.com/article/the-conservative-movement.

3. Richard Hofstadter, "The Pseudo-Conservative Revolt," in *The New American Right*, ed. Daniel Bell (New York: Criterion Books, 1955), 43.

4. Hofstadter, "Pseudo-Conservatism Revisited—1965," in *The Paranoid Style and Other Essays* (New York: Knopf, 1965), 86–87.

5. While Andrew Hartman argues, contrary to the connotation Hofstadter gave "status" relative to "interest politics," that the issues at the heart of the culture wars were "real and compelling" rather than "sideshows," both find that cultural questions touching upon American identity have been central to our politics. Hartman, *A War for the Soul of America: A History of the Culture Wars* (Chicago: University of Chicago Press, 2015), 1, 2.

6. Jack Pole, "Richard Hofstadter," in *Clio's Favorites: Leading Historians of the United States, 1945–2000*, ed. Robert Allen Rutland (Columbia: University of Missouri Press, 2000), 80.

7. Hofstadter, "The Paranoid Style in American Politics," in *The Paranoid Style and Other Essays*, 29–30.

8. Stephen J. Whitfield and, more recently, Jennifer Ratner-Rosenhagen and Tim Lacy have written illuminating reconsiderations of *Anti-Intellectualism in American Life* and anti-intellectualism itself. See Ratner-Rosenhagen, "Anti-Intellectualism as Romantic Discourse," *Daedalus* 138, no. 2 (Spring 2009): 41–52; Lacy, "Against and Beyond Hofstadter: Revising the Study of Anti-Intellectualism," in *American Labyrinth: Intellectual History for Complicated Times*, ed. Raymond Haberski Jr. and Andrew Hartman (Ithaca, NY: Cornell University Press, 2018), 253–70; and Whitfield, "Second Thoughts: 'The Eggheads and the Fatheads,'" *Change* 10, no. 4 (April 1978): 64–66.

9. Philo A. Hutcheson, "Richard Hofstadter (6 August 1916–24 October 1970)," in *Twentieth-Century American Cultural Theorists*, ed. Paul Hansom, *Dictionary of Literary Biography*, vol. 246 (Detroit: Gale Group, 2001), 218.

10. As Hofstadter's Columbia colleague European historian Peter Gay put it in response to *The Age of Reform*: "Let me state the question baldly: to what extent is your piece an *a priori* construction?" In other words, to "what extent do you start with an aristocratic picture of what society should be like, and then come out with your indictment of Populism? . . . As your piece now stands, its aristocratic assumptions show." Gay to Hofstadter, undated, box 3, Richard Hofstadter Papers, Rare Book and Manuscript Library, Columbia University Library (hereafter cited as RHP), quoted in David S. Brown, *Richard Hofstadter: An Intellectual Biography* (Chicago: University of Chicago Press, 2006), 107.

11. George Sokolsky, "These Days . . . They Never Had It So Good," *Washington Post and Times Herald*, June 22, 1955, 15.

12. William Phillips and Philip Rahv, "Our Country and Our Culture, Part One," *Partisan Review* 19, no. 3 (May–June 1952): 282, 284.

13. Kevitt had a significant role in Hofstadter's writing, raising the broader question of the extent to which male scholars' literary production rests upon the often invisible labor of women, frequently their wives. Feminist critics in the 1960s called attention to this dynamic both to highlight gendered assumptions and inequalities built into conceptions of the intellectual and to devise alternative modes of work that might change these disparities. See chapter 4 for discussion of this broader point, and on the debate

about Kevitt's role specifically, see Allison Miller, "'Thanks Are Due Above All to My Wife': When It Comes to Intellectual Partnerships, Sometimes an Acknowledgment Is Enough," *Chronicle of Higher Education*, February 11, 2018, https://www.chronicle.com/article/Thanks-Are-Due-Above-All-to/242517; and Tim Lacy, "'Mrs. Hofstadter' and the Myth of the Heroic Lone Scholar," *U.S. Intellectual History Blog*, January 18, 2018, https://s-usih.org/2018/01/mrs-hofstadter-heroic-lone-scholar-myth/.

14. Phillips and Rahv, "Our Country and Our Culture, Part One," 284. On this point, see Neil Jumonville, *Critical Crossings: The New York Intellectuals in Postwar America* (Berkeley: University of California Press, 1991).

15. Phillips and Rahv, "Our Country and Our Culture, Part One," 284.

16. Phillips and Rahv, 284.

17. Christopher Lasch, foreword (1973) to *The American Political Tradition and the Men Who Made It*, by Richard Hofstadter (1948; repr., New York: Vintage Books, 1989), xv. Richard Pells has argued that this period nevertheless yielded "more provocative and imaginative criticisms of . . . society than one can find in the manifestos of either the 1930s or the 1960s." Pells, *The Liberal Mind in a Conservative Age: American Intellectuals in the 1940s and 1950s* (Middletown, CT: Wesleyan University Press, 1989), x. George Cotkin describes the variety of intellectuals' purposes served by criticism of mass culture in "The Tragic Predicament: Postwar American Intellectuals, Acceptance, and Mass Culture," in *Intellectuals in Politics: From the Dreyfus Affair to Salman Rushdie*, ed. Jeremy Jennings and Anthony Kemp-Welch (London: Routledge, 1997), 248–70.

18. Phillips and Rahv, "Our Country and Our Culture, Part One," 285.

19. Cultural and political shifts repositioning "the intellectuals" relative to "the people" had antecedents earlier in the century. Cf. Michael Kazin, *A Godly Hero: The Life of William Jennings Bryan* (New York: Anchor Books, 2006). On the 1930s, see Michael Denning, *The Cultural Front: The Laboring of American Culture in the Twentieth Century* (London: Verso, 1998).

20. See Andrew Ross, *No Respect: Intellectuals and Popular Culture* (New York: Routledge, 1989), chaps. 1, 2. Critics of "the culture of consumption" also implicated capitalism, not just the aesthetic choices it fostered, but in such a way that humanistic, democratic concerns came to the fore rather than economic analyses. Richard Wightman Fox and T. J. Jackson Lears, eds., *The Culture of Consumption: Critical Essays in American History, 1880–1980* (New York: Pantheon, 1983), represents the continuation of this critical tradition, with its roots in midcentury dissenters like C. Wright Mills.

21. William Leuchtenburg, interview with the author, April 7, 2011. Theodor W. Adorno's *The Authoritarian Personality* (1950) also exerted significant influence on Hofstadter and other intellectuals concerned with mass culture. Hofstadter borrowed some of the conceptual apparatus that he used to analyze the "radical right" directly from

Adorno's work. For a discussion of *The Authoritarian Personality* and its reception in the United States, see Rolf Wiggershaus, *The Frankfurt School: Its History, Theories, and Political Significance* (Cambridge, MA: MIT Press, 1998), 408–30.

22. Hannah Arendt, *Totalitarianism: Part Three of The Origins of Totalitarianism* (1951; repr., San Diego, CA: Harvest Books, 1994), 21, 50.

23. Arendt, 29–30. While Hofstadter's view of the masses largely accorded with Arendt's, he seemingly overlooked her concern with intellectuals' susceptibility to the same forces that shape those masses. This feature of Arendt's thinking was more evident in the work of Raymond Aron, Jacques Barzun, and, later, Irving Kristol.

24. Arendt, 155; Irving Howe, "This Age of Conformity," *Partisan Review* 21, no. 1 (January–February 1954): 7–33. K. A. Cuordileone makes this point about gender in *Manhood and American Political Culture in the Cold War* (New York: Routledge, 2005), 118–24.

25. Phillips and Rahv, "Our Country and Our Culture, Part One," 282; Edmund Wilson, *Europe without Baedeker: Sketches among the Ruins of Italy, Greece and England* (1947), quoted in Phillips and Rahv, 283.

26. Jacques Barzun's *The House of Intellect* (New York: Harper and Brothers, 1959) took a critical view of intellectuals. "The real disaster haunting the intellectual today," he wrote, "is that the alienation, the disinheriting, the loss of authority have occurred, not between the intellectuals and the rest—the commercial rump—of society, but among the intellectuals themselves and as a result of their own acts" (9).

27. "The Loyalty Oath Controversy, University of California, 1949–1951," University of California Digital History Archives, 2006, http://sunsite.berkeley.edu/~ucalhist /archives_exhibits/loyaltyoath/. On McCarthyism and the academy, and on intellectuals' responses to McCarthyism, see Ellen W. Schrecker, *No Ivory Tower: McCarthyism and the Universities* (New York: Oxford University Press, 1986), and Michael Paul Rogin, *The Intellectuals and McCarthy: The Radical Specter* (Cambridge, MA: MIT Press, 1967).

28. This phenomenon was not limited to Hofstadter. Michael Paul Rogin noted that "many pluralists [his term for liberal intellectuals like Hofstadter, Bell, Riesman, and Lipset] published books in the late 1940s sharply at variance with their views of a few years later. Hofstadter, for example, ended his introduction to *The American Political Tradition* . . . by defending himself against 'pietistic biographers' of our national heroes. . . . Seven years later, Hofstadter focused on the dangerous American tendency to be suspicious of power and overcritical of political leadership." Rogin, *The Intellectuals and McCarthy*, 292n1. See also Howard Brick, *Daniel Bell and the Decline of Intellectual Radicalism: Social Theory and Political Reconciliation in the 1940s* (Madison: University of Wisconsin Press, 1986).

29. Hofstadter to Swados, October 9, 1939, box 31, folder 17, Harvey Swados Papers (MS 218), Special Collections and University Archives, University of Massa-

chusetts Amherst Libraries (hereafter cited as HSP); Brown, *Richard Hofstadter*, 25. On these years in Hofstadter's life, see also Susan Stout Baker, *Radical Beginnings: Richard Hofstadter and the 1930s* (Westport, CT: Greenwood Press, 1985).

30. Hofstadter, *The American Political Tradition*, xxxvii; Lasch, foreword to *The American Political Tradition*, xiii.

31. Schlesinger observed that "Hofstadter perceived the [entrepreneurial] consensus from a radical perspective, from the outside, and deplored it"; other so-called "consensus" historians "perceived it from the inside and celebrated it." Schlesinger, "Richard Hofstadter," in *Pastmasters: Some Essays on American Historians*, ed. Marcus Cunliffe and Robin W. Winks (New York: Harper and Row, 1969), 289–90. Deploring the dominant business outlook himself eight years after Hofstadter's book, Schlesinger criticized the distinction between "Men of Affirmation" and "Men of Protest" in *Time* magazine's portrayal of American intellectuals. While the former offered "benign approval of an America in which the business community wields the political power," the latter were depicted as "grouches and expatriates, grumbling in the outer darkness." Schlesinger, like Hofstadter before him, appreciated these dissenters. He noted, however, that "one generation's Man of Protest is likely to be the next generation's Man of Affirmation"—an apt description of Schlesinger's own situation in the 1960s, if his position in the Eisenhower years stands as a dissenting one. Schlesinger, "*Time* and the Intellectuals" (1956), in *The Politics of Hope and The Bitter Heritage: American Liberalism in the 1960s* (Princeton, NJ: Princeton University Press, 2008), 287, 289.

32. Hofstadter, *The American Political Tradition*, xxxvii.

33. Lionel Trilling, preface and "Freud and Literature" (1940, rev. 1947), in *The Liberal Imagination: Essays on Literature and Society* (1950; repr., Garden City, NY: Doubleday Anchor Books, 1953), 10, 64. "Maturity" appears as a theme throughout the volume.

34. Hofstadter, *The American Political Tradition*, 179 (emphasis added), 180.

35. Hofstadter, xxxix, 178. The distinction made here between the politician and the reformer calls to mind Max Weber's "Politics as a Vocation," where the "ethic of ultimate ends" is opposed to the "ethic of responsibility."

36. Hofstadter, with quotations from Phillips, 209.

37. Hofstadter, 210; Plato, *The Apology*, 30e.

38. Barton J. Bernstein, "The Republicans Return," in *The Coming to Power: Critical Presidential Elections in American History*, ed. Arthur M. Schlesinger Jr. (New York: Chelsea House, 1972), 406–10. While Hofstadter's embrace of the Stevenson-Sparkman ticket in 1952 suggests that civil rights was not a decisive issue for him at the time, his position had changed by 1965, when he undertook a rare-for-him act of overt political engagement: joining the march from Selma to Montgomery, Alabama. "That the normally circumspect Hofstadter" traveled to Alabama, Sean Wilentz observed, "suggested just how deep the outrage at Jim Crow repression had become." Wilentz, "What Was Liberal History?," review of *Richard Hofstadter: An Intellectual Biography*, by David S. Brown, *New Republic*, July 10, 2006, 21.

39. Bernstein, "The Republicans Return," 410–12.

40. Bernstein, 412.

41. "Reminiscences of Frank Freidel: Oral History, 1972," 4, Richard Hofstadter Project, Columbia Center for Oral History Collection (hereafter cited as CCOHC); "Reminiscences of Elisabeth Earley: Oral History, 1972," 6, 14, CCOHC; Hofstadter to Swados, October 3 [context suggests 1940], box 31, folder 17, HSP.

42. "Reminiscences of Frank Freidel," 6–7; "Stevenson Backed by Columbia Group," *New York Times*, October 2, 1952, 21; Melvin L. Ember, Donald L. Hymes, Allan E. Jackman, Jerry G. Landauer, Norman Marcus, Rolon W. Reed, Barry Schweid, and Nicholas K. Wolfson, "Ike and Adlai," *Columbia Daily Spectator*, October 1, 1952, 2.

43. "Nixon Fund Vicious, Say 23 at Columbia," *New York Times*, October 6, 1952, 10; "Two N.Y. Papers Spotlight Clash between Nixon and Columbia Professors," *Christian Science Monitor*, October 15, 1952, 6. For a vivid account of the 1952 campaign and Nixon's speech, particularly its "telepopulism," see Kevin Mattson, *Just Plain Dick: Richard Nixon's Checkers Speech and the "Rocking, Socking" Election of 1952* (New York: Bloomsbury, 2012).

44. "Two N.Y. Papers Spotlight Clash between Nixon and Columbia Professors," 6.

45. "I don't think we even thought twice about that," Leuchtenburg remembered of the historians' weighing in on the campaign. "We just took it for granted that we had a special knowledge of American politics and American government, and despite the fact that we were acting in a partisan fashion, we were autonomous individuals acting as scholars. And I can see that, on the point of view of the Eisenhower people or in the point of view of neutral observers that there is an inconsistency in that position." Leuchtenburg, interview. Though Nevins was an accomplished academic historian, he lacked the credential that had come to symbolize expertise: the PhD. See Ian Tyrrell, *Historians in Public: The Practice of American History, 1880–1970* (Chicago: University of Chicago Press, 2005), chap. 4.

46. "Two N.Y. Papers Spotlight Clash between Nixon and Columbia Professors," 6.

47. Volunteers for Stevenson on the Columbia University Faculties and Staff, "We Are for Stevenson Because . . . ," *New York Times*, October 16, 1952, 21. The statement overlooked the extent to which Stevenson, by accepting the segregationist Sparkman as his running mate, had surrendered to the unsavory side of his own party.

48. Leuchtenburg, interview.

49. "Election of Eisenhower Is Urged by 714 on Various Columbia Staffs," *New York Times*, October 23, 1952, 1, 26; Leuchtenburg, interview. Buchler had a distinguished career in philosophy and with the ACLU. Gay, who switched from political science to history, became a prominent historian of European thought. Seabury also straddled history and political science, becoming in time a neoconservative adviser to the Reagan administration.

50. "Professors in Politics," *Washington Post*, October 20, 1952, 8.

51. W. T. de Bary, letter to the editor, *New York Times*, October 17, 1952, 26.

52. Brown calls it "curious" that Hofstadter used "Columbia, or at least its name and reputation, to further the cause of a political candidate. This is precisely the kind of nonacademic activity that he felt undermined the mission of the university." Brown, *Richard Hofstadter*, 85.

53. "Reminiscences of H. Stuart Hughes: Oral History, 1972," 10, 15, 21, CCOHC. On Hofstadter's modes of political engagement after 1952, Leuchtenburg "doubt[ed] very much that he ever went around ringing doorbells, handing out literature," but he did recall Hofstadter's involvement with the "Stern Gang," a group of intellectuals who met at historian Fritz Stern's apartment near Columbia to draft a letter to Lyndon Johnson expressing their opposition to the Vietnam War. As noted, he also traveled to Alabama in 1965. Leuchtenburg, interview.

54. "Reminiscences of Frank Freidel," 8–9.

55. Hofstadter, *Anti-Intellectualism in American Life* (New York: Vintage, 1963), 3–4.

56. Louis Bromfield, "The Triumph of the Egghead," *Freeman* 3 (December 1, 1952): 158; Hofstadter, *Anti-Intellectualism*, 9–10.

57. Hofstadter, *Anti-Intellectualism*, 9 (emphasis in original); Bernstein, "The Republicans Return," 416.

58. See Seymour E. Harris, "Economics of Higher Education," *American Economic Review* 43, no. 3 (June 1953): 344. Hofstadter wrote about threats to intellectual freedom posed by lay governance of colleges and universities (often by businessmen) and about the indifference of America's practical business culture to the life of the mind. Yet his institutional homes were supported by the dollars of big business. At a time when he was turning away from popular power, Hofstadter may have seen in business a welcome, if unlikely, ally in the cause of intellect.

59. John D. Millett, foreword to *The Development and Scope of Higher Education in the United States*, by Richard Hofstadter and C. DeWitt Hardy (New York: Columbia University Press, 1952), vii.

60. Hofstadter, "The Development of Higher Education in America," in *Development and Scope*, by Hofstadter and Hardy, 11–12, 13.

61. Hofstadter, 22, 36–37.

62. Hofstadter, 67, 98.

63. Hofstadter, 107. Hofstadter did not mean "democracy" in the meritocratic sense of broad participation open to talents rather than restricted by class. Indeed, "if by democracy we mean equality or recruitment among the intellectually able without regard to the limitations of their purses, American colleges and universities could welcome an extension of it," he wrote. Democracy in this instance meant a leveling down of quality rather than an opening up of opportunity. Hofstadter, 107–8.

64. Hofstadter, 107, 110, 111.

65. Hofstadter, 101–2.

66. Hofstadter, 104 (emphasis in original).

67. Hofstadter, "The Age of the College," in *The Development of Academic Freedom in the United States*, by Richard Hofstadter and Walter P. Metzger (New York: Columbia University Press, 1955), 41, 151, 216.

68. Hofstadter, 261.

69. Daniel J. Singal has argued against the interpretation that McCarthy and the "radical right" drove Hofstadter to "lose faith in popular democracy per se," pointing out Hofstadter's "continued strong sympathy for working-class and minority movements." For Singal, Hofstadter's thinking flows from a cosmopolitanism that predated the rise of McCarthy. That view largely accords with Brown's, which emphasizes regional tensions. Similarly, Singal argues that "Hofstadter did not take an antidemocratic stance as much as an antivillage stance." In Hofstadter's writings on American higher education in the 1950s, however, the threat to intellectual values comes not from the provincial quality of education, but from its quantitative expansion, which he equates with democratization. Hofstadter's fear is not that village culture can turn menacing, or even that such culture can be telegraphed to the national stage by the likes of a McCarthy, but rather that in a democratic culture the intellect has no independent force or power of its own and may therefore be outnumbered, whether in HUAC hearings, on college campuses, or at the polls. Singal, "Beyond Consensus: Richard Hofstadter and American Historiography," *American Historical Review* 89 (October 1984): 990–93; Brown, *Richard Hofstadter*, xiv–xvi.

70. Richard Gillam, "Richard Hofstadter, C. Wright Mills, and 'the Critical Ideal,'" *American Scholar* 47 (Winter 1977/78): 70–71 (emphasis in original).

71. "Reminiscences of Frank Freidel," 8.

72. Hofstadter's other notable institutional affiliation during this period was the American Committee for Cultural Freedom, an organization of anti-communist intellectuals that was linked to the international Congress for Cultural Freedom, which received funds, it was later revealed, from the CIA. See Brown, *Richard Hofstadter*, 82–83.

73. Hofstadter, "The Age of the College," 151, 246–47.

74. Brown, *Richard Hofstadter*, 86.

75. Hofstadter, "Democracy and Anti-Intellectualism in America," *Michigan Alumnus Quarterly Review* 19, no. 21 (August 8, 1953): 282, 281, 295.

76. Hofstadter, 286.

77. Hofstadter's argument here echoes Tocqueville's claims about the tyranny of the majority in American democracy: "In America the majority has enclosed thought within a formidable fence. A writer is free inside that area, but woe to the man who goes beyond it. Not that he stands in danger of an *auto-da-fé*, but he must face all kinds of unpleasantness and everyday persecution." Tocqueville, *Democracy in America*, 255.

78. Hofstadter, "Democracy and Anti-Intellectualism," 288.

79. Hofstadter, 295.

80. Hofstadter, 295.

81. "Populism" as opposed to "populism" distinguishes the former—the nineteenth-century movement—from popular politics more broadly.

82. Hofstadter, *The Age of Reform: From Bryan to F.D.R.* (New York: Knopf, 1955), 19. As with almost everything Hofstadter wrote between 1952 and 1964, the 1952 Stevenson defeat was mentioned early on in *Age*: intellectuals had become "far more conscious of those things they would like to preserve than . . . those things they would like to change. The immense enthusiasm that was roused among American intellectuals by such a circumspect and sober gentleman as Adlai Stevenson in 1952 is the most outstanding evidence of this conservatism." This passage illustrates Hofstadter's argument that in the wake of the New and Fair Deals liberal intellectuals came to see themselves as struggling to conserve the established order against a nominal conservatism that was, in fact, radical in its demands for sweeping changes to dismantle the New Deal and either wage outright war on communism or pull back from the United Nations and internationalism altogether. Hofstadter, 13.

83. Hofstadter, 18–19.

84. Hofstadter, 17.

85. Hofstadter, 4, 5, 20.

86. Hofstadter's interpretation of Populism has been criticized on many counts, and one of the most frequent claims is that he overlooks the extent to which Populists accurately diagnosed their concrete economic problems and advanced a forward-thinking reform agenda—an "interest politics"—to meaningfully address those problems. See, for example, Charles Postel, *The Populist Vision* (New York: Oxford University Press, 2007), 9.

87. Hofstadter, *Age of Reform*, 19.

88. Hofstadter originally wrote the essay in 1954, giving it as a lecture at Barnard College. For Daniel Bell's description of the "radical right," see his "Interpretations of American Politics," in *The New American Right*, ed. Daniel Bell (New York: Criterion Books, 1955), 14–15.

89. Hofstadter, "The Pseudo-Conservative Revolt," 35, 47. While Hofstadter drew "heavily" upon Adorno's "enlightening study," he did "have some reservations about its methods and conclusions." He called attention, in particular, to Edward Shils's contention that the study's questionnaires "were designed not to disclose the authoritarian personality as such but rather the 'Right'—the nativist-fundamentalist Authoritarian." The authors, accordingly, overlooked evidence of Left authoritarianism in their data. Hofstadter, "The Pseudo-Conservative Revolt," 54n1; Shils, "Authoritarianism: 'Right' and 'Left,'" in *Studies in the Scope and Method of "The Authoritarian Personality,"* ed. Richard Christie and Marie Jahoda (Glencoe, IL: Free Press, 1954), 38. For a more recent critical discussion of the survey methods upon which Adorno's work was based, see Wiggershaus, *The Frankfurt School*, 408–24. For Adorno's discussion of pseudo-conservatism, see T. W. Adorno, Else Frenkel-Brunswik, Daniel J. Levinson, and R. Nevitt Sanford, *The Authoritarian Personality* (New York: Harper and Brothers, 1950), chap. 17.

90. Michael Paul Rogin has applied this strand of Hofstadter's reasoning to Hofstadter himself: "If McCarthy is damned for concern with noneconomic questions, what can one say of his educated, eastern opponents?" Rogin points out that Hofstadter and other contributors to *The New American Right* "fear McCarthyism as a movement of new wealth against established institutions. Their fear of McCarthyism parallels progressive anxieties. In thus reflecting progressive concerns, Riesman, Nathan Glazer, and Hofstadter not only exhibit status politics but the particular status politics of the progressives." Rogin, *The Intellectuals and McCarthy*, 20.

91. Hofstadter, "The Pseudo-Conservative Revolt," 51.

92. Taylor Caldwell to Hofstadter, January 11, 1956, box A, folder 6, RHP.

93. "Taylor Caldwell, Prolific Author, Dies," *New York Times*, September 2, 1985, 26; Caldwell to Hofstadter, January 11, 1956, box A, folder 6, RHP. Caldwell and Hofstadter had some significant things in common: both were from Buffalo and earned their undergraduate degrees at the University of Buffalo. They each had extensive publishing records. Hofstadter's father was an immigrant; Caldwell herself was one, having been born in Manchester, England. While in 1956 Caldwell charged Hofstadter with elitism, in 1976 she told a *New York Times* reporter, who labeled her an "outright elitist," that "both men and women should be tested for literacy and intelligence before they vote." Nan Robertson, "Irrepressible, Prolific Taylor Caldwell," *New York Times*, December 11, 1976, 39.

94. Caldwell to Hofstadter, January 11, 1956, box A, folder 6, RHP.

95. Hofstadter, "The Pseudo-Conservative Revolt," 48, 50.

96. Hofstadter's religious affiliation is complicated. His father, Emil, was Jewish, while his mother, Katherine, was Lutheran and baptized her son in that church. After his mother died, Hofstadter's maternal aunt enrolled him as an Episcopalian. Brown, *Richard Hofstadter*, 9–10.

97. Alfred Kazin, *New York Jew* (Syracuse, NY: Syracuse University Press, 1996), 238.

98. Hofstadter, "Pseudo-Conservatism Revisited—1965," 83–84; Hofstadter, "Democracy and Anti-Intellectualism," 286.

99. Hofstadter, "The Pseudo-Conservative Revolt," 53–54.

100. Sokolsky, "These Days . . ."; Clement C. Sullivan, letter to the editor, *New York Times*, November 27, 1955, 368.

101. C. Vann Woodward, "The Populist Heritage and the Intellectual," *American Scholar* 28 (1959): 231–40, quoted here as published in Woodward, *The Burden of Southern History* (New York: Random House, 1960), 144.

102. Woodward, *Burden of Southern History*, 165–66.

103. Woodward, 166. Michael Kazin renews Woodward's stance, arguing for the ongoing importance of the populist idiom and urging rapprochement between intellectuals and popular politics, with the former emphasizing "the harmonious, hopeful, and pragmatic aspects of populist language" over "the meaner ones." Kazin, *The Pop-*

ulist Persuasion: An American History, rev. ed. (Ithaca, NY: Cornell University Press, 2017), 290.

104. "The Paranoid Style" itself was first delivered as the Herbert Spencer Lecture at Oxford in 1963 and originally published in *Harper's* in 1964.

105. Hofstadter, *Anti-Intellectualism*, 3 (emphasis in original).

106. Hofstadter, "Democracy and Anti-Intellectualism," 284–85.

107. Hofstadter, "Democracy and Anti-Intellectualism," 284; C. Wright Mills, "Our Country and Our Culture, Part Two," *Partisan Review* 19, no. 4 (July–August 1952): 447.

108. Mills, "Our Country and Our Culture, Part Two," 448.

109. Mills, 448, 450. Even as Mills wrote about the dormant state of politics, the most sweeping movement for justice in his time—the civil rights movement—was getting under way. Mills indicated, as late as 1960, that he had not been attentive to the African American freedom struggle. See Daniel Geary, "'Becoming International Again': C. Wright Mills and the Emergence of a Global New Left, 1956–1962," *Journal of American History* 95, no. 3 (December 2008): 734.

110. "Reminiscences of H. Stuart Hughes," 16.

111. Mills, "Letter to the New Left," in *The Politics of Truth: Selected Writings of C. Wright Mills*, ed. John H. Summers (New York: Oxford University Press, 2008), 263; Mills, "Our Country and Our Culture, Part Two," 450.

Chapter Two

1. There is an extensive literature on Mills's life and work, including Richard Gillam, "C. Wright Mills and the Politics of Truth: *The Power Elite Revisited*," *American Quarterly* 26 (October 1975): 461–79; Rick Tilman, *C. Wright Mills: A Native Radical and His American Intellectual Roots* (University Park: Pennsylvania State University Press, 1984); Irving Louis Horowitz, *C. Wright Mills: An American Utopian* (New York: Free Press, 1983); James Miller, "Democracy and the Intellectual: C. Wright Mills Reconsidered," *Salmagundi* 70–71 (Spring–Summer 1986): 82–101; Guy Oakes and Arthur J. Vidich, *Collaboration, Reputation, and Ethics in American Academic Life: Hans H. Gerth and C. Wright Mills* (Urbana: University of Illinois Press, 1999); Kathryn Mills with Pamela Mills, eds., *C. Wright Mills: Letters and Autobiographical Writings* (Berkeley: University of California Press, 2000); Kevin Mattson, *Intellectuals in Action: The Origins of the New Left and Radical Liberalism, 1945–1970* (University Park: Pennsylvania State University Press, 2002), chap. 2; John H. Summers, "New Man of Power," introduction to *The Politics of Truth: Selected Writings of C. Wright Mills*, ed. John H. Summers (New York: Oxford University Press, 2008), 3–12; Daniel Geary, *Radical Ambition: C. Wright Mills, the Left, and American Social Thought* (Berkeley: University of California Press, 2009); and Stanley Aronowitz, *Taking It Big: C. Wright Mills and the Making of Political Intellectuals* (New York: Columbia University Press, 2012).

2. C. Wright Mills, *The Causes of World War Three* (New York: Simon & Schuster, 1958), 126, 7.

3. Mills, 144, 40, 169. This view opposed that of Reinhold Niebuhr, who argued that liberals too readily attributed "the evils in human nature and history . . . to social institutions or to ignorance or to some other manageable defect in human nature or environment." This sense of a fixable world obscured the tragic, intractable problems of human life—the bonds of fate. Niebuhr, *The Irony of American History* (Chicago: University of Chicago Press, 2008), 4.

4. Mills, *Causes of World War Three*, 170–71.

5. Mills, 135–36 (emphasis added). Russell Jacoby claims to have coined the term "public intellectual" in *The Last Intellectuals* (1987). It is difficult to see, however, what he adds to Mills's use of it here, three decades earlier. Jacoby, introduction to the 2000 edition of *The Last Intellectuals* (New York: Basic Books, 2000), xvi.

6. H. Stuart Hughes to Martin Greenberg, November 21, 1958, box 3, folder 55, Henry Stuart Hughes Papers (MS 1446), Manuscripts and Archives, Yale University Library (hereafter cited as HSH Papers); Martin Greenberg to Hughes, January 13, 1959, box 3, folder 55, HSH Papers.

7. Hughes, "A Politics of Peace: Reflections on C. Wright Mills's 'The Causes of World War III,'" *Commentary* 22 (February 1959): 119–20. That Hughes affirmed Mills's "diagnosis" is unsurprising, for key elements of it had been staked out by Hughes several years earlier, when he forecast "the triumph of the political concepts associated with force and irrational sentiment, the necessarily elitist organization of society, and the basically illusory character of social reform—and with it the discrediting of politics as reason in action, the virtue of majorities, and progress as social faith." Like Mills, Hughes found that intellectuals, "who might be supposed to stand exclusively for the abstract cause of liberty, are by a thousand hidden strands, unconsciously perhaps or even against their will, tied in with existing relations of wealth and class." Thus, Mills's book renewed and stated more strongly Hughes's own appraisal of that situation while, crucially, connecting it to a clarion call for intellectuals' political activity. Mills's book also raised the stakes for Hughes by sharpening his attention to the atomic bomb. Hughes, "The End of Political Ideology," *Measure* 2 (Spring 1951): 155–56.

8. Hughes, "A Politics of Peace," 121, 120 (emphasis in original). Hughes stopped short, however, of endorsing what he took to be Mills's push for unilateral American nuclear disarmament, which he called "willful self-exposure." Hughes, "A Politics of Peace," 126.

9. C. Wright Mills to H. Stuart Hughes, February 13, 1959 (emphasis in original); Hughes to Mills, April 23, 1959, box 5, folder 115, HSH Papers.

10. Hughes to Mrs. C. W. Mills, March 23, 1962, box 4, folder 105, HSH Papers; Mills, *Causes of World War Three*, 135.

11. On the links between the Committee of Correspondence and the emerging New Left, see Daniel Geary, "The New Left and Liberalism Reconsidered: The Com-

mittee of Correspondence and the Port Huron Statement," in *The Port Huron Statement: Sources and Legacies of the New Left's Founding Manifesto*, ed. Richard Flacks and Nelson Lichtenstein (Philadelphia: University of Pennsylvania Press, 2015), 83–94. The quotation is from the *Newsletter of the Committee of Correspondence*, no. 10 (September 10, 1960), quoted in Geary.

12. Hughes, notes for "Individual Responsibility in the Nuclear Age," November 28 and December 13, 1961, accession 2000-M-086, box 5, folder 47, HSH Papers; Mills, *Causes of World War Three*, 137, 133 (emphasis in original).

13. Hughes, notes for "Individual Responsibility in the Nuclear Age" (emphasis in original).

14. Mills, *Causes of World War Three*, 140.

15. On the campaign and its role in Massachusetts liberalism, see Stephen J. Whitfield, "Democratic Dynasties: The Historical Meaning of the 1962 U.S. Senate Race in Massachusetts," *Journal of the Historical Society* 12 (2012): 447–78, and Lily Geismer, *Don't Blame Us: Suburban Liberals and the Transformation of the Democratic Party* (Princeton, NJ: Princeton University Press, 2015), chap. 5.

16. Hughes, *Gentleman Rebel: The Memoirs of H. Stuart Hughes* (New York: Ticknor and Fields, 1990), 313–14; Hofstadter, *Anti-Intellectualism in American Life* (New York: Vintage, 1963), 401.

17. "A Statement by Stuart Hughes, Independent Candidate for United States Senator from Massachusetts, 1962," box 11, folder 28, HSH Papers; Hofstadter, *Anti-Intellectualism*, 196. On the professions becoming in the decades after World War Two "increasingly disconnected from functions perceived to be central to the public welfare and more exclusively connected to the idea of 'expert knowledge,'" see Steven Brint, *In an Age of Experts: The Changing Role of Professionals in Politics and Public Life* (Princeton, NJ: Princeton University Press, 1994) (quotation on p. 8). Brint's "age of experts" has recently been followed by Tom Nichols's "death of expertise." Nichols argues that traditional skepticism of experts has been supplanted by outright rejection of their claims and denigration of their persons on behalf of the notion—familiar to Tocqueville—that no one may claim knowledge superior to that of any other. Nichols, *The Death of Expertise: The Campaign against Established Knowledge and Why It Matters* (New York: Oxford University Press, 2017). Writing ten years before Brint and thirty-three before Nichols, Thomas L. Haskell declared: "All of us defer to the authority of experts," though with "an undertone of fear and resentment" and the sense that "we probably ought to withhold our deference more often than we do." Haskell, ed., *The Authority of Experts: Studies in History and Theory* (Bloomington: Indiana University Press, 1984), ix.

18. Hughes, *Gentleman Rebel*, 313 (emphasis added).

19. Hughes, 249.

20. Hughes, 185, 108; Hofstadter, *Anti-Intellectualism*, 196; Hughes, *An Essay for Our Times* (New York: Knopf, 1950), 64. In his analysis of European history, Hughes found that until the 1920s "no sharp division between literature and social science

had been drawn, and the intellectual still felt himself as free as Goethe to roam at will throughout the varied domains of human activity." During that decade, however, the intellectual as literary generalist was supplanted by more specialized alternatives: "the new school of logical positivism," on the one hand, and "the advocates of social 'commitment,'" on the other. From these perspectives, the old wide-ranging moralist stood for "dilettantism" and "intolerable frivolity." A self-described "Edwardian," however, Hughes sympathized with this older notion of the intellectual. Hughes, *Consciousness and Society: The Reorientation of European Social Thought, 1890–1930* (New York: Vintage Books, 1958), 405.

21. Hughes, *Gentleman Rebel*, 85, 192.

22. Hughes, *Consciousness and Society*, 26; Godfrey Hodgson, "Better Red . . . in Boston," *Observer* (London), September 2, 1962, 6.

23. Hughes, *Gentleman Rebel*, 189.

24. Hughes thought such broad-mindedness should also characterize the intellectual historian: "In intellectual history even more than in other branches of historical investigation, the play of group passions has no proper place. The only fitting attitude is that of the cosmopolitan, detached intellectual." Hughes, *Consciousness and Society*, 26.

25. Hughes, *Gentleman Rebel*, 206; Seymour Martin Lipset, "Political Controversies at Harvard, 1636–1974," in *Education and Politics at Harvard* (New York: McGraw Hill, 1975), quoted in Hughes, 208. See also Peter Novick, *That Noble Dream: The "Objectivity Question" and the American Historical Profession* (New York: Cambridge University Press, 1988), 330, 330n17.

26. Hughes, *Gentleman Rebel*, 209, 223, 229. Novick reports that Hughes's appointment in the history department at Stanford, where he went after leaving Harvard, "was held up until he could be queried on his current political beliefs," for there was doubt about him in the department. When Hughes later returned to Harvard, there was still concern within its history department about his "lack of 'political sagacity.'" Novick, *That Noble Dream*, 330, 330n17.

27. Hughes, "The Intellectual as Corrupter," *New Leader*, July 7, 1952, 16, 18.

28. Hughes, 17–18.

29. Hughes, "Corrupter," 18; Hughes, *Gentleman Rebel*, 224; Hughes, "The Scholar Cornered: Why We Had No Dreyfus Case," *American Scholar* 30, no. 4 (Autumn 1961), 476; Hughes, *Gentleman Rebel*, 225.

30. Hughes, "Is the Intellectual Obsolete?" *Commentary* 22, no. 4 (October 1956): 314.

31. Hughes, 314–15 (emphasis in original).

32. Hughes, 315.

33. Hughes, 316–19.

34. Hughes, 319 (emphasis in original).

35. Russell Kirk, letter to the editor, *Commentary* 23, no. 1 (January 1957): 82.

36. Kirk, 82–83.

37. Hughes, "Obsolete?" 319, 318.

38. Hughes, "The Turn of the Tide: Western Diplomacy in the Sputnik Era," *Commentary* 25, no. 3 (March 1958): 187.

39. 85 Cong. Rec. H2509 (daily ed. February 20, 1958) (extension of remarks by Sen. Humphrey).

40. Mills, *Causes of World War Three*, 129, 125.

41. Mills, 129 (emphasis in original).

42. Hughes, "Dreyfus Case," 478 (emphasis in original); Mills, *Causes of World War Three*, 39.

43. Hughes, *Gentleman Rebel*, 250; *The Liberal Papers*, ed. James Roosevelt (Garden City, NY: Doubleday Anchor Original, 1962), back cover. This volume was the published result of the Liberal Project, which aimed "to create a greater identification and dialogue of ideas between liberal intellectuals and politicians." Marcus G. Raskin to Hughes, September 27, 1960, box 4, folder 92, HSH Papers.

44. Russell Johnson to Hughes, October 20, 1959, box 4, folder 84, HSH Papers.

45. Clarence Pickett to Hughes, November 18, 1959, box 5, folder 123, HSH Papers; Hughes, "Dreyfus Case," 474.

46. Charles A. Barker to Hughes, February 27, 1959, box 1, folder 13, HSH Papers (emphasis added); Hughes, notes for "War and the Mind of Man: The Erosion of the Political Response," December 11, 1959, accession 2000-M-086, box 5, folder 47, HSH Papers; James Roosevelt, introduction to *The Liberal Papers*, 5 (emphasis added); Michael Maccoby and David Riesman, "The American Crisis," in *The Liberal Papers*, 47.

47. Hughes, "Opening Remarks to Bear Mt. Meeting," March 10, 1960, accession 2000-M-086, box 5, folder 47, HSH Papers.

48. Jean Mosher to Hughes, March 31, 1962; Hughes to Mrs. Carl Mosher, April 10, 1962, box 9, folder 4, HSH Papers.

49. Hughes, "Remarks at Tamiment Conference on Mass Culture," June 3, 1959, accession 2000-M-086, box 5, folder 47, HSH Papers; Hughes, "Mass Culture and Social Criticism," *Daedalus* 89, no. 2 (Spring 1960): 388–89.

50. Hughes, "Mass Culture," 391–92.

51. Hughes, 393.

52. Hughes, "Dreyfus Case," 479.

53. "The Unhelpful Fringes: The Present-Day Radicals, Left or Right, Bring Us Neither Hope nor Realism," *Life*, May 12, 1961, 32.

54. John Martinson to Hughes, May 14, 1961, box 4, folder 104, HSH Papers.

55. Martinson to Hughes, May 14, 1961, box 4, folder 104, HSH Papers; Raquel Wood, "In Memoriam," *FNVW Non-Violent Times*, Spring 2009, 7, fnwv.org.

56. Hughes, "Dreyfus Case," 479.

57. "Teddy and Kennedyism," *Time*, September 28, 1962, http://www.time.com/time/magazine/article/0,9171,940066-1,00.html.

58. Dwight and Hildagarde Baum to Hughes, March 21, 1962, box 9, folder 2, HSH Papers.

59. Hughes to Marjory Stuart Hughes, April 29, 1961, box 19, folder 50, HSH Papers; Hughes, *Gentleman Rebel*, 27, 240.

60. Hughes, "On Being a Candidate," *Commentary* 35, no. 2 (February 1963): 123.

61. Hughes to Marjory Stuart Hughes, March 18, 1962, box 19, folder 51, HSH Papers.

62. Elliot Cohen, a letter writer from Jamaica, New York, endorsed the idea that the other candidates were second rate. He advised Hughes to "hammer away at the fact that your opponents are attempting to ride in on the basis of affinity and consanguinity and that this fact is an oblique indictment of our society—in this day and age when, purportedly, the best men should make the decisions for us." Elliot A. Cohen to Hughes, March 23, 1962, box 9, folder 2, HSH Papers.

63. Hughes to Marjory Stuart Hughes, March 18, 1962, box 19, folder 51, HSH Papers.

64. Jerome S. King to Hughes, March 26, 1962, box 9, folder 4, HSH Papers; Murray L. Bob to Hughes, March 30, 1962, box 9, folder 2, HSH Papers; Hughes to Carey McWilliams, March 21, 1962, box 9, folder 4, HSH Papers.

65. Susan M. Magri to Hughes, March 25, 1962, box 9, folder 4, HSH Papers; Joseph C. Duval to Hughes, March 25, 1962, box 9, folder 2, HSH Papers; Lawrence Martin to Hughes, March 29, 1962, box 9, folder 4, HSH Papers (emphasis added); William H. Gribble to Hughes, March 22, 1962, box 9, folder 3, HSH Papers.

66. Gray Adams to Hughes, March 21, 1962, box 9, folder 2, HSH Papers; Ruth M. Dadourian to Hughes, March 21, 1962, box 9, folder 2, HSH Papers; Barbara Sessions to Hughes, March 29, 1962, box 9, folder 5, HSH Papers; Hughes, "Dreyfus Case," 479.

67. Paul Gagnon to Hughes, March 23, 1962, box 9, folder 3, HSH Papers.

68. "Statement by H. Stuart Hughes," press conference, Hotel Bellevue, Boston, March 27, 1962, box 11, folder 31, HSH Papers.

69. Hughes to Mrs. Peter Dillard, March 30, 1962, box 9, folder 2, HSH Papers; Hughes, *An Approach to Peace and Other Essays* (New York: Atheneum, 1962), 5–6.

70. Donald Mintz, "A Book for Today," *Washington Star*, May 14, 1962, box 13, folder 64, HSH Papers; Theodore Roszak, "A Call for Martyrs," *Nation*, August 25, 1962, 76.

71. Mills, *Causes of World War Three*, 141 (emphasis in original).

72. Hughes to George Steiner, May 31, 1962, box 9, folder 5, HSH Papers; F. C. Hunnius to Hughes, May 1, 1962, box 9, folder 2, HSH Papers; Dr. Sunder Mansukhani to Hughes, June 4, 1962, box 9, folder 4, HSH Papers.

73. Hughes to Mrs. John W. Root, April 16, 1962, box 9, folder 2, HSH Papers; Jerome Grossman to Hughes, April 2, 1962, box 9, folder 3, HSH Papers; Hughes to George Steiner, May 31, 1962, box 9, folder 5, HSH Papers.

74. Alfred C. Klahre to Hughes, April 5, 1962, box 10, folder 15, HSH Papers;

"This Is Education?" *Bucyrus* (OH) *Telegraph-Forum*, April 22, 1964, box 16, folder 1, HSH Papers.

75. Hughes, *Approach to Peace*, 4.

76. Hughes, "Commitment," talk given to Harvard SANE Students, February 10, 1960, accession 2000-M-086, box 5, folder 47, HSH Papers. The tension between detachment and commitment applied to the historian as well as the intellectual, and Novick points to Hughes as one who saw the disciplinary role of both dispositions. "If it was less frequently urged that historians approach their work totally purged of values," Novick wrote of the postwar period, "it was often demanded that those values be kept under tight rein. H. Stuart Hughes thought values were useful for the historian if 'mastered,' 'transcended,' 'controlled.'" Novick, *That Noble Dream*, 407.

77. Allen Forbes Jr. to George Sommaripa, June 8, 1962, box 9, folder 3, HSH Papers; David Riesman to Hughes, April 17, 1962, box 9, folder 5, HSH Papers.

78. Hughes, "Thoughts on the Campaign," July 13, 1962, box 11, folder 34, HSH Papers (emphasis in original).

79. Luliova Barker to Hughes, April 22, 1962, box 9, folder 2, HSH Papers; Edith L. Bunker to Hughes, September 19, 1962, box 10, folder 13, HSH Papers.

80. "Memo re: I. Speech on Boston Common II. Suggestion for Strategy during the Campaign," unsigned and undated, box 9, folder 3, HSH Papers.

81. Jim Lieberman to Hughes, July 16, 1962, box 9, folder 9, HSH Papers.

82. "The Political Scene. Hughes Lauds Workers; His 118,437 Names Pass," *Sunday Republican* (Springfield, MA), August 5, 1962; "First since Wallace," National Affairs, *Newsweek*, August 6, 1962, 20.

83. Peter J. Kumpa, "Rare Outlook Faces Voters," *Baltimore Sun*, September 10, 1962, 7; William Buckley, Richard Clurman, H. Stuart Hughes, Frank McGee, Chalmers Roberts, and Lawrence E. Spivak, *Meet the Press*, National Broadcasting Company, aired August 12, 1962, transcript, box 10, folder 15, HSH Papers; Jerome Grossman to Karaway Kenton, August 30, 1962, box 9, folder 9, HSH Papers; Mary Farquharson to Hughes, August 12, 1962, box 9, folder 8, HSH Papers; Richard Frantz to Hughes, August 13, 1962, box 9, folder 8, HSH Papers; Alan Kapelner to Hughes, August 13, 1962, box 9, folder 9, HSH Papers; John W. Pitts to Hughes, August 13, 1962, box 9, folder 10, HSH Papers.

84. Edward P. Eichler, "Hughes on the Hustings," box 10, folder 19, HSH Papers; Virginia E. Bartell to Hughes, October 22, 1962, box 10, folder 18; Nick Norris to Hughes, undated, box 10, folder 21; Hughes to Norris, October 19, 1962, box 10, folder 21, HSH Papers.

85. Hughes, "On Being a Candidate," 129; "Memo re: I. Speech on Boston Common," box 9, folder 3, HSH Papers.

86. A scholar of Italian intellectual history, Hughes read Antonio Gramsci's work before it was available in English and cited Gramsci's time in Turin, where "in the factories he made the acquaintance of intelligent, highly trained, and class-conscious

workers with whom an intellectual like himself—acquainted with poor people from childhood—could maintain a creative exchange of ideas." Hughes, perhaps, failed to do the same because his childhood had not prepared him for it. Hughes, *Consciousness and Society*, 100.

87. *Gentleman Rebel* is the title of Hughes's memoirs.

88. Hughes, "Being a Candidate," 126; Nick Norris to Hughes, undated, box 10, folder 21, HSH Papers; Hughes, "Being a Candidate," 129. On the limitations of Massachusetts suburban liberals' political-coalition building, see Geismer, *Don't Blame Us*, 13–14.

89. Press release, October 19, 1962, box 11, folder 31, HSH Papers. The Hughes for Senate Committee also included a number of intellectual and artistic lights: Isaac Asimov, Henry Steele Commager, Lewis Coser, Archibald MacLeish, Herbert Marcuse, Barrington Moore Jr., David Riesman, Norman Rockwell, Carey McWilliams, Lewis Mumford, and Benjamin Spock. "A Statement by Stuart Hughes, Independent Candidate for United States Senator from Massachusetts, 1962," box 11, folder 28, HSH Papers; invitation to reception for Hughes at the home of Mr. and Mrs. William A. Bernat, October 21, 1962, box 10, folder 20, HSH Papers.

90. "Lodge Will Meet Hughes in Debate; Kennedy Refuses," *Harvard Crimson*, September 25, 1962, http://www.thecrimson.com/article/1962/9/25/lodge-will-meet -hughes-in-debate/?print=1; undated press release, box 11, folder 31, HSH Papers.

91. Press release, October 22, 1962; "Stuart Hughes, Independent Candidate for U.S. Senate, Today Issued a Peace Plan for Cuba," press release, October 23, 1962, box 11, folder 31, HSH Papers.

92. Peter Shepherd to Hughes, October 29, 1962, box 10, folder 22, HSH Papers; Allan A. Ryan Jr. to Hughes, October 29, 1962, box 10, folder 21, HSH Papers; Peter Irons, Edward Knappman, and Dawn Lander, *Peace and Politics 1962*, box 11, folder 32, HSH Papers.

93. "The Candidates for Senator," *Berkshire (MA) Eagle*, November 3, 1962, 18; Joel I. Cohen, "Peace and Politics: The Hughes' [sic] Campaign," *Brown Daily Herald*, December 3, 1962, 6; Karl Miller, "Left of the Frontier," *New Statesman*, November 2, 1962, 628; Hughes, *Gentleman Rebel*, 257.

94. Hughes, "Commitment," talk given to Harvard SANE students, February 10, 1960, accession 2000-M-086, box 5, folder 47, HSH Papers; Marjory Collins, "Summary of Statements and Answers to Questions by H. Stuart Hughes to Audiences in Amherst, Northampton, Deerfield, and Williamstown, 4/27–4/29/62," box 11, folder 34, HSH Papers; Hughes to the *Daily Evening Item* (Lynn, MA), April 24, 1962, box 9, folder 4, HSH Papers.

95. "3 Reasons Why Your Vote for Stuart Hughes Will Count," box 11, folder 32, HSH Papers; "For United States Senate Stuart Hughes, an Expert in Foreign Policy," box 11, folder 32, HSH Papers; *Meet the Press* transcript, box 10, folder 15, HSH Papers.

96. Julien Benda, *The Treason of the Intellectuals* (1927), trans. Richard Adlington

(1928; repr., New York: W. W. Norton, 1969), 44; "Channel 2 Panel of 5 Candidates—July 12," 1962, box 11, folder 34, HSH Papers; "Nation: Keeping the Pledge," *Time*, January 4, 1963; Hughes, "Plymouth Heritage Day Speech," October 20, 1962, box 11, folder 35, HSH Papers. Hughes had written about Benda in *Consciousness and Society*, chap. 10.

97. "Put Hughes on the Ballot," box 11, folder 32, HSH Papers; "Stuart Hughes for Senator: An Open Mind for an Open Future," box 11, folder 32, HSH Papers; Edgar Snow to Hughes, August 30, 1962, box 10, folder 17, HSH Papers; Louise Reilly to Hughes, July 14, 1962, box 9, folder 10, HSH Papers; Rev. O. R. Williams to Hughes, August 12, 1962, box 9, folder 12, HSH Papers.

98. "Hughes for Senate Committee Press Release," October 22, 1962, box 11, folder 31, HSH Papers; Hughes to Marjory Stuart Hughes, May 26, 1962, box 19, folder 51, HSH Papers; Hughes, *Gentleman Rebel*, 251.

99. Miller, "Left of the Frontier," 627; James F. Droney, "Crimson of Harvard, Blue of Yale Helped Color Wartime OSS," *Boston Sunday Herald*, May 13, 1962, A5.

100. Ed Friedman, "Saturday Night Debate with Lodge on the Cold War," September 29, 1962, box 11, folder 35, HSH Papers.

101. The Hughes campaign complained that "it is the least qualified candidates who are in a position to pay for maximum T.V. exposure." "Hughes for Senate Committee Press Release," October 8, 1962, box 11, folder 31, HSH Papers; Cohen, "Peace and Politics," 4. Elizabeth Warren's 2020 presidential campaign generated probing discussion of candidates as teachers. See, for instance, Rebecca Traister, "Elizabeth Warren's Classroom Strategy," *The Cut*, August 6, 2019, https://www.thecut.com/2019/08/elizabeth-warren-teacher-presidential-candidate.html.

102. "3 Reasons Why Your Vote for Stuart Hughes Will Count," poster, box 11, folder 32, HSH Papers; "Staff Meeting October 3," box 11, folder 36, HSH Papers.

103. Allen Klein questions for Hughes; Hughes to Klein, July 13, 1962, box 9, folder 9, HSH Papers; Sevallon Brown, "He Just Might Trip Up Brother Ted," *Providence (RI) Journal*, September 16, 1962; Kumpa, "Rare Outlook"; Hughes to Klein, June 8, 1962, box 9, folder 4, HSH Papers.

Chapter Three

1. David Halberstam's *The Best and the Brightest* (New York: Random House, 1972) was an early, influential, and critical account of this group. By the time of the book's appearance, many of its readers were prepared to see the title as ironic rather than, as it may have sounded a decade earlier, straightforward.

2. Arthur M. Schlesinger Jr., *A Thousand Days: John F. Kennedy in the White House* (Boston: Houghton Mifflin Company, 1965), 143.

3. That literary skill also served Schlesinger, for the book allowed him to put a favorable gloss not only on the administration but also his work for it.

4. Schlesinger, *Thousand Days*, 423.

5. Martin Agronsky, Douglas Kiker, Arthur M. Schlesinger Jr., and Mike Wallace, *Face the Nation*, CBS News, aired May 8, 1966, transcript, box 77, folder 7, Arthur M. Schlesinger Jr. Papers, 1922–2007, New York Public Library (hereafter cited as NYPL).

6. Schlesinger, *Thousand Days*, 111; Kennedy, no citation given, quoted in Schlesinger, 76.

7. Schlesinger's view owes much to Reinhold Niebuhr and to George F. Kennan's *American Diplomacy* (1951), the locus classicus of the realist/idealist binary. See John Lewis Gaddis, *George F. Kennan: An American Life* (New York: Penguin, 2011), 434–37, 555–56.

8. Robert F. Barsky, *Noam Chomsky: A Life of Dissent* (Cambridge, MA: MIT Press, 1997), 119–20, 124. Barsky has also written an estimate of Chomsky's public, political role: *The Chomsky Effect: A Radical Works Beyond the Ivory Tower* (Cambridge, MA: MIT Press, 2007). Chris Knight's *Decoding Chomsky: Science and Revolutionary Politics* (New Haven, CT: Yale University Press, 2016) argues that separation between Chomsky's politics and his linguistics is driven by dissonance between the former and Chomsky's location at MIT, a hub of military research. *The Cultural Logic of Computation* (Cambridge, MA: Harvard University Press, 2009) by David Golumbia also emphasizes the division between Chomsky's politics and his linguistics, situating the latter in terms of the development of neoliberal ideology—a frequent target of Chomsky's political criticism that, Golumbia argues, his scholarship nonetheless fostered.

9. Chomsky, quoted in Richard Falk, "Letters from Prison—American Style: The Political Vision and Practice of Noam Chomsky," in *Noam Chomsky: Critical Assessments*, ed. Carlos P. Otero (London: Routledge, 1994), 3:596n1.

10. Chomsky, "The Responsibility of Intellectuals," *New York Review of Books*, February 23, 1967, as printed in Chomsky, *American Power and the New Mandarins* (New York: Pantheon, 1969), 325. The *New York Times* piece cited by Chomsky is "Schlesinger Says He Lied to Times," *New York Times*, November 25, 1965, 8.

11. The important question becomes speaking truth to whom? Richard Aldous counts "among Schlesinger's greatest assets . . . his ability to speak truth unsparingly to power and influence." Chomsky is concerned with speaking truth not only to power but also to the public. Aldous, *Schlesinger: The Imperial Historian* (New York: W. W. Norton, 2017), 207.

12. Chomsky, "The Responsibility of Intellectuals, Redux: Using Privilege to Challenge the State," *Boston Review*, September 1, 2011, http://bostonreview.net/noam-chomsky-responsibility-of-intellectuals-redux.

13. "White House's List of Nixon 'Enemies,'" *Los Angeles Times*, June 28, 1973, 33.

14. Schlesinger to Marcus Cunliffe, July 9, 1968, box 32, folder 3, NYPL.

15. Schlesinger, *A Life in the Twentieth Century: Innocent Beginnings, 1917–1950* (New York: Houghton Mifflin, 2000), 89; Schlesinger to Cunliffe, July 9, 1968, box 32, folder 3, NYPL.

16. Schlesinger to Cunliffe (on Niebuhr), July 9, 1968, box 32, folder 3, NYPL; Schlesinger, *A Life*, 250.

17. Schlesinger, *A Life*, 251–52, 253.

18. John Dewey was no stranger to the disposition toward war himself. "Squeamishness about force is the mark not of idealistic but of moonstruck morals," Dewey wrote in the run-up to American involvement in World War One. Dewey, "Force and Coercion" (1916), in Dewey, *The Middle Works, 1899–1924*, vol. 10: *1916–1917*, ed. Jo Anne Boydston (Carbondale: Southern Illinois University Press, 1980), 249.

19. This view, Bruce Kuklick reports, was also a reaction to Wilsonianism: "Policy intellectuals assumed by the 1940s that the United States must pursue an internationalist and interventionist role but that the tough-minded must overrule the high-minded." Kuklick, *Blind Oracles: Intellectuals and War from Kennan to Kissinger* (Princeton, NJ: Princeton University Press, 2006), 12–13.

20. Sean Wilentz has noted how Schlesinger's Niebuhrian liberalism, which "understood the moral blindness and arrogance of supposing that the future will yield easily to its acumen," had, in the case of Vietnam, "[fallen] victim to these human frailties." Whereas for Chomsky this outcome was reason to reject Schlesinger's liberalism, Wilentz argues that it "makes that liberalism more pertinent . . . as a paradoxical caution." Wilentz, foreword to Schlesinger, *The Politics of Hope and The Bitter Heritage: American Liberalism in the 1960s* (Princeton, NJ: Princeton University Press, 2008), xxxiv.

21. Schlesinger, *A Life*, 268. Schlesinger and other OWI writers ultimately left because they could not "'tell the full truth'" there. Quoted in Aldous, *Schlesinger*, 74.

22. Schlesinger, *The Vital Center: The Politics of Freedom* (1949; repr., New York: Da Capo, 1988), xvii–xviii.

23. Schlesinger, "The Future of Socialism: III, The Perspective Now," *Partisan Review* 19 (May–June 1947): 236–37.

24. As K. A. Cuordileone observes, "Schlesinger presumed the ability to *see through* the left intellectual's worship of proletarian muscle, but what is striking is the absence of self-consciousness about *The Vital Center's* own unconcealed adulation of virility. Here the charge that the progressive's political stances serve as emotional compensation for his deficiencies as a mere intellectual more properly belonged to Schlesinger's critics." Cuordileone, *Manhood and American Political Culture in the Cold War* (New York: Routledge, 2005), 25–26 (emphasis in original). Paul M. Buhle and Edward Rice-Maximin note "the marked gender tilt of Niebuhr's" work, claiming that "Niebuhr's rhetorical hypermasculinity captured the self-image of the 1950s pen-pushing intellectuals who fretted about the reputed omnipresence of homosexuals in the national life of the mind and sought to demonstrate their own political virility through muscular prose." Buhle and Rice-Maximin, *William Appleman Williams: The Tragedy of Empire* (New York: Routledge, 1995), 74.

25. Christopher Lasch, *The New Radicalism in America: The Intellectual as a Social Type, 1889–1963* (1965; repr., New York: W. W. Norton, 1997), 286, 289.

26. Koestler's statements appeared in the *New York Times*, June 27, 1950, 19. He is quoted in Christopher Lasch, *The Agony of the American Left* (New York: Vintage, 1969), 65–66.

27. Schlesinger, "The Highbrow in Politics," *Partisan Review* 20, no. 2 (March–April 1953): 165.

28. Schlesinger, "New Frontiers of Political Liberalism," Democratic Midwest Conference, Detroit, MI, March 26, 1960, box P-7, Arthur M. Schlesinger, Jr. Personal Papers (#206), John F. Kennedy Presidential Library (hereafter JFKL).

29. Robert Frost, no citation given, quoted in Schlesinger, *Thousand Days*, 3; Schlesinger, *Thousand Days*, 104, 111.

30. Schlesinger, *Thousand Days*, 104.

31. John F. Kennedy, "Harvard Commencement Speech," June 14, 1956, Papers of John F. Kennedy, Presidential Papers, President's Office Files, JFKPOF-135-016, JFKL.

32. Louis B. Wright to JFK, January 16, 1961, Papers of John F. Kennedy, Presidential Papers, White House Staff Files of August Heckscher (#8.9), box 040, JFKL.

33. Schlesinger, *Thousand Days*, 210–12.

34. Schlesinger to JFK, February 6, 1961, box WH-66, Arthur M. Schlesinger, Jr. Personal Papers (#206), JFKL.

35. Tevi Troy's *Intellectuals and the American Presidency: Philosophers, Jesters, or Technicians?* (Lanham, MD: Rowman & Littlefield, 2002) examines the instrumental, image-sculpting value of White House intellectuals to modern presidents, beginning most clearly with Kennedy and Schlesinger.

36. McGeorge Bundy, National Security Action Memorandum No. 31, Memorandum of discussion on Cuba, March 11, 1961, Box WH-31b, Arthur M. Schlesinger, Jr. Personal Papers (#206), JFKL; Schlesinger, *A Thousand Days*, 240; Schlesinger to JFK, March 10, 1961, box WH-66, Arthur M. Schlesinger, Jr. Personal Papers (#206), JFKL.

37. Schlesinger to JFK, February 11, 1961, the National Security Archive, George Washington University, http://www.gwu.edu/~nsarchiv/bayofpigs/19610211.pdf.

38. Schlesinger, *Thousand Days*, 245–46; John P. McKnight to [USIA] Director [Edward R. Murrow], March 22, 1961, box WH-31b, Arthur M. Schlesinger, Jr. Personal Papers (#206), JFKL.

39. Bertram B. Johansson, "U.S. Urges Cuba to Sever Red Link," *Christian Science Monitor*, April 4, 1961; Max Lerner, "In the Margin," *New York Post*, April 8, 1961; Editorial, *Chicago Daily News*, April 5, 1961.

40. Editorial, *Gazette and Daily* (York, PA), April 7, 1961.

41. Lerner, "In the Margin."

42. "Washington Opens Fire on Fidel Castro," *Newsweek*, April 10, 1961, 57.

43. Schlesinger, Memorandum for the President, April 5, 1961; Schlesinger, Memorandum for the President, April 10, 1961, box 19, folder 5, NYPL.

44. Schlesinger, Memorandum for the President, April 10, 1961, box 19, folder 5, NYPL (emphasis in original).

45. Schlesinger, *Thousand Days*, 261; Schlesinger to Kennedy, April 6, 1961 (1) and (2), box WH-5, Arthur M. Schlesinger, Jr. Personal Papers (#206), JFKL.

46. "Schlesinger Says He Lied to Times," 8.

47. Schlesinger, *Thousand Days*, 296.

48. Schlesinger, 255.

49. Schlesinger, 256.

50. Schlesinger, *The Crisis of Confidence: Ideas, Power and Violence in America* (Boston: Houghton Mifflin, 1969), 95.

51. Schlesinger, *Thousand Days*, 285–86. The Mills statement is from the *Militant*, May 1, 1961, quoted in Schlesinger, 286.

52. The "Open Letter to President Kennedy" was not a strictly Harvard affair. Endorsed by scholars from other Boston-area institutions, including MIT, Boston University, and Brandeis, the document stated that "it is now a matter of record that the attempt at counter-revolution was planned, organized, and directed by an agency of the United States Government. This agency, acting in secret and deceiving both the American people and the Cuban rebels—particularly the most democratic among those rebels—has blundered in an inexcusable and almost inconceivable manner. But this was more than a failure of *technique*; it was a failure of *policy* itself." "Open Letter to President Kennedy," *New York Times*, May 10, 1961, 48 (emphasis in original).

53. Schlesinger, draft letter to signers of the Harvard Cuba statement, undated; Seymour E. Harris to McGeorge Bundy and Schlesinger, May 26, 1961, box P-3, Arthur M. Schlesinger, Jr. Personal Papers (#206), JFKL.

54. Hughes to Vittorio Calef, May 29, 1961, box 1, folder 21, Henry Stuart Hughes Papers (MS 1446), Manuscripts and Archives, Yale University Library (hereafter HSH Papers).

55. James Reston, "How Cambridge Flunked the First Test," *New York Times*, April 28, 1961, 30.

56. Ronald Hilton, letter to the editor, *New York Times*, May 15, 1961, 30, with annotation, box W-5, Arthur M. Schlesinger, Jr. Personal Papers (#206), JFKL.

57. Max Lerner, "Disenchanted," *New York Post*, May 1, 1961.

58. Peter Lisagor, "The Egghead on the New Frontier," *New York Post*, May 14, 1961.

59. Schlesinger, "The Administration and the Left," *New Statesman*, February 8, 1963, 185.

60. Schlesinger, 185.

61. Schlesinger, *Crisis of Confidence*, 94.

62. Schlesinger to JFK, August 30, 1961, box W-5, Arthur M. Schlesinger, Jr. Personal Papers (#206), JFKL.

63. Schlesinger, "Administration and the Left," 186.

64. Noam Chomsky, "The Radical Intellectual," lecture, Haven Center, Madison, WI, April 8, 2010, https://chomsky.info/20100408/.

65. Chomsky, interview with the author, March 9, 2012. Chomsky regarded what he saw in the 1930s and early 1940s as part of a larger historical phenomenon of "working people educating themselves."

66. Barsky, *Noam Chomsky*, 51.

67. Chomsky, "Radical Intellectual."

68. Chomsky, "Creation and Culture," Alternative Radio, recorded November 25, 1992, quoted in Barsky, *Noam Chomsky*, 79; Chomsky, interview.

69. Chomsky, interview. "Masscult," as Dwight Macdonald defined it, "offers its customers neither an emotional catharsis nor an aesthetic experience, for these demand effort. The production line grinds out a uniform product whose humble aim is . . . merely distraction. It may be stimulating or narcotic, but it must be easy to assimilate. It asks nothing of its audience. . . . And it gives nothing." Macdonald, "Masscult and Midcult," in *Masscult and Midcult: Essays against the American Grain* (1960; repr., New York: New York Review Books, 2011), 4–5.

70. Wilhelm von Humboldt, *Humanist without Portfolio: An Anthology of the Writing of Wilhelm von Humboldt*, trans. Marianne Cowan (Detroit: Wayne State University Press, 1963), 33, quoted in Barsky, *Noam Chomsky*, 113. See also Kasim Küçükalp, "Wilhelm von Humboldt (22 June 1767–8 April 1835)," in *Orientalist Writers*, ed. Coeli Fitzpatrick and Dwayne A. Tunstall, *Dictionary of Literary Biography*, vol. 366 (Detroit: Gale, 2012), 144.

71. Charlotte B. Evans, "Wilhelm von Humboldt (22 June 1767–8 April 1835)," in *German Writers in the Age of Goethe, 1789–1832*, ed. James N. Hardin and Christoph E. Schweitzer, *Dictionary of Literary Biography*, vol. 90 (Detroit: Gale, 1989), 203.

72. Barsky, *Noam Chomsky*, 86; Schlesinger, *Thousand Days*, 162.

73. See, for example, Chomsky, review of *Verbal Behavior*, by B. F. Skinner, *Language*, 35, no. 1 (1959): 26–58.

74. Chomsky, "The Case against B. F. Skinner," *New York Review of Books*, December 30, 1971, https://chomsky.info/19711230/; Chomsky, *Language and Politics*, ed. C. P. Otero (Montreal: Black Rose, 1988), 190, quoted in Barsky, *Noam Chomsky*, 100.

75. Chomsky to Barsky, March 31, 1995, quoted in Barsky, *Noam Chomsky*, 105.

76. Sherry Gershon Gottlieb, *Hell No, We Won't Go! Resisting the Draft during the Vietnam War* (New York: Viking, 1991), xix; "Noam Chomsky Interviewed by Eleanor Wachtel," *Queen's Quarterly* 101, no. 1 (1994): 66.

77. Chomsky, *New Mandarins*, iii; Schlesinger, *The Bitter Heritage: Vietnam and American Democracy, 1941–1966* (Boston: Houghton Mifflin Company, 1967), iii. Schlesinger published a revised version of the book with a new final chapter in 1968.

78. Schlesinger, *Bitter Heritage*, 1, 31–32 (emphasis in original).

79. Schlesinger, "Vietnam: What Should We Do Now?" *Look*, August 9, 1966, 31.

80. Schlesinger, "Vietnam and the End of the Age of the Superpowers," *Harper's*, March 1969, 44; Schlesinger, "The Necessary Amorality of Foreign Affairs," *Harper's*, August 1971, 72, 74; Schlesinger, "Traditional Objectives and Policies of the U.S.," lecture, Air War College, September 2, 1953, box 412, folder 1, NYPL.

81. Schlesinger, "Necessary Amorality," 77.

82. Chomsky, introduction to *New Mandarins*, 3, 9.

83. Schlesinger, *Bitter Heritage*, 43, 34; Chomsky, introduction to *New Mandarins*, 3–4.

84. Chomsky, introduction to *New Mandarins*, 10.

85. Chomsky, 10–11.

86. Chomsky, letter to the editor, *New York Review of Books*, March 27, 1969, http://www.nybooks.com/articles/archives/1969/mar/27/the-ethics-of-intervention/.

87. Chomsky, letter to the editor, *New York Review of Books*, March 27, 1969; Chomsky, "The Logic of Withdrawal," in *New Mandarins*, 221.

88. Chomsky, "Logic of Withdrawal," 243–44.

89. Chomsky, "Objectivity and Liberal Scholarship," in *New Mandarins*, 60; Chomsky, "Logic of Withdrawal," 252.

90. Chomsky, "The Responsibility of Intellectuals," in *New Mandarins*, 329; Chomsky, "Logic of Withdrawal," 267; Alfred Jules Ayer, *Language, Truth, and Logic* (New York: Dover, 1952), 111.

91. Reuben Eisenstein, letter to the editor, *Commentary* 49, no. 4 (April 1970): 17; Schlesinger, "Three Cheers for Professor Chomsky—but Not Just Now," *Washington Post Book World*, March 23, 1969, 5. Twenty years later, this issue was still very much alive for Schlesinger, who wrote in his journal for October 1, 1989: "Last night [Harold Pinter] became rather truculent about the fact that the *New York Review of Books* . . . no longer publishes Noam Chomsky. He had read Chomsky with care, he said, and admired the precision with which he analyzed the iniquity of American foreign policy. I said that Chomsky fabricated quotations (I had in mind the fake Truman quote I exposed many years ago), that I would not believe the baseball scores in a Chomsky piece . . . and that no serious person in the United States took Chomsky seriously once outside his field of linguistics." Schlesinger, *Journals: 1952–2000*, ed. Andrew Schlesinger and Stephen Schlesinger (New York: Penguin, 2007), 680.

92. Dennis H. Wrong, "Chomsky: Of Thinking and Moralizing," *Dissent* 17, no. 1 (January–February 1970): 78.

93. Schlesinger, letter to the editor, *Commentary* 48, no. 6 (December 1969): 4, 10.

94. Chomsky, letter to the editor, *Commentary* 49, no. 2 (February 1970): 6, 14.

95. Schlesinger, *Bitter Heritage*, 105, 49.

96. Robert R. Tomes, *Apocalypse Then: American Intellectuals and the Vietnam War, 1954–1975* (New York: New York University Press, 1998), 153; Chomsky, letter to the editor, *Commentary*, February 1970, 14.

97. Chomsky, "The Bitter Heritage: A Review," in *New Mandarins*, 295.

98. Chomsky, "Objectivity and Liberal Scholarship," 26; Zbigniew Brzezinski,

"America in the Technocratic Age," *Encounter*, January 1968, quoted in Chomsky, "Objectivity and Liberal Scholarship," 30.

99. Chomsky, "Some Thoughts on Intellectuals and the Schools," in *New Mandarins*, 317. "Free-floating" is a translation of the German term to which Karl Mannheim applied this gloss: "This unanchored, *relatively* classless stratum is, to use Alfred Weber's terminology, the 'socially unattached intelligentsia' (*freischwebende Intelligenz*)." Mannheim, *Ideology and Utopia: An Introduction to the Sociology of Knowledge* (1929), trans. Louis Wirth and Edward Shils (1936; repr., London: Routledge, 1948), 137–38 (emphasis in original).

100. Tomes observed that "surprisingly, it was not the generals and technocrats who would absorb the most fervent brunt of radical contempt, but liberal intellectuals." Tomes, *Apocalypse Then*, 75.

101. Chomsky, "Responsibility of Intellectuals," 324.

102. Chomsky, 325.

103. "Schlesinger Says He Lied to Times," 8.

104. "Schlesinger Backs Cuba 'Cover Story,'" *New York Times*, November 29, 1965, 16; Schlesinger, letter to the editor, *Listener*, December 18, 1969, 858.

105. "Schlesinger Backs Cuba 'Cover Story,'" 16. Aldous rebuts criticism like Chomsky's by noting the "obvious point that Schlesinger was no longer a critic: as a special assistant to the president, he was a government official"; and "that governments mislead the press, the public, allies . . . is hardly news." Unlike his wartime resignation from OWI, Schlesinger responded to the Bay of Pigs "with a certain maturity in the middle of a crisis not of his own making, showing a willingness not to quit the arena to return to a spectator's seat at the first sign of trouble." Aldous, *Schlesinger*, 237–38.

106. Yorick Wilks, "Weeping for a Country," *Listener*, October 30, 1969, 604; Schlesinger, letter to the editor, *Listener*, December 18, 1969, 858; Chomsky, letter to the editor, *Listener*, January 15, 1970, 88.

107. Schlesinger to JFK, June 30, 1961, "CIA Reorganization," box WH-69, Arthur M. Schlesinger, Jr. Personal Papers (#206), JFKL.

108. Schlesinger, letter to the editor, *Listener*, December 18, 1969, 859; Julien Benda, *The Treason of the Intellectuals* (1927), trans. Richard Adlington (1928; repr., New York: W. W. Norton, 1969). Benda's book was widely invoked if imperfectly understood. Though American intellectuals largely construed Benda's notion of "treason" as intellectuals' abandonment of abstract contemplation or compromise of its principles for the sake of political involvement, Benda pointed most insistently to those intellectuals who rejected the universalist reason of the Enlightenment in order to extol nationalism with irrationalist vigor. While Benda may have criticized Schlesinger for trimming intellectual values on behalf of government service, this kind of "treason" to truth appears less troubling from his perspective than that of intellectuals who, rather than spreading falsehoods for the nation, conflate truth itself with the nation. On reception of Benda, see David L. Schalk, "*La Trahison des clercs*—1927 and Later,"

French Historical Studies 7, no. 2 (1971): 245–63. For critique of Benda, see also H. Stuart Hughes, *Consciousness and Society: The Reorientation of European Social Thought, 1890–1930* (New York: Vintage Books, 1958), chap. 10.

109. Chomsky, letter to the editor, *Listener*, January 15, 1970, 89.

110. Schlesinger, *Crisis of Confidence*, 88.

111. Schlesinger, 92.

112. Lionel Abel, "Seven Heroes of the New Left," *New York Times*, May 5, 1968, SM30. The other six were Albert Camus, Paul Goodman, Che Guevara, Regis Debray, Frantz Fanon, and Hebert Marcuse.

113. Schlesinger, *Crisis of Confidence*, 86.

114. Schlesinger, 89. In 2007 Chomsky noted that Niebuhr "was once called 'the theologian of the establishment.' And the reason is because he presented a framework which, essentially, justified just about anything they wanted to do. His thesis is dressed up in long words and so on (it's what you do if you're an intellectual). But what it came down to is that, 'Even if you try to do good, evil's going to come out of it; that's the paradox of grace.'—And that's wonderful for war criminals." Chomsky, interviewed by Gabriel Matthew Schivone, "On Responsibility, War Guilt and Intellectuals," *Counterpunch*, August 3, 2007, https://chomsky.info/20070803/.

115. Schlesinger to Hubert H. Humphrey, March 25, 1966, box 67, folder 3, NYPL; Chomsky, interview with author.

116. In 2006 Chomsky spoke of "our intuitive moral judgments" in relation to just war theory. Noam Chomsky, "Just War Theory," lecture, US Military Academy, West Point, NY, April 20, 2006, https://chomsky.info/20060420/.

117. Schlesinger, *Crisis of Confidence*, 89.

118. Schlesinger, "Necessary Amorality," 73, 77.

119. Schlesinger, 73, 77.

120. H. Stuart Hughes, "Statement at Speak-Out on Vietnam: March 25, 1966," box 5, folder 132, HSH Papers.

121. *Causes, Origins, and Lessons of the Vietnam War, Before the United States Senate Committee on Foreign Relations*, 92nd Congress, 60 (May 10, 1972).

122. Schlesinger, *Thousand Days*, 922, 724.

123. *Causes, Origins, and Lessons*, 103; Chomsky, interview.

124. *Causes, Origins, and Lessons*, 103.

125. *Causes, Origins, and Lessons*, 100.

126. Chomsky, letter to the editor, *New York Review of Books*, March 27, 1969.

127. *Causes, Origins, and Lessons*, 84.

128. Schlesinger, "The Role of Intellectuals in a Democracy Undergoing Radical Change," lecture, American Association of Advertising Agencies, White Sulphur Springs, WV, April 24, 1970, box 334, folder 3, NYPL.

129. Chomsky, interview. The Schlesinger editorial is "Good Foreign Policy a Casualty of War," *Los Angeles Times*, March 23, 2003. While Schlesinger's position on Iraq

looked to Chomsky like evidence of the former's changing views, Schlesinger's position on Vietnam continued as recently as 2017 to stand in Chomsky's mind for the limited range of dissent among American intellectuals, who "can choose to be responsible experts"—like "Arthur Schlesinger" worrying "that escalation . . . would prove to be too costly"—or "'wild men in the wings,' who raise objections of principle . . . not merely tactical questions about feasibility and cost." Noam Chomsky, preface to *The Responsibility of Intellectuals* (New York: New Press, 2017), 7–8, 12.

Chapter Four

1. Guy Alchon, "Lasch, Christopher," in *American National Biography*, vol. 13, ed. Mark C. Carnes and John A. Garraty (New York: Oxford University Press, 1999), 217; Richard Fox, "A Tribute to Christopher Lasch," Annual Meeting of the American Historical Association, San Francisco, January 8, 1994, quoted in Robert Westbrook, "In Retrospect: Christopher Lasch, *The New Radicalism*, and the Vocation of Intellectuals," *Reviews in American History* 23, no. 1 (1995): 177.

2. Casey Blake and Christopher Phelps, "History as Social Criticism: Conversations with Christopher Lasch," *Journal of American History* 80 (March 1994): 1313.

3. Eric Miller, *Hope in a Scattering Time: A Life of Christopher Lasch* (Grand Rapids, MI: William B. Eerdman's Publishing, 2010), 21, 24. For additional biographical material and discussion of Lasch's work after 1970, see David S. Brown, *Beyond the Frontier: The Midwestern Voice in American Historical Writing* (Chicago: University of Chicago Press, 2009), 149–72.

4. Blake and Phelps, "Conversations with Lasch," 1317; Richard Hofstadter to Lasch, March 19, 1957, box 1, folder 4, Christopher Lasch Papers, Department of Rare Books, Special Collections, and Preservation, University of Rochester (hereafter CL Papers). Lasch ultimately wrote on American liberals' responses to the Russian Revolution.

5. Blake and Phelps, "Conversations with Lasch," 1317.

6. Blake and Phelps, 1319.

7. Blake and Phelps, 1320–21; William Leuchtenburg to Lasch, May 5, 1958, box 1, folder 5, CL Papers. The equation of taking a position with being a man (i.e., not a "eunuch") indicates the gendered construction of the intellectual enfolded into these men's language. On gendered language in Lasch's writing, see Linda Gordon, Persis Hunt, Elizabeth Pleck, Rochelle Goldberg Ruthchild, and Marcia Scott, "Historical Phallacies: Sexism in American Historical Writing," in *Liberating Women's History: Theoretical and Critical Essays*, ed. Berenice A. Carroll (Urbana: University of Illinois Press, 1976), 59–62.

8. Lasch to Leuchtenburg, August 22, 1961, box 1, folder 5, CL Papers.

9. Lasch, "Is Conservatism the Real Enemy?," review of *The Futilitarian Society*, by William J. Newman, *St. Louis Post-Dispatch*, August 2, 1961, 2C.

10. Lasch quoted this passage from Benjamin Ginzburg's "Against Messianism," *New Republic*, February 18, 1931, in his "Radicals of the Thirties: Their Literature, Not Politics, Seen as Real Issue," review of *Writers on the Left: Episodes in American Literary Communism*, by Daniel Aaron, *St. Louis Post-Dispatch*, February 11, 1962. Lasch would quote the same material again in *The New Radicalism*.

11. Lasch, "Radicals of the Thirties," 4D.

12. Lasch to Schlesinger, December 20, 1954, box 1, folder 7, CL Papers; Lasch to Schlesinger, June 30, 1962, box 1, folder 11, CL Papers.

13. Lasch, "Arthur Schlesinger and 'Pragmatic Liberalism,' Part 1: The Cult of the Hard Boiled," *Iowa Defender*, April 29, 1963, 1, 8.

14. Lasch, "Arthur Schlesinger and 'Pragmatic Liberalism,' Part 2: The Uses of Realism," *Iowa Defender*, May 6, 1963, 4.

15. The Lasch-Taylor partnership produced in the end one article: "Two 'Kindred Spirits': Sorority and Family in New England, 1839–1846," *New England Quarterly* 36 (March 1963): 23–41.

16. Berenice M. Fisher, "The Wise Old Men and the New Women: Christopher Lasch Besieged," review of *Haven in a Heartless World: The Family Besieged*, by Christopher Lasch, *History of Education Quarterly* 19, no. 1 (Spring 1979): 137–38. Though she canvassed his other writings, Fisher wrote primarily in response to Lasch's *Haven in a Heartless World*, which, pointing to a "decline of paternal authority," linked gender politics to experts and intellectuals in a manner reminiscent of Irving Kristol's critique of the New Class. Lasch, *Haven in a Heartless World* (1977; repr., New York: Basic Books, 1979), 74. As Marie Jo Buhle put it, Lasch saw feminists as having "colluded with various reformers to transfer paternal authority to outside experts and to the impersonal state." Buhle, *Feminism and Its Discontents: A Century of Struggle with Psychoanalysis* (Cambridge, MA: Harvard University Press, 1998), 282. See also Wini Breines, Margaret Cerullo, and Judith Stacey, "Social Biology, Family Studies, and Antifeminist Backlash," *Feminist Studies* 4, no. 1 (February 1978): 43–67; and Ilene Philipson, "Experts, Instincts, and the Family," *Socialist Review* 8, nos. 4–5 (July–October 1978): 255–63.

17. Lasch, "Arthur Schlesinger and 'Pragmatic Liberalism,' Part 3: The Historian as Politician," *Iowa Defender*, May 13, 1963, 1, 4; Lasch, "The Bored," review of *Abundance for What? and Other Essays*, by David Riesman, *Progressive*, September 1964, 50. In 1959 Schlesinger had lauded Walter Lippmann for insisting "in the heat and clamors of the present on the indispensability of the long view." Schlesinger out of power thus sounded a note similar to the one Lasch now struck against him in it. Arthur M. Schlesinger Jr., "Walter Lippmann: The Intellectual *vs*. Politics" in *The Politics of Hope and The Bitter Heritage: American Liberalism in the 1960s* (Princeton, NJ: Princeton University Press, 2008), 194.

18. Staughton Lynd, "Jane Addams and the Radical Impulse," *Commentary* 32, no. 1 (July 1961): 59; Lasch to Lynd, September 8, 1962, box 1, folder 10, CL Papers.

19. The Addams quote is from Jane Addams, "A Function of the Social Settle-

ment," *Annals of the American Academy of Political Science* 13 (May 1899): 339; Lasch to Lynd, September 8, 1962, box 1, folder 10, CL Papers.

20. Lynd, "Jane Addams and the Radical Impulse," 55; Lasch to Lynd, October 22, 1962, box 1, folder 10, CL Papers.

21. Lasch to Lynd, October 22, 1962, box 1, folder 10, CL Papers.

22. Lasch to Lynd, October 22, 1962.

23. Lasch to Lynd, October 22, 1962.

24. Lynd, "Jane Addams and the Radical Impulse," 55; Lasch to Lynd, October 22, 1962, box 1, folder 10, CL Papers.

25. For a critical appraisal of Lasch's work on Addams, see Gordon et al., "Historical Phallacies."

26. Lasch's notes for *The New Radicalism*, box 9, folder 18, CL Papers; Hofstadter to Lasch, September 27, 1964, box 9, folder 26, CL Papers.

27. Lasch to Hofstadter, October 3, 1964, box 9, folder 26, CL Papers.

28. Hofstadter to Lasch, October 9, 1964, box 9, folder 26, CL Papers (emphasis in original).

29. Lasch to Alfred Knopf, November 12, 1963, box 1, folder 12, CL Papers.

30. Lasch, *The New Radicalism in America: The Intellectual as a Social Type, 1889–1963* (1965; repr., New York: W. W. Norton, 1997), ix–x.

31. Lasch, 64.

32. Lasch, 168.

33. Lasch, 169.

34. This argument compares to the "diplomacy of the intellectuals" on Cuba, where Schlesinger's white paper was hailed as a new era in international relations, when arguments sallied forth rather than armies. For a brief moment between the white paper and the Bay of Pigs, there was hope that rational methods might replace violent ones in the Cold War contest for hearts and minds. For Lasch, that hope simply masked the class interest of intellectuals. If so, however, were not nonviolent methods still preferable to violent ones? If a class interest should triumph, why not that of intellectuals rather than, say, business—in whose interest violence was often deployed to block anti-capitalist forces? As it turned out with Schlesinger, however, the ultimate issue was not violence or nonviolence, business-class interests or intellectual-class ones; it was intellectuals' role in legitimating violence. After all, Schlesinger's white paper was not the alternative to invasion; it was the prelude for it.

35. Lasch, *New Radicalism*, 169, 147.

36. Lasch, 290–91, 298 (emphasis in original).

37. Lasch, 289.

38. Lasch, 313–15.

39. Lasch, 315, 316–17 (emphasis in original).

40. Lasch, 317.

41. Miller, *Hope in a Scattering Time*, 89; Leuchtenburg to Lasch, July 5, 1965, box

1, folder 18, CL Papers; Lasch to Robert and Zora Lasch, March 15, 1966, box 2, folder 4, CL Papers.

42. Michael Harrington, "Pragmatists and Utopians," *Commonweal*, September 3, 1965, 623.

43. Alfred Kazin, review of *The New Radicalism in America*, by Christopher Lasch, *New York Review of Books*, May 20, 1965, https://www.nybooks.com/articles/1965/05/20/radicals-and-intellectuals/.

44. Lasch, *New Radicalism*, xvi; Edward T. Chase, review of *The New Radicalism in America*, by Lasch, *Nation*, May 24, 1965, 564–65; Daniel Aaron, review of *The New Radicalism in America*, by Lasch, *New York Times Book Review*, June 13, 1965, 38; Peter Filene, "Alienation vs. Involvement," *Reporter*, June 17, 1965, 42–43.

45. August Heckscher, review of *The New Radicalism in America*, by Lasch, *Saturday Review*, June 12, 1965, 42.

46. Schlesinger to Hook, March 2, 1966, box 4, folder 3, Arthur M. Schlesinger Jr. Papers, 1922–2007, New York Public Library; Schlesinger, "Intellectuals under Fire," review of *The New Radicalism in America*, by Lasch, *Sunday Times* (London), February 27, 1966, 30.

47. Schlesinger, "Intellectuals under Fire," 30. Schlesinger's pluralist view of intellectuals' roles had a functional element. He later wrote that "the intellectual in government . . . can count on the legion of incorruptibles left behind to act with relish as his conscience and his critics." The latter "has some effect in helping" the former "to keep straight." Arthur M. Schlesinger Jr., *The Crisis of Confidence: Ideas, Power and Violence in America* (Boston: Houghton Mifflin, 1969), 95.

48. Benjamin DeMott, "Building Barricades Out of Bookracks," review of *The New Radicalism in America*, by Lasch, *Washington Post Book Week*, June 27, 1965, 6, 18.

49. Fred Rue Jacobs to Lasch, September 1, 1965; Lasch to Jacobs, October 12, 1965, box 1, folder 17, CL Papers; William Stanton to Lasch, July 19, 1966, box 2, folder 5, CL Papers.

50. Samuel Haber, "Is There an Intellectual in the House!!!!," paper presented at the Organization of American Historians Annual Meeting, Cincinnati, OH, April 28, 1966, box 9, folder 30, CL Papers.

51. Lasch, "OAH Cincinnati session reply '27 min,'" paper presented at the Organization of American Historians Annual Meeting, Cincinnati, OH, April 28, 1966, box 9, folder 30, CL Papers. Given Lasch's concerns about the anti-democratic tendencies of expertise, his definition here appears descriptive rather than normative. He had written of State Department officials visiting his campus in Iowa: "These people really hate democracy; they wish nothing so much as that everybody should shut up and let the experts have things their own way." Lasch to Robert and Zora Lasch, March 15, 1966, box 2, folder 4, CL Papers. On the other hand, Lasch valued particular forms of expertise. Toward the end of his overtly activist period, he continually worried about his tenuous grasp on the latest developments in his own line of expertise: American history.

52. Lasch, "OAH Cincinnati session reply."

53. Lasch, "OAH Cincinnati session reply." The Steffens quote is from his letter to Dot Hollister, March 26, 1921, cited in *New Radicalism in America*, 278.

54. Leuchtenburg to Lasch, January 26, 1966, box 2, folder 5, CL Papers.

55. Leuchtenburg to Lasch, July 5, 1965, box 1, folder 18, CL Papers.

56. Lasch to Leuchtenburg, July 17, 1965, box 1, folder 18, CL Papers.

57. Lasch to Leuchtenburg, July 17, 1965.

58. Lasch to Leuchtenburg, July 17, 1965.

59. Lasch to Leuchtenburg, July 17, 1965.

60. Lasch, "Democratic Vistas," review of *The Crossroads Papers*, ed. Hans J. Morgenthau, and *Seeds of Liberation*, ed. Paul Goodman, *New York Review of Books*, September 30, 1965, https://www.nybooks.com/articles/1965/09/30/democratic-vistas/.

61. E. Jeffrey Ludwig, letter to the editor, *New York Review of Books*, November 11, 1965, https://www.nybooks.com/articles/1965/11/11/the-banality-of-liberalism-3/ (emphasis in original); Lasch, letter to the editor, *New York Review of Books*, November 11, 1965, https://www.nybooks.com/articles/1965/11/11/the-banality-of-liberalism-3/.

62. John F. Withey, letter to the editor, *New York Review of Books*, November 11, 1965, https://www.nybooks.com/articles/1965/11/11/the-banality-of-liberalism-2/ (emphasis in original); Lasch, letter to the editor, *New York Review of Books*, November 11, 1965 (emphasis in original).

63. Lasch, letter to the editor, *New York Review of Books*, November 11, 1965.

64. But how did intellectuals arrive at the values that formed the basis of their commitment to "committed scholarship"? An exchange between Lasch and Benjamin Ginzburg sheds light on this question. "I realize today that the term 'intellectual' or 'scholar' as I used it at that time [of his 1931 *New Republic* piece] properly refers to the man who has absorbed in himself the central moral-religious experience of the race," Ginzburg told Lasch. This absorption happens "through religious training, study and reflection, or through developing an artistic sensibility in literature, or through study and reflection on the 'humanistic' side of human history (or through all three methods combined). The intellectual in this sense—if we still want to continue to use the term—is to be distinguished from the social scientist and the historian who deal only with the material side of human affairs (and who are also called intellectuals)." Since "the intellectual as you and I have used the term is one who absorbs the central moral-religious or spiritual experience of the race—something which cannot be taught or accepted on the authority of an expert but only by direct spiritual communication (like a candle lighting other candles), then it is folly to expect him to know all the detailed economic and sociological facts which are within the purview of the social scientific expert" who "provid[es] the techniques or means to carry out spiritual policy." Ginzburg to Lasch, November 22, 1965, box 2, folder 3, CL Papers. "What you say about the real function of the 'intellectual' in your letter helps to clarify matters," Lasch replied, "and it is somewhat discouraging to reflect that it is a definition which most so-called

intellectuals today would find embarrassing." Lasch to Ginzburg, January 3, 1966, box 2, folder 3, CL Papers.

65. Fisher, "Lasch Besieged," 139.

66. Fisher, 141; Alice Echols, *Daring to Be Bad: Radical Feminism in America, 1967–1975* (1989; repr., Minneapolis: University of Minnesota Press, 1998), 149–51.

67. Ellen Willis, *The Essential Ellen Willis*, ed. Nona Willis Aronowitz (Minneapolis: University of Minnesota Press, 2014), 16.

68. Echols, *Daring to Be Bad*, 181.

69. Fisher, "Lasch Besieged," 141.

70. As he later wrote, "After 1965, American involvement in Vietnam converted [the peace movement] into a mass movement embracing a wide spectrum of opinion from pacifists to violent revolutionaries. . . . The civil rights movement also changed its character at mid-decade. . . . Around 1966, the movement became more militant in its tactics and in its program." Lasch to Dale Jacobs, October 26, 1970, with attached "WORLD BOOK ENCYCLOPEDIA DRAFTS," box 2, folder 20, CL Papers.

71. Lasch, "The Decline of Dissent," *Katallagete* 1 (Winter 1966–67): 11–17, reprinted in *The Agony of the American Left* (New York: Vintage, 1969), 29; Lasch to Robert Silvers, October 25, 1965, box 2, folder 1, CL Papers.

72. As part of its involvement, the CIA channeled funds through the Congress for Cultural Freedom to *Encounter*, an Anglo-American journal founded by Irving Kristol and Stephen Spender. See, for instance, Sylvan Fox, "Stephen Spender Quits Encounter: British Poet Says Finding of CIA Financing Led to His Leaving Magazine," *New York Times*, May 8, 1967, 1; Lasch, "The Cultural Cold War: A Short History of the Congress for Cultural Freedom," in *The Agony of the American Left*, 94.

73. Noam Chomsky, "The Responsibility of Intellectuals," *New York Review of Books*, February 23, 1967, as printed in Chomsky, *American Power and the New Mandarins* (New York: Pantheon, 1969), 348; Lasch, "The Cultural Cold War," 97–98.

74. Lasch, "Democratic Vistas."

75. Isabel Condit to Lasch, January 26, 1968, box 2, folder 10, CL Papers.

76. I am grateful to Benjamin Seitelman for pointing out the Rumsfeld connection.

77. Lasch to Robert and Zora Lasch, January 25, 1968, box 2, folder 11, CL Papers.

78. Lasch to Strauss, August 20, 1968, "Brief Description of the Book," box 10, folder 1, CL Papers.

79. David I. Bruck, "From the Shelf: The Agony of the American Left," *Harvard Crimson*, March 25, 1969, http://www.thecrimson.com/article/1969/3/25/the-agony-of-the-american-left/.

80. Lasch, "The Revival of Political Controversy in the Sixties," in *The Agony of the American Left*, 212; Bruck, "From the Shelf."

81. Staughton Lynd, letter to the editor, and Lasch reply, *New York Review of Books*, September 12, 1968, https://www.nybooks.com/articles/1968/09/12/the-future-of

-radicalism/. While Lasch saw little wisdom in independent candidacies, like the one he refused in Illinois, the formation of a new party was different: it was less ephemeral, a better forum for working out ideas, and more likely to generate lasting change.

82. David Marr to Lasch, July 12, 1968, box 2, folder 12, CL Papers; Ed Trory to Lasch, undated, box 2, folder 13, CL Papers (emphasis in original); Robert Brustein to Lasch, March 30, 1969, box 2, folder 14, CL Papers; Tom Blandy to Lasch, August 23, 1970, box 2, folder 18, CL Papers; B. Hal Eskesen to Lasch, undated, box 2, folder 18, CL Papers.

83. J. T. Gault to Lasch, March 29, 1969, box 2, folder 15, CL Papers; David Jones to Lasch, July 6, 1968, box 2, folder 11, CL Papers (emphasis in original); Peter Israel to Lasch, July 31, 1968, box 2, folder 11, CL Papers (emphasis in original).

84. Paul Lauter to Lasch et al., undated, box 2, folder 12, CL Papers; Gar Alperovitz to Lasch, March 11, 1968, box 2, folder 9, CL Papers; Lasch to Alperovitz, March 27, 1968, box 2, folder 9, CL Papers.

85. Lasch to Alperovitz, May 23, 1968, box 2, folder 9, CL Papers.

86. Lasch to Alperovitz, April 7, 1969, box 2, folder 14, CL Papers.

87. Lasch to Alperovitz, April 7, 1969.

88. Peter Israel to Lasch, July 31, 1968, box 2, folder 11, CL Papers.

89. Lasch, "March 4 Talk," box 13, folder 23, CL Papers. Although this six-page, typed document is undated, it refers to protests that took place in 1969.

90. Lasch to Eugene Genovese, November 8, 1968, box 2, folder 10, CL Papers.

91. Lasch to Dwight Macdonald, February 22, 1969, box 2, folder 16, CL Papers.

92. Lasch and Eugene Genovese, "Beyond the New Left," typs. w. manu. rev., 238, box 13, folder 30, CL Papers.

93. Lasch and Genovese, "Beyond the New Left," 4.

94. Lasch to Genovese, November 8, 1968, box 2, folder 10, CL Papers.

95. Lasch and Genovese, "Beyond the New Left," 6.

96. Lasch to Mike Wreszin, February 3, 1966, box 2, folder 5, CL Papers.

97. David Kettler, "The Vocation of Radical Intellectuals," Politics and Society 1 (Autumn 1970): 26.

98. Kettler, 39.

99. For Chomsky, appeals to reason are democratic because they are predicated upon the rational capability shared by all human beings. Robert F. Barsky quotes Chomsky as saying, "It does not require very far-reaching, specialized knowledge to perceive that the United States was invading South Vietnam. And, in fact, to take apart the system of illusions and deception which functions to prevent understanding of contemporary reality [is] not a task that requires extraordinary skill or understanding. It requires the kind of normal skepticism and willingness to apply one's analytical skills that almost all people have and that they can exercise. It just happens that they exercise them in analyzing what the New England Patriots ought to do next Sunday instead of

questions that really matter for human life, their own included." Noam Chomsky, *The Chomsky Reader*, ed. James Peck (New York: Pantheon, 1987), 35, quoted in Barsky, *Noam Chomsky: A Life of Dissent* (Cambridge, MA: MIT Press, 1997), 114.

100. Irving Howe thought Lasch's influence was considerable. "I think you may have a good deal more influence right now with the students than any of us at *Dissent*," he told Lasch. Howe to Lasch, June 1, 1968, box 2, folder 11, CL Papers.

101. Willis, *Essential Ellen Willis*, 15–16.

102. Toni Cade Bambara, preface to *The Black Woman: An Anthology*, ed. Toni Cade Bambara (New York: Mentor Books, 1970), 9, 11–12. On the context for and significance of this volume, see Brittney C. Cooper, *Beyond Respectability: The Intellectual Thought of Race Women* (Urbana: University of Illinois Press, 2017), 113–19.

103. Kettler, "The Vocation of Radical Intellectuals," 47–48. Kettler put the distinction between counsel and leadership into practice at Ohio State when, in the wake of the Kent State shootings on May 4, 1970, the campus erupted in protest. "We sat on the ground for hours on the day after Kent State between squads of armed Guardsmen and up to 2000 brick-toting students," he told Lasch. Amid "five thousand occupying troops on campus," Kettler spoke "to a large assembly of students and urge[d] them to push for a free and open university instead of one which is shut down. These public performances happen as a direct and immediate response to situations which look threatening and I try scrupulously to avoid taking on the role of student-leader—although there are days when the distinctions waver. In any case, I am satisfied that I functioned within the general guidelines I tried to work out in the 'Vocation . . .' paper." Kettler to Lasch, July 29, 1970, box 2, folder 20, CL Papers.

104. Lasch to Kettler, October 9, 1969, box 2, folder 15, CL Papers.

105. Lasch and Genovese, outline/first draft of "Beyond the New Left," typs. w. manu. rev., 3–4 (emphasis in original), box 13, folder 22, CL Papers. This is not the same document as that cited earlier under the title "Beyond the New Left." Whereas that document is a full draft manuscript, this one appears to be an earliest draft or outline. For the authors' views on the threat of fascism, see p. 11 of the outline/first draft.

106. Lasch and Genovese, "Beyond the New Left," 239, 5.

107. Lasch and Genovese, outline/first draft of "Beyond the New Left," 5–6.

108. Lasch and Genovese, outline/first draft of "Beyond the New Left," 8, 7.

109. Lasch to Kettler, September 17, 1969, box 2, folder 15, CL Papers (emphasis in original).

110. Lasch to Kettler, September 25, 1969, box 2, folder 15, CL Papers.

111. Lasch to Genovese, September 13, 1969, box 13, folder 24, CL Papers.

112. Lasch to Genovese, September 13, 1969 (emphasis in original).

113. Lasch to Genovese, January 3, 1970, box 2, folder 19, CL Papers. In his account of the tumultuous 1969 American Historical Association meeting and the fractures within the discipline that it manifested, Peter Novick describes "the polarization of left historians into two distinct and mutually hostile camps": one that included Lasch,

Genovese, and James Weinstein, and another composed of Lynd, Howard Zinn, Jesse Lemisch, and others. Among the differences between the camps was a longer-term approach by the former and a more immediate, activist orientation among the latter. Their sense that revolution was not imminent led Lasch and Genovese's circle to favor work that, while intended as political intervention, would prefigure a radical movement or society rather than serving, as Lynd believed may be the case, a movement on the cusp of realizing the new society. Peter Novick, *That Noble Dream: The "Objectivity Question" and the American Historical Profession* (New York: Cambridge University Press, 1988), 417–38 (quote on 428).

114. Lasch to Robert and Zora Lasch, March 26, 1970, box 0, folder 38, CL Papers.

115. Lasch to Richard Hofstadter, October 22, 1970, box 2, folder 20, CL Papers.

116. Lasch, "Hofstadter," 2 pages of handwritten notes clipped to Lasch's October 22, 1970, letter to Hofstadter, box 2, folder 20, CL Papers.

117. Lasch, *New Radicalism*, 295.

118. That evening "Lasch did not 'talk much,' he recalled in a 1993 interview, 'being overawed by this distinguished company, and feeling a little uncomfortable too because of having written so much about the perils of intellectuals as advisers to people in power. I wasn't sure whether I should even be there in the first place.'" Miller, *Hope in a Scattering Time*, 241.

119. Though Lasch would not intervene in this later period as he did in the late 1960s, it was not, Natasha Zaretsky has shown, for lack of readers encouraging him to do so. The logic of social criticism was still at work. Zaretsky, *No Direction Home: The American Family and the Fear of National Decline, 1968–1980* (Chapel Hill: University of North Carolina Press, 2007), 213–14.

120. Lasch to Robert and Zora Lasch, March 26, 1979, box 0, folder 38, CL Papers.

121. Robert B. Westbrook argues that Lasch's later work is characteristic of Michael Walzer's ideal of "connected criticism." "In his last years," Westbrook writes, "Lasch connected himself to American culture in profound fashion, finding (some would say constructing) an indigenous, 'populist' tradition to which he gave his provisional loyalty." Westbrook, "In Retrospect: Christopher Lasch," 188. See also Michael Walzer, *Interpretation and Social Criticism* (Cambridge, MA: Harvard University Press, 1993) and *The Company of Critics: Social Criticism and Political Commitment in the Twentieth Century*, 2nd ed. (New York: Basic Books, 2002).

Chapter Five

1. Irving Kristol, "Colloquium on the Urban Intellectual, I: From Plato to Marx," box 26, folder 23, Irving Kristol Papers, 1946–2001 (Mss. 1036), Wisconsin Historical Society, Madison, WI (hereafter IK Papers).

2. Kristol's collaborator Daniel Bell described this phenomenon in *The Coming of Post-Industrial Society: A Venture in Social Forecasting* (New York: Basic Books, 1973). I

use "New Class" for the theorized entity and "new class" to indicate an emerging social group not yet theorized as the New Class. Kristol's usage varies. In a single column in 1977, he uses both of the above. Kristol, "On Corporate Philanthropy" (1977), in *Two Cheers for Capitalism* (New York: Basic Books, 1978), 145.

3. Kristol to William O. Miller, October 4, 1976, box 1, folder 34, IK Papers; Gail Pitts, "Businessmen Losing Out in Idea War, Editor Says," *Denver Post*, February 21, 1977.

4. Richard Weaver's *Ideas Have Consequences* (1948) had pilloried philosophical relativism. If his argument did not endure, Weaver's title nonetheless became a rallying cry for postwar conservatives seeking a renewed intellectual basis for their politics. See George H. Nash, "The Influence of *Ideas Have Consequences* on the Conservative Intellectual Movement in America," in *Steps toward Restoration: The Consequences of Richard Weaver's Ideas*, ed. Ted J. Smith III (Wilmington, DE: Intercollegiate Studies Institute, 1998), 81–124.

5. Kristol, "American Historians and the Democratic Idea," *American Scholar* 39, no. 1 (Winter 1969–70): 102 (emphasis in original); Peter Steinfels, "The Reasonable Right," *Esquire*, February 13, 1979, 24.

6. See Sidney Blumenthal, *The Rise of the Counter-Establishment: From Conservative Ideology to Political Power* (New York: Times Books, 1986); and J. David Hoeveler Jr., *The Postmodernist Turn: American Thought and Culture in the 1970s* (New York: Twayne, 1996), 145.

7. Kristol to Richard Randall, January 24, 1974, box 26, folder 17, IK Papers (emphasis in original). Kevin Mattson has characterized this strand of Kristol's thought as "sermonizing," which others on the Right moved past, sharpening Kristol's "critique of the 'new class' into populist anti-intellectualism and antiacademic stances . . . by throwing overboard his elitism, sophistication, and most certainly his hand-wringing tone." Mattson, *Rebels All! A Short History of the Conservative Mind in Postwar America* (New Brunswick, NJ: Rutgers University Press, 2008), 90, 86.

8. Kristol to Randall, November 12, 1973, box 26, folder 23, IK Papers.

9. Josiah Lee Auspitz, "Intellectuals and Power," *Commentary* 55, no. 5 (May 1973): 86, 88.

10. Kristol, "The Shaking of the Foundations," in *On the Democratic Idea in America* (New York: Harper and Row, 1972), 23–24.

11. Kristol, *Neo-Conservatism: The Autobiography of an Idea* (New York: Free Press, 1995), 3–5; J. David Hoeveler Jr., *Watch on the Right: Conservative Intellectuals in the Reagan Era* (Madison: University of Wisconsin Press, 1991), 81; Barry Gewen, "Irving Kristol, Godfather of Modern Conservatism, Dies at 89," *New York Times*, September 18, 2009, http://www.nytimes.com/2009/09/19/us/politics/19kristol.html?pagewanted=all &_r=0.

12. Kristol, "From 'Memoirs of a Trotskyist' by Irving Kristol," *Arguing the World*, http://www.pbs.org/arguing/nyintellectuals_krystol_2.html.

13. Gertrude Himmelfarb's scholarship and Kristol's writing pursued many of the same themes, including middle-class morals and manners, the tension between personal freedom and social order, the disruptive or stabilizing potential of intellectuals, and capitalism as a driver of revolutionary cultural as well as economic change. Himmelfarb's studies of Victorian life—particularly *Lord Acton: A Study in Conscience and Politics* (1952), *Victorian Minds* (1968), *On Liberty and Liberalism: The Case of John Stuart Mill* (1974), and *The Idea of Poverty: England in the Early Industrial Age* (1984)—provided in the form of deeply researched intellectual histories ideas that also reverberated in Kristol's essays and editorials about contemporary American life during these same years. Kristol told Daniel Bell that Himmelfarb (known to family and friends as Bea) was his most formidable critic: "Bea thinks it's publishable," he reported of an article draft, "and once I get past her, I'm usually home scott free." Kristol to Daniel Bell, July 30, 1968, box 20, folder 40, IK Papers.

14. "US Army Units," *Holocaust Encyclopedia*, United States Holocaust Memorial Museum, http://www.ushmm.org/wlc/en/article.php?ModuleId=10006161; Gewen, "Irving Kristol"; Kristol, *Neo-Conservatism*, 13.

15. Kristol, "'Civil Liberties,' 1952—A Study in Confusion," *Commentary* 13, no. 3 (March 1952): 229.

16. Kristol, "'Civil Liberties,' 1952," 234–35; Christopher Lasch, *The New Radicalism in America: The Intellectual as a Social Type, 1889–1963* (1965; repr., New York: W. W. Norton, 1997), 316.

17. Kristol, "'Civil Liberties,' 1952," 229, 234–35.

18. Reports of the CIA funding *Encounter* had appeared in the *New York Times* in 1966, but the scandal gained momentum the following year. See Tom Wicker, John W. Finney, Max Frankel, and E. W. Kenworthy, "Electronic Prying Grows: CIA Is Spying from 100 Miles Up," *New York Times*, April 27, 1966, 1, 28. On the unfolding of the scandal, see Tity de Vries, "The 1967 Central Intelligence Agency Scandal: Catalyst in a Transforming Relationship between State and People," *Journal of American History* 98, no. 4 (March 2012): 1075–92.

19. Kristol stated that his refusal would not have been motivated by any specific objection to the CIA but, rather, a desire to protect his "reputation as an independent writer and thinker" and to avoid becoming "a functionary in a large organization," particularly the government. Though he reprinted this statement in 1995's *Neo-Conservatism: The Autobiography of an Idea*, Kristol's service on corporate boards in the intervening years at least qualifies his position. There is a large literature on the CCF, and it touches on the question of whether Kristol had in fact known—or should have known—of the CIA's role. At the center of that debate is a letter Kristol wrote to Dwight Macdonald suggesting that the latter's highly critical article, "America, America," had been rejected with a view toward the political preferences of foundation officers who controlled *Encounter*'s funds. Kristol, "Memoirs of a 'Cold Warrior,'" *New York Times Magazine*, February 11, 1968, SM25. Kristol's letter to Macdonald is quoted in

Michael Wreszin, *Rebel in Defense of Tradition: The Life and Politics of Dwight Macdonald* (New York: Basic Books, 1994), 342. See also the letters by Norman Birnbaum, Kristol and Stephen Spender, Nicolas Nabokov, and Macdonald in *Universities and Left Review*, Autumn 1958, 5, and Spring 1959, 60–61.

20. Christopher Lasch, "The Cultural Cold War: A Short History of the Congress for Cultural Freedom," in *The Agony of the American Left* (New York: Vintage, 1969), 72; Kristol, "'Civil Liberties,' 1952," 230 (Commager was Lasch's father-in-law); Lasch, "The Cultural Cold War," 73.

21. Lasch, "The Cultural Cold War," 94.

22. Kristol, "Memoirs of a 'Cold Warrior,'" SM92, SM94, SM98.

23. Context suggests that the magazine Kristol referred to was the *New York Review of Books*. Kristol, "Memoirs of a 'Cold Warrior,'" SM98.

24. Kristol, "The Philosopher's Hidden Truth," review of *Persecution and the Art of Writing*, by Leo Strauss, *Commentary* 14, no. 4 (October 1952): 394.

25. Kristol, 394.

26. Kristol, "God and the Psychoanalysts," *Commentary* 8, no. 5 (November 1949): 443.

27. Kristol, "The Philosopher's Hidden Truth," 394.

28. Kristol, "Two Varieties of Democracy," *Commentary* 14, no. 3 (September 1952): 289; Kristol, preface to *On the Democratic Idea in America*, ix.

29. Kristol to Lionel Trilling, January 15, 1963, and Kristol to Lionel Trilling and Richard Hofstadter, May 17, 1966, box 20, folder 23, IK Papers.

30. Lionel Trilling, preface to *Beyond Culture, Essays on Literature and Learning* (New York: Viking, 1965), xii–xiii.

31. Trilling, xiii, xvi.

32. Trilling, xv.

33. Kristol, "The Drift of Things," *Encounter*, January 1962, 110.

34. Kristol, "Big Government and Little Men," *New Leader*, November 26, 1962, 14.

35. Kristol, "The Politics of 'Stylish Frustration,'" *New Leader*, April 1, 1963, 11.

36. Kristol, "My Friend, the Professor," *New Leader*, November 11, 1963, 14–15 (emphasis in original).

37. Joseph Kraft and Kristol, "A Preliminary Memo from Irving Kristol and Joseph Kraft," attached to Daniel J. Boorstin to Kristol, July 28, 1960, box 14, folder 16, IK Papers.

38. "Middle-Aged Meliorists," *Time*, March 4, 1966, http://content.time.com/time/magazine/article/0,9171,835224,00.html.

39. Kristol to Lionel Trilling, May 10, 1965, box 17, folder 41, IK Papers; Daniel Bell, *The End of Ideology: On the Exhaustion of Political Ideas in the Fifties* (1960; repr., New York: Free Press, 1965), 393, 402–3. Kristol was not entirely persuaded by Bell's thesis. In 1983 he wrote: "Someone who is not of the Left will declare that all these

ideological categories are outmoded, and the time has come to proceed with the business of politics in some kind of pragmatic, nonideological way." These pronouncements "usually represent little more than an effort, in a spirit of resignation, to ratify the views of the more moderate left as a new consensus." Kristol, *Reflections of a Neoconservative: Looking Back, Looking Ahead* (New York: Basic Books, 1983), ix.

40. Daniel Bell, "The New Class: A Muddled Concept," in *The New Class?* ed. B. Bruce-Briggs (New York: McGraw-Hill, 1981).

41. Ivan Szelenyi and Bill Martin, "Three Waves of New Class Theories," *Theory and Society* 17, no. 5 (September 1988): 649.

42. Ivan Szelenyi, "Gouldner's Theory of Intellectuals as a Flawed Universal Class," *Theory and Society* 11, no. 6 (November 1982): 785.

43. Mikhail Bakunin, *Bakunin on Anarchy*, trans. Sam Dolgoff (New York: Knopf, 1972), quoted in Noam Chomsky, *Towards a New Cold War: Essays on the Current Crisis and How We Got There* (New York: Pantheon, 1982), 61.

44. A branch of New Class theory associated with Yugoslav intellectual Milovan Djilas focused on the Eastern Bloc, but Kristol suggested this strand was not particularly influential for him by referring to Barry Bruce-Briggs, who wrote: "While the term 'the new class' was suggested by Djilas, no serious American writer has claimed that any group here is comparable to the Communist party bosses of Eastern Europe." Bruce-Briggs indicated that American usage of the term began with Daniel Patrick Moynihan in *Public Interest* in 1972. Thomas Bethell to Kristol, March 17, 1979, and Kristol to Bethell, March 21, 1979, box 2, folder 8, IK Papers; Bruce-Briggs, "An Introduction to the Idea of the New Class," in *The New Class?*, ed. Bruce-Biggs, 1. See also Joshua Muravchik, "Theories of the New Class," *World Affairs* 144, no. 2 (Fall 1981): 157.

45. Szelenyi, "Gouldner's Theory of Intellectuals," 785.

46. See Szelenyi and Martin, "Three Waves of New Class Theories," 654–55.

47. Joseph Schumpeter, *Capitalism, Socialism, and Democracy* (1942; repr., New York: Harper and Brothers, 1950), 143, 144.

48. Schumpeter, 146, 151.

49. Schumpeter, 122, 147, 153–54.

50. Schumpeter, 153–54.

51. Robert Dahl, review of *Two Cheers for Capitalism*, by Irving Kristol, *New Republic*, June 3, 1978, https://newrepublic.com/article/69474/two-cheers-capitalism; Robert Lekachman, "Proposition 13 and the New Conservatism," *Change*, September 1978, 24; William Wolman, "A Dubious Defense of Free Enterprise," *Business Week*, May 8, 1978, 16.

52. "Biographical Note," David T. Bazelon Papers, University of Delaware Special Collections Department, http://www.lib.udel.edu/ud/spec/findaids/bazelon/; David T. Bazelon, *Power in America: The Politics of the New Class* (New York: New American Library Company, 1967), 199; Christopher Lasch, "Same Old New Class," review of

Power in America: The Politics of the New Class, by David T. Bazelon, *New York Review of Books*, September 28, 1967, https://www.nybooks.com/articles/1967/09/28/same-old-new-class/.

53. Lasch, "Same Old New Class."

54. John Kenneth Galbraith, *The New Industrial State* (Boston: Houghton Mifflin, 1967); Muravchik, "Theories of the New Class," 162.

55. Michael Harrington, *Toward a Democratic Left: A Radical Program for a New Majority* (New York: Macmillan, 1968), 266, 291, 285. Galbraith and Harrington follow Karl Mannheim's view of intellectuals "free-floating" above the materially determined outlook of other groups.

56. On evangelicals, see Kristol, "Conservative Christians: Into the Fray," *Wall Street Journal*, December 22, 1995, A8.

57. Richard J. Whalen, review of *Two Cheers for Capitalism*, by Irving Kristol, *American Spectator*, November 1978, 36.

58. Two important contributions to that body of thought after Kristol's main essays on it are Barbara and John Ehrenreich's "The Professional-Managerial Class," *Radical America* 11, no. 2 (March–April 1977): 7–31; and Alvin W. Gouldner's *The Future of Intellectuals and the Rise of the New Class: A Frame of Reference, Theses, Conjectures, Arguments, and an Historical Perspective on the Role of Intellectuals and Intelligentsia in the International Class Contest of the Modern Era* (New York: Seabury Press, 1979).

59. Eileen Shanahan, "Rise in States' Tax on Incomes Urged," *New York Times*, February 6, 1966, 1; Douglas Robinson, "750 in Rally Here to Protest War," *New York Times*, February 6, 1966, 4; "Lynd's Passport Canceled by U.S.," *New York Times*, February 6, 1966, 7.

60. "A Band of New York Intellectuals Meets with Prof. Schlesinger for Talk-In on Vietnam," *New York Times Magazine*, February 6, 1966, SM12, SM72.

61. "A Band of New York Intellectuals," SM72, SM75.

62. Kristol, "The Troublesome Intellectuals," *Public Interest* no. 2 (Winter 1966): 5–6 (emphasis in original).

63. Kristol, "American Intellectuals and Foreign Policy," *Foreign Affairs* 45, no. 4 (July 1967): 607, 595–96.

64. Kristol, 596, 606–7.

65. Annotated copy of Noam Chomsky's "The Responsibility of Intellectuals," box 1, folder 4, IK Papers; Kristol, "American Intellectuals and Foreign Policy," 600–601 (emphasis in original).

66. Kristol, "American Intellectuals and Foreign Policy," 597–98.

67. Kristol, 596, 605.

68. Kristol, 605, 602, 609.

69. Kristol, 606–8.

70. Kristol, "Decentralization for What?" *Public Interest* no. 11 (Spring 1968): 17–18.

71. Kristol to Robert Short and David Ginsburg, May 8, 1968, box 14, folder 17, IK Papers.

72. Kristol to William Kristol, July 9, 1968, box 14, folder 17, IK Papers.

73. Irving Howe and Irving Kristol, "The New York Intellectuals," *Commentary* 47, no. 1 (January 1969): 12, 16.

74. Jason Epstein to Kristol, February 12, 1968, box 14, folder 17, IK Papers.

75. Kristol, "The Shaking of the Foundations," 23–24.

76. Kristol, 28–29; Kristol to Seymour M. Lipset, May 22, 1968, box 22, folder 26, IK Papers.

77. Kristol to Arnold Beichman, July 15, 1969, box 17, folder 14, IK Papers.

78. Kristol, *Neo-Conservatism*, 32.

79. "Henry Luce Professorship on Urban Values," box 26, folder 23, IK Papers.

80. Kristol, reading list for "Colloquium on Urban Civilization: Its Problematics, Its Values and Its Potential," December 31, 1969, box 26, folder 21, IK Papers; Richard Hofstadter, "Two Cultures: Adversary and/or Responsible," *Public Interest* no. 6 (Winter 1967): 74; Kristol to Hiram Haydn, December 8, 1969, box 1, folder 36, IK Papers, published in "Neglected Books," *American Scholar* 39, no. 2 (Spring 1970): 330.

81. Lionel Trilling, "Reality in America," in *The Liberal Imagination: Essays on Literature and Society* (1950; repr., Garden City, NY: Doubleday Anchor Books, 1953), 22; Kristol, "American Historians and the Democratic Idea," 103.

82. Kristol, "Urban Civilization and Its Discontents," *Commentary* 50, no. 1 (July 1970): 30.

83. Kristol, 34, 35.

84. Kristol, 35; Kristol, "Machiavelli and the Profanation of Politics" (1961), in *Reflections of a Neoconservative*, 127.

85. Kristol, "'When Virtue Loses All Her Loveliness'—Some Reflections on Capitalism and 'The Free Society'" (1970), in *On the Democratic Idea in America*, 94, 97, 98, 104.

86. Kristol, 105–6.

87. Kristol, "A Foolish American Ism—Utopianism," *New York Times Magazine*, November 14, 1971, SM103; Kristol, "Pornography, Obscenity and the Case for Censorship," *New York Times Magazine*, March 28, 1971, SM112–13.

88. Robert L. Bartley, "Irving Kristol and Friends," *Wall Street Journal*, May 3, 1972, 20.

89. Carroll Kilpatrick, "The 'Real' President Nixon Is Still Seen in Silhouette," *Washington Post*, August 22, 1972, A13; William Chapman, "The White House Discovers an Intellectual to Its Liking," *Washington Post*, April 15, 1973, A2.

90. Damon Linker, "Irving Kristol's Other Journey," *New Republic*, September 19, 2009, http://www.newrepublic.com/blog/damon-linker/irving-kristols-other-journey#.

91. Bartley, "Irving Kristol and Friends," 20.

92. Norman Podhoretz, "Between Nixon and the New Politics" (1972), in *The New York Intellectuals Reader*, ed. Neil Jumonville (New York: Routledge, 2007), 408.

93. Podhoretz, 409.

94. Edward Shils, "The Prospects of Civility," *Encounter*, November 1972, 34.

95. Shils, 35, 36–37.

96. Shils, 37.

97. Bartley, "Irving Kristol and Friends," 20.

98. Jeremy Campbell, "Jeremy Campbell Reports from Washington," *Evening Standard* (London), November 29, 1972; Rowland Evans and Robert Novak, "The Ceasefire Police," *New York Post*, November 18, 1972, 29.

99. James R. Dickenson, "Nixon's Man in the Middle," *National Observer*, December 30, 1972, 1; Campbell, "Jeremy Campbell Reports."

100. Dickenson, "Nixon's Man in the Middle," 1, 16.

101. Podhoretz, "Between Nixon and the New Politics," 410.

102. Bartley, "A Most Improbable 'Conservative,'" *Wall Street Journal*, November 19, 1970, 18.

103. According to Barry Bruce-Briggs, "Three very influential American intellectuals adopted and developed the term" New Class in 1972: Moynihan in *Public Interest*, Kristol's "About Equality" in *Commentary*, and Podhoretz also writing there. Bruce-Briggs, "An Introduction to the Idea of the New Class," 1.

104. Kristol, "About Equality," *Commentary* 54, no. 5 (November 1972): 41; John Rawls, *A Theory of Justice* (Cambridge, MA: Harvard University Press, 1971).

105. Kristol, "About Equality," 42.

106. Kristol, 42–43.

107. Kristol, 43 (emphasis in original).

108. Kristol, 43.

109. Kristol, 44.

110. Kristol, 44.

111. Kristol, 45; Kristol, introduction to *Reflections of a Neoconservative*, xiv–xv.

112. Michael Novak, "Novak: The Rise of Unmeltable Ethnics, Part I," *First Things*, August 31, 2006, https://www.firstthings.com/web-exclusives/2006/08/novak-the-rise -of-unmeltable-e.

113. Kristol, "About Equality," 45.

114. Kristol, 47 (emphasis in original).

115. Michael Walzer, "In Defense of Equality," *Dissent* 20, no. 4 (Fall 1973), in *The New York Intellectuals Reader*, ed. Jumonville, 357, 359.

116. Geoffrey Norman, "The Godfather of Neoconservatism (and His Family)," *Esquire*, February 13, 1979, 42.

117. Spiro T. Agnew to Kristol, July 5, 1973, box 1, folder 32, IK Papers.

118. According to the *Village Voice*, Kristol "sits on the boards of numerous cor-

porations." Richard Goldstein, "The War for America's Mind," *Village Voice*, June 8, 1982, 16. After a 1986 meeting that included Kemp and a small circle of prospective supporters, economist Irwin Stelzer told Kristol: "In a sense, you were the most powerful man in the room, being the source of the ideas Jack was espousing, and providing a common intellectual ground on which all the participants in the luncheon could stand. I mention this not to flatter you, but to emphasize my point that underlying intellectual credibility and respectability do matter, even though voters don't dig too deeply into some of these issues. They need to be satisfied that a candidate has, so that they need not." I. M. Stelzer to Kristol, May 22, 1986, box 15, folder 4, IK Papers.

119. Kristol, "Utopianism, Ancient and Modern" (1973), in *Two Cheers for Capitalism*, 169–70; Kristol, "The Adversary Culture of Intellectuals" (1979), in *Neo-Conservatism*, 122.

120. Kristol, "Business and the 'New Class'" (1975) and "The Frustrations of Affluence" (1973), in *Two Cheers for Capitalism*, 27, 37.

121. Kristol, "The Adversary Culture of Intellectuals," 112; Kristol, "Business and the 'New Class'" (emphasis in original), and "Taxes, Poverty, and Equality" (1974), in *Two Cheers for Capitalism*, 29, 225.

122. Christopher Lasch, *The Revolt of the Elites and the Betrayal of Democracy* (New York: W. W. Norton, 1996), 35.

123. Kristol, "Utopianism, Ancient and Modern," 170.

124. Kristol, "Horatio Alger and Profits" (1974), in *Two Cheers for Capitalism*, 84.

125. Kristol, "The Credibility of Corporations" (1974) and "The Corporation as a Citizen" (1974), in *Two Cheers for Capitalism*, 118, 92.

126. Kristol, "The Credibility of Corporations," 114.

127. Kristol, "The Shareholder Constituency" (1974) and "The Corporation and the Dinosaur" (1974), in *Two Cheers for Capitalism*, 147, 75.

128. Kristol, "On Corporate Philanthropy," 142–45 (emphasis in original).

129. Kristol, 145.

130. Daniel Bell, *The Cultural Contradictions of Capitalism* (New York: Basic Books, 1976); Kristol, "Capitalism, Socialism, and Nihilism" (1973), in *Two Cheers for Capitalism*, 66–67.

131. On the differences between Friedman and Hayek and those between Kristol and Friedman, see Angus Burgin, *The Great Persuasion: Reinventing Free Markets since the Depression* (Cambridge, MA: Harvard University Press, 2015), 207–13.

132. Kristol, "Horatio Alger and Profits" and "On 'Economic Education'" (1976), in *Two Cheers for Capitalism*, 88, 99.

133. Kristol, "On Corporate Philanthropy," 145; and "Capitalism, Socialism, and Nihilism," 66.

134. Kristol, preface to *Two Cheers for Capitalism*, xi.

135. Kristol, "'The Stupid Party'" (1976), in *Two Cheers for Capitalism*, 130–32, 134–35.

136. Kristol, "Reforming the Welfare State" (1976); "Horatio Alger and Profits"; and "Of Populism and Taxes" (1972), in *Two Cheers for Capitalism*, 248, 88, 227.

137. Kristol, "Of Populism and Taxes," 229, 231; and "Utopianism, Ancient and Modern," 170.

138. "Report of the Organizing Committee, William E. Simon, Chairman," box 25, folder 18, IK Papers.

139. On the ultimate selection of the name for the organization, Kristol favored something "'low profile.'" Kristol to Leslie Lenkowsky and [F. A.] O'Connell, November 22, 1977, box 25, folder 18, IK Papers.

140. See Leslie Lenkowsky to Robert Goldwin, May 12, 1978, box 25, folder 19, IK Papers.

141. Kristol, "Draft of fundraising letter," box 25, folder 19, IK Papers.

142. Kristol and William E. Simon, "Statement of Purpose," in *IEA Annual Report* (1980), 3, and "What Does IEA Do?" in *IEA Annual Report* (1980), 19, box 25, folder 31, IK Papers.

143. "Reagan for President News," April 17, 1980, and Kristol to Ronald Reagan, July 1, 1980, box 14, folder 28, IK Papers; "The New American Establishment: Irving Kristol, the Politics of Ideas," *U.S. News & World Report*, February 8, 1988, 64; Goldstein, "The War for America's Mind," 16; Walter Goodman, "Irving Kristol: Patron Saint of the New Right," *New York Times*, December 6, 1981, SM90; Phillip Marcus to Kristol, December 12, 1984, box 25, folder 37, IK Papers.

144. "Returning to the Roots of Freedom: President Reagan's Inspirational Speech to His College Alma Mater in Eureka, Ill.," *New York Post*, February 7, 1984, 33.

145. Kristol, "Capitalism, Socialism, and Nihilism," 70; Howe, quoted in Goodman, "Irving Kristol," SM90.

146. "Is America Moving to the Right? Ought It? A Conversation with Irving Kristol and Arthur Schlesinger, Jr.," *Across the Board*, February 1979, 70–71.

147. "The President's News Conference," August 12, 1986, Ronald Reagan Presidential Library and Museum, https://www.reaganlibrary.gov/research/speeches/081286d.

Chapter Six

1. Theodore H. White, "The Action Intellectuals (Part I)," *Life*, June 9, 1967, 44; Ponchitta Pierce, "Problems of the Negro Woman Intellectual," *Ebony*, August 1966, 144–49. On Pierce's article, its reception, and its legacy, see Brittney C. Cooper, *Beyond Respectability: The Intellectual Thought of Race Women* (Urbana: University of Illinois Press, 2017), 102–21.

2. Nell Irvin Painter noted that formulations of "the race" to which African American intellectuals have been deemed responsible are based on "two assumptions no longer so openly embraced: that it is possible to speak of African-Americans in the singular—as what used to be called 'the Negro' and now most often appears as 'the black

community'—and that the [intellectuals] in question possess the authority to speak for the whole African-American race." Painter, "A Different Sense of Time," *The Nation*, May 6, 1996, 38.

3. "Perhaps no major black intellectual had his door knocked on more often than Ralph Ellison," Jerry Grafio Watts has written, "precisely because he was viewed by some as having gone AWOL from the Negro freedom movement. Contrary to Ellison's claims, the division of labor [between novelists and activists] existed in his head, not in the heads of the Negroes." Watts, *Heroism and the Black Intellectual: Ralph Ellison, Politics, and Afro-American Intellectual Life* (Chapel Hill: University of North Carolina Press, 1994), 93. Robin D. G. Kelley also breaks down that division by showing how artistic and imaginative intellectual work has been at the heart of radical re-visionings of the world across the African diaspora. Just as the "poetics of struggle" shapes political vision and action, it is shaped by the experience of social movements. Kelley, *Freedom Dreams: The Black Radical Imagination* (Boston: Beacon Press, 2002), 10.

4. James Baldwin, *The Fire Next Time* (New York: Dial Press, 1963); Ta-Nehisi Coates, *Between the World and Me* (New York: Spiegel & Grau, 2015); Douglass, *Frederick Douglass, Oration, Delivered in Corinthian Hall, Rochester, July 5th, 1852* (Rochester, NY: Lee, Mann & Co., 1852).

5. While regarding "the nostalgia accusation" against his book as wrongheaded, Russell Jacoby noted that it had nonetheless "become almost the standard line about" it. Jacoby, introduction to the 2000 edition of *The Last Intellectuals: American Culture in the Age of Academe* (New York: Basic Books, 2000), xviii–xix.

6. Cornel West and Michael Lerner, *Jews and Blacks: Let the Healing Begin* (New York: G. P. Putnam's Sons, 1995), 18; West interviewed by Peter Osborne, *A Critical Sense: Interviews with Intellectuals*, ed. Peter Osborne (New York: Routledge, 1996), 128; West interviewed by Amy Goodman, *Democracy Now*, September 30, 2009, http://www.democracynow.org/2009/9/30/dr_cornel_west_on_his_new.

7. West, *The Ethical Dimensions of Marxist Thought* (New York: Monthly Review Press), xviii; West interviewed by Osborne, *A Critical Sense*, 129.

8. West interviewed by Osborne, 130.

9. West, *Ethical Dimensions*, xx.

10. West, afterword to "Symposium on Sheldon Wolin," *Theory & Event* 10, no. 1 (2007), *Project MUSE*, doi:10.1353/tae.2007.0051.

11. West interviewed by Osborne, *A Critical Sense*, 130.

12. West, *Ethical Dimensions*, xxiv.

13. History and Mission, Union Theological Seminary in the City of New York, http://www.utsnyc.edu/about/union-theological-seminary-history-mission; Timeline, History and Mission, Union Theological Seminary in the City of New York, http://www.utsnyc.edu/about/history-mission/timeline#six.

14. Cornel West with David Ritz, *Brother West: Living and Loving Out Loud, a Memoir* (New York: Smiley Books, 2009), 92, 94, 151.

15. bell hooks, "Introduction to Cornel West," in *Breaking Bread: Insurgent Black Intellectual Life*, hooks and West (Boston: South End Press, 1991), 24.

16. "Scholar Cornel West on His Work," West interviewed by Bill Moyers, *A World of Ideas*, PBS, April 1, 1990, https://billmoyers.com/content/cornel-west/.

17. K. Anthony Appiah, "A Prophetic Pragmatism," *Nation*, April 9, 1990, 496–97.

18. W. E. B. Du Bois, *The Souls of Black Folk* (Chicago: A. C. McClurg and Company, 1903), 3.

19. Daniel T. Rodgers, *Age of Fracture* (Cambridge, MA: Harvard Belknap, 2011), 2–3; Noam Chomsky, "The Responsibility of Intellectuals," in *American Power and the New Mandarins* (New York: Pantheon, 1969), 325.

20. Thomas S. Kuhn, *The Structure of Scientific Revolutions* (Chicago: University of Chicago Press, 1962). Kuhn himself resisted these implications of his work, holding to the view that whatever considerations prompted scientists to adopt one theory or another were internal to science and the evaluative standards of the scientific community. "Despite Kuhn's personal commitment to an internalist posture," Peter Novick nevertheless points out, "his attack on the view that theory choice was algorithmic opened the door to serious consideration of 'externalities' which could be shown to have been important if not decisive in determining scientific truth at different times and places." Novick, *That Noble Dream: The "Objectivity Question" and the American Historical Profession* (New York: Cambridge University Press, 1988), 534–35.

21. François Cusset, *French Theory: How Foucault, Derrida, Deleuze, & Co. Transformed the Intellectual Life of the United States*, trans. Jeff Fort (Minneapolis: University of Minnesota Press, 2008), 28–32.

22. John Rajchman, foreword to *The Chomsky-Foucault Debate on Human Nature*, by Noam Chomsky and Michel Foucault (New York: New Press, 2006), vii.

23. Chomsky and Foucault, *The Chomsky-Foucault Debate*, 15–16, 17.

24. Chomsky and Foucault, 50, 54–55, 58.

25. West, "Religion and the Left" (1984), in *Prophetic Fragments* (Grand Rapids, MI: William B. Eerdmans, 1988), 20.

26. Tables 198 and 237, *Digest of Education Statistics 2011*, U.S. Department of Education, Institute of Education Sciences, National Center for Education Statistics, http://nces.ed.gov/programs/digest/d11/index.asp.

27. West, *Ethical Dimensions*, xvii.

28. West, "Decentering Europe: The Contemporary Crisis in Culture" (1991), in *Beyond Eurocentrism and Multiculturalism*, vol. 1, *Prophetic Thought in Postmodern Times* (Monroe, ME: Common Courage Press, 1993), 137.

29. Joyce Appleby, Lynn Hunt, and Margaret Jacob, *Telling the Truth about History* (New York: W. W. Norton, 1994), 2.

30. Peter Burke, *The French Historical Revolution: The Annales School 1929–89* (Stanford, CA: Stanford University Press, 1990), 110–11.

31. West, *The American Evasion of Philosophy: A Genealogy of Pragmatism* (Madison: University of Wisconsin Press, 1989), 4.

32. West, "Decentering Europe," 137–39; Matthew Arnold, *Culture and Anarchy* (1869; repr., New Haven, CT: Yale University Press, 1994), 5.

33. James B. Gardner and George Rollie Adams, eds., *Ordinary People and Everyday Life: Perspectives on the New Social History* (Nashville: American Association for State and Local History, 1983); West, "The Prophetic Tradition in Afro-America" (1984) and "On Christian Intellectuals" (1984), in *Prophetic Fragments*, 49, 271; David L. Smith, Chet Lasell, Eleanor Holmes Norton, Paula Giddings, Sterling Stuckey, Wahneema Lubiano, and Cornel West, "A Symposium on the Life and Work of Sterling Brown," *Callaloo* 21, no. 4 (Autumn 1998): 1066.

34. Neil Postman, *Amusing Ourselves to Death: Public Discourse in the Age of Show Business* (1985; repr., New York: Penguin, 2006), 28; Thomas Bender, *Intellect and Public Life: Essays on the Social History of Academic Intellectuals in the United States* (Baltimore: Johns Hopkins University Press, 1993), 144; West, *American Evasion*, 177.

35. West, "Theory, Pragmatisms and Politics" (1991), in *Keeping Faith: Philosophy and Race in America* (New York: Routledge, 1993), 94.

36. Allan Bloom, *The Closing of the American Mind: How Higher Education Has Failed Democracy and Impoverished the Souls of Today's Students* (1987; repr., New York: Touchstone, 1988), 346; Richard Hofstadter, "214th Columbia University Commencement Address, June 4th 1968. Transcript," *Columbia University Libraries Online Exhibitions*, https://exhibitions.library.columbia.edu/exhibits/show/1968/item/9566.

37. Jacoby, *Last Intellectuals*, 6, ix, 12, 26.

38. Michael Eric Dyson wrote that *Last Intellectuals* gave the term "fresh currency in the late '80s." Jacoby went further, suggesting that he "was the first to use this term," putting it "into circulation." As noted earlier, Mills used it in *The Causes of World War Three* (New York: Simon & Schuster, 1958). Dyson, *Race Rules: Navigating the Color Line* (New York: Vintage, 1997), 48; Jacoby, *Last Intellectuals*, xvi.

39. Jacoby, *Last Intellectuals*, 5.

40. Jacoby, *Last Intellectuals*, xvi; Dick Flacks, "Making History and Making Theory: Notes on How Intellectuals Seek Relevance," in *Intellectuals and Politics: Social Theory in a Changing World*, ed. Charles C. Lemert (Newbury Park, CA: Sage, 1991), 12; Jacoby, *Last Intellectuals*, 198.

41. Jeffrey Escoffier, "Pessimism of the Mind: Intellectuals, Universities and the Left," *Socialist Review* 18, no. 1 (January–March 1988): 125.

42. Escoffier, "Pessimism of the Mind," 125, 127, 129–30.

43. Robert S. Boynton, "The New Intellectuals," *Atlantic Monthly*, March 1995, 53–54.

44. Jonathan Scott Holloway calls Crummell's 1897 speech to the American Negro Academy "the birth of the twentieth-century black intellectual tradition" of responsi-

bility for "saving" the race. Holloway, "The Black Intellectual and the 'Crisis Canon' in the Twentieth Century," *Black Scholar* 23, no. 1 (Spring 2001): 2. Hazel V. Carby notes that Frances Ellen Watkins Harper's *Iola Leroy* preceded and "prefigured" both Crummell's speech and Du Bois's work on the "concept of a black intelligentsia." Carby, *Reconstructing Womanhood: The Emergence of the Afro-American Woman Novelist* (New York: Oxford University Press, 1987), 84.

45. Henry Louis Gates Jr., "Parable of the Talents," in *The Future of the Race*, Henry Louis Gates Jr. and Cornel West (New York: Knopf, 1996), 4, 6, 10; Gates and West, *The Future of the Race*, viii, x; E. Franklin Frazier, *Black Bourgeoisie* (Glencoe, IL: Free Press, 1957); Nathan Hare, *The Black Anglo-Saxons* (New York: Marzani and Munsell, 1965). Evelyn Brooks Higginbotham has shown that the term "talented tenth" originated with Henry Morehouse, a white leader in the American Baptist Home Missionary Society. Higginbotham, *Righteous Discontent: The Women's Movement in the Black Baptist Church, 1880–1920* (Cambridge, MA: Harvard University Press, 1993), 25. Henry Louis Gates Jr. discusses the term's background in "Who Really Invented the 'Talented Tenth'?" *The Root*, February 18, 2013, https://www.theroot.com/who-really -invented-the-talented-tenth-1790895289. For a history and critique of elite racial uplift ideology in the first half of the twentieth century, see Kevin K. Gaines, *Uplifting the Race: Black Leadership, Politics, and Culture in the Twentieth Century* (Chapel Hill: University of North Carolina Press, 1996).

46. Gates and West, *The Future of the Race*, xi.

47. Du Bois, "The Talented Tenth" (1903), in *The Future of the Race*, Gates and West, 133, 140, 145, 156–57.

48. Du Bois, "The Talented Tenth Memorial Address" (1948), in *The Future of the Race*, Gates and West, 162–63, 169. On Du Bois's evolving view of the Tenth, see Joy James, *Transcending the Talented Tenth: Black Leaders and American Intellectuals* (New York: Routledge, 1997), 18–27.

49. "The Victorian three-piece suit . . . worn by W. E. B. Du Bois . . . signified his sense of intellectual vocation, a sense of rendering service by means of critical intelligence and moral action," West wrote. "The shabby clothing worn by most black intellectuals these days may be seen as symbolizing their utter marginality behind the walls of academe and their sense of impotence in the wider world of American culture and politics." West, *Race Matters* (Boston: Beacon Press, 1993), 40. Carby observes that "to define this appearance as the *only* acceptable confirmation of intellectual vocation, critical intelligence, and moral action is also to secure these qualities as irrevocably and conservatively masculine." Hazel V. Carby, *Race Men* (Cambridge, MA: Harvard University Press, 2000), 21.

50. West, "Black Strivings in a Twilight Civilization," in *The Future of the Race*, Gates and West, 58. Du Bois did famously claim that American society had much to learn from African Americans, but West saw that claim as part of his elitism. "While the Afro-American masses are busy giving the world its meekness, humility and jovial-

ity," West wrote, "the Talented Tenth is provided leadership and guidance. . . . In other words, the Untalented Ninetieth possess the idealized gift of spirit, while the Talented Tenth acquire the essentials of power, namely education and skills." West, "Philosophy and the Afro-American Experience," *Philosophical Forum* 9, nos. 2–3 (Winter–Spring 1977–78): 130.

51. West, "Black Strivings in a Twilight Civilization," 58, 60, 64–65, 67–68. Patricia Hill Collins observes that "the journalistic forms [Ida B. Wells Barnett] chose to communicate her ideas were not associated with 'scholarship.' Because scholars typically categorized Wells Barnett more as a public *activist* and Du Bois as a public *intellectual*, her ideas remain marginalized, her groundbreaking analysis of the workings of the color line generally dismissed. Foreshadowing the current situation, Du Bois claimed the mantle of black public intellectual, whereas, until recently, black intellectual history largely ignored Wells Barnett." Collins, "Black Public Intellectuals: From Du Bois to the Present," *Contexts* 4, no. 4 (Fall 2005): 24 (emphasis in original).

52. West, "Black Strivings in a Twilight Civilization," 68.

53. West, 70–71.

54. Gates and West, *The Future of the Race*, xvii.

55. West, "Black Strivings in a Twilight Civilization," 71.

56. See "Harold W. Cruse," *New York Review of Books*, https://www.nybooks.com /contributors/harold-w-cruse/.

57. Harold Cruse, *Crisis of the Negro Intellectual: A Historical Analysis of the Failure of Black Leadership* (1967; repr., New York: Quill, 1984), 475, 565. For critique, contextualization, and reappraisal of Cruse, see Cooper, *Beyond Respectability*, 102–3, 113–15; Hortense J. Spillers, "The Crisis of the Negro Intellectual: A Post-Date," *boundary 2* 21, no. 3 (Autumn 1994): 65–116; and Jerry Watts, ed., *Harold Cruse's "The Crisis of the Negro Intellectual" Reconsidered* (New York: Routledge, 2004).

58. Cruse, *Crisis of the Negro Intellectual*, 9, 475.

59. Cruse used Mills's "cultural apparatus" to designate "an organized network of functions that are creative, administrative, propagandistic, educational, recreational, political, artistic, economic, and cultural." Cruse, 474.

60. Cruse, 65.

61. Cruse, 549, 557, 560 (emphasis in original).

62. Cruse, 565.

63. Christopher Lasch to Robert Silvers, December 11, 1967, box 2, folder 8, Christopher Lasch Papers, Department of Rare Books, Special Collections, and Preservation, University of Rochester (hereafter CL Papers).

64. Christopher Lasch, "A Special Supplement: The Trouble with Black Power," *New York Review of Books*, February 29, 1968, https://www.nybooks.com/articles/1968 /02/29/a-special-supplement-the-trouble-with-black-power/.

65. Cruse to Lasch, June 29, 1968, and Lasch to Cruse, July 21, 1968, box 2, folder 10, CL Papers.

66. "'Black Power' Statement by National Committee of Negro Churchmen," *New York Times*, July 31, 1966, 143 (emphasis in original); James H. Cone, "Black Consciousness and the Black Church: A Historical-Theological Interpretation," *Annals of the American Academy of Political and Social Science* 387 (January 1970): 51–52.

67. Jeffrey L. Klaiber, "Prophets and Populists: Liberation Theology, 1968–1988," *The Americas* 46, no. 1 (July 1989): 2.

68. Cone, "Black Consciousness and the Black Church," 53; West, "Black Theology of Liberation as Critique of Capitalist Civilization," *Journal of the Interdenominational Theological Center* 10, no. 2 (1983): 71.

69. Michel Foucault, *Power/Knowledge: Selected Interviews and Other Writings, 1972–1977*, ed. Colin Gordon, trans. Colin Gordon et al. (New York: Pantheon, 1980), 129.

70. Foucault, *Power/Knowledge*, 126; Foucault, *Language, Counter-Memory, Practice*, ed. Donald Bouchard, trans. Bouchard and Sherry Simon (Ithaca, NY: Cornell University Press, 1980), 208.

71. Antonio Gramsci, *The Modern Prince and Other Writings*, trans. by Louis Marks (New York: International Publishers, 1968), 118; Gramsci, *Selections from the Prison Notebooks of Antonio Gramsci*, ed. and trans. Quintin Hoare and Geoffrey Nowell Smith (New York: International Publishers, 1971), 7.

72. Kevin Mattson has proposed, alternatively, that "postmodern conservative intellectuals" were particularly well suited to this moment. Mattson, *Rebels All! A Short History of the Conservative Mind in Postwar America* (New Brunswick, NJ: Rutgers University Press, 2008), chap. 3.

73. West, "Philosophy and the Afro-American Experience," 125.

74. West, 123–24, 145n17.

75. West, 143, 148n48, 122; "*The Philosophical Forum*, A Quarterly Journal," Department of Philosophy, Weissman College of Arts and Sciences, Baruch College, http://www.baruch.cuny.edu/wsas/academics/philosophy/PhilosophicalForum.htm.

76. West, "Philosophy and the Afro-American Experience," 146n19.

77. West, "Socialism and the Black Church," *New York Circus* 3, no. 5 (1979): 8.

78. The term also suggested biological or racial essences, which loom large in the history of racist thought, and its application to African American intellectuals was therefore fraught when it seemed to emphasize shared biology and not, as West did, shared historical experience.

79. West, "Black Theology and Marxist Thought," in *Black Theology: A Documentary History 1966–1979*, ed. Gayraud Wilmore and James Cone (Maryknoll, NY: Orbis Press, 1979), 561.

80. West, 564.

81. Martin Kilson, "The New Black Intellectuals," *Dissent* 16 (July–August 1969): 307, 309 (emphasis in original); The Brainwaves Video Anthology, "Cornel West—Teachers Make a Difference—Martin Kilson," YouTube Video, March 22, 2017, https://www.youtube.com/watch?v=AlV7kyHvVBM. "What Malcolm X, Stokely Carmi-

chael, Huey Newton, and other paraintellectuals shared," Simon Wendt observed, "was the fact that the basis for their nationalist thinking was a 'lived' rather than 'learned' analysis of the problems that confronted black America." For West, organic intellectuals' perspective had to be *both* lived and learned. Wendt, "Intellectual Predicaments: Black Nationalism in the Civil Rights and Post–Civil Rights Eras," in *Black Intellectual Thought in Modern America: A Historical Perspective*, ed. Brian D. Behnken, Gregory D. Smithers, and Simon Wendt (Jackson: University Press of Mississippi, 2017), 171.

82. Angela Davis, *Lectures on Liberation* (New York: N.Y. Committee to Free Angela Davis, 1971), 14.

83. West, review of *Philosophy and the Mirror of Nature*, by Richard Rorty, *Union Seminary Quarterly Review* 37, nos.1–2 (Fall 1981–Winter 1982): 182–84.

84. West, "A Philosophical View of Easter" (1980), in *Prophetic Fragments*, 263.

85. Perhaps as a response to West's criticism, Rorty specified his loyalties in "Postmodernist Bourgeois Liberalism," *Journal of Philosophy* 80, no. 10 (October 1983): 583–89.

86. West, "The Politics of American Neo-Pragmatism," in *Post-Analytic Philosophy*, ed. John Rajchman and Cornel West (New York: Columbia University Press, 1985), 267, 271–72.

87. West, "Nietzsche's Prefiguration of Postmodern American Philosophy" (1981), in *The Cornel West Reader* (New York: Basic Books, 1999), 209–10; West, *Prophesy Deliverance!* (Philadelphia: Westminster Press, 1982), 111; West, "The Historicist Turn in Philosophy of Religion" (1985), in *Keeping Faith*, 129.

88. West, "The Dilemma of the Black Intellectual," 67.

89. West, 69–70 (emphasis in original).

90. West, 71–72.

91. West, 76, 78.

92. West, 81. Alan Wolfe provided an alternative version of the self-authorizing intellectual when he wrote: "My authority for being an intellectual comes only from me, and to be true [to] that authority, I have to be true to myself." While Foucault described intellectuals who by propounding an ideology of universal reason underwrote their own authority as bearers of such reason, Wolfe conveyed the concept found in Benjamin Ginzburg, Mills, and Lasch of what Richard Gillam called "the critical ideal"—the autonomous mind as source of the authoritative voice. Wolfe, *An Intellectual in Public* (Ann Arbor: University of Michigan Press, 2003), 379.

93. West, "The Dilemma of the Black Intellectual," 81–82.

94. West, 82–83.

95. Moreover, "poor people, already suspicious of rhetorics of science which surreptitiously manipulate and control them, come to see many Marxist organizations as what, in part, they are: anti-democratic hierarchical groupings which merely express the modern European will to power." West, *Prophesy Deliverance!*, 100.

96. West, "The Dilemma of the Black Intellectual," 84.

97. West, 84–85; "The Political Intellectual" (1987), West interviewed by Anders Stephanson, in *The Cornel West Reader*, 285.

98. West, "The Crisis in Theological Education" (1987) and "On Franz Hinke-lammert's *The Ideological Weapons of Death*" (1986), in *Prophetic Fragments*, 277, 204.

99. "The Political Intellectual," 290; West, "The Dilemma of the Black Intellectual," 85.

100. "The Political Intellectual," 280, 293 (emphasis in original); West, "Prophetic Theology" (1988), in *Beyond Eurocentrism and Multiculturalism*, vol. 2, *Prophetic Reflections: Notes on Race and Power in America* (Monroe, ME: Common Courage Press, 1993), 226.

101. West, "The Dilemma of the Black Intellectual," 84; on the essay's reception, see the introduction to "The Dilemma of the Black Intellectual," in *The Cornel West Reader*, 302.

102. West, *American Evasion*, 5–6.

103. West, 5, 8.

104. West, 10–11, 36–37.

105. West, 55, 62, 101.

106. West, 114, 125, 131, 137, 147.

107. West, 178–79.

108. West, 178, 180; West, "South Africa and Our Struggle," in *Prophetic Reflections*, 186.

109. West, *American Evasion*, 238, 207.

110. West, 210, 229–30.

111. West, 212–13.

112. West, 212–13. John Dewey's "Creative Democracy—The Task Before Us" (1939) presented democracy not as a set of formal institutions, but as "a way of personal life" characterized "by faith in the capacity of human beings for intelligent judgment and action if proper conditions are furnished." Dewey, "Creative Democracy—The Task Before Us," (1939), in *John Dewey: The Later Works, 1925–1953*, vol. 14: *1939– 1941: Essays, Reviews, and Miscellany*, ed. Jo Ann Boydston (Carbondale: Southern Illinois University Press, 1988), 227.

113. West, *American Evasion*, 213.

114. West, 231–32.

115. Prophetic truth is not transcendental truth, which West rejected; it must rather be the truth of a people—as embodied in their history. This kind of prophecy is that which Michael Walzer commends as "connected criticism." West, *American Evasion*, 233; Walzer, *Interpretation and Social Criticism* (Cambridge, MA: Harvard University Press, 1993).

116. West, *American Evasion*, 234.

117. Rick Bales, "Resurrecting Labor," *Maryland Law Review* 77, no. 1 (2017): 5,

fig. 1; "The Party's (Largely) Over, Political Parties' Membership Is Withering: That's Bad News for Governments, but Not Necessarily for Democracy," *Economist*, October 21, 2010, http://www.economist.com/node/17306082; Robert D. Putnam, *Bowling Alone: The Collapse and Revival of American Community* (New York: Simon & Schuster, 2000), 27.

118. West's conception of "organic" differed from Gramsci's, which was grounded in economic class. West held to a looser, more cultural formulation, yet it was also stricter, for it could conjure the sense that organicism had to be existentially felt or experienced—like religious conversion.

119. Responding to West's work, Robert B. Westbrook described the "prophetic wing of the black church," as "one of the few incipient dialogical communities that continues to afford some resistance to the constriction of democratic life." Westbrook, "Democratic Evasions: Cornel West and the Politics of Pragmatism," *Praxis International* 13, no. 1 (April 1993): 10.

120. Richard Rorty, "The Professor and the Prophet," *Transition*, no. 52 (1991): 75.

121. Rorty, 76, 78.

122. Appiah, "A Prophetic Pragmatism," 498.

123. Howard Brick, review of *The American Evasion of Philosophy*, by Cornel West, *Journal of American History* 79, no. 2 (September 1992): 687.

124. "Scholar Cornel West on His Work."

125. "A World of Ideas," West interviewed by Moyers, in *The Cornel West Reader*, 294.

126. West with Ritz, *Brother West*, 169–70.

127. West, *Race Matters*, 11–14.

128. West, 35, 43, 40, 46 (emphasis in original).

129. West with Ritz, *Brother West*, 170; Kuumba Ferrouillet Kazi, "Cornel West Talking about *Race Matters*," *Black Collegian* 24, no. 1 (1993): 24.

130. Michael Eric Dyson, review of *Prophetic Fragments*, by Cornel West, *Theology Today* 45, no. 4 (January 1989): 453; West, introduction to "The Dilemma of the Black Intellectual," in *The Cornel West Reader*, 302.

131. bell hooks, *Ain't I a Woman: Black Women and Feminism* (Boston: South End Press, 1981). Building upon Hazel Carby's work, Patricia Hill Collins points out "how gender politics frames the very categories of public, private, and intellectual." This "much-needed gender critique" highlights "the distinctions between public intellectuals who garner attention in a male-defined 'public sphere' and 'domestic intellectuals'"—largely women—"whose activities support those in the public limelight." Collins, "Black Public Intellectuals," 25.

132. hooks, "Black Women Intellectuals," in *Breaking Bread*, 148–50; Carol E. Henderson, "Bell Hooks (25 September 1952–)," in *Twentieth-Century American Cultural Theorists*, ed. Paul Hansom, *Dictionary of Literary Biography*, vol. 246 (Detroit: Gale

Group, 2001), 221. Whereas for Mills and Hofstadter the life of the mind is part of a fully realized selfhood, for hooks the life of the mind is a mode of achieving a hard-won selfhood.

133. hooks, "Black Women Intellectuals," 150.

134. hooks, 150.

135. hooks, 151, 155. "Housework, childcare, or a host of other caretaking activities has made it difficult for women to make intellectual work a central priority," while on the basis of women's work in these areas, men have been able to prioritize intellectual labor. hooks, 156.

136. hooks, 155, 158, 153.

137. hooks, 152.

138. hooks, "Introduction to Cornel West" and "Cornel West Interviewed by bell hooks," in *Breaking Bread*, 24, 45. hooks and West published an edition of *Breaking Bread* with new material in 2017.

139. Popular culture was the domain, moreover, "where Black people have been able to articulate their sense of the world in a profound manner." "Cornel West Interviewed by bell hooks," 37.

140. hooks, "Introduction to Cornel West," 23; Rosemary Cowan, *Cornel West: The Politics of Redemption* (Malden, MA: Polity, 2003), 8 (emphasis in original).

141. "bell hooks Interviewed by Cornel West," "Black Women Intellectuals," and "Introduction to Cornel West," in *Breaking Bread*, 71, 163, 75, 25–26. Carol E. Henderson reports that *Ain't I a Woman* sold upward of eighty thousand copies, "an astounding feat for an academic book of this type." Henderson, "Bell Hooks," 223.

142. "Cornel West Interviewed by bell hooks," 29; hooks, "Introduction to Cornel West," 25.

143. "Cornel West Interviewed by bell hooks," 29; West, "Introduction to bell hooks," in *Breaking Bread*, 59; "bell hooks Interviewed by Cornel West," 72–73; Henderson, "Bell Hooks," 223.

144. "bell hooks Interviewed by Cornel West," 73.

145. hooks, "Introduction to Cornel West, " 21–22; "Cornel West Interviewed by bell hooks," 42.

146. Eugene Rivers, "On the Responsibility of Intellectuals in the Age of Crack," *Boston Review* 17, no. 5 (September–October 1992), http://bostonreview.net/archives /BR17.5/rivers.html.

147. Anthony Appiah, Margaret Burnham, Henry Louis Gates Jr., bell hooks, Glenn Loury, Eugene Rivers, and Cornel West, "On the Responsibility of Intellectuals," *Boston Review* 18, no. 1 (January–February 1993), http://bostonreview.net/archives /BR18.1/responsibility.html (emphasis in original).

148. Appiah et al., "On the Responsibility of Intellectuals."

149. Appiah et al. (emphasis in original).

150. Appiah et al.

151. Regina Austin, Margaret Burnham, Selwyn Cudjoe, bell hooks, Randall Kennedy, and Eugene Rivers, "The Responsibility of Intellectuals in the Age of Crack," *Boston Review* 19, no. 1 (February–March 1994), http://bostonreview.net/archives/BR19.1/responsibility.html.

152. Michael Bérubé, "Public Academy: A New Generation of Black Thinkers Is Becoming the Most Dynamic Force in the American Intellectual Arena since the Fifties," *New Yorker*, January 9, 1995, 73.

153. Boynton, "The New Intellectuals," 56; Bérubé, "Public Academy," 74.

154. Boynton, "The New Intellectuals," 56; Bérubé, "Public Academy," 77–78.

155. Boynton, "The New Intellectuals," 56; Seth Forman, letter to the editor, *New Yorker*, February 6, 1995, 6–7. As Patricia Hill Collins puts it: "Black intellectuals who identified too closely with so-called black special interests by becoming champions of African-American issues risked being accused of an inability to see beyond their own special interests. There is no way to win against this logic." Collins, "Black Public Intellectuals," 23–24.

156. Boynton, "The New Intellectuals," 56; Bérubé, "Public Academy," 77.

157. Boynton, "The New Intellectuals," 65–66, 68; Bérubé, "Public Academy," 79; Appiah et al., "On the Responsibility of Intellectuals" (emphasis in original). For critical appraisal of the relationship in this period between intellectuals and popular culture, see Andrew Ross, *No Respect: Intellectuals and Popular Culture* (New York: Routledge, 1989); and John Michael, *Anxious Intellects: Academic Professionals, Public Intellectuals, and Enlightenment Values* (Durham, NC: Duke University Press, 2000).

158. Bérubé, "Public Academy," 78–79.

159. Leon Wieseltier, "All and Nothing at All," *New Republic*, March 6, 1995, http://www.newrepublic.com/article/books/88939/cornel-west-race-america-book-review.

160. See, for instance, Andrew Delbanco, "The Decline of Discourse," *New York Times*, April 16, 1995; Henry Louis Gates Jr., letter to the editor, *New Republic*, April 10, 1995, 4; or Sean Wilentz, "Race, Celebrity, and the Intellectuals," *Dissent* 42, no. 3 (Summer 1995): 293–99.

161. Ellen Willis, "Wieseltier vs. West: Debate Matters," *Village Voice*, March 21, 1995, 8; name withheld, letter to the editor, *New Republic*, April 3, 1995, 6.

162. Elizabeth Maguire, letter to the editor, *New Republic*, April 3, 1995, 7; West, quoted in Jack E. White, "Philosopher with a Mission," *Time*, June 7, 1993.

163. Adolph Reed, "What Are the Drums Saying Booker? The Current Crisis of the Black Intellectual," *Village Voice*, April 11, 1995, 31–35 (emphasis in original).

164. Reed, 32.

165. "Chekhov, Coltrane, and Democracy," West interviewed by David Lionel Smith (1998), in *The Cornel West Reader*, 551.

Conclusion

1. Robert Boynton, "Obama and the Blues," *Rolling Stone*, March 20, 2008, https:// www.rollingstone.com/culture/culture-news/obama-and-the-blues-240917/; Lisa Miller, "'I Want to Be Like Jesus,'" *New York*, May 4, 2012, http://nymag.com/news /features/cornel-west-2012-5/.

2. "Cornel West on the Election of Barack Obama," West interviewed by Amy Goodman, *Democracy Now*, November 19, 2008, https://www.democracynow.org/2008 /11/19/cornel_west_on_the_election_of.

3. Michael Kruse, "'He Brutalized for You,'" *Politico*, April 8, 2016, https://www .politico.com/magazine/story/2016/04/donald-trump-roy-cohn-mentor-joseph -mccarthy-213799?o=0.

4. Michael Tomasky, "Barack Obama and the Intellectual as President," *Democracy*, January 6, 2016, https://democracyjournal.org/alcove/barack-obama-and-the -intellectual-as-president/; Kevin Mattson, "The Intellectual as President," *Chronicle of Higher Education*, September 25, 2016, https://www.chronicle.com/article/The -Intellectual-as-President/237860; Michael Kruse, "Trump Reclaims the Word 'Elite' with Vengeful Pride," *Politico*, November/December 2018, https://www.politico.com /magazine/story/2018/11/01/donald-trump-elite-trumpology-221953; Walter G. Moss, "The Crassness and Anti-Intellectualism of President Donald Trump," *History News Network*, March 18, 2018, https://historynewsnetwork.org/article/168305.

5. Kruse, "Trump Reclaims the Word 'Elite'"; David A. Graham, "The Paradox of Trump's Populism," *Atlantic*, June 29, 2018, https://www.theatlantic.com/politics /archive/2018/06/the-paradox-of-trumps-populism/564116/.

6. Danny Shea, "David Brooks: Sarah Palin 'Represents a Fatal Cancer to the Republican Party,'" *Huffington Post*, November 8, 2008, updated December 6, 2017, https://www.huffingtonpost.com/2008/10/08/david-brooks-sarah-palin_n_133001 .html; Katie Couric and Brian Goldsmith, "What Sarah Palin Saw Clearly," *Atlantic*, October 8, 2018, https://www.theatlantic.com/ideas/archive/2018/10/what-sarah-palin -understood-about-politics/572389/.

7. David Brooks, "The Follower Problem," *New York Times*, June 11, 2012, https:// www.nytimes.com/2012/06/12/opinion/brooks-the-follower-problem.html.

8. Brooks quoted in Shea, "David Brooks."

9. Lynn Sanders makes this argument in "Against Deliberation," *Political Theory* 25, no. 3 (1997).

10. Eric Liu, "How Donald Trump Is Reviving American Democracy," *Atlantic*, March 8, 2017, https://www.theatlantic.com/politics/archive/2017/03/how-donald -trump-is-reviving-our-democracy/518928/; Eric Levitz, "Trump Has Turned Millions of Americans into Activists," *New York*, April 6, 2018, http://nymag.com/intelligencer /2018/04/trump-has-turned-millions-of-americans-into-activists.html.

11. Yoni Appelbaum, "'I Alone Can Fix It,'" *Atlantic*, July 21, 2016, https://www.theatlantic.com/politics/archive/2016/07/trump-rnc-speech-alone-fix-it/492557/.

12. Rodney M. Sievers, *The Last Puritan? Adlai Stevenson in American Politics* (Port Washington, NY: Associated Faculty Press, 1983), x; "Obama on Super Tuesday: 'Our Time Has Come,'" *Washington Post*, February 6, 2008, http://www.washingtonpost.com/wp-dyn/content/article/2008/02/06/AR2008020600199.html.

13. C. Wright Mills, *The Causes of World War Three* (New York: Simon & Schuster, 1958), 125.

14. Mills, 7; "Obama on Super Tuesday."

INDEX

Harvard University (*continued*)
of Fellows, 92–93, 108, 110; W. E. B.
DuBois Institute, 208
Haskell, Thomas L., 282n17
Haven in a Heartless World (Lasch), 298n16
Hayek, Friedrich, 198
Heckscher, August, II, 139–40
Heidegger, Martin, 227
Henderson, Carol E., 324n141
Higginbotham, Evelyn Brooks, 318n45
Higgins, James, 201
Hilton, Ronald, 105
Himmelfarb, Gertrude, 166, 307n13
Hiss, Alger, 24, 182–83
Hitler, Adolf, 45, 182
Ho Chi Minh, 122
Hofstadter, Dan, 20
Hofstadter, Richard, 1, 3, 10, 12, 14–16,
21–22, 24, 54–56, 58–59, 62, 67, 109–
10, 127, 131–34, 137, 160, 163, 183–
84, 199–200, 203, 206, 214, 216, 254,
270n1, 271–72n13, 273n28, 277n72,
278nn88–89, 279n90; *Age of Reform*,
19, 25, 40, 43–44, 49–50, 128; agitator-
intellectual, 27–28; American political tradition, critique of, 26; *American
Political Tradition and the Men Who
Made It*, 19, 25, 27, 160, 273n28; and
anti-intellectualism, 18, 34–35, 45,
109, 135, 155; *Anti-Intellectualism in
American Life*, 1, 10, 19, 34, 40–41,
50, 57, 131; big business, 276n58; at
Columbia University, 19, 29–33, 39–
41; and communism, 31; on conformity, 45; critical ideal, adherence to,
39–40; cultural politics, 18; culture
war, waging of, 18–19; death of, 160;
on democracy, 276n63; "Democracy
and Anti-Intellectualism in America,"
40–41; *The Development and Scope of
Higher Education in the United States*,
19, 35, 50; *Development of Academic
Freedom in the United States*, 19, 38,
41, 50; dynamic of dissent, 17; edu-

cation work on, 35–39, 42–43; elites,
criticism of, 27; elitism, charges of,
279n93; entrepreneurial view, 26, 127,
274n31; industrial capitalism, critique
of, 40; influences on, 272n21; on intellect, 50–51; intellect, as outnumbered,
277n69; intellect, bolstering status of,
40, 45; intellectualism, commitment
to, 26; intellectuals, role of, 19–20,
41–42, 51; interest politics, 44, 271n5,
278n86; and liberalism, 26; life of the
mind, championing of, 40, 42, 323–
24n132; overt political engagement
of, 274n38; paranoid style, 17–19; *The
Paranoid Style and Other Essays*, 50;
"The Paranoid Style in American Politics," 17, 19, 40; popular politics and
intellectualism, tension between, 50;
populist mentality, as foe, 40; pseudo-
conservatism, 18, 47; "The Pseudo-
Conservative Revolt," 19, 44; public
sphere, 39, 46–47, 52; religious affiliation of, 279n96; status anxiety, accusation of, 46; status politics, 44; Stern
Gang, 276n53; symbolic politics, 18;
tyranny of majority, 277n77; at Wellfleet, 19, 33, 40–41, 47–48
Holloway, Jonathan Scott, 317–18n44
Hook, Sidney, 140, 183, 234–35
hooks, bell, 9, 13, 15, 204, 207–9, 218, 242,
246–47, 249, 257; *Ain't I a Woman:
Black Women and Feminism*, 241, 244–
45, 324n141; *Breaking Bread: Insurgent Black Intellectual Life*, 243; life of
the mind, and selfhood, 323–24n132;
women and intellectual labor, 324n135
Hoover, Herbert, 72, 92–93
House of Intellect, The (Barzun), 273n26
House Un-American Activities Committee (HUAC), 24–25, 30–31, 46,
277n69
Howe, Irving, 23, 166, 178, 182, 202, 248,
304n100; *A Margin of Hope: An Intellectual Autobiography*, 215

Iola Leroy (Harper), 317–18n44

Iraq War, 2, 124

Iron Curtain, 167

isolationism, 44, 178

Israel, Peter, 152–53

Italy, 60

Jackson, Andrew, 11; Jacksonian democracy, 39, 41

Jackson, Henry "Scoop," 188

Jackson, Michael, 209

Jacob, Margaret, 212

Jacobs, Fred Rue, 141

Jacoby, Russell, 204, 207, 217, 240, 248, 252, 315n5; *The Last Intellectuals*, 10, 15–16, 215–16, 218, 225, 241, 281n5, 317n38; public intellectual, coining of, 281n5

Jacoby, Susan, 3

James, William, 48, 125, 167, 234

Jameson, Fredric, 245

Japan, 124

Jefferson, Thomas, 213

Jewish Americans, 13

Jim Crow, 252

John Birch Society, 46

Johnson, Lyndon B., 110–11, 120, 134, 139, 276n53

Johnson, Russell, 67–68

Johnson, Samuel, 221

Jones, David, 152–53

Jordan, Michael, 209

Journal of Black Studies, 214

Kafka, Franz, 60

Kahn, Herman, 72

Kant, Immanuel, 116

Kapelner, Alan, 81

Kazi, Kuumba Ferrouillet, 240–41

Kazin, Alfred, 47–48, 139, 279–80n103

Kelley, Robin D. G., 269n32, 315n3

Kemp, Jack, 194, 312–13n118

Kennan, George: *American Diplomacy*, 289n7

Kennedy, Edward M. "Ted," 57, 72, 82, 85–86, 89

Kennedy, John F., 72–73, 80, 83, 86–87, 90–91, 93–94, 101–2, 104–6, 110, 117–19, 122, 125, 139, 155; Bay of Pigs failure, responsibility for, 103; brain trust of, 89, 98; and Camelot, 137; and intellectuals, 96–100, 107, 171; as man of action, perception of, 96; missile gap, 65, 96; new thinking, trumpeting of, 98; "Open Letter to President Kennedy," 292n52

Kennedy, Joseph P., 86

Kennedy, Robert F., 89

Kennedy Presidential Library, 89

Kent State shootings, 304n103

Kerry, John, 3

Kettler, David, 154–59, 304n103

Kevitt, Beatrice, 20, 271–72n13

Keyes, Alan, 246

Keynes, John Maynard, 7

Khrushchev, Nikita, 83

Kierkegaard, Søren, 66–67

Kilson, Martin: on paraintellectuals, 229

King, Jerome S., 73

King, Martin Luther, Jr., 138

King, Rodney, 209, 239

Kirk, Russell, 65; *The Conservative Mind*, 64

Kissinger, Henry, 16, 72

Klahre, Alfred C., 77

Klein, Allen, 87

Knopf, Alfred, 134, 150

Koestler, Arthur, 95

Korea, 65

Korean War, 24, 28

Korff, Baruch, 86

Kraft, Joseph, 172

Kristol, Irving, 15, 95, 136, 162, 165, 169–71, 189, 193, 204–6, 217, 221–22, 255, 273n23, 302n72, 307n13, 308–9n39, 309n44, 312–13n118; as champion of "the people," 163; "Civil Liberties," 167–68; at *Commentary*, 166; conservative ideal, 186; corporate America,

Means, Gardiner: *The Modern Corporation and Private Property*, 173
"Memoirs of a Cold Warrior" (Kristol), 168, 182
Merton, Robert, 18
#MeToo movement, 12
Meyeroff, Hans, 60
Middle America, 163
Milbank, Jeremiah, 201
military-industrial complex, 132, 135
millennial Christianity, 176
millennialism, 177
Miller, Eric, 138
Miller, Karl, 83–84, 86
Millett, John D., 35
Mills, C. Wright, 29, 54, 56–57, 66, 76, 104–5, 134, 206, 216, 223, 234–36, 259–60, 280n109, 281n7, 281n8, 319n59, 321n92; *The Causes of World War III*, 53, 55, 65, 75; corporate capitalism, critique of, 51; critical ideal, adherence to, 39; "Letter to the New Left," 52; life of the mind, 323–24n132; *The Power Elite*, 53; public intellectual, as term, 281n5; *White Collar*, 175
Mills, Yaroslava Surmach, 55–56
Mintz, Donald, 75
Model Cities Program, 181
Modern Corporation and Private Property, The (Berle and Means), 173
modernity, 164–65, 185–87; crisis of, 183, 195
Montgomery, AL, 138
Montgomery Bus Boycott, 70, 222
Moore, Barrington, Jr., 287n89
moral imagination, 27
moralism, 94, 115, 121
moralists, 9, 85, 120–23
Morehouse, Henry, 318n45
Morrison, Toni, 206, 208–9
Mosher, Jean, 69
Moss, Walter, 253
movement politics, 51–52
Moyers, Bill, 208–9, 239, 244

Moynihan, Daniel Patrick, 309n44, 312n103
mugwump culture, 57–58
Mumford, Lewis, 287n89
Murray, Pauli, 205
Murrow, Edward, 98–99
Muste, A. J., 108

Naderites, 196
National Association for the Advancement of Colored People (NAACP), 82
National Committee of Negro Churchmen, 224
National Committee for a Sane Nuclear Policy (SANE), 68
National Institute for Mental Health, 171
nationalism, 44, 196
National Liberation Front, 110
National Review (magazine), 202
National Security Act (1947), 7
Nature and Destiny of Man (Niebuhr), 93
Nazism, 8, 178
Nehru, Jawaharlal, 76–77
neoconservatism, 136, 162, 165–66, 192, 203, 217; neoconservative revolution, 202
Neo-Conservatism: The Autobiography of an Idea (Kristol), 307–8n19
Neumann, Franz, 60
Nevins, Allan, 30, 275n45
New Bedford, MA, 81
New Class, 8–9, 15, 163, 164–65, 167–68, 170, 172, 176, 178, 181, 190, 192–201, 203–4, 298n16, 309n44; as educated masses, 175; genealogy of, 173, 177, 187; as muddled concept, 173; as separate class, 188; as term, adoption of, 312n103
New Deal, 1, 6–7, 21, 24, 26–27, 29, 34–35, 40, 62, 183, 223, 278n82; Brains Trust, 63
New Frontier, 90, 101, 140
New Haven, CT, 47–48
New Industrial State, The (Galbraith), 176

Schlesinger, Arthur M., Jr. (*continued*)
brand of, 93–95; masculinity and, 94–
95, 290n24; "Men of Affirmation" and
"Men of Protest," 274n31; moral principles, assessment of, 120–21; press,
misleading of, 99, 117–19; as prototypical mandarin, 15, 92, 116–17, 119–
20; public persona, 98; Republicans,
critique of, 95; Senate Committee on
Foreign Relations, testimony of, 121–
23; *A Thousand Days: John F. Kennedy
in the White House*, 89, 91, 118, 122;
tough-mindedness of, 94; and Vietnam War, 107, 111–13, 115–16, 120–
22, 296–97n129; *The Vital Center*, 94,
290n24
Schumpeter, Joseph, 15, 177, 182, 187;
Capitalism, Socialism, and Democracy,
174–75
Seabury, Paul, 32, 275n49
Second Red Scare, 182, 253
segregation: demonstrations against, 70;
residential, 222
Segundo, Juan Luis, 224
Selma, AL, 138
Selma to Montgomery march, 274n38
Senate Committee on Foreign Relations,
121
Servicemen's Readjustment Act (1944).
See GI Bill
Sessions, Barbara, 74
sexism, 13, 243
Shakespeare, Frank, 201
Shakespeare, William, 2
Shepherd, Peter, 83
Shils, Edward, 188–89, 278n89
Signs (journal), 214
Silent Generation, 252
silent majority, 190
Silvers, Robert, 148, 223
Simmons, Ruth, 208
Simon, William E., 200–201
Singal, Daniel J., 277n69
Skinner, B. F., 110, 114

social criticism, 126
social Darwinism, 17
socialism, 174
"Socialism and the Black Church" (West),
208
social media, 2, 256
social movements, 205, 235–36
social thought, 210
Socrates, 28
Sokolsky, George, 20, 49
Sontag, Susan, 178, 181
South Africa, 208, 239
Southeast Asia Treaty Organization,
114
South Vietnam, 111–12, 114, 303–4n99
Soviet Union, 83, 95–96, 104. *See also*
Russia
Sowell, Thomas, 246, 249
Sparkman, John, 28, 274n38, 275n47
Spender, Stephen, 302n72
Spengler, Oswald, 60
Spivak, Lawrence, 84
Spock, Benjamin, 287n89
Sputnik, 65
Stalin, Joseph, 21, 120
Stanton, William, 141
status politics, 279n90; vs. interest politics,
18, 44, 271n5
Steffens, Lincoln, 142
Steinfels, Peter, 164
Stelzer, Irwin, 312–13n118
Stern, Fritz, 276n53
Stevenson, Adlai, 24, 29–30, 32–35,
39, 41, 43, 47, 52, 54–55, 62, 64–65,
79, 81, 95, 107, 109, 127, 129, 163,
203, 253, 274n38, 275n47, 278n82;
as egghead, 259; as intellectual, 1–2,
31; as midwestern patrician, 28; *New
York Times* advertisement, 31; 1956
campaign, 62; as original "egghead,"
2–3, 14
Stockman, David, 194
Stone, Sly, 214
Strauss, Harold, 153

Willis, Ellen, 15, 147, 155–56, 250
Wilson, Edmund, 24, 39, 48
Wilson, Woodrow: Inquiry group, 266–67n18; Wilsonianism, 290n19
Winfrey, Oprah, 209
Wisconsin, 25
Withey, John F., 145
Wittgenstein, Ludwig, 227
Wolfe, Alan, 270n1, 321n92
Wolin, Sheldon: "Political Theory as a Vocation," 208
Wolman, William, 175
women intellectuals, 16, 23, 130, 146–47, 217. *See also* African American women intellectuals

Women's International League for Peace and Freedom, 79
women's studies, 214
Woodward, C. Vann, 49–50, 279–80n103
World War I, 132, 267n22
World War II, 4, 6–7, 9, 11, 16, 20, 24, 35, 59, 93, 175, 178, 203, 205, 209, 234, 257–58
Wright, Louis B., 98

xenophobia, 127

Zaretsky, Natasha, 305n119
Zinn, Howard, 304–5n113
Zuccotti Park, 256